Aspects of
Nineteenth-Century Ontario

photo by Margaret Martin

Aspects of
Nineteenth-Century Ontario

Essays Presented to James J. Talman
Edited by F.H. Armstrong,
H.A. Stevenson, J.D. Wilson

Published in association with
The University of Western Ontario
by University of Toronto Press

Contents

Contents

Maps

Foreword

It is a pleasure for me to take up the invitation extended by James Talman's professional colleagues and write these few words at the beginning of a book which they have conceived as a lasting tribute to their friend and mine.

Jamey Talman, in my opinion, has made his mark with distinction in several lines of work, and I believe he richly deserves this tribute. I say that as a layman who has been in a position to observe his effectiveness over a long number of years. During the time I was a member and later the chairman of the Board of Governors at Western, I found it stimulating to work with Dr Talman. He was a 'team man' even when he was not completely in agreement with some of the decisions being taken by the Board. For the good of the team he would cheerfully produce alternatives, compromises, or counter-measures and advocate them strongly. It is to his credit that Western embarked on several new directions that later on were praised as far-sighted and significant.

The greatest legacy the new library now contains, in my view, is the collection of Canadiana that was built up so resolutely by Dr Talman. He always had faith in the lasting importance of this, his favourite project. I recall with deep personal pleasure many, many conversations on this subject; quite often I was privileged to enjoy a share of the excitement and enthusiasm with which he greeted the acquisition of new material for the collection.

One other vivid memory I have of my good friend goes back to the last days of the Second World War when the groundwork was being laid at Western for the first degree course in journalism in Canada. He was active in helping to plan the programme of studies and then taught the first course in the History of Canadian Journalism.

I mentioned above that I always regarded friend Talman as a 'team man.' That is why I think it is so right and appropriate that this book has been written by a team of contributors. I congratulate them on their achievement; it is indeed a fine tribute to the man whose life and life-style inspired it.

Col. D.B. Weldon / Chairman Emeritus of the Board of Governors

Foreword

For thirty-five years, James John Talman has been a familiar figure on Western's campus. To many of us, he is best known as the University's chief librarian who for some twenty years presided over the modern expansion period of the UWO library system. During those low-budget years, his ingenuity and expert knowledge of the field overcame adversity to the extent that our library holdings grew enormously in quality and quantity. Indeed, his persistent efforts to achieve excellence in a growing university have culminated in the establishment of the new D.B. Weldon Library.

James Talman is best known to his academic colleagues as a scholar and teacher of immense productivity and talent. His interest in the history of Western Ontario has provided the world of scholarship with salty insights into the rollicking days of the region – a period which, in many ways, exemplifies the expansive love of life of its author. To the many thousands of undergraduate and graduate students who have witnessed his humane erudition and mastery of his subject, he is a warm friend and a respected, multi-faceted scholar.

The University and the larger community have benefited enormously by his membership on Senate, his early command of the UWO Contingent, COTC, and his long service to the library and historical professions at large.

Most of all, James Talman has become a symbol to his colleagues of loyalty to Western, a loyalty that takes precedence over his pride of discipline and his many professional affiliations.

I join his friends and admirers in wishing him long life, and the same zest for living and labour that has marked his whole distinguished career at this University.

D. Carlton Williams / President, The University of Western Ontario

Preface

The reasons for writing and publishing these essays in honour of James J. Talman have been made abundantly clear in the tributes paid him on the preceding pages by Colonel D.B. Weldon and President D.C. Williams as well as in Professor Hugh A. Stevenson's biography. His friends, colleagues, and students who have co-operated in producing this volume join in celebrating James Talman's achievements as an historian, a librarian, an archivist, a journalist, and as a man.

Preparation for this book began immediately after his retirement as chief librarian in the summer of 1970. It was decided to invite contributions of recent research from long-time friends and associates of Dr Talman, from established scholars, from junior historians, and from his students, some of whom are pioneering new approaches to Ontario history as he and his close friend Fred Landon did some four decades ago. Then, because his special field of interest – the theme of nineteenth-century Ontario, particularly its social, intellectual, and cultural aspects – seemed to emerge so naturally, it was decided to encourage contributions reflecting these and related themes, though each author was free to choose his own subject and to treat it in his own way. The result is a variety of topics and historical methodologies ranging from narrative to quantification history.

The insights of disciplines other than history are apparent in that some contributors hold appointments in geography and English departments, and two are not academics at all. Such diversity of approach symbolizes James Talman's own career which at various times saw him teaching American and Latin American history, the history of journalism, the Canadian history survey, as well as his specialty, the history of Ontario. On the whole, the contributors represent second and third generations of Canadian scholars working in fields which Talman did so much to establish, and in some cases with the very materials he helped to preserve as Ontario archivist and as librarian at Western, where he built the university's Regional Collection into an outstanding resource for the history of southwestern Ontario. Taken together the articles cover the entire nineteenth century and in fact extend, in one or two cases, back into the eighteenth and forward into the twentieth centuries. The main thrust, however, remains the middle years of the century to which James Talman has devoted most of his research and writing.

The articles have been arranged according to both chronology and similarity of theme. The first three are concerned with the early development of the province and are followed by several others dealing with the urban development and business interests of a gradually maturing community. Professors Wightman and Gagan have examined practical aspects of an emerging rural society by studying construction materials employed and the relationship between credit and land holding as a sample case study. Two examples of early social historical research, one by Fred Landon and the second a joint article by James Talman and his friend the Rev. M.A. Garland, illustrate the pioneering scholarship done at the University of Western Ontario more than thirty years ago; Smith's article by comparison is illustrative of current research into the intellectual history of Ontario. These are followed by two articles concerning education mid-way through the nineteenth century and two others dealing with widely differing aspects of an increasingly literate society, as seen through contemporary newspapers and the publication of county atlases toward the latter part of the century. New Ontario, in two northern regions of the province, is the subject of articles by Elizabeth Arthur and Morris Zaslow which examine provincial development through the contributions and careers of individual politicians and a little-known civil servant of ubiquitous talents. The outreaching religious influences of Ontario Methodism to less developed areas of western Canada are examined by George Emery. The collection is concluded by Carl Klinck, one of Jimmie Talman's oldest and most respected colleagues, in a survey of the intellectual community which nineteenth-century Ontario produced and the legacy of scholarship it left for those of Talman's and succeeding generations to expand. Klinck's article provides an appropriate backdrop for the publication of Talman's extensive bibliography of scholarly and journalistic writing.

In conceiving the *Festschrift*, the editors were consciously aware that, while he would be honoured by the tribute paid him in being presented with these articles, James Talman would be equally thrilled by the realization that this volume might provide insights for local historians and a useful reference work for scholars, students, and general readers interested in regional aspects of Canadian history. We hope that this book will provide a background for university courses dealing with Ontario history and, as well, will become a useful addition to the collections of high school and public libraries. Herein would lie the ultimate tribute to James J. Talman.

Special thanks are due to the Board of Governors of the University of Western Ontario whose generous grant in aid of publication made the volume possible; to Dr R.J. Rossiter, vice-president (academic) and provost, Dr J.G. Rowe, dean of arts, and to Dr Robert N. Shervill, executive assistant to the president of the University of Western Ontario, for their sage advice and enthusiastic support throughout the project; to Rosemary Shipton of the University of Toronto Press for her editorial assistance; Sheila Lui, formerly reference librarian at Althouse College; and not least to the colleagues and friends of James J. Talman who so willingly contributed their talents to honour the achievements of a valued associate. Finally, it is with regret that we note the passing of one of our contributors, Max L. Magill, who died on 5 March, 1973 in Toronto.

FHA
HAS
JDW
June 1973

Aspects of
Nineteenth-Century Ontario

James John Talman
Historian and Librarian

Hugh A. Stevenson

Just to the right of the front entrance, along the narrow hall leading to the main office of the old Lawson Memorial Library, an abundance of clues pointed to the kind of man one might expect to find at its end in the chief librarian's office. The drab walls were hung with an array of historical memorabilia: delicate water colours of local scenes, autographed portraits of prominent Canadians, and an occasional framed proclamation, or a yellowed clipping from a famous Canadian newspaper announcing an historical event. At the corridor's end one entered a small anteroom and was confronted by a counter guarded by several secretaries. Over one's right shoulder, conveniently out of sight, was the office of the chief librarian. Beside it, within peripheral vision of callers at the counter, was the assistant librarian's room, door always open, with Lillian Benson hovering busily over the legendary eight to ten inches of papers, books, and files littering her desktop.

The young ladies who worked in the outer office had several common characteristics. They were efficient, loyal, courteous, and usually attractive. Politely but firmly they always protected their employer's time. Beyond the rewards of salary, employment on the library staff brought with it considerable unofficial fringe benefits, for 'JJ' always had time for friendly advice and help with personal problems when need be. Cordial relations prevailed in a casual working atmosphere among the professional librarians and clerical personnel. Long hours and cramped working conditions were compensated for with kindness and consideration, the opportunity to accumulate over-time for overseas trips, and, not least, the staff could set aside class time for study toward degrees.

The reception one received at the office counter depended rather naturally on the nature of one's business. Routine enquiries were dealt with promptly by the office staff assisted by Miss Benson, who seemed always to have an ear tuned to goings-on in the outer office. Regular callers always received personal treatment; important visitors with appointments from outside the university community were extended extra promptness and pleasantries. Reasonable complaints were listened to and assuaged but malcontents received short shrift and sometimes a stinging rebuff from the chief librarian if he happened to overhear and saw fit to intercede. Nobody ever received an indifferent reception.

The chief librarian's door was usually open. While he hated to interrupt dictation of correspondence, he frequently did so. Except for the brief period of annual madness occasioned by budget preparation, he was always available to colleagues and students, particularly if the latter took the trouble to make an appointment. As one entered the office, first impressions of its occupant gleaned from the hall were immediately confirmed. The south and east walls were shelved and laden with books. Those on the south wall adjacent to his desk were a mixture of bibliographic and literary references, Canadiana and current reading. The east wall, punctuated in the middle by a seldom-used door, housed handsomely bound editions of Canadiana, among them standard references in Canadian and Ontario history. The west wall was taken up by high windows, with a view across the playing fields to the mixed architecture of Huron College. The desk Jimmie Talman used for day-to-day business sat in the southwest corner, flanked by chairs for visitors, just out of sight from the outer office. Without doubt, the north wall was the most spectacular. An immense high desk, designed for tall stools or to be stood at, spanned the wall space and dominated the entire room. Its gently sloping top invariably displayed a collection of yellowing documents, boxed reels of microfilm, archival file boxes, letterbooks, and, overpowering the rest, bound folios of nineteenth-century Canadian newspapers piled one upon the other. Someplace along its top a small working space would be sufficiently clear of this orderly disarray of historical clutter to show a colleague a recent discovery or to stand with a student while examining an essay.

Once inside the chief librarian's office, academic visitors, whether student or colleague, received much the same kind of welcome. Quite often the preface to business would be a casual greeting followed by a clipped, almost breathless lecture on the demands placed on a chief librarian's time, somewhat longer for students than colleagues, and then to the point. Once issues were joined, the discussion seldom terminated without a course of action decided upon or a decision being reached. And despite the prefatory lecture on business, it was seldom so serious that there was no time to describe an amusing experience, deal with a query from the outer office, share with delight and interest in the good fortune of others or express concern for mutual friends and acquaintances. Nothing gave Talman as much delight as staging and winning a coup for the library. It might be as small as the acquisition of a much-sought after book at a good price or as significant as winning an encounter in the administrative offices of Stevenson Hall. The magnitude of the incident in no way diminished the pleasure he took in sharing news of the victory with associates. Only carpers and budget cuts spoiled the delightful style and good nature with which Jimmie Talman normally conducted library business and pursued his scholarly interests.

Dr Talman always took immense pleasure in his work and enjoyed the physical environment of the library, his office, and his associations with colleagues and students. Even though the library expanded greatly through his efforts and the assistance of his staff, JJ's working routines changed little. The office remained the same until late in his career when the leather-covered oak furniture characteristic of Western's executives offices replaced the older, more individualized appointments of an earlier era in Western's history that was passing.

Jimmie Talman's association with the university began as an undergraduate registered at Huron College on 30 September 1921. The event marked a point of transition in his life from the influence of his family, where many of his life-long interests were kindled, to the influence of Western, its scholars, and the friends he made while attending and serving the university. Throughout his graduate education and early career, his experience as a librarian and historian, he never lost contact with the institution he returned to serve during its most pronounced period of growth. On the contrary, as his career grew the ties with Western became stronger, now spanning more than half a century from the time he was a freshman.

Fred Landon, who had directed the library since his original appointment in 1923, was made vice-president of the university in 1946. James J. Talman, his protégé, colleague, and friend for more than twenty years, succeeded 'Mr Landon,' as he always called him, as chief librarian in 1947. Individually and together these two men built the library system at the University of Western Ontario from an insignificant, inadequately housed collection to one befitting a large university of scholarly significance and international stature.[1]

Talman's immediate family origins were delightfully romantic and rather adventurous, leaving similar qualities in his own personality which have always been evident in the sheer joy with which he approached scholarly investigation and met the challenges of associations with varied circumstances and new people. It began in the chance meeting of a second officer and a school girl on a British passenger ship en route from her home in South Africa to England at a time when, despite Cecil Rhodes' admonitions to the contrary, the sun had begun to set on Britain's vast overseas empire.

The ship's officer, Stephen Talman, had served under sail in Britain's merchant fleet since he was seventeen. After volunteering in Cape Town he had just completed a tour of service during the Boer War with Brabant's Horse, a somewhat notorious regiment of irregular cavalry, fighting for preservation of English rule in the Cape Colony. The school girl, seven years his junior, came from one of the Cape's oldest English families, who were well established on the land and well connected in local colonial government circles.

In time Winifred Ross finished her schooling and in 1903 married Stephen Talman, who sought and received a land post with Bucknell's, his shipping company, to avoid the long separations of a seaman from his family. Neither side of the family approved particularly of the match. The Talmans in England felt it was 'unfortunate' that Stephen had married a 'colonial,' while the Ross clan in South Africa saw little advantage to union with an experienced but grounded mate off sailing ships with no particular prospects. From the beginning the young couple went their own way. Their first child, James John, was born 15 September 1904, in Beira, Mozambique (Portuguese East Africa), where Stephen supervised the off-loading of steel for the Victoria Falls bridge in Rhodesia.

James' birth started the new parents on a twentieth-century odyssey typical of many whose lives were caught up in the fortunes of Britain's overseas possessions. Beira may have had the advantage of romance and colour and offered the security of a good job as agent for a major shipping company, but it was not a suitable environment for a middle-class Englishman of small means and his wife to raise children. In 1906 the young family sought a new start in South Africa, with Stephen first employed supervising the planting of trees for the Cape Colony Forestry Department. In less than a year he undertook the management of a run-down orange farm near Cape Town which belonged to Mrs Talman's uncle. By 1910 the orange groves had been restored and the prospering operation was returned to direct management by the owner. Again James Talman's father moved his family, now grown to include two girls, this time to Kimberley where he became a mechanic and lathe operator for De Beers Diamond Mines.

Here both James and his father began to study: the bilingual child, having learned Afrikaans from his nursemaid and servants on the orange farm, was enrolled at an English-speaking kindergarten; the father engaged himself in a mail-order course of studies toward qualification as a civil engineer through the International Correspondence School in Scranton, Pennsylvania. Stephen succeeded in his qualifying examinations and was recognized as a registered engineer by the South African Institute of Civil Engineers. At De Beers he moved from the machine shop to the drafting room, firmly convinced that education was an essential ingredient to success and determined that his children should have every advantage to learn. The trouble in Kimberley was that education cost too much, £1 a week per child.

The free education available in Australia and Canada beckoned the family to greener pastures. Stories of rich gold mines developing in Cochrane, Ontario, mining experience, a new diploma and certification in enginering, and strong enough family connections to provide a letter of introduction made Canada their choice. Australia seemed too far from the centre of things for the Talmans and it did not have the advantage of Laurier's well-publicized statement that the twentieth century belonged to Canada. Fortified with a letter of reference to Sir William Mulock from the Hon. Sir James Sivewright, one of Mrs Talman's relations in South Africa, and sporting maple leaf badges supplied to immigrants, the family arrived in Toronto on 19 March 1913 in their fifth attempt in a decade to find a permanent home. The emotional and material insecurity of stepping off a train in a strange country, not knowing where one would sleep that night, left a marked impression on James. It united him psychologically with the thousands of others who came to Canada in similar circumstances, and later gave a richness to his insights into pioneer society. Initially, the family secured lodgings in Mrs Houston's boarding house on Wood Street on the advice of a kindly ticket agent at Union Station. Maple Leaf Gardens is now located on the site of Mrs Houston's residence. A short time later they moved to a rented terrace cottage situated nearby on the north side of Wood Street near Yonge.

By contrast, with full Edwardian dignity, Sir William Mulock received them at dinner where he made a lasting impression on the children by eating a pear on which he had squashed a pesky house fly during the main course. The insect had been ceremoniously dispatched by a blow from a decorative ivory handled, wire whisk swatter delivered to Sir William's hand by his butler. With the same style and in true gentlemanly fashion he offered to put Stephen up for several clubs. But reality persisted and James' father secured employment with the City of Toronto Works Department as an engineer in street maintenance and construction.

Within a few weeks of the family's having found this degree of security, a chance opportunity brought James' father an offer to become chief engineer for the Hollinger Mining Company – provided he could leave for Cochrane that very evening. The job offer was declined since no time was allowed to give his civic employers decent notice. Because he felt children should be raised in the country, and as an economy measure, in the spring of 1914 Stephen moved the family to a small farm in Halton County on a crossroad south of Acton. There were other ventures too. Stephen commuted to Toronto for a while on a weekly basis, then farmed full time, worked with the Dominion Rubber Company in Kitchener-Waterloo for several years, and completed his working life with twenty-five years' employment in the Toronto waterworks. The last two jobs involved more moves for the family but by then James was well along in his schooling. Stephen and Winifred Talman's odyssey ended when they arrived in Ontario. There the family established itself putting down roots in a locale which would have a marked influence on James' career.

Although Jimmie attended Church Street School in Toronto during 1913–14, the countryside near Guelph provided the real environment of his boyhood. Their stone farmhouse was substantial, having attached to it a separate centre-hall designed frame structure which had originally been the Kennedy Tavern. In this quiet rural environment James grew up attending ss 10 in Esquesing Township, and subsequently rode a bike five miles to and from the Acton Continuation School. In this fashion, boarding in town only one month in the winter because funds were not available for more, he finished his junior matriculation at Acton. For a short time after beginning his senior matriculation year (Grade 13) he continued, by adding a daily train ride to Guelph to his five-mile stint on the bicycle. But, after a few months, the family moved to Waterloo and James finished his public education at the Kitchener-Waterloo High Shool.

By the time he had finished Continuation School his father's faith in education and the family habit of reading avidly had become firmly rooted in the boy's mind. He had devoured all of Parkman, most of Scott's works, and Prescott's books on Mexico and Peru before leaving his one-room rural school. When he was ten his father presented him with Emily P. Weaver's *Counties of Ontario* which they studied together. In addition Marriot's *Settlers in Canada,* based on his own travels, novels such as *Two Years Before the Mast,* and the books available at the Acton public library made James a compulsive reader and no doubt helped to generate his avid interest in Canadian history.

His choice of career as a Canadian historian, however, emerged much later. James did not know what to do with himself when he finished high school. Teaching after normal school was the quickest route to an income, but a small one; his father leaned toward seeing his son become a businessman, where he felt there was real money to be had, or, second best, an archaeologist. The latter career choice was undoubtedly based on stories of romantic exploits in far-off lands father and son had read together. Despite these paternal views, James held the notion that he was cut out to be a chemical engineer. The idea, however, seemed less appealing after he spent an extremely boring day, arranged by his father, dogging the head chemist at the Dominion Rubber Company through his routine of making tests. Finally, for his initial choice of vocation, James turned to the influence of their minister, Canon (later Dean) P.N. Harding, and family tradition.

For two generations on his father's side men of the Talman family had been trained either as engineers like his grandfather or seamen in England's famous ship schools. Earlier, however, since the sixteenth century, they had taken degrees at Oxford or Cambridge and given themselves in service to the church. Which church depended on the extent to which various members of the family had been influenced by the Oxford movement. James' father had attended King's School, Canterbury. Then, owing to the untimely death of his father in a shooting accident, Stephen was sent to hms *Conway,* anchored off Birkenhead in the mouth of the Mersey, for a practical secondary education and eventual apprenticeship with the merchant fleet. Even if James had been interested, Southwestern Ontario offered no opportunities of following a maritime career; he chose the Church of England.

Two weeks after his seventeenth birthday he entered Huron College in London as a theological student, sincere in his willingness to explore the theoretical aspects of the vocation, but uncertain of his own ability to fulfil the practical requirements of the calling.

His work as an undergraduate went well. Summers were spent preaching in the small parishes of rural Ontario: Glanworth, Belmont, and Dorchester as one circuit, in Wheatley near Leamington and at St Luke's in Yarmouth Heights on the eastern outskirts of St Thomas. The latter job allowed James to spend two days a week reading in James H. Coyne's excellent library of Canadian and Ontario history. The summer he was twenty-one he worked his way overseas on a cattle boat. These were pleasant years but by the time he graduated with a Bachelor of Arts degree in 1925 he was no closer to a definite choice of career than when he arrived at Western. He was still too young to be ordained and in any event he had doubts that he was cut out for successful service as a parish priest. He felt he had little to offer regular church-goers spiritually and nothing to contribute to the drudgery of bake sales and like parish duties. Without making an irrevocable decision concerning advanced work in theology James, in the meantime, chose to take a second degree in history.

At this point rather ironic and distinctly secular circumstances had a marked impact on Jimmie Talman's future. They led him to become an historian of the country in which his family had found a home, an academic librarian serving the area in which he grew to manhood, and into an extremely happy marriage. His life-long friendships with fellow students like the Rev. M.A. Garland, John Elliott, and Goldwin Smith stem from this period.

During his studies as an undergraduate, Western's historians, Dr A.G. Dorland and Professor Landon, had influenced him greatly, kindling an interest both in Canadian and church history. Whether their tutelage or the companionship of Ruth Davis, who was employed in the university library, had a stronger influence is a moot point. In any event the time spent in the stacks located in the University College, reading history for his Master's degree, served a treble purpose: it fostered his close association with the library collection at Western, nurtured in him the love for historical research, and heightened his interest in the librarian for whom he so often waited at the end of her working day. Ruth Davis was born in Buffalo, New York, and at an early age moved with her parents to London where her father was engaged in the insurance business. She attended the public schools of the city, graduating from the London Collegiate Institute with a junior matriculation and a scholarship to attend the University of Western Ontario where she obtained her BA in 1923 and an MA in history in 1925.

In 1927 James completed his Master's degree, having written a thesis on 'The Position of the Church of England in Upper Canada 1791–1840' which reflected perfectly the young man's two predominant interests. He was, however, still undecided regarding a final choice of career. The master's thesis supervised by Professor Landon had brought him into contact with A.H. Young who, although a distinguished Professor of German at Trinity College, Toronto, also had a deep interest in Canadian church history. Through Young, James saw the possibility of becoming a theological scholar and he was both accepted and offered a scholarship by the General Theological Seminary in New York. But Landon and Young also pointed out the possibility of his doing a PHD in history at the University of Toronto or at Wisconsin. He and Landon had often discussed the possibility of applying Frederic Jackson Turner's frontier thesis in the Canadian setting. The obvious place to apply for a scholarship was Wisconsin where F.L. Paxson, a Turner disciple, could act as mentor.

Finally, Talman's decision was made on practical grounds but for a year there remained considerable uncertainty about it. Finances were of crucial importance but history was more appealing than theology. In Toronto he might live at home, his family having moved back to the city while James was at Western. Also, Dr Young had offered to prepare him for the German examinations for the PHD. However, attending a university as conservative and pretentious as the University of Toronto was not without its difficulties. Its aspiration to academic leadership in the country and in attracting singularly talented scholars to its faculty tended to foster an atmosphere of aloofness. In addition, the city itself was hardly known for its warm hospitality to newcomers. At first the university was not sure it wanted Talman as a student.

The History Department, administered by Chester Martin, doubted its own desire to give the PHD. The calendar, however, advertised it and a search of the records indicated two precedents. With the help of scholars like George Brown and Young who had befriended him, Talman overcame this initial barrier and was enrolled in 1928 but without financial assistance. During that first year in Toronto, James applied for and received two scholarships. Wisconsin offered $350 plus fees, but at Toronto, acting on a suggestion by George Brown, he won the Alexander Mackenzie Fellowship in history paying $700 and fees. By 1929 any question that Toronto would be his choice of university to study for a doctorate was removed. Through an individual programme of studies there he was brought into contact with some of Canada's leading historians.

He studied historiography with Ralph Flenley, and took his major in Canadian history in a seminar given by William Stewart Wallace, university librarian and head of graduate research in Canadian studies. From George Brown, the only non-Oxford scholar in the department at the time, he took a minor in American history. His programme also included an 'outside course' in politics. As so often happens it was the young men in the department, particularly George Brown and Donald Creighton, who saw Jimmie Talman over the rough spots in his doctoral work. Except for sound advice from Stewart Wallace who was always very helpful, and, of course, Fred Landon, who had given him a letter of reference to Wallace, he was left much on his own to complete his thesis. For a topic he chose social history as reflected in the accounts written by early travellers to Canada: 'Social Conditions in Upper Canada, 1815-1840.'

The transition from the friendly, rather intimate, scholarly relationships which he had come to enjoy at Western to the more aloof and impersonal life at Toronto was a difficult adjustment for James. Even though it was a lonely period it had its value and compensations. Above all else he learned to work hard and independently – both very necessary qualities for historical researchers. And not everyone was stand-offish. As promised, Dr Young helped him through the German examinations and encouraged Talman to assist him in checking over a biography of the Rev. John Stuart, (1740-1811) of Kingston which he was writing at the time. The two men spent many pleasant hours during Talman's regular visits to Trinity College reading and discussing the second and third drafts of Young's chapters on the Loyalist clergyman's life. This association enabled their friendship to grow until Young died in 1935; the manuscript, practically ready for the press when Talman had helped with it, mysteriously disappeared in the confusion of settling Young's estate, a disappointing loss to scholarship which made it impossible for James to conclude what little remained to be done and publish it posthumously in memory of his friend.

During the nearly three years as a doctoral student at Toronto, James became friendly with Vera and George Brown and the artist, Charles W. Jefferys, well known for his Canadian historical scenes. Their homes and Dr Young's suite at Trinity were the only residences James visited socially on a regular basis. Then, too, there was Ruth who had remained in London working at the Western library under Mr Landon and in her father's insurance office until James finished his degree. Regularly he made the trip to London to visit her in an old car affectionately named 'Eloise' or by rail, taking advantage of special weekend rates. In this period of hard work there was always good reason to maintain a close connection with Western – to consult both Professor Landon and the excellent collection of Canadiana he was building for the library. By then Talman had begun to publish too, his first article having appeared in the London and Middlesex Historical Society *Transactions* in 1927, to be followed in 1929 by another article for the society, and in the same year one for the Canadian Historical Association, *Annual Report*.

When he graduated with his doctorate in 1930 there was no question of an academic career; the depression had set in and university positions were not to be had for specialists in Canadian social history. Fortunately, during his last year as a graduate student, he had done part-time editorial work for the General Board of Religious Education of the Anglican church. This developed into a permanent job which enabled him to marry Ruth in 1930 and settle in Toronto. At first they resided in an apartment on Jarvis Street near Bloor; a short time later they were able to move to a rented house in North Toronto. James Davis Talman was born in 1931; their second son Richard was born three years later. Both sons in time took Bachelor's degrees in mathematics and Master's degrees in physics at the University of Western Ontario where James (PHD Princeton) is presently a full professor in the Department of Applied Mathematics. Richard obtained his PHD at California Institute of Technology and is now a full professor in physics at Cornell.

Fortunately JJ's editorial work allowed time to continue doing the historical research which kept him abreast of academic developments. In 1931 he published two articles in the Ontario Historical Society *Papers*, one of which, written in collaboration with the Rev. M.A. Garland, is reprinted in this volume. In later years it became a matter of some considerable wry speculation among his colleagues whether or not Jimmie Talman researched the 'pioneer drinking habits' while Rev. Garland delved into the 'temperance agitation.' Such was his reputation for purity in research and one is left to speculate if this marked the beginning of Jimmie Talman's renown as a connoisseur of excellent spirits and fine food, particularly well-aged Canadian cheddar, probably the most palatable staple among the victuals served in the best of Upper Canada's drinking establishments prior to 1840! That he was an unofficial but frequently employed wine taster for the Ontario Liquor Control Board chemist during his time as archivist of the province lends some little credibility to the supposition. Forty years later the cellars of Dr R.N. Shervill, executive assistant to the president, and Dr Talman contained the best rum in London, the result of a joint private enterprise to import the finest available stock from Barbados (Doorly's Fine Old).

When, in 1931, Col. Alexander Fraser, archivist for the Province of Ontario, sought an assistant, Professor Landon recommended James Talman and on 1 July he assumed his new duties as a specialist in historical documents at a salary of $1800. On Fraser's retirement in 1934, Talman, whose reputation as a scholar had begun to be established, succeeded him as provincial archivist. Within a year a chance accident which disabled a political appointee made him legislative librarian as well. While Mitch Hepburn as premier, not one for tidiness and detail among his civil service, never got around to confirming the latter appointment officially, Talman held both positions on one salary until 1939. Despite the constant frustrations of little money to administer two government agencies, neither of which ever held any claim to priorities with the Hepburn administration, his five years as archivist and legislative librarian were not without their significance and rewards. For a scholar deeply interested in such disparate aspects of the history of Ontario as loyalists and railways, it is difficult to imagine a better place to work during the severe years of the depression. His passion for research and work with books could be fulfilled entirely. This marked the beginning of his career as a scholarly librarian and gave him the experience which accounted for his return to Western as assistant librarian in 1939.

These twists of fate – the unfortunate slipping of an elderly gentleman on an icy winter street, Mitch Hepburn's indifference (or perhaps his zeal for economy in getting two jobs done for the price of one), and, above all, circumstances of an academic struggling to make a career during the depression – launched Talman as a librarian. Dr Hartley Thomas, a long-time colleague of Talman at Western and historian of the UWO contingent of the COTC, provided us with a much less plausible reason for his successful career as a librarian. With just a little tongue-in-cheek so characteristic of Thomas' own delightful sense of humour, he pointed out that Corporal J.J. Talman, No 1 Platoon, UWO Contingent, COTC in the school year 1924–5 had been promoted to Headquarters as orderly room sergeant, 'a good job that persumably [sic] made him prospective University librarian.'[2]

As archivist and legislative librarian Talman had spent the quiet, frustrating years of the depression consolidating his career and developing new personal interests. He joined the University Lodge of the Masonic Order in 1930, an association which he maintained and enjoyed always. In time he went 'through the chairs' becoming master of the Tuscan Lodge, London in 1950, grand senior warden in 1959, and a member of the Board of General Purposes since 1962. Actually, the membership in University Lodge gave him an association with academics which he missed in his day-to-day preoccupation with books and historical documents. On coming to Western he did not join a lodge until encouraged to do so by Nelson Hart. Here the lodge became the reverse of what it had been before, an escape from the pressures and narrowness of an exclusively academic existence. In Tuscan Lodge his friendship warmed with Professors Nelson Hart, Jack A. Gunton, J.W. Burns, and to a lesser extent with Dr Fred Miller. Through the lodge in Toronto he became very good friends with William Dunlop, who was director of extension and in public relations work for the University of Toronto when they first met in 1929. Later, between 1951 and 1959, Dunlop became minister of education for Ontario in the Frost government. The two men maintained a close friendship until Dunlop's death in 1961.

Many professional relationships either developed or matured from this period, too: for example, his associations with Dr W. Kaye Lamb, provincial archivist in British Columbia, who later became dominion archivist, and W. Stewart Wallace, chief librarian at the University of Toronto and long-time secretary of the

Champlain Society. Frequent visits to Ruth's parents in London during the thirties provided ample opportunities to keep in touch with friends at Western and to gain greater familiarity with the southwestern Ontario countryside. Most important, he continued an active programme of research and publication on Upper Canadian history, its newspapers, the development of printing, the role of the Church of England and politics in the frontier society. His articles appeared in the *Canadian Historical Review*, the *Journal of Southern History*, the *American Historical Review*, and the Transactions of The Royal Society of Canada. When, in 1938, the possibility of a university posting finally arose, Dr Talman's reputation as a competent, experienced scholar and academic librarian was firmly established.

Actually two tentative positions emerged, the first as an assistant to Mr Landon in the library at Western, the second as chief librarian at the University of British Columbia. There had been casual talk with both during 1938 but neither university was in a position to make a concrete offer until 1939. The University of Western Ontario moved first, Fred Landon and A.T. Little, chairman of the Board of Governors, concluding their negotiations with Talman before UBC made a definite offer. It is unlikely, however, that Talman would have gone to British Columbia in any event. The opportunity to work closely with Landon and follow his research interests was entirely too strong to make Vancouver an attractive alternative. Years later the same reasoning kept him at Western when Queen's University tried to attract him during 1946-7 to head their library.

The outbreak of World War II coincided with Dr Talman's appointment as assistant librarian and made his tour in that office extra busy and more varied than the title would suggest. He began teaching almost immediately, replacing Professor Landon in his intramural course in American history during an illness; from that time on he taught Canadian and American history regularly in the extension programme. In 1940 his commission as lieutenant in the Canadian army was activated, marking the revival of his association with the COTC. During the war he participated in training successive classes of officers who passed through the unit. Between 1947 and 1954 Lt-Col. James Talman served as commanding officer of the UWO Contingent and in 1953 was awarded the Canadian Forces Decoration.[3] In addition to military duties and his regular job, which included picture hanging in The McIntosh Gallery, James edited several significant works on Canadian history. With the assistance of Lillian Benson he edited *The Papers and Records* of the Ontario Historical Society for two years and also acted as the society's president between 1937 and 1940.

Once he joined the university his activities never ceased to be varied and stimulating. As the library collection grew steadily and the university expanded in size, more and different opportunities to teach presented themselves, including Canadian history, the first history of journalism taught at Western, a unique course in the history of the Americas, and a likewise unique half-course in Latin American history and in library science. Throughout, he continued his Masonic activities and in so doing increased his knowledge of the communities of the fourteen counties served traditionally by Western in its early days as a regional university. He became a popular speaker at alumni functions and the meetings of local historical societies, as well as contributing regularly as a journalist in the columns of Ontario newspapers, especially *The London Free Press*. As his journalistic articles testify, Talman made a major contribution as a publicist for Canadian history, by writing extensively for large numbers of readers and reaching them effectively through the columns of their local newspaper. This aspect of his scholarship fostered interest significantly in Canadian identity and brought the university closer to its surrounding community. It helped set a higher standard for local history and provided an example of carefully researched popularization which has not been emulated enough by scholars in this country.

When Talman became chief librarian in 1947 the direction of his activities did not change; they merely quickened in pace. In 1949 he was elected a Fellow in the prestigious Royal Society of Canada; he served as president of the Ontario Library Association in 1945-6 and as treasurer of the Canadian Library Association between 1955 and 1958, a period when the organization needed a firm administrative hand managing its budget. In 1955 his fellow historians honoured him by electing him to the presidency of the Canadian Historical Association. A year later formal recognition for his years of teaching, research, and publications came in the form of a professorship in both the History Department and the Faculty of Graduate Studies at Western.

While continuing to write scholarly articles he served as chairman of the Governor General's Award Board between 1956 and 1959 and as a member of the Historic Sites and Monuments Board of Canada from 1961 to 1973. In the summer of 1957 he travelled to Ghana with the student-faculty summer seminar of World University Service of Canada. His most outstanding contribution to the development of Canadian scholarly libraries was unquestionably his long chairmanship of the Microfilm Project of the Canadian Library Association between 1954 and 1971. By 1968, after twenty-two years in operation, the project had made available microfilm of 3619 years of newspapers distributed over 231 titles. Positive prints as an aid to scholarship had been purchased by eighty-four Canadian and sixty-five United States libraries.[4]

One of his most personally rewarding experiences came in 1953 when he and his wife collaborated in writing *'Western' – 1878–1953* to commemorate the seventy-fifth anniversary of the founding of the University of Western Ontario. Part of the history was based on Ruth Davis's Master's thesis completed years earlier, the remainder represented new research. Ruth always acted as critic-in-residence for James' publications, never completely approving of her husband's system of taking innumerable notes on scraps of paper and writing in brief excerpts from them, which only when put together formed a unified piece. The differences in their research and writing styles must have made for interesting scholarly discussions; both authors maintain steadfastly that they enjoyed the experience immensely. James and Ruth Talman also collaborated on an article entitled 'The Canadas (1763–1812)' for the *Literary History of Canada* (1965) edited by their friend Carl F. Klinck. A few years later, Klinck and Talman worked together again, co-editing and introducing a large work, *The Journal of Major John Norton 1816* (1970), for the Champlain Society.

Dr Talman's major contribution to the University was in the period after he became chief librarian in 1947. The library system had outgrown its quarters and at the same time the university faced a period of expansion which characterized many of Dr G. Edward Hall's years as president from 1947 to 1967. The record of library expansion is a lasting tribute to Dr Talman and his staff: between 1947 and 1969 sixteen new reading rooms were stocked with books and opened to students and faculty; two major additions to Lawson Library were contracted, the north wing in 1954 and the south addition in 1961–2; completely new libraries for law (1960–1), the School of Business Administration (1961–2), Althouse College of Education (1965–6), and natural sciences (1965–6) were opened; the Stevenson Medical Library opened in 1962–3 and the entire medical library was moved from South Street to the Health Sciences Centre in 1964–5; additions were made to the law, business administration, and health sciences libraries in 1968–9; and construction was begun for the new D.B. Weldon Library.

During the twenty-three years he was chief librarian, acquisitions, special collections, budgets, and staff expanded remarkably. A collection of 172,474 volumes in 1947 (housed in Lawson, the medical libraries, and a small reading room staffed by a part-time member at the Institute of Public Health) grew to a total of 1,546,849 volumes which included many non-book and photographically reproduced resources of particular interest to the university and its surrounding community. Dr Talman's vigorous policy of overseas purchasing greatly expanded the breadth and depth of scholarship represented by Western's library holdings. This activity secured the internationally famous Milton collection for the university. The annual library budget rose spectacularly from a total of $39,720 (1947–8) to approximately $3,175,000 in the 1969–70 fiscal year, as well as additional expenditures from special funds. The Regional History Collection begun by Dr Landon was expanded greatly under Dr Talman's direction, providing the university with a rich and distinctive specialty closely identified with its locale. Over the years it has come to be well known and respected among Canadian scholars and local historians. That the Regional Collection has been preserved in proper facilities, with room for expansion, in the D.B. Weldon Library is a fitting tribute to the insight and imagination of the two men who nurtured it.[5]

Throughout James Talman's career there had always been rewards and honours. The work itself, from which he drew singular pleasures, provided the most substantial satisfactions. Yet there were others too – some distinctly personal, others which signified Canadian and international recognition for his scholarship and achievements as a librarian. Life in London provided ample opportunity for involvement with the community, an excellent locale to raise a family to maturity, and closeness to the countryside where so many of his scholarly interests drew him. There was time for the quiet pleasures of walking his German short-haired pointer in the natural beauty of Western's campus on Sunday afternoon; there was always good company too, particularly in the Friday afternoon 'teas' held in the Connaught restaurant (fondly dubbed the 'greasy spoon' by its patrons) near the old *Free Press* building on Richmond Street where for years a select group connected with the newspaper, including Bud Wild, John Elliott, Burke Martin, and Jim Dunn, met with Arthur Ford and any celebrity who might happen to be visiting the city. Tea drinking prevailed until lunch at Campbell's restaurant and tavern took its place; regardless of meeting place the companionship remained at a consistently high level, women being admitted as guests on only two occasions over the years.

In addition to the distinctions already mentioned, the University of Waterloo bestowed on him the Honorary Doctor of Letters degree at its first convocation in 1960, recognizing his achievements as an historian and his assistance to the university while it had been an affiliate of Western. His alma mater, Huron College, in recognition of his writing its centennial history, made him an Honorary Fellow in 1963 and in 1968 the Ontario Historical Society awarded him its highest distinction, the Cruikshank Medal. The award, itself being named for one of Ontario's earliest and most productive historians, was made in recognition of Talman's major contributions to the society and the study of Ontario history. In 1970 the Queen invested him into the Order of the British Empire in recognition of his many years of service in arranging co-operative book exchanges and displays between Canadian libraries and those in other nations of the Commonwealth.

During that summer the university marked his formal retirement by holding a gala reception for friends and close associates at Gibbons Lodge, official residence of the president. After an extremely pleasant afternoon of conviviality, in a brief informal ceremony Dr D. Carlton Williams presented Dr Talman with the traditional commemorative silver. As the gift emerged from its wrapping and the distinctive royal blue cloth bag of Birks jewellers became visible, Jimmie Talman exclaimed, 'How splendid! Seagram's Crown Royal.' The spontaneous outburst could not have been more fitting and characteristic of his good nature.

Formal retirement by no means marked the end of JJ's activity as a teacher and historian. Since then he has continued to teach in both the undergraduate and graduate programmes. His well-known graduate course in Ontario history continues to be a popular offering; between 1946 and 1972 he supervised a total of twenty-two graduate theses in history. As a member of the Board of Trustees for the Ontario Historical Studies Series since 1971 he has continued to influence the province's history by assisting with the most significant attempt ever made to record its development. Retirement has allowed him more time to devote to his own research as his studies of nineteenth-century Ontario continue the remarkable record of productive scholarship he established over more than forty years.

At its 212th Convocation in the fall of 1972 The University of Western Ontario bestowed its highest distinction in awarding Dr James J. Talman, scholar-librarian, the degree of Doctor of Laws (LLD) in recognition of his excellent scholarly achievements and to honour his outstanding contribution to the university and the community it serves.

NOTES

1 The details of early library and university development have been recorded in William F. Tamblyn, *These Sixty Years* (London, 1938) and James J. Talman and Ruth Davis Talman, *'Western' – 1878–1953* (London 1953). For a full account of Dr Fred Landon's career see also Frederick H. Armstrong, 'Fred Landon, 1880–1969,' and Hilary Bates, 'A Bibliography of Fred Landon,' *Ontario History*, LXII, 1, March 1970, 1–4 and 5–16 respectively.

2 Hartley Munro Thomas, *U.W.O. Contingent C.O.T.C.: The History of the Canadian Officers' Training Corps at The University of Western Ontario* (London, 1956), 60

3 Ibid., 141 ff

4 James J. Talman, 'Twenty-two Years of the Microfilm Newspaper Project,' *Canadian Library*, xxv, 2, Sept.-Oct. 1968, 147–8

5 *The President's Report 1970*, Part 2 (London 1970), 87–100

The Settlement of Western District
1749-1850

Leo A. Johnson

The development of settlement in any area seldom follows a regular and unin-
terrupted pattern. In this, Western District, today the counties of Essex, Kent, and
Lambton, was no exception.[1] The decision of the potential settler to locate in an
area is the product of many factors, among which economic, geographic, social,
and ideological considerations loom very large. Moreover, the decision to settle is
affected not only by the personal hopes and aspirations of the settler, but by the
plans and policies of governments as well. From this complex interplay of personal
and public interests – an interplay whose texture is constantly changing – emerges
the settlement patterns of an area. So it was in Western District.

The first white settlement in what was to be the Western District was an outgrowth of the French trading and military establishment at Detroit (a name which,
in the early years, was applied to both sides of the river). In the century-long
struggle for predominance in the fur trade, the French and English vied for control
of strategic locations. By 1700 Antoine Laurnet, Sieur de Lamothe Cadillac, commandant of Michilimackinac from 1694 to 1697, had convinced French authorities that a military and trading post and an agricultural community should be
established at Le Detroit, as the river and area between Lakes Erie and Huron
was called. Thus in the summer of 1701 a little contingent of soldiers and potential
settlers under the command of Cadillac built a warehouse, chapel, and dwellings
on the north shore of the Detroit River,[2] and called the settlement Fort Pon-
chartrain. This name soon fell into disuse, and was replaced by the original designation, Detroit, which it has retained ever since.

In spite of Cadillac's enthusiasm for the site, the little settlement grew slowly.
It was not until 1748, when the Marquis de la Galissonière, governor of Quebec,
decided to build a chain of forts in the west in order to cut off the British and
Iroquois fur traders, that Detroit took on new importance. To make the military
expansion economically feasible, it was decided to increase greatly the agricultural
production of the Detroit area, and to accomplish this a major expansion of population would be necessary.

In 1749, as a means of encouraging settlers to move to Detroit, La Galissonière caused a proclamation to be read through every parish along the St Lawrence River. It promised that 'Every man who will go to settle at Detroit will receive gratuitously one spade, one axe, one ploughshare, one large and one small auger. Other tools will be advanced to be paid for in two years only. The settler will also be given a cow, which he shall return at the time of increase; the same for a sow. Seed will be advanced the first year, to be returned at the third harvest. The women and children will be supported for one year.'[3] In 1749 several families travelled from Quebec, and these were joined by other civilians who had been living in the fortified town of Detroit and by a number of discharged soldiers. These settlers took up land both around the fort at Detroit and across the river around present-day Windsor. In accordance with the promises made in the proclamations, land and provisions were given the settlers. For those who established themselves across the river from Detroit, land was surveyed on the Quebec plan – long, narrow farms measuring 3 by 40 arpents[4] fronting on the river.

For a variety of reasons, while the settlement on the south side of the Detroit River grew, it did not prosper. In 1749 land had been granted to twenty-two settlers although only ten appear to have actually taken it up. Many of those who had been sent to Detroit the previous year had gone to seek their fortune elsewhere, while others 'contented themselves with eating the rations that the King gave them.'[5] Those who stayed to struggle with the forest found life difficult indeed. The land given to the first settlers was the poorest quality of yellow sand with a thin cover of loam. Those who seriously desired to cultivate land were forced to move farther south or towards Lake St Clair. Moreover, the Ohio posts never created a large demand for produce, with the result that prices were low while shipping costs meant that the only effective market was the army provision stores at Detroit. It was not long before the locality became known as *Côte de Misère* – Misery Settlement.[6]

With the growth in the number of settlers, the French spread out along the Detroit shore from *Ile aux Dindes* (Turkey Island) to the entrance to Lake St Clair. In time three communities developed, separated by Indian settlements: *Petite Côte*, the earliest settlement, stretched from the Anderdon–Sandwich boundary to a stream called *Le Ruisseau de la Vieille Riene*, which was the southern boundary of a large Huron village; *La Côte des Hurons* lay between the Huron village and a large Odawa (Ottawa) village; and *La Côte des Outaouais* stretched from the Odawa village to Lake St Clair. It was not until the British acquired control of the area that any large change in this pattern occurred.

The transfer of the area from French to English control was made almost without event on 29 November, 1760. By the terms of the capitulation of Montreal on 8 September, 1760 all the western posts including Detroit had been ceded to

England. Thus when the British force lead by Major Robert Rogers arrived at Detroit seven weeks later, there was nothing for the French garrison to do but to hand over the fort, and to march southward to Philadelphia where they embarked for France. Thus ended the era of French rule on the western frontier.

For the French settlers along the Detroit River, the first twenty years under British rule meant little change in their lives. The fur trade with the Indians continued as it had under French control, and markets for produce remained poor and prices low. In the late 1770s a few English traders and farmers began to take an interest in the Thames Valley,[7] but few settled. It was not until the American revolutionary war was nearing a close that the British merchants and military commanders, particularly those at Detroit, began to look at the area with renewed interest.

A number of these Detroit merchants, evidently believing that the government would have to expand settlement on the Canadian side of the Detroit River, began to purchase large tracts of land from the Indians along the Thames River. In 1780 a colourful Indian woman, Sarah Ainse,[8] who had been a trader on the Mohawk River and Great Lakes, bought from the Chippewas the whole north bank of the Thames from Lake St Clair to the forks (present day Chatham) and 5.9 miles in depth. At the same time Charles Gouin acquired the south bank from the mouth of the river up to Jeannette's Creek, and the next year the Detroit merchants, Garret Teller and William Park, purchased the land from Jeannette's Creek to the Chatham forks.[9] It was the intention of these speculators to divide their acquisitions into farm lots and sell them to the expected influx of settlers displaced by the revolutionary war. More seriously from the government's point of view, Jacob Schieffelin, secretary of the Indian Department at Detroit, had, by the use of liquor, persuaded a number of local Indian chiefs to sell him the entire area of Malden Township. From an official stand, the latter deal was the last straw.

In the years after the defeat of the French, the British continued to depend upon Indian alliances for much of their military strength. Thus it was necessary for the British government to follow a 'good neighbours' policy with the Indians – particularly as it applied to the acquisition of land. In 1775 the colonial authorities had instructed Governor Carleton that 'No purchases of Lands belonging to the Indians, whether in the Name and for the Use of the Crown, or in the Name and for the Use of propriataries of Colonies be made but at some general Meeting, at which the principal chiefs of each Tribe, claiming a property in such Lands, are present ...'[10] Clearly all the purchasers of Indian lands in Western District had failed to follow these rules. The government's response to Schieffelin's demand that his purchase be recognized was swift and to the point. On 26 April, 1784 Carleton's successor, Governor Haldimand, wrote Lieutenant-Governor Hay, commandant at Detroit:

In answer to the other subjects of your letter, I have to acquaint you that the claims of individuals, without distinction, upon Indian Lands at Detroit, or any other part of the Province are INVALID, and the mode of acquiring lands by what is called Deeds of Gift, is to be entirely discountenanced, for by the King's instructions, no private Person, Society, Corporation, or Colony, is capable of acquiring any property in lands belonging to Indians, either by purchase of, or grant of conveyance from the said Indians ...

These instructions lay totally aside the claim of Mr. Schieffelin ... even had he obtained it by less unworthy means than he did.[11]

By the same reasoning, the purchases of Sarah Ainse, Charles Gouin, and Teller and Park were invalid as well. These were not dealt with, however, until a later date.[12]

In 1783, while Schieffelin was struggling to assert his claim to Malden, quite a different group of people were taking possession of the area. A small group of loyalist Indian interpreters, led by Captains Matthew Elliot and William Caldwell, had been granted farms along the Detroit River in Malden by the Indians resident in the area. While it would appear that these grants suffered the same disability as did that to Schieffelin, Haldimand gave his support.[13] To legalize their possession, however, it would be necessary to arrange a surrender of the area to the crown.

In 1784 Captain Caldwell's company of Butler's Rangers, which had seen service at Detroit, was disbanded, and at Caldwell's invitation, a number decided to settle on the shores of Lake Erie. In 1787 the Erie shore was surveyed and ninety-seven lots laid out between the Detroit River and present-day Kingsville. In this survey lots 68, 69, and 70 (the site of the present town of Colchester) were reserved for a townsite. This settlement, called the 'New Settlement' or the 'Two Connected Townships' (Colchester and Gosfield), did not, however, immediately prosper. In January 1789 Major John Smith reported that only twenty-nine lots of the original ninety- seven were settled, while twenty-two were occupied by sham settlers. Poor crops and the failure of the government to supply the expected provisions and implements were partially to blame, although speculation by Detroit merchants appears to have been a major problem.[14]

During the late 1780s settlement began to spread up the Thames River from Lake St Clair as the speculators began to sell off portions of holdings. The reason that so many potential settlers were willing to take a chance on having only 'Indian title' to their lands was the severe shortage of surveyed lots in Essex County. Rather than wait, the settlers decided to purchase lots from the Thames River speculators. The government, seeing that control of the situation was slipping from its hands, was finally forced to act.

The first major surrender of lands by the Indians was made on 19 May, 1790.

It covered all of Essex and Kent, with the exception of the Gores of Chatham and Camden, and the township of Anderdon.[15] In return the Indians received £1200 Quebec currency in trade goods.[16] A survey of Essex County was ordered immediately, and the Land Board began to accept applications for lands in the surrendered area, as well as issuing certificates to settlers in the areas which had been occupied since 1749.[17] To accommodate the backlog of potential settlers, the south shore of Lake St Clair was surveyed and opened to settlement. Maps I and II show the extent of settlement first in 1754 and then in 1790 after the St Clair survey.

The progress made in opening new areas for settlement was almost entirely frustrated by the operations of the merchant speculators of Detroit and Sandwich. In 1787 Major Robert Mathews of Detroit described the problem on the Western Frontier: 'Individuals procure immense tracts of lands upon Indian Grants, sell it out in detail to poor wretches for £100 for three acres in front and 40 deep for which the Farm is at the same time mortgaged. The settler labours for a few years with only half his vigour, paying and starving all the time: and ultimately for debts on every hand is obliged to give his Land. In Trade, the lowest of the profession resort to these obscure places. They are without education or sentiment and many of them without common honesty ...[18] Because of a shortage of capital among the new settlers, even those who acquired their land directly from the government soon found themselves hopelessly in debt to the much denounced 'Shopkeeper Aristocracy.' The most conspicuous example of such speculation was revealed when John Askin, a Detroit merchant, wrote his friend D.W. Smith, the surveyor general, that he had acquired about eighty lots, most of them along the Lake St Clair shore.[19] The combination of speculation and the economic difficulties of the area would retard the development of Essex County for a long time.

The early settlement of Kent County to the east would demonstrate many of the same problems which had developed in Essex. The government's method of dealing with both settlers and speculators on the Thames was to sweep aside the 'legal' basis of their claims and then to allow them land on exactly the same terms as anyone else. They were, however, allowed to retain possession of farms upon which they had made improvements and a few were granted additional lands where it was felt that some particular sacrifice had been made to encourage settlement. Thus, while Sarah Ainse's claims to the north shore of the Thames were rejected, she was offered 1600 acres in Dover Township in recognition of her work in encouraging settlement.[20] Similarly the Detroit merchants, Meldrum and Park (the successor firm of Teller and Park) received more than 2000 acres in Camden, Harwick, and Raleigh townships.

With the opening of the townships along the Thames all of those who had waited impatiently for lands quickly took up farms along the river. The swampy

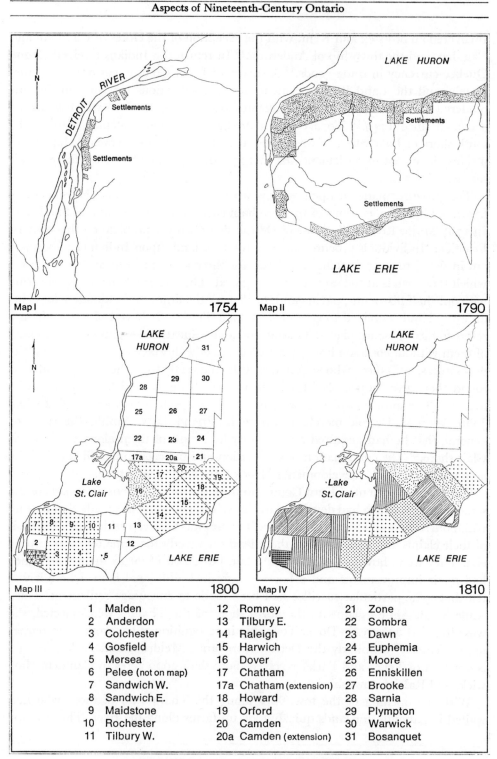

1	Malden	12	Romney	21	Zone
2	Anderdon	13	Tilbury E.	22	Sombra
3	Colchester	14	Raleigh	23	Dawn
4	Gosfield	15	Harwich	24	Euphemia
5	Mersea	16	Dover	25	Moore
6	Pelee (not on map)	17	Chatham	26	Enniskillen
7	Sandwich W.	17a	Chatham (extension)	27	Brooke
8	Sandwich E.	18	Howard	28	Sarnia
9	Maidstone	19	Orford	29	Plympton
10	Rochester	20	Camden	30	Warwick
11	Tilbury W.	20a	Camden (extension)	31	Bosanquet

TOWNSHIPS OF THE WESTERN DISTRICT

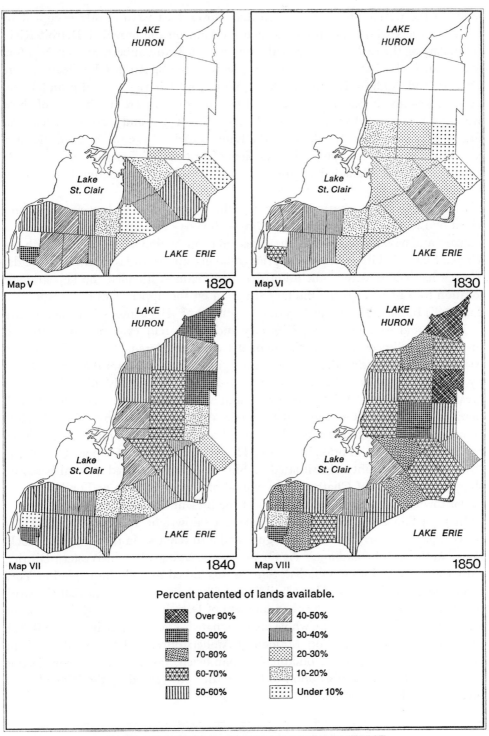

LAND SETTLEMENT IN THE WESTERN DISTRICT

lands in the western part of Raleigh and Dover East were mostly occupied by French settlers who were unable to acquire land on the crowded Detroit River front. Among the early patents issued were those to Jean Faubert, Francis Mouton, and Francis Thebott in Dover East; Alexis Langois, Andres Beniteau, Pierre Demers, and Andrew Lefleur in Dover West; and Charles Gerardin and Bonaventure Reaume in Raleigh.[21] These settlers, of course, were neighbours of those who had bought land from the speculators before 1790, and who had been confirmed in possession of their land by the Land Board. Above the French, the river lots were settled by loyalists and ex-soldiers of British and German ancestry.[22] By 1792 when Upper Canada had just been separated from Quebec, most of the river lots were claimed.

The greatest spur to early settlement of the Thames Valley, however, was provided by Lieutenant-Governor John Graves Simcoe's enthusiasm for the area as a military and naval stronghold in the expected continuation of the struggle with the United States. While at Montreal, prior to taking up his duties in Upper Canada, Simcoe had come to the conclusion that the Thames provided the key strategic location to control both the military situation on the upper lakes and trade with England's Indian allies in the American Northwest.[23] His winter trip from Niagara to Detroit and back between 4 February and 10 March, 1793 merely confirmed his ideas. As Simcoe wrote to Lieutenant-Governor Alured Clark of Quebec on 31 May, 1793: 'During the course of the Winter I walked from the Grand River by the route of La Tranche (or Thames) to Detroit; and I fully substantiated the great consequences of this internal communication between the countries which border on the Lakes Ontario and St. Clair. And for the purpose of civilization, command of the Indians & general defense, I am decidedly of opinion, that on the confluence of the main branches of the Thames the Capital of Upper Canada, as soon as possible, ought to be situated ...' Simcoe's plans included a naval base and shipyard at the site of Chatham, the capital of Upper Canada at London, and a major town (which he called Oxford) at the present site of Woodstock.[24]

In 1794 Simcoe ordered William Baker, a shipwright at Detroit, to build six boats capable of carrying six-pound guns and a storehouse 'in the form of a Blockhouse' at the site of Chatham.[25] Again, as was the case so often in Western District, early rosy expectations soon faded. Simcoe was forced to build his capital at York (Toronto), and the costs of boat-building at Chatham were so high that the work was stopped in 1795. With the abandonment of Detroit by the British in 1796, the Indian trade declined and the whole area stagnated. Even the moving of the British troops to the newly-built Fort Malden at Amherstburg, and the building of the court house and municipal buildings at Sandwich, failed to create any lasting prosperity.[26] Later, the disruption to local settlement caused by the War of 1812 only worsened the situation.[27]

Because of the delay for the settler in patenting his lands, caused by the necessity of performing settlement duties and acquiring the money to pay the various fees, the collapse in the economy of Western District did not immediately show up in levels of land patents taken out. As Table 1 shows, in the first three years (1797–9) after the government had finally solved all the problems of the land department,[28]

TABLE 1

Lands patented by township in Western District 1797–1820[29]

	1797–1800	1800–5	1805–10	1810–15	1815–20
ESSEX					
Malden	11,168	2402	269	188	184
Anderdon					
Colchester	4557	5596	7994	2252	2190
Gosfield	2084	5217	5903	4700	2200
Mersea					
Pelee Is.					
Sandwich	2912	14,524	5272	1290	1829
Maidstone	1789	8198	4091		
Rochester	198	6675	1000	200	
Tilbury W		1200	1491	3600	200
Total	22,808	47,016	32,529	12,230	10,003
KENT					
Romney		5000			
Tilbury E		570	800	853	
Raleigh	5219	6673	1500	2300	
Harwich	2172	21,443	5558	4740	2530
Dover	5475	7361	5773	120	
Chatham	1667	4195	1569		
Howard	1800	5340	420		1770
Oxford	200				200
Camden	1408	3246	1052		300
Total	17,941	53,828	16,672	8013	4800

40,749 acres of land were patented in Essex and Kent. This increased to 100,844 in the 1800–5 period when most of the earliest settlers were completing their settlement duties. After 1805 patenting declined to 49,201 acres in 1805–10 and 20,243 acres in the period 1810–15. Table 2 points out that population showed the same pattern of slow growth between 1805 and 1820 as did land patenting. In contrast to the slow growth in Western District, Home District, whose main centre, the Town of York, had been made the capital, was experiencing rapid growth. Thus between 1805 and 1820, Markham Township grew from 889 to 1789, York Township, from 494 to 1672 (and York Town from 473 to 1240), and outlying townships such as Pickering and Whitby grew from 96 and 104 to 575 and 505 respect-

TABLE 2

Population by township, Western District 1805–20[30]

	1805	1818	1820
Sandwich, Maidstone, and Rochester	1453	1911	2064
Malden	424	777	806
Colchester	250	418	396
Gosfield ⎫	220	361	336
Mersea ⎭			130
Raleigh ⎫	386	717	NA
Tilbury E & W and Dover E & W ⎭			
Chatham and Harwich ⎫	423	289	473
Camden and Howard ⎭			
Orford		NA	784

ively. The Western District had begun the century as one of the most developed regions in the province, but by 1820 was falling rapidly behind.

As Maps III, IV, and V show, the slow growth was not created to any great degree by either a scarcity of land or speculation. While absentee owners had, no doubt, created considerable disruption by getting control of the most accessible lands along Lake St Clair and the Thames River, there was still a great deal of land available behind the front concessions. Indeed, in 1800, in most areas except Malden Township, less than 10 per cent of the available land (that is, outside the two-sevenths of all land reserved for crown and clergy purposes) had been patented, while in 1820, with the exception of Malden (80–90 per cent patented), Sandwich (50–60 per cent), and Harwich (50–60 per cent), less than half the available land had been taken up.

In 1817 Robert Gourlay inquired into the economic and social problems of the province, and some of his findings warrant notice here. In reply to his question, 'What, in your opinion, retards the improvement of your township in particular ...?' the settlers made it clear that they saw four major difficulties which caused the slow growth. These were absentee ownership of lands, the presence of crown and clergy reserves, lack of a large population, and distance from markets.[31] With immense tracts of land available in more desirable parts of the province, which were free except for fees, there was little incentive for immigrants to purchase lands from their loyalist or speculator owners in Western District or to move so far from the best markets. This problem would continue to trouble the area for years to come.

In line with the government's policy of removing the Indians from Southern Ontario, a provisional treaty was signed with the local tribes on 9 March, 1819 covering Sombra, Dawn, and Zone, and parts of Enniskillen Township. This treaty was confirmed 8 July, 1822 in a second treaty which omitted Sombra. In searching

TABLE 3
Lands patented by township in Western District 1820–50[32]

	1820–5	1825–30	1830–5	1835–40	1840–5	1845–50
ESSEX						
Malden		200	2088	2995	300	
Anderdon				1688	1775	269
Colchester	661		508	13,497	568	12,624
Gosfield	1866	548	1505	11,003	1991	3236
Mersea	400	600	2301	6171	1901	8017
Pelee Is.						
Sandwich E & W	2945	3859	2275	7164	4782	4815
Maidstone		3743	200	1257	2252	3442
Rochester	200	3202	25	314	842	4885
Tilbury W		1556	183		1971	9968
	6072	13,708	9085	44,089	16,382	47,256
KENT						
Romney	420		2462	1200	408	4795
Tilbury E	665	3491	860	900	1100	19,812
Raleigh	3372	800	800	3949	6542	21,201
Harwich	1700	600	5400	12,259	2488	102
Dover E & W		1050	1000	8515		
Chatham	950	2775	8100	22,209	3475	3075
Howard	4614	600	5449	14,005	2054	850
Oxford	1000	2000	2730	6815	1070	5017
Camden			400	1441	736	1762
	12,721	11,316	27,401	71,293	17,873	56,614
LAMBTON						
Zone & Euphemia	2950	750	1567	2424	6764	19,630
Sombra	3000	11,020	4940	31,221	622	13,308
Dawn	11,373	12,450	18,100	24,300	5830	7100
Moore			1549	35,810	3194	600
Enniskillen				53,058	5750	650
Brooke			600	127,970	2106	2700
Sarnia			1289	15,173	14,600	1101
Plympton			538	45,089	5088	4134
Warwick			1233	29,920	8111	5659
Bosanquet			9180	54,992		7500
	17,323	24,220	38,996	419,957	52,065	62,382

old treaties it was discovered that Sombra had, in fact, been surrendered on 7 September, 1796, but had never been surveyed or opened to the public.[33] Sombra was surveyed in 1820 and Dawn in 1831.[34] While a number of settlers immediately took up some of the more desirable locations (for example Francis Baby, Duncan MacDonald, Samuel Burnham, and Abraham Smith in Sombra, and Job Hall in Dawn), there was little immediate demand for lots in the area. As Table 3 shows, only 17,323 acres were patented in the three new townships (Sombra, Dawn, and Zone) between 1820 and 1825, and another 24,220 acres between 1825 and 1830.

In 1825 the balance of the northern area of Western District was surrendered by the Indians.[35] These townships were surveyed and thrown open for settlement between 1826 and 1829, with Bosanquet being reserved for the Canada Company as part of the Huron Tract. Those surveying the newly-opened area found that a few squatters had lived there for several years. For example in Moore, Mahlon Burwell, the surveyor, discovered fifteen French-speaking and five English-speaking families.[36] For the first decade the seven new townships (Moore, Anniskillen, Brooke, Sarnia, Plympton, Warwick and Bonsanquet) attracted little attention from settlers. As Table 3 shows, a total of only 14,389 acres were patented in the new area up to 1835, and 9180 acres of this was patented by the Canada Company in Bosanquet for speculative purposes.

In addition to the purchases from the Indians of new areas, the government made fundamental changes in land policy that affected old-settled areas as well. The most important of these changes – the taxation of wild lands, the ending of free grants (except those already due to loyalist and military claimants), and the decision to sell the crown and clergy reserves – had great effects in central areas such as Home District. There the taxation of wild lands and the opening up of the reserves had the effect of allowing a much more compact settlement, and resulted in a great increase in population in long-settled areas.[37] This was not the case in Western District. Up to 1835 there was very little increase in patenting in the old areas, only Harwich and Chatham showing any large-scale patenting. This, however, relates to the rise of Chatham as the metropolitan centre for the newly-opened areas rather than the freeing-up of new lands in old areas.

A comparison of Maps v and vi (1820 and 1830) shows how little immediate advantage was felt in Western District from the opening of the crown and clergy reserves. In almost every township the proportion of lands patented of lands available had declined. The combination of slow growth and the opening of the reserves meant that in 1830, of the whole area, only Malden was more than 50 per cent patented, while Mersea, Tillbury East and West, Romney, Raleigh, Dover East and West, Chatham, Howard, Oxford, Camden, Zone, Sombra, and Dawn were all less than 30 per cent patented. In addition the whole new area, acquired in 1825, was yet to begin the patenting process.

The slow development of land acquisition was paralleled by the slow rate of population growth in Western District between 1820 and 1835. While other areas were experiencing a period of dynamic growth and rapid expansion, Western District remained in the depressed state which had been general from the beginning of settlement. For example, while Sandwich and Malden grew from 2017 and 1224 persons in 1825 to 2618 and 1459 respectively in 1835, other centres in

TABLE 4
Population by township, Western District 1820–50[38]

	1820	1825	1830	1835	1840	1851
ESSEX						
Malden	806	{1124	{1211	{1459	1969	4195
Anderdon					241	1199
Colchester	396	545	695	868	1059	1870
Gosfield	336	415	552	943	1006	1802
Mersea	130	243	321	439	696	1193
Pelee Is.[1]						
Sandwich E & W	{2064	2017*	2247	2618	3062	4928
Maidstone		{236	{271	{523	547	1167
Rochester					376	788
Tilbury W	467[9]			496[2]	219	675
KENT						
Romney		{290	365	158	231	{1023
Tilbury E[2,9]					312	
Raleigh		395	582	1077	1563	2460
Harwich	473[10]	458[3]	320	656	1397	2627
Dover E & W[9]		791[4]	602	790	1094	1723
Chatham[3,10]			255	363	509	1723
Howard	784[11]	{404	690	1134	1524	2798
Oxford			223	415	536	1566
Camden[11]		271[5]	437[6]	216	308	1434[7]
LAMBTON						
Zone & Euphemia†,[6]				674	993	1457[8]
Sombra[4]			517	524	786	738
Dawn[5,6]				409	694	556
Moore				471	643	1258
Enniskillen						238
Brooke						511
Sarnia					359	1384
Plympton				261	467	1511
Warwick					630	2069
Bosanquet						1093

*Figures are for 1826.

†Zone and Euphemia were a single township named Zone until 1850.

1 Pelee Island was, in 1850, still unorganized. There were, however, several families resident there in 1850, both employed as lighthouse keepers and as squatters farming the land. For example, in 1844 W. H. Smith noted that about 600 acres were under cultivation on the Island and the population was about fifty.

2 Tilbury E & W were combined in 1835.

3 Harwick and Chatham were combined in 1825.

4 Dover E & W and Sombra were combined in 1825.

5 Camden and Dawn were combined in 1825.

6 Camden, Zone, Euphemia, and Dawn were combined in 1830.

7 Camden and Zone were combined in 1851.

8 Figures are for Euphemia alone in 1851.

9 Tilbury E & W and Dover E & W were united in 1820.

10 Harwich and Chatham were united in 1820.

11 Howard and Camden were united in 1820.

Western Ontario grew much more rapidly. Thus, during the same period London Township (in Middlesex) grew from 1606 to 3533, Stamford from 1498 to 2459, and North and South Dumfries (in Brant) from 1330 to 4309. In Western District, only Raleigh and Howard, which grew from 395 and 404 to 1077 and 1134 respectively, showed the same dynamism.

In Western District, up to 1835, there were three main problems which retarded settlement and economic growth: distance from the main markets and difficult transportation to them; a lack of high value crops and a proper agricultural technology to grow them; and the new land policies which tended to concentrate new settlement in more central areas.[39]

In spite of the disruptions caused by the severe depression of 1837–8, the Rebellion of 1837 and subsequent 'Patriot' invasions, the period 1835–50 would completely reverse the old pattern of stagnation and shattered hopes. With the opening of the Erie and Welland canals, the Lake Erie area finally achieved access to the European grain markets that had previously proved so valuable to the more eastern farmers. Moreover, with settlers filling up the better lands in more central areas, after 1840 more and more newcomers were forced to turn their attention westward. The result was a 'boom' such as had never before been experienced in the area. Thus, as Table 4 shows, a massive wave of settlers poured into the area. Villages such as Amherstburg and Sandwich, which had been dormant for generations, became hives of activity, and Chatham, which had already begun to develop between 1825 and 1835, now became a booming, brawling, frontier metropolis.

In all this growth, only one act by the government created serious local difficulty. In 1835 and 1836 those speculators and loyalist and military claimants holding free land rights fought back against the long series of legislative changes which had lessened their value by wild land taxes and the reimposition of settlement duties. Confronted with a bill which asserted the control of the Assembly over land regulations, Lieutenant-Governor Sir John Colborne and the Executive Council abolished the settlement duties on all loyalist and militia claims already located.[40] The result was a land-rush of catastrophic proportions by absentee owners. Table 3 shows that in just five years (1835–40) 535,339 acres were patented in Western District. In this area the situation in Brook Township presented the most spectacular case with 103,400 acres patented in 1835 alone. In 1836 Plympton with 22,905 acres, Enniskillen with 28,500, and Dawn with 20,800 acres patented were the most severely affected. In the old areas, while patent rates were much lower, townships such as Colchester, Gosfield, Harwich, Chatham, and Howard showed large amounts of land-rush patents. Patenting rates dropped off between 1840 and 1845, but between 1845 and 1850 increased once again. During the latter period, however, patenting activity reflected an increased population rather than speculation.

As Maps VII and VIII show, by 1850 the process of land acquisition was largely completed, although in many localities population density was still relatively low – reflecting the large amounts of absentee-owned lands that still existed although the large-scale inflow of settlement continued.[41] By 1850, however, the essential pattern for later years had been established. Henceforth the process would be one of purchasing absentee-owned lands and filling vacant areas by draining marshes and building roads. The periods of great change were over until the rise of large manufacturing centres, and new farming technology would again create dynamics to which population distribution would be forced to respond.

The settlement of Western District, like that of other areas in Upper Canada, therefore, was shaped both by external forces and events, and by local conditions and developments. Because of the area's location on the frontier, far distant from the seats of power and commerce at York, Kingston, and Montreal, its early impetus as a military and trading centre for the American Northwest soon faded, and it lapsed into poverty and neglect. The early history of Western District, then, was one of shattered hopes and frustrated ambitions. It was not until after 1835 when new transportation routes were opened, and the waves of British emigration had finally reached the area, that the modern agricultural landscape would take shape. The settlement of Western District, in the context of pioneer Ontario, had been among the most difficult to acomplish. The 'Clear Gritism' of its inhabitants in the 1850s reflected the independence of mind which that struggle had bred.

NOTES

1 The western portion of the colony of Quebec was divided into four districts in 1788. These districts were called Luneburg (later Lunenburg), Micklenburg, Nassau, and Hesse, but were almost immediately renamed Eastern, Midland, Home, and Western districts. When Upper and Lower Canada were separated in 1791, the districts were retained as the basis of local government in Upper Canada. In 1798 the four original districts were subdivided into eight with Johnstown, Newcastle, Niagara, and London districts being created. With this division Western District was reduced to the general area covered by the present-day counties of Essex, Kent, and Lambton. The latter area forms the basis for the present study. For a good study of the development of district boundaries see G.W. Spragge, 'The District of Upper Canada 1788–1849,' Ontario Historical Society, *Papers and Records* [OHSPR], XXXIX, 1947, 91–100.

2 The terms 'north' and 'west' shores were used interchangeably because of the sharp bend in the Detroit River between Lake St Clair and Lake Erie.

3 Quoted in Ernest J. Lajeunesse, ed., *The Windsor Border Region, Canada's Southermost Frontier: a collection of Documents* (Toronto 1960) lii-liii

4 The arpent, a French land measure, equals approximately 191.8 English feet. Thus the farms measured 575.4 feet wide and 7672 feet long, and contained approximately 102 English acres. See ibid., xli

5 Diary of Father Joseph Pierre Bonnecamps, sj, reproduced in ibid., 57

6 Ibid., lxix-lxx

7 According to F.C. Hamil, *The Valley of the Lower Thames* (Toronto 1951), 10, the first English settler on the Thames was likely John Peck who settled in 1778, while Jean Baptiste Lacroix (1779) and David Lynd (1780) followed close behind.

8 For an interesting account of Sarah Ainse's career, see F.C. Hamil, 'Sally Ainse, Fur Trader,' Algonquin Club (Detroit), *Historical Bulletin*, III, 1939

9 Hamil, *The Valley of the Lower Thames*, 11

10 Quoted in Gilbert C. Paterson, 'Land Settlement in Upper Canada 1783–1840,' *Sixteenth Annual Report of the Public Archives ... of Ontario* (Toronto 1921), 220

11 Lajeunesse, ed., *Windsor Border Region*, 157–8

12 Two interesting examples of the kinds of exploitive land deals with the Indians were those made for Mersea Township and Pelee Island. On 6 May 1788 James Allan, William Caldwell and J. Caldwell received an area '11 miles by six miles north of Lake Erie' for '999 years renewable' for 'three bushels of Indian corn annually or value thereof.' In a similar bargain made on 1 May 1788 the Indians had leased Pelee Island to Thomas McKee for 999 years on terms. See ibid., Appendix IV, 332

13 Ibid., 159

14 Ibid., cxii

15 Anderson had been surrendered by the Indians on 15 May 1786 to Alexander McKee to be held in trust for themselves. This legality was entered into in order to prevent unscrupulous speculators such as Schieffelin from getting control of the Huron lands by illegitimate means. See Government of Canada, *Indian Treaties and Surrenders* (2 vols., Ottawa 1891), I, Treaty no 116

16 Ibid., Treaty no 2. Map III shows the areas covered by the major Indian land surrenders.

17 Lajeunesse, ed., *Windsor Border Region*, cxi

18 Major Robert Mathews, Detroit, to Governor Haldimand, 3 Aug. 1787, quoted in Lillian F. Gates, *Land Policies of Upper Canada* (Toronto 1968), 43

19 See John Askin to D.W. Smith, 1797, reproduced in Lajeunesse, ed., *Windsor Border Region*, 186

20 See Hamil, *The Valley of the Lower Thames*, 22–3. The lots offered were numbers 9 to 16, Concession I. These were patented 29 June 1794, but the patents were rescinded in 1798 when the Executive Council reversed Simcoe's ruling in the case. These and future patent data are from Provincial Secretary's Paper, 'Land Patents to 1850,' Public Archives of Ontario, microfilm.

21 'Land Patents to 1850'

22 Hamil, *The Valley of the Lower Thames*, 21

23 Fred Landon, *Western Ontario and the American Frontier* (Toronto 1967), 12–14

24 J.G. Simcoe to Alured Clark, 31 May 1793, in E.A. Cruikshank, ed., *The Correspondence of Lieutenant-Governor John Graves Simcoe* (5 vols., Toronto 1923–31), I, 338; Landon, *Western Ontario and the American Frontier*

25 J.G. Simcoe to William Baker, 9 Oct. 1794, *Simcoe Papers*, III, 116–7

26 Lajeunesse, ed., *Windsor Border Region*, cxxi

27 Hamil, *The Valley of the Lower Thames*, 78–104

28 See Theodore D. Regehr, 'Land Ownership in Upper Canada 1783–1796: A Background to the First Table of Fees,' *Ontario History*, LV, 1, 40–6

29 It should be noted that neither Anderdon nor Oxford were open for settlement. These were still Indian reserves occupied by Hurons and the Moravian-lead Delawares respectively. In addition, Dover East had been closed to free settlement from 1803 to 1818 because of Lord Selkirk's Baldoon experiment. Patent data are calculated from 'Land Patents to 1850.'

30 Census data are from 'Provincial Secretary's Papers,' RG 5, B 26, vols. 1–7

31 Robert F. Gourlay, *A Statistical Account of Upper Canada* (London 1822), I, 271–301

32 For a more detailed discussion of land policy, land patenting, and settlement see Leo A.

Johnson, 'Land Policy, Population Growth and Social Structure in the Home District, 1793–1851,' *Ontario History*, LXIII, 1, March 1971, 41–60.

33 *Indian Treaties and Surrenders,* I. See Treaties no 7, 21, 280½ and 25.

34 See Jan T. Elford, *A History of Lambton County* (Sarnia 1967), 75, 96

35 *Indian Treaties and Surrenders*, I. See Treaties no 27½ (a provisional surrender covering the area signed 26 April 1825) and 29, the confirmatory treaty signed 10 July 1825.

36 Elford, *History of Lambton County*, 83

37 Johnson, 'Land Settlement ... in Home District,' 55, see maps for 1830 and 1840

38 Census data are from Public Archives of Canada, Provincial Secretary's Papers, RG 5, B 26, vols. I to IV; and *Journals of the Legislative Assembly of Upper Canada*, 1824–40.

39 Hamil's discussion of the attempt of farmers in Western District to establish an export market for tobacco is particularly instructive. Lacking a viable local market either for grain or produce, the farmers found it necessary to adopt an alternative crop, but lacked the proper skills required to process it properly. It took almost a generation to make it a steady source of income. See the discussions in Hamil, *The Valley of the Lower Thames*

40 Gates, *Land Policies of Upper Canada*, 137

41 See *Census of the Canadas, 1861* (Ottawa 1862), I, Table 1

The Origins of Local Government

G.P. deT. Glazebrook

The early system of local government in what is now the Province of Ontario originated in the first years of settlement and remained little changed until the larger towns were given elected bodies at the beginning of the 1830s. 'Local government' is a phrase which may be misunderstood. It is the government of an area, having in the main to do with such public affairs as are regional rather than national (or provincial). It may be conducted in whole or in part by elected authorities but not necessarily so. Shared jurisdiction is common. Like national government, local government need not have any elected element.

The form of local government that was to prevail, virtually unaltered, for nearly forty years was established between 1783 and 1791, in the years between the Anglo-American treaty of peace and the division of the Province of Quebec. The original model for the institutions was the local government of England. To some extent that model, in the form which it had taken in the late eighteenth century, was followed with little alteration; but in other respects the modifications earlier made in British colonies had some influence. Although nearly all the first English-speaking settlers came from the Thirteen Colonies, local institutions were not in their baggage. Both the legislature and public of Nova Scotia had argued over local government but in the end New England forms were rejected. In the Province of Quebec, under British civil rule, British and French practices were ingeniously combined.

In England the areas for local government were the county, the parish, and the borough. Throughout the country only pockets of democracy were to be found. In the county the officials, all appointed, were drawn from the landed gentry. The lord lieutenant was the senior, followed by the sheriff and the high constable. The burden of administration, however, was borne by justices of the peace, sitting singly, in pairs, or in the courts of quarter sessions of the peace. The parishes, of which the boundaries were ill-defined, had superseded the old manors and hundreds. A large proportion of them had come under the control of 'select' or 'close' vestries, that is, of oligarchies. They nominated overseers of the poor, overseers of highways, constables, and other officials, for which approval by the justices was frequently required. The boroughs, too, had been falling into the hands of small groups. In addition to these standing bodies were those established by the central government to undertake specific duties. Of these the ones that were most relevant to Upper Canada were the turnpike trusts.[1]

In the old North American colonies the structure was somewhat different, partly because of local conditions, partly because local government had started there before the trend toward oligarchy was marked. Those colonies, however, were not in a single pattern. In the south the parish had a minor role, the major one being played by the county, with the county court corresponding to quarter sessions in England. The middle colonies placed more emphasis on the township, but it was in New England that the town, or township, meeting was dominant. Continuity was maintained by 'selectmen' elected to direct the work of officials in the intervals between general meetings.[2] The township was adopted as the local district in Nova Scotia, but the efforts of groups to have the New England town meeting introduced were unsuccessful.

When the Province of Quebec, out of which Upper Canada was carved in 1791, came under British civil rule, the arrangements made for local government reflected the English ones of the day, but modified to fit the French traditions. At the outset authority was given to the governor and his council to appoint sheriffs and justices of the peace, the latter meeting in courts of quarter sessions or acting in ones or twos. For the towns of Quebec and Montreal they might make police rules, the word 'police' being regularly used in Quebec, and subsequently in Upper Canada, in its sense of a body of rules or regulations. Complaints, however, were made about the administration of towns, groups of men in both Montreal and Quebec advocating incorporation.

Outside the towns each parish was directed to nominate six men from which list the governor would appoint the required number, they to be sworn into office by justices of the peace. Such officials would carry out the duties of constables, overseers of roads, coroners, and fence viewers. Control of weeds and stray cattle was covered in ordinances. Prevention of fire, the assize of bread, and maintenance of standards for flour to be exported were dealt with in other ordinances. What in Quebec had been called the corvée and in Upper Canada statute labour was the subject of a lengthly ordinance of 1777.

Those United Empire Loyalists who chose to settle in the western part of the Province of Quebec were placed in the vicinities of the old French forts at Kingston and Niagara. Apart from a handful of fur traders, the only other white inhabitants of the whole land from the end of the seigneuries to the American border were the French farmers near the Detroit River. In that area, however, both under French and early British rule, local government seems to have been of the simplest nature. After 1763 a justice of the peace was appointed but the commandant at Detroit exercised semi-military rule.[3] Local government in French-speaking Quebec in the

British regime may be more usefully studied in the eastern parts of the province. The institutions and practices which developed in the west arose in the Loyalist settlements.

Apart from the fort at Niagara and the remains of the French fort at Kingston, the places chosen for the refugees from the revolutionary war were untouched by man except for the presence of a few Indians, from whom the land was bought by the crown. The newcomers were, therefore, pioneers, devoting their energies to clearing land for farms and the building of little towns.

In contrast with Nova Scotia, western Quebec was not a haven for New Englanders. Most of the Loyalists who founded Upper Canada had lived in New York where local government was a compromise between the county system of Virginia and the town meeting of Massachusetts. They were not likely to advocate institutions they had never known, but neither did they show much interest in transplanting those they had. The Loyalists were never backward in asking for what they wanted, believing that they had earned the gratitude of the British government. They sought, and many of them obtained, financial compensation for the loss of their possessions and prospects in the old colonies. They expected, and were awarded, land, and were critical of any break in the flow of free rations and of tools for farming and building.

In the political field they asked for an elected assembly, freehold instead of seigneurial tenure, and for the separation of the west of the province, what is now Southern Ontario, from the District of Montreal. Suggestions were made that there be officials to look after local matters, as compared to provincial ones, but generally without showing any preference between appointment and election. There is nothing to suggest a general demand for local self-government. It may be that the evidence is misleading. The spokesmen were of the more educated class, men who became leaders and magistrates. The larger numbers were deep in the woods, struggling to make farms; and if they had political views those are not recorded. All that can be said with confidence is that expressed opinion gives no support for the assertion, commonly made, that the Loyalists initiated what has been described as a long struggle for elected local bodies.

The settlement of large groups of Loyalists began in 1784 on the Niagara Peninsula and more extensively on the upper St Lawrence and the eastern end of Lake Ontario. In the next four years the whole western area was a part of the District of Montreal, so that whatever local government was exercised would be under the authority of ordinances. Some work on roads was certainly done but, unfortunately, little is known about local government in this period. Individual justices of the peace were appointed to the area from 1784, and so in all probability were captains of militia. The former certainly acted as judges but there is nothing to show that they took any part in administration. It is not until 1788 when the letters patent were issued creating new districts that the operation of local government can be followed. In these new districts – labouring under the absurd names of Luneburg, Mecklenburg, Nassau, and Hesse – a framework was quickly erected.

On the same day on which the patent was signed a general commission of the peace for the District of Mecklenburg in the Kingston area was also signed.[4] Probably similar documents were drawn for the other districts. Such commissions were, apart from names, verbatim copies of those in England which applied to counties. Each was addressed by the king to a large number of persons of whom many held high office but were not residents of the area in question. The last names were those of the magistrates who would in fact 'keep our peace.' Although not mentioned in the commission every court of quarter sessions accepted it as its general authority, and in some courts the documents were read aloud at the opening of a sitting.

No legislation was needed to establish courts of quarter sessions for they had been authorized and at work in older parts of the province for several years. They were courts of law, hearing minor civil and criminal cases. Their functions in local government were, as explained by Sidney and Beatrice Webb in their *Study of English Local Government*, not administrative but judicial, in the sense that they were enforcement of the laws which imposed obligations on the king's subjects. As the name implies the courts were required to meet in general sessions four times a year, but in some districts the volume of business made adjournments to further days necessary and in some cases special sessions were held between quarters.

In the District of Nassau, which was for practical purposes the Niagara area, the court was called together promptly in October 1788. It seems to have been the first, followed by Luneburg and Mecklenburg on the St Lawrence in 1789.[5] For a short time the courts of quarter sessions were the only bodies responsible for local affairs in the western districts. They were given little if any guidance but could invoke the authority of ordinances. A reference in the Nassau minutes at the beginning of 1789 shows that commissioners of roads and pathmasters, who had been directing the obligatory road work in conformity with ordinances, came under the general direction of the court.

The courts of magistrates faced problems as they arose, and to a considerable extent seem to have used their own judgment, with some reference to opinion in the townships. They placed restrictions on the sale of liquor, sought to preserve the sanctity of Sunday, made provision for orphans and illegitimate children, deliberated on whether domestic animals might run at large, appointed constables, and looked after roads. It has often been said, at the time and later, that the justices of the peace, appointed officials, were unrepresentative of the people at large. Certainly they were atypic, as were all the judges. On the other hand most of them, probably all, had other occupations which brought them in touch with people and conditions of all kinds. Certainly they dominated local government; and whether in the circumstances of the province at the time that was desirable must be a matter of opinion. They must, however, be credited with starting township bodies and forcing or keeping them in operation when they faltered (which often happened).

In January 1789, less than three months after the first sitting, the quarter sessions of Nassau issued, without explanation, an order of court requiring that on the first Tuesday of April a meeting was to be held in each township of the district for the purpose of electing such public officers as the magistrate present should direct. The result is recorded explicitly only in the case of Township Number 6 (later Grimsby) where the inhabitants had a town meeting in 1790, 'according,' as the minutes read, 'to an order from court.' They may also have met in 1789 but the first two pages of the township record have been lost. The only other township in the district of which the earliest proceedings have been found is Louth, but unfortunately they were edited by a town clerk with a curious sense of logic. The first meeting, held in May 1793, he attributed to the statute which was not even introduced into the legislature until June.

At the eastern end of what was to be Upper Canada only two townships are known to have had such early meetings. In Sidney (now in Hastings County) they began in 1790, but in this case the town clerk was even more imaginative. Having secured by public subscription a blank book in 1800, he proceeded to rewrite the early record, to the effect that the meeting of 1790 arose out of the act of 1793. Adolphustown (now in Lennox and Addington) began its impressive annual meetings in 1792 without any explanation of their commencement.[6] Considering the sad destruction of documents it is quite possible, and indeed probable, that other townships called the people together before 1793, although, of course, only a few were sufficiently populated at that time.

Thus, the evidence showing how town meetings began is lacking in depth. Direct mention is to be found in quarter sessions only in the case of Nassau and in townships only in Grimsby. Further clues are concealed either by the absence of documents or by the arbitrary way in which proceedings were written. Nevertheless, the evidence is firm. Township meetings were called on the order of courts, the authority of which in local matters was unquestioned, and not because of spontaneous outbursts of democratic zeal. Indeed, it is more likely that such gatherings were unpopular with many of the people of a township. Travelling was difficult and time-consuming, and many of those who were elected to office did their best to escape unprofitable tasks.

By 1790 the essential parts of the machinery of local government had been developed and were in operation at least in some areas. In respect of towns, however, the architects of the days when the western district was still part of Quebec made no more progress than did those of early Upper Canada. Loyalists at camp in Sorel in 1784 asked for a borough at Kingston comparable to those in the

Province of New York.[7] In 1791 an ordinance extended the powers of the justices over the towns of Quebec and Montreal to any town or village in the province, explicitly empowering the justices to make police regulations over a wide field. Nothing was done, however, to take advantage of this authority which came on the eve of the division of the province.

The first legislature of Upper Canada, meeting at Newark in 1792, was overwhelmingly Loyalist. The assembly, elected on a wide franchise, was made up, according to the first lieutenant-governor, John Graves Simcoe, of 'the most active characters in the several Counties'; nor did he find that either house was as subject to direction as he thought proper. One would suppose that if the Loyalists had been anxious to have democratic institutions for local affairs they would have said so and acted accordingly. Perhaps some of them did express such sentiments, but in the absence of any newspaper it is impossible to follow the debate. All that the cryptic journals record is the decision of majorities, and they show no crusade for democracy.[8]

In the first session the issue was joined between those who wished to retain the existing township system and those who preferred a more conservative one. Ephraim Jones, justice of the peace for Luneburg and member of the assembly for Grenville, introduced a bill 'to authorize town meetings for the purpose of appointing divers parish officers.' Although no one has apparently seen the text or even a description of its contents, it has for some reason been deduced that a measure more democratic than that finally adopted was proposed. There is no reason to suppose so. Jones would have been fully familiar with the operation of town meetings and was probably merely proposing that they be continued under the new regime. The other bill, the author of which is unidentified, provided that 'divers Public Officers' be appointed by the justices of the peace. Both bills were read twice and then dropped.

In the session of 1793 the same difference of opinion seems to have obtained; but, according to Simcoe, majority opinion was in favour of election of local officers, and he saw no serious objection to such a mild devolution of power. Neither, it seems, did the British authorities, in spite of their fear of anything that smacked of American democracy. After passing between the two houses and being amended, an act emerged 'To provide for the Nomination and Appointment of Parish and Town Officers within this Province' (33 Geo. III, c 12). There were no parish officers except to the extent that churchwardens could be considered as such, nor was the parish a unit for government. The recognized local divisions were districts and townships. Simcoe's proclamation of 16 July 1792 divided the southern part of the province into nineteen counties, but these had only slight relationship to local government, being established as ridings and militia units.

Perhaps the chief interest of the statute of 1793 is that it was the first written description of the main features of the township system as it had been practised, with some minor variations that can be identified and perhaps others that cannot in view of the lack of information on pre-1793 meetings. Each township with not less than thirty householders was to hold each March a meeting called by a constable under a warrant signed by two justices of the peace. The sole purpose, according to the act, was to elect a number of officials.

The legislature failed to make any special provision for the government of towns, although Richard Cartwright of Kingston made an attempt. In 1794 he introduced into the Legislative Council a bill 'to enable the magistrates of the respective districts to regulate the Police of the several Towns within the Province.' In effect this was the gist of the ordinance of 1791, already mentioned. After being read a second time the bill disappeared into limbo. Simcoe would have gone further by incorporating Kingston and Newark but was turned down flat by the secretary of state, Portland, who obviously did not understand the problem and concluded only that such municipalities were not proper in a colony. Nor did he like Simcoe's companion proposal, that there be a lieutenant for each county; but since that was already embodied in an act for the regulation of the militia (33 Geo. III, c 1) he placed no absolute ban.[9]

This was the sole original contribution of the legislature, and then only to implement an idea put forward by the lieutenant-governor. It was not a success. Lieutenants were appointed over several years, suitable men being chosen, but they never lived up to Simcoe's expectations. Thus, the effective machinery of local government was much as it had been before 1792, with the important exception that there was a provincial legislature which took an increasingly active part in local government, either by instructions to quarter sessions and town meetings or by direct means.

Successful operation was dependent on two principal conditions: the willingness of competent individuals to accept public office and the financial resources at their disposal. For the district offices it was not always possible to find enough suitable men, a problem met even in England with its old landowning class. The positions of sheriff and high constable were financially unrewarding. The same was true of justices of the peace, but here elements of prestige and responsibility were compensating factors. At times and in places not enough magistrates were present for the many tasks they had to perform. Some were idle. On rare occasions courts of quarter sessions were delayed when the bench could not be even partially filled, but on the whole this was not a problem, even if the justices dwindled to two. Complaints that magistrates could not be found for such purposes as administering oaths were many and well founded. If inconvenience and delays resulted, however, it did not necessarily follow that the system itself was faulty. The province did not have enough people of any kind, including the educated class from which judges of all kinds were ordinarily drawn.

Township officials were far more numerous but could be taken from a wider range of the population. No knowledge of the law was required and little formal education for those who, for the most part, were concerned with the affairs of the countryside. Roads and bridges, the placing and specifications of fences, straying domestic animals, prevention of grass or forest fire, and control of weeds were the subjects with which they were mostly concerned. The town clerks' spelling was frequently subjective but the meaning was clear enough. The real difficulty was the unpopularity of most of the positions, which took time and brought little return in cash. Payment was nearly always in fees rather than salary. Case after case came up in quarter sessions of men who had refused office or who had failed in their duties.

The first system of district taxation was a failure. Under the statute of 1793 (33 Geo. III, c 3) the township assessors were directed to classify the inhabitants according to their real and personal property. Any one below £50 was at first excused but later required to pay two shillings. For higher categories, from £50 to £100 and so on, fixed sums were assigned. When the lists were made up and signed by two justices of the peace the collectors took the field. It was soon found that returns were falsified by connivance between householders and assessors and that they varied wildly when new assessors examined the same properties. Amending bills of 1798 and 1800 were reserved and it was not until 1803 that a new statute (43 Geo. III, c 12) went into effect.

Under the new plan, which lasted for many years, arbitrary values were placed on real and personal property. An acre of arable land, for example, was worth £1, a milch cow £3, a town lot £10, and so on in a list that was several times amended by subsequent acts. When everything was added up the court of quarter sessions decided the rate of taxation, up to a statutory maximum of a penny in the pound, in relation to estimated expenditure. Although the townships supplied the assessors and collectors they had very little revenue of their own. What there was came from fines on persons breaking their regulations and sometimes from subscriptions for special purposes. As time went on the provincial grants, largely for roads and bridges, became more frequent.

Such was the system. Its ancestry was remarkably mixed. The role of the magistrates, in and out of quarter sessions, was adopted directly from contemporary England. Both Simcoe and Russell, the administrator in his absence, had hoped that the lieutenants of counties would keep an eye on the magistrates so that weak spots could be bolstered, but there is no indication that they did so, and in any case the office of lieutenant existed for only a few years. As the original four districts were subdivided, the area for which each court of quarter sessions was responsible became of more manageable size. Some of the courts were busier than others and the proportion of time devoted to local government varied.

In contrast with what could be criticized as the oligarchic or class rule of the magistrates, the town meeting was an example of direct democracy. It bore no exact resemblance to any similar institution elsewhere, the closest comparison, perhaps, being with the Quebec parish. It has been too quickly written off (perhaps by writers who have never lived in farming country) on the grounds that it dealt only with stray cattle and the height of fences, and that it had no control over the officials which it elected. The importance of the election itself is seldom stressed. For early years the records of too few townships have been preserved to allow for firm conclusions on their effectiveness. Furthermore, the minutes speak only of 'an annual meeting of the inhabitants,' making it impossible to tell how representative they were. The populations, of course, were small, but as all the early meetings were in private houses they cannot have been large.

Too little is known, but enough to show that the township organization was flexible in that the nature of its use depended on the degree of enterprise exhibited by those who were active in public affairs. It was possible to do the minimum – elect officers and go home for a year, the practice sometimes regarded as the usual one. In some townships, however, a great deal more was done, and frequently with a blind eye to the letter of the law. Instructions were given to officials in connection with the relief of poverty, there being nothing comparable to the English poor laws, and in supervising the destruction of thistles. At times the townships operated the wolf bounty entirely on their own resources. Occasionally they held special meetings to consider some local need and might contribute private money to it. Given the type of rural area at the beginning of the nineteenth century, it will be seen that the township could, if it desired, take in hand the majority of the problems.

The yawning gap in the system of local government was the absence of any special provision for the administration of towns. Early projects had been frustrated by London and the provincial legislature acted only when pressed from outside. The situation was not quite as bad as it might appear. The courts of quarter sessions were well aware that they could not give enough attention to the particular needs of towns, but most of the justices were urban and familiar with local wants. Indeed, as residents they had selfish reasons for attempting improvement. They did what they could. In the Home District, for example, the court forbade in 1800 obstruction of streets, and in the following year issued regulations designed to prevent or control fires.[10]

For some years the course followed was that which had met with less than success in the Province of Quebec: to give to the justices wide authority over the management of towns, together with power to fine those who broke the rules they had laid down. A temporary pattern developed out of a petition to the assembly in 1816 signed by 'the Magistrates and Inhabitants of the Town of Kingston,' then the principal urban centre. They asked for 'a well regulated Police established by law' in view of the fact that authority did not exist to cover such questions as street repairs and fire protection.[11]

The legislature responded quickly with a statute (56 Geo. III, c 33) passed on 1 April. It authorized quarter sessions to make such regulations as they thought necessary under a number of headings; to raise, by assessment on property, up to £100 a year for fire equipment and other improvements; and to inflict fines up to forty shillings for breaches of the regulations. The ink was hardly dry on the paper before the Midland court issued its series of rules. The Kingston act was followed in 1817 by a similar one for York, Sandwich, and Amherstburg, and by another one in 1819 for Niagara.

The question of 'police towns,' although late in the day, marked some advance toward more efficient government by extending the powers of the magistrates and providing them with modest funds, but the defects were glaring. The towns remained under district and township government with no officials or standing bodies concerned exclusively with them. In 1825 the legislature made a half-hearted attempt to remedy the situation by passing an act (6 Geo. IV, c 6) under which justices of the peace living in a police town were directed to meet twice a week. The magistrates in the Town of York went one step further in the following year by establishing a police office which they would attend at fixed hours in rotation and in which there was a clerk. They protested, however, that, in view of their several occupations, the plan was not practical and asked that a salaried chairman of quarter sessions be appointed who would daily attend to the affairs of the town.[12] Thus, the wheel had gone full circle, back to the argument made by Peter Russell in 1799 that full-time officials were needed for the towns.[13]

This was at last accepted but associated with the even earlier proposals that the governing body of a town be elected by its citizens. Dissatisfaction with the rule of the magistrates had been on two grounds, sometimes combined, sometimes not. One was that they did not give consistent attention to a town, and with that they themselves agreed. The other was that they were appointed, and outside the control of the people. A desire for local self-government had grown only slowly but by the 1820s was a significant force.

The first police town in the new style, one that conceded popular government, was Brockville. Established by an act of 1832 (2 Wm IV, c 17) it had a Board of Police, a body corporate, consisting of five members, two to be elected in each of two wards and the fifth appointed by those four. The board would then choose one of its members as president. The corporation was to make by-laws in a given list of subjects, and might levy an assessment of not more than two pence in the pound. It would appoint such officers, and at such salaries, as it saw fit. This important step marks the beginning of the modern system of municipal government. Further towns and villages followed before long: Hamilton, Belleville, Cornwall, Port Hope, Prescott, and others. York, however, chose an alternative course, being incorporated as the City of Toronto in 1834. Kingston became an incorporated town in 1838.

Long ignored, the urban communities had secured a form of government designed to devolve both power and responsibility on their own people. Farmers and villagers, comprising the great part of the population, continued to be under the original system of district and township government. It does not necessarily follow that they suffered as a result, or even that the majority of them wanted institutions comparable to those in the towns. It had always been obvious that the courts of quarter sessions and town meetings were better adapted to rural than to urban society, and yet if self-government was thought to be better for some parts of the province it could be argued that it was better also for the others.

One important change in the township system was made by a statute of 1835 (5 Wm IV, c 8). Town meetings were called upon to choose a board of three commissioners to which were given direction of road building and some lesser functions formerly vested in quarter sessions. That act, however, was repealed in 1838. For a time, then, the jurisdiction of the courts of quarter sessions was curtailed in favour of the townships. It was further limited by the creation of a number of private companies to build roads, bridges, and harbours; and also by the increasing activity of the province itself in those fields.

Lord Durham may be forgiven for his singularly inaccurate description of local government in Upper Canada since he was concerned to exaggerate its defects in order to strengthen his argument for reform. It is more difficult, however, to understand why later writers have accepted it literally. The one city and nearly all the towns had municipal government not essentially different from modern forms. The provincial legislature did not manage 'the private business of every parish,' and at no time has there been more criticism of provincial intervention in local affairs than in the present age. Justices of the peace were frequently condemned, and no doubt often with good reason. But has it been proved that the elective system automatically screened out the lazy, the incompetent, and the corrupt? Change was overdue in view of the altered character of Upper Canada; but on the whole the men of the old regime, of the earlier pioneer decades, wrought well.

NOTES

1 The outstanding authority is the series of volumes by Sidney and Beatrice Webb under the general title of *English Local Government*. Of a number of short studies see W. Eric Jackson, *The Structure of Local Government in England and Wales* (London 1966).

2 George E. Howard, *An Introduction to the Local Constitutional History of the United States* (2 vols., Baltimore 1899); Herman G. James, *Local Government in the United States* (New York 1928)

3 Ernest J. Lajeunesse, ed., *The Western Border Region, Canada's Southernmost Frontier: a Collection of Documents* (Toronto 1960), lxxvi ff

4 The text of the Mecklenburg commission was published by R.V. Rogers in Vol. VIII of Ontario Historical Society, *Papers and Records*.

5 The minutes of the court of quarter sessions of Nassau, 1788–90, are in the Metropolitan Toronto Central Library; those for Luneburg, 1789–1802, in the Ontario Archives. The minutes for Mecklenburg cannot now be found but extracts from them were published by Adam Shortt in a series of articles on 'Early Records of Ontario' in the *Queen's Quarterly* 1899–1901. Proceedings of the court of Hesse before 1799 have not been found.

6 The minutes for Grimsby and Louth are in the Ontario Archives; those for Sidney in the Public Archives of Canada. The minutes for Adolphustown were published in *Ontario Sessional Paper* 32, 1897–8.

7 Richard A. Preston, ed., *Kingston before the War of 1812: a Collection of Documents* (Toronto 1959), 55

8 *Report of the Bureau of Archives for the Province of Ontario*, 1909

9 The correspondence on municipalities and lieutenants of counties is in E.A. Cruikshank, ed., *The Correspondence of Lieutenant-Governor John Graves Simcoe* (5 vols., Toronto 1923–31), Vols. III and IV.

10 The proceedings of the court are in *Report of the Department of Public Records and Archives of Ontario*, 1932

11 *Report of the Bureau of Archives for the Province of Ontario*, 1912, 177

12 The memorial is in Edith G. Firth, ed., *The Town of York, 1815–1834: a Further Collection of Documents of Early Toronto* (Toronto 1966), 272

13 E.A. Cruikshank and A.F. Hunter, eds., *The Correspondence of the Honourable Peter Russell, with allied documents relating to the Administration of the Government of Upper Canada during the official term of Lieutenant-Governor Simcoe* (3 vols., Toronto 1932–6), I, 229

Robert Baldwin and Decentralization 1841-9

C.F.J. Whebell

For upwards of a hundred and twenty years, the foundation of the system of local government in Ontario has been the Baldwin Act of 1849; and though changes are now in train, these have not yet taken the form of a systematic restructuring. But the Baldwin Act and its associated territorial changes are not widely understood. On what basis did the government of the day formulate the local government system that was embodied in the Baldwin Act (properly the Municipal Corporations Act) and its companion, a Territorial Divisions Act?[1] Did some fundamental principle or theory of territorial organization provide a coherent conceptual foundation for this durable legislation? Or was this system founded on the pragmatism of the seasoned politician and the expediency of the political situation of the 1840s? This paper investigates the rationale for the system of local government areas that has existed since 1849. Such an aim necessitates an exploration of at least the first level or layer of the politics of Canada near the middle of the nineteenth century.

Undoubtedly these questions would have been settled by historians long since but for two factors. In the second Baldwin-LaFontaine ministry (1848–51) the dominant issue was the Rebellion Losses bill, which was making its stormy passage through the legislature at the same time as the municipal reforms; newspaper space and contemporary comment were therefore pre-empted by the former, at the expense of discussion of the local government issue. Second, but arising from the Rebellion Losses issue, was the burning of the legislature buildings in Montreal, while the Municipal Corporations bill was in committee, and therefore much documentation that should have been in the records was destroyed.

It is reasonable to assume that, without the dominating issue of the Rebellion Losses bill, the municipal government reform bill would have attracted much more notice and left clearer traces in the records. From the very beginning of the Province of Upper Canada there had been a current (or at least undercurrent) of politics that provided a pull towards local government, and a certain amount of tension between the governing elites and the rest of the population. The first session of the Legislative Assembly of Upper Canada in 1792 introduced a bill permitting specific, if trivial, exercise of local government at the township level. In explanation of this event to a government that was understandably sensitive to any hints of republicanism, Lieutenant-Governor Simcoe wrote to London: 'They seemed rather to have a stronger attachment to the Elective principle for all Town affairs, than may be thought altogether adviseable; and a Bill for that purpose was allowed to be postponed without much difficulty.'[2]

The following year a bill to the same end was in fact passed.[3] The lieutenant-governor's report at this time was as follows:

A Bill for the choice of Parish and Town Officers by the election of the inhabitants had been proposed at the first meeting of the Legislature, but was deferred under the Idea that Town Meetings should not be too much encouraged. To give the nomination altogether to the Magistrates was found to be a distasteful measure – many well-affected settlers were convinced that Fence Viewers, Pound Keepers and other Petty Officers to regulate matters of local Policy would be more willingly obeyed if named by the House keepers – and especially that the Collector of the rates should be a person chosen by themselves that if default was made, they could not arraign the Magistrates.

It was therefore thought adviseable not to withhold such a gratification to which they had been accustomed, it [the Town Meeting] being in itself, not unreasonable, and only to take place one day in the year.'[4]

The popular interest in local 'Town' (ie, township) meetings thus exemplified has been generally considered to have been brought into Upper Canada by Loyalist refugees from the New England and middle colonies. At the same time a more centralized form of juridical-administrative system was imposed by the British government – that of rule by magistrates in quarter sessions. The areas organized into townships as survey units expanded territorially along with or ahead of the spread of settlers onto the land of Upper Canada.[5] Undoubtedly, the tendency towards township government was strengthened by the isolation of widely scattered pockets of settlement combined with difficulties of travel.[6] This clear need for spatial decentralization under pioneer conditions, where access to centres of governance was difficult, also affected the quarter sessions system. As the total areal extent of settlement increased, it became necessary to increase the number of districts from the original four in 1788[7] to eight in 1801–2. On this occasion the distance-time constraint was cited as a prime consideration, so that 'none of His Majesty's subjects in this province will be at a greater distance from the place to which the discharge of his public duty calls him than an easy days journey.'[8] Related to the thin spread of settlement was a shortage of 'qualified' (in terms of property and social class) persons to act as magistrates, as such individuals tended to concentrate in the major urban places while owning land and even holding constituencies in the remoter sections.[9]

One can thus envisage a two-tier local political system, democratic at the township level through the town meeting, and authoritarian at the district level through the appointed magistrates. Over the half-century that followed the establishment of township government, the former survived and grew in strength, reinforced by the radical movement in the 1830s to the point where, briefly, township government displaced the magistrates with elective commissioners holding the power (1835–8). Following the post-rebellion Tory resurgence in 1838 this form of township governance was repealed and the district magistrates resumed control, but the ideal of township-level representative government was evidently very well established by the late 1830s.[10]

Meanwhile, at the authoritarian level some changes were occurring. The rise of European liberalism was beginning to erode the very core of centralized authority in the British empire. The 'free trade' theory and its concomitant notion of decreasing the financial dependence of her colonies on Britain may have been, at bottom, a strategy to maximize British commercial gains in the exploitation of colonial resources; but it found ready co-operation amongst the rising middle classes of colonies as widely separated as New South Wales and Upper Canada.[11] Decentralization of decision-making power within the British empire (particularly control of patronage) was the goal of radicals and reformers, and 'responsible government' was seen as the avenue towards that goal. Robert Gourlay was advocating this innovation as early as 1822, and with the activities of W.L. Mackenzie a few years later it became a perennial issue in Upper Canada.

In Britain a new set of local governments had been created by reforming legislation by 1835. Prior to that time the mode of local governance had been by justices of the peace (magistrates) which had, by the beginning of the nineteenth century, become 'an Inchoate County Legislature, formulating new policies in respect of the prevention of crime, the treatment of criminals, the licensing of ale-houses, the relief of destitution, the maintenance of roads and bridges, the assessment of local taxation, and even the permissible habits of life of whole sections of the community.'[12] Here, too, the problem of a shortage of competent magistrates provided sources of difficulty in working this system, established in an agrarian epoch, during one of burgeoning population and increasing urban growth. In the 1830s a number of changes were made in the pattern, chiefly those pertaining to making parish councils elective (the parish was the lowest functional unit) and those establishing Poor Law Unions under appointed overseers.[13] As for urban places (boroughs), a drastic reform took place in 1835 in that the enormous variety in the modes of governance of the boroughs (mostly oligarchic) was replaced by a standardized elective system.[14] This English Municipal Corporations Act can be regarded as a logical outgrowth of the great Reform Bill of 1832 since it extended the political power of the middle classes into their own immediate milieu, the urban system.[15]

Attempts were made to gain elective county councils in this period, but failed to overcome the opposition of landed interests.[16] There can be little doubt, therefore, that local representative institutions and decentralization of political power were aspects of the *zeitgeist* and that such information was flowing to Canada through newspapers, letters, and travellers. Indeed, Robert Baldwin was in England in the midst of this period of reform activity, and appears to have been in contact with Joseph Hume, one of its leaders.[17]

The close relationship of local government change with more general reform-cum-radical tendencies was evident in the English case. The municipal reforms alluded to above were directly influenced by Bentham's work,[18] and the link between this school of thought and Upper Canada was provided in 1838 by Edward Gibbon Wakefield,[19] the earl of Durham himself, and especially Charles Buller, Durham's secretary. Wakefield and Buller considered colonial government to be equivalent to municipal government (Wakefield used the expression 'Canada, which is a municipality'). 'The parallel to the colonial problem was, they thought, to be found in the [English] municipalities reconstructed by Imperial Act in 1835 ...'[20] Small wonder, then, that Durham recommended municipal government for Canada[21] (though such provision was not included in the Union bill as the result of pressure)[22] and that Sydenham pushed through the 1841 District Councils Act[23] as a means of furthering such decentralization of power. This Act also had the important practical effect of reducing the workload of the legislature, for even a cursory inspection of the orders of the day for either the Legislative Council or the Legislative Assembly in this period reveals an immense quantity of essentially local business – road petitions, welfare cases, licence appeals, bylaws referred for approval, and so on.

If people like Gourlay, Mackenzie, Wakefield, and Buller were exotics carrying the innovations of the English radical-reform doctrines of the day, Robert Baldwin was a more autochthonous variety of reformer, born in the country in 1804 into a family which had reform leanings even then, and his father, William Warren Baldwin, was active in political matters in opposition to the then deeply-entrenched 'Family Compact.'[24] From this background Robert Baldwin developed a view of responsible government that was not directly derivative of the Benthamites and others in England, since he saw such an evolution of self-government in terms of the benefits to the people of Canada rather than to the government of Great Britain. In his letter to Colonial Secretary Lord Glenelg in 1836, Baldwin wrote '... my native Country [Canada's] prosperity is necessarily to be an object of the most intense Anxiety.'[25] This same letter, however, contains no reference to municipal institutions, nor does any other utterance of Robert Baldwin at this time, but he can hardly have been insensible to issues of municipal government, either at the township level (as a member of a family that owned widely-scattered parcels of land) or at district level (as an active Reform politician whose goal was to dislodge the Family Compact). It seems very probable that this apparent neglect of municipal matters is not a real oversight, but that the subject is subsumed in some larger part of the issues of responsible government – for example patronage – or the right of appointment to various offices.[26] Such offices included the magistracy (the quarter sessions system of district governance) and various officers and functionaries including surveyors, tax collectors, superintendents of public works, and road commissioners. Quite a large part of the letters in the Baldwin Papers of the Toronto Public Library are from individuals soliciting such appointments. The value of these appointive offices to the incumbents is suggested by the fact that in 1849 the emoluments of the county registrar for York (Samuel Ridout) were 'not much under Two thousand pounds per Annum';[27] and while this may be an extreme case, there was at least a measure of financial security even for the customs collector at some tiny port in an economy that was very short of ready cash.[28]

Sydenham's District Councils Act of 1841 was viewed by the Baldwin clique with mixed feelings. On the one hand it brought the elective principle down to local level and this was to be approved of; on the other the chairman of each council was a crown appointment, while the control of finance was denied to the elective councils, the district treasurer being still associated with the quarter sessions. William Warren Baldwin wrote to his son in this respect: 'Let the Township Meetings elect one District Council Man – from 15 to 20 townships would furnish a council of as many members, this is quite enough – buy [sic] annually chosen; ... these councils should choose their own Warden or head man ... [and] ... the council to be the controllers and auditors of all costs – and under this warrant the Treasurer should pay all drafts of the Bench of Magistrates.'[29] He also reported the attitude of Robert Baldwin's own constituents in the Fourth Riding of York County (the 'North Riding' colloquially): 'The Municipal Bill is very much disliked in the north riding – I made no comment on it; it was their own voluntary judgment of it – they say all the Bills add more and more power to the Govr & take away from the people ...'[30]

In addition to the ideological reservations the Reform leaders had with respect to the Municipal Councils Act, they saw their position as middle-class landowners threatened by the taxation of wild land. This possibility was of course promoted assiduously by the radical group, who had little vested interest in land as a form of wealth. It was also clearly favourable to the Buller-Wakefield approach to colonization from the standpoint of advantages to Britain: the forced release of land from speculators' holdings with concomitant lowering of prices would facilitate the export of surplus population from the British Isles. The Baldwin group saw it this way:

We apprehend that it [the District Councils Act] is a mode of carrying out the principle – if such a word is applicable upon the occasion – divide and govern – it may *appear* to add to our importance when in fact it may materially diminish our influence through our Representatives in the United Parliament ... a latent suspicion that such will be their construction that the prefect or head man appointed by the Govr will be armed with such powers, as may with him carry the same influence within minor assemblies, that he [the Governor] so successfully uses in another assembly – the 100 acres men probably forming a majority in these minor assemblies may not have much hesitation in taxing heavily the unproductive lands of the larger holder of acres – by these means we may all be reduced to a level, and then the Head be the better enabled to prescribe and enforce his own terms.[31]

Mr. Buller has effected one of his experimental schemes – I mean the Establishment of the Municipal Councils – not satisfied with this great innovation made with his avowed purpose of imposing a tax so heavy on the uncultivated land that the owners should be unable to pay & thus get the land into the hands of Gov't. – and without even waiting a reasonable time for the exercise – and that of this innovation he proposes to take the lands from private owners by some more prompt and devouring plan ...[32]

'We are now fighting the battle of the *middle classes* against the aristocracy – all our commissions will be attacked on the score of unfit people – that is, not *gentlemen* ...';[33] the author (Francis Hincks) went on to recommend the appointment of some middle-class Tories to the magistracy to confound such criticism. Robert Baldwin's own views on the District Councils bill are not extant in the form of a direct statement, but he appears to have fought a stiff though futile rearguard action, clause by clause, against a number of its provisions.[34]

In the rural districts the working of the District Councils Act was not an unqualified success: 'farmers taxes that was five Dollars last year is twenty this and no one understands it ... I have taken a great deal of pains and trouble to Explain to many that it was not your [Baldwin's] wish that law was in force and that you detested it and would get it removed from the statute book.'[35]

After the Reformers as a group had achieved power in 1842 as the first Baldwin-LaFontaine ministry (though not yet in the mode of a responsible government), they introduced a pair of bills, one to establish municipal corporations, the other to abolish districts and set up in their stead unions of counties which would be separated as the growth of their respective populations warranted. The full text of these bills has not been found, and the reports of debate are fragmentary. The former bill referred to townships, towns, counties, and cities (but not to villages) as the corporate entities and, with the companion, seem very much a foretaste of the bills of the 1848–9 period. In a crisis of confidence with Governor Sir Charles Metcalfe, however, the ministry resigned and so these bills did not pass into law.[36]

The Baldwin group, no doubt aided by petitions from local sources, kept up the pressure, and in 1846 the Tory government of W.H. Draper brought in a bill to provide for the election of district wardens by the council members.[37] This bill in its first form did not provide for the election of treasurers, and drew criticism on this account. In the debate on second reading, J.H. Price referred to the situation of the Home District Council: 'That council had done a vast amount of good in its District, but it did not work harmoniously in consequence of not having the power of electing its own officers, and the result of it was, that they did not grant regular salaries, but voted a sum annually in the shape of gratuities to their officers, and have resolved not to grant them a regular salary until they have the right of election.'[38] The amended version did in fact provide for the appointment of such officers by the councils.

Baldwin was ready to take credit for this result. In a broadsheet on the occasion of the election of 1847 addressed 'To the Electors of the Fourth Riding of the County of York,' he makes the following claim: 'But it is sometimes asked what have the Liberals done for the country! Let the questioner look back into the history of the last thirty years. Is it not to their exertions that the people are indebted for the recognition of their rights as British subjects to a practical influence upon the administration of their government – for the Municipal Councils, and through them for the control and management of their local taxes ...'[39] But apart from this reference there is no mention of municipal affairs as any issue of principle in the election, and there is no evidence that local government was a plank in itself in the Reform platform – though it was still subsumed in the issue of patronage, since the quarter sessions based on district territories continued to function, and the appointment of magistrates still remained with the executive. On this count at least Baldwin had unfinished business in local government matters. And though there has been found no record of how Baldwin viewed the local government territories as such, the territorial issue has a nexus with that of local responsible government because the territorial basis for the magistracy system was the district. This nexus probably explains the motivation for his unsuccessful bill to abolish districts, and with them the magistracy system, in 1843. But what, conceptually, *ought* to comprise a territorial unit did not, apparently, exercise Baldwin or his associates. This is not to say that there was not a good deal of interest and agitation in such matters in other quarters, and it is necessary to turn to this, the other major element in the Baldwin Act of 1849.

During the life of Upper Canada, the number of districts had grown from four to twenty, though a few did not begin functioning before the Union of 1841. The number of townships had increased from a matter of a few dozens in 1791 to more than 370 in 1845.[40] While not all of the latter number were occupied it is clear that there had been an explosive increase in the number of town meetings and in the township-centred aspects of the work of the quarter sessions. The growth in the Upper Canadian population, from perhaps 20,000 in 1791 to nearly a million in 1841, would of itself contribute an immense increase in the magistrates' case loads.

The increase in the numbers of people and the townships to contain them also necessitated a far wider spread of settlements. The scattered settlements of 1802 were serviced by eight district centres according to the principle of 'an easy day's journey.' The easy day's journey in the 1840s covered a much greater distance where the roads had been improved by grading, surfacing, or planking; but these tended to be feeder roads to the main town and cities along the major transport corridors.[41] A petition from the Bathurst District for the setting off of its northern portion (Renfrew County) indicates that a trip of sixty-five miles over 'almost impassable' roads required two days, and much of the district was even farther away from the capital, Perth.[42] On the other hand, in more densely settled areas it was the amount of business which underlay the notions of distance. A petition from Brantford and vicinity to be set off from the Gore District implied that a journey of up to thirty-five miles to Hamilton consumed too much valuable time, and for even a moderately sized district (see Map 2) the pressure on one administrative centre was too great; 'upwards of forty civil suits having been left untried, for want of time, at the last Gore assizes.'[43]

Throughout much of the area of Canada West, therefore, isolation of local communities by distance and bad roads still obtained, and with it a pragmatic requirement for continued if not increased decentralization. Map 1 shows the extent of the area between the outer fringe of small communities, many of which were populated by merely scores rather than hundreds of people. Further, there was by no means close settlement all along roads, which are used on this map as a crude surrogate for accessibility. Lord Durham's report makes reference to these problems, especially as regards the social fragmentation resulting from difficult communications, as 'many petty local centres, the sentiments and the interests (or at least what are fancied to be so) of which, are distinct, and perhaps opposed.'[44]

There was indeed pressure for stronger local rural government which took the form of arguments for incorporating the townships. As an example of the local view, the following petition from the Western District Council was sent to the Legislative Assembly: '... this Council, in accordance with its former prayer, beg leave to assure your honourable House that your Memorialists are fully aware of the benefits that has [sic] accrued to this Province from the Municipal Council

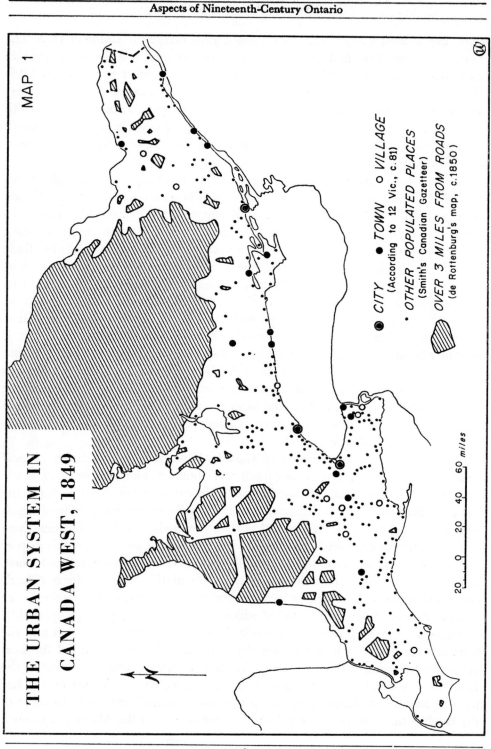

MAP 1

THE URBAN SYSTEM IN
CANADA WEST, 1849

● CITY ● TOWN ○ VILLAGE
       (According to 12 Vic., c. 81)

· OTHER POPULATED PLACES
   (Smith's Canadian Gazetteer)

▨ OVER 3 MILES FROM ROADS
   (de Rottenburg's map, c.1850)

20   0   20   40   60 miles

Acts, and they further hope that your honourable body will extend the Boon by granting the prayer of their former Petitioners, viz., for Township municipalities and that the said Law may be in accordance with true British principles.'[45] The London District Council also petitioned for township councils and a 'Court of Wardens.'[46]

Another indication of the need for decentralization was mentioned in the Toronto *Globe* which, in its report of the debate on the Municipal Corporations Bill in 1849, at second reading, reported the speech of F. Hincks:

'At present the concerns that the districts had to manage were often of an entirely township character. There were, for example, the schools. The funds for those establishments were collected by the District Council; but they were divided among the townships. The same thing happened with local improvements. In fact, the representatives of each township, to a great extent, managed the whole business of that township himself. Now, these people travelled often fifty or sixty miles to transact this business, which could be done much better on the spot.'[47]

But while the township leaders, and especially the more remote ones, were pressing for full municipal status for this ancient level of local government, there were others whose interests lay at the district level. Map 2 shows the district territories as at 1849, together with the later counties. It can be seen that many districts were huge, and others were of awkward shapes. Most districts had, of course, a district capital around which the district had been formed during the 1791–1841 period. Many had, however, at least one other town of some size (compare Maps 1 and 2), and in such towns had arisen a middle class that was fully cognizant of the commercial 'spin-offs' of the district capital function. From these people came petitions to divide the district, and bills were presented to the legislature by members for the purpose of dividing districts. As brief and unsystematically chosen examples, the following are indicative of this trend:

1 Bill 1154 of 1839, which was suspended, would have divided Peterborough County into two parts, in response – according to the preamble – to a petition. (The same division was actually effected by a Territorial Divisions Act of 1851.)

2 Act 10–11 Vic., c 39, which was not proclaimed, was to set off the District of Kent from the Western District, with Chatham as the district town. The preamble refers to '... the increase of the population of the Western District its geographical situation position and its vast resources in fertility of soil and inland navigation and the great distance of many parts from the District Town [Sandwich] ...' That this may have resulted from pressure from Chatham is suggested by a counter-petition in 1843 from Canadians [sic] in Sandwich against some petition from Chatham to have the district offices removed there: '... il n'y a aucunne nécessité quelconque pour transporter les Edifices Publiques &c. de Sandwich à Chatham

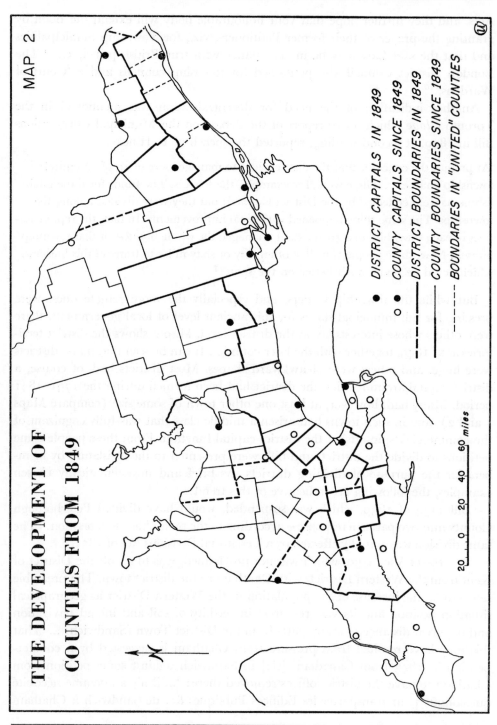

MAP 2

THE DEVELOPMENT OF
COUNTIES FROM 1849

● DISTRICT CAPITALS IN 1849
○ COUNTY CAPITALS SINCE 1849
━ ━ DISTRICT BOUNDARIES IN 1849
━━━ COUNTY BOUNDARIES SINCE 1849
─ ─ ─ BOUNDARIES IN "UNITED" COUNTIES

20 0 20 40 60 miles

et que ce transport et cette innovation seroit d'ailleurs très injuste et très *impolitique,* sans compter qu'il seroit la cause de la ruine, d'un grand nombre de Canadiens, habitans ce Comté ...'[48]

3 A further petition from the Western District Council, asking the Legislative Council to divide the district further by setting off the ten northern townships into yet another district (later Lambton County). This said in part: 'Your petitioners would respectfully shew to your Honorable Body that from the geographical position of that portion of the said County of Kent comprising the Ten northern townships, the rapid increase of population therein and the extreme distance of many of its settlements from Chatham ...'[49] This petition was eventually fulfilled in the 1851 Territorial Divisions Act.

4 A bill (no 148 of 1847) sponsored by Mr Jessup, to divide the Johnstown district into two, using the apparently stereotyped preamble: 'Whereas from the increase of the population of the Johnstown District, its geographical position and its resources in fertility of soil, and the great distance of many parts thereof from the District Town [Brockville] ...' and erect the eastern portion, the County of Grenville, into the District of Bruce, with Prescott as the District town.[50]

5 Petition sent by the Gore District Council opposing a Gazetted proposal 'to detach from this District certain Townships therein named, for the purposes of forming a new District,' and in particular refuting any distance claim: '... the present limits of this District are not so large as to make it inconvenient for the inhabitants of the most distant Townships to attend at the District Town [Hamilton] ...'[51] When this same issue came up in connexion with the Territorial Divisions bill of 1849, the debate was reported in part as follows: 'There had been some agitation in favour of the formation of the District of Brant, but it commenced and was confined solely to the Township of Brantford, for the aggrandizement of which the Bill was chiefly introduced.' There was also reference to land speculation in town lots in Brantford.[52]

6 The reduction of the Gore District was also effected by the division of its southern part to be a portion of a new county unit, Haldimand, which was also to include parts of the Niagara and Talbot districts. Though not heavily populated at this time, Haldimand had excellent economic prospects through the functioning of the Grand River Navigation Company system which formed a developmental axis through its territory. The desire for District status is indicated in a reference by Baldwin in a letter noting that the County (Riding) of Haldimand seems dissatisfied with the reform party: 'I am not aware of the grounds on which it rests except so far as it seems to take for its foundation the non-erection of the Co. into a separate District.'[53] Certainly another reason for Baldwin's breaking up the Gore District (into four portions, actually) would be to reduce the power base of Sir Allan MacNab. In the debate on this point, there was 'a keen opposition' by Sir Allan.[54]

7 An Act, 12 Vic., c 96, which 'from the great extent of the District of Huron as at present constituted and the consequent distance of some parts of it from the District Town [Goderich]' divided it up into three parts, to be the counties of Huron, Bruce, and Perth. Evidently the controlling faction of the council disapproved of this idea, as the council had earlier voted a petition against the division of the district.[55]

8 A bill to erect a County of Grey.[56]

9 A bill to divide the District of London.[57]

The origin of the concept of a hierarchy of urban places, provided for in the Municipal Corporations bill of 1849 – police villages, villages, towns, and cities – must remain a matter for speculation. Certainly there had already been a great number of *ad hoc* incorporations of urban places, starting with boards of police and extending to full city charters. As F.H. Armstrong observes: 'By the end of the Upper Canadian period most towns of any size had been incorporated, but, though the legislation was gradually showing more sophistication in its wording, no overall plans had been adopted. The same system was continued under the union until 1847 when a limited scheme for the incorporation of small towns came into force (10 & 11 Vic., c 42).'[58]

The general inconsistency in the incorporation system was referred to during debate on the 1849 bill: 'The bill proposed first to incorporate villages, towns, and cities; that was a great good, for application was being constantly made for incorporations of this kind, each one containing some new crochet'[59] and '... one of the greatest objects to be gained by the bill, was the classification of the municipalities, and the uniformity of the law respecting each class. At present the acts of incorporation formed a complete chaos of inconsistent enactments.'[60]

It is perhaps curious that Baldwin is not reported as having much to say on this bill that has ever since carried his name. His principal comment was in relation to local institutions having 'the effect of creating a school of practical statesmen.'[61] This is certainly a Benthamite statement, and the basic idea of a uniform set of laws for urban places probably derives from the British Municipal Corporations Act of 1835. Baldwin was, as noted, in England in 1836, during the first year of operation of this act, and must have taken cognizance of its existence and its provisions.[62] And certainly the linkage of responsible government with local councils was made in the debate, though by H.J. Boulton who referred to the lack of responsible government in the district councils and to the fact that 'things were too much regulated by backstairs influence.'[63]

There is, of course, the power appeal towards the middle classes referred to earlier. That the Tories were in particular concerned about the implications of the bill is suggested by a report to the Toronto City Council by a committee struck to consider its provisions. The report used particularly strong language in criticism of the provision that qualification of aldermen and councillors should be freehold premises to an annual rental value of £60, 'actually occupied by himself in the ward for which he is a candidate.'[64] In view of the normal tendency of a social elite in larger urban places to cluster in certain sections or neighbourhoods, this provision may have been intended to loosen their grip on urban ward politics made possible under the larger property franchise without residence requirement. Here may be a parallel with the middle class achieving wider political influence in the province through the breaking up of the large, magistrate-dominated districts.

In conclusion, then, this attempt to probe into the political circumstances surrounding the establishment in 1849 of a very long-lived system of local government areas, both rural and urban, has established that there was probably a coherent political philosophy and strategy behind the *forms* of government adopted. The principle of responsible government was a facet of this, but underlying it was the deeper reality of a rising middle class struggling for a share of political power. The Municipal Corporations bill or Baldwin Act was a weapon in this struggle, especially as it demolished the magistracy as a perpetual power base for the Tories. But it must be noted that there were other weapons unsheathed in the same year: an Elections Act, an Assessment Act, a School Act, as well as various public works items. These in combination seem to have finished the old Toryism for good; but the evaluation of their total impact requires a deeper probe into the politics of the day than has been attempted here.

As for the actual *territorial* units created by the Baldwin Act and other legislation in the few years after 1849, their creation involved mostly political pragmatism and expediency. To abolish the district system was a blow to Toryism, indeed, but the actual units created rather reflected the local pressures and petitions received. Probably in adjudicating between petitions and proposals from opposing interest groups, Baldwin would favour the more 'liberal' (*vide* the case of Sir Allan MacNab's Gore District). Otherwise the changes he made in the territorial map were minimal (see Map 2, comparing the discarded district boundaries – heavy dashed lines, with those that have continued as county boundaries – heavy solid lines). Only one former district capital has since been replaced by another town as the county seat – Niagara yielded to St Catharines – even so not until 1866.[65] In local pressures, then, Baldwin was acting in a 'responsive' way, and thus illustrates the general principle that local political territories are creatures of their core centres, and not the opposite.

Since, then, there appears to have been no fundamental underlying principle of political geography by which the county system was deliberately designed, an empirical generalization previously proposed by the writer from a more general overview seems to be supported as an 'ascriptive' model of human territorial behaviour.[66] There is not yet in being any comprehensive theory of local government territories and probably each set of circumstances will require different models. The political decentralization that was so necessary in the context of the communications of 1849 hardly obtains today; in fact, the seeds of the Baldwin Act's ultimate obsolescence were contained in another act of the same year, the Railway Guarantee Act.[67] The ribbons of steel that followed this generated great urban growth along the main corridors, but they also weakened the demographic base for viable local representative institutions through migration and rural depopulation.[68] Today's innovations are tomorrow's constraints, and there is a constant need for reformers to overcome the constraints of obsolescent political systems. But can every age count on producing a Robert Baldwin who, on the matters discussed here at least, manifested a superb blend of idealistic principle and realistic pragmatism?

NOTES

1 12 Vic., c 81 and 12 Vic., c 78 respectively
2 E.A. Cruikshank, ed., *The Correspondence of Lieutenant-Governor John Graves Simcoe* (5 vols., Toronto 1923-31), I, 250, Simcoe to Dundas, 4 Nov. 1792
3 32 Geo. III, c 12
4 Cruikshank, ed., *Simcoe Papers*, II, 53-4. Simcoe to Dundas, 16 Sept. 1793. Also created in 1792 was a set of counties with restricted formal functions. Used as territorial units for legislative representation, militia organization, and legal registry, they were never the main theatre of local political activity. But it is an interesting speculation that, through the parliamentary and militia usage which touched many people's lives, a sort of territorial identity came to be associated with the county names – which were always different from those of the superior districts, even when the two areas were conterminous – and that Baldwin was responsive to this aspect of local political feeling in his legislation.
5 For more detail as to this spatial process, see C.F.J. Whebell, 'Core Areas in Intrastate Political Organization,' *Canadian Geographer*, XII, 1968, 99–112
6 J.J. Talman, 'Travel in Ontario before the coming of the Railway,' *Ontario History*, XXIX, 1933, 85–102
7 The establishment of Upper Canada in 1791 resulted in no change in the areas of these districts and little change in their mode of operation
8 Public Record Office [PRO], CO 42/323, f 45, Remarks by J. Elmsley (chief justice) in a dispatch from Peter Russell to Portland, 11 Aug. 1798
9 Cruikshank, ed., *Simcoe Papers*, II, 32. Chief Justice Elmsley complains of the lack of Grand and Petty jurors
10 Shortt, A., 'Municipal History 1791–1867,' in *Canada and its Provinces* (23 vols., Toronto, 1914–17), XVIII, 429. It seems very possible that the 'Commissioners' idea derived from the British Poor Law Unions begun in 1834
11 C.M.H. Clark, *Select Documents in Australian History, 1851–1900* (Sydney 1955), 322, the 'Grand Remonstrance' of the New South Wales Legislative Council, 1851
12 S. and B. Webb, *The Parish and the County*, 482, quoted in H.J. Laski, ed., *A Century of Municipal Progress* (London 1935), 22
13 Ibid., 35. The change was effected by (UK) 4 & 5 Wm IV, c 76. The commissioners were empowered to order unions of parishes (Section 26).

14 Ibid., 55–6. The Act, (UK) 5 & 6 Wm IV, c 76, did not include any gradations of urban places (all were included under the generic 'borough'), though some smaller places, listed by name, were not entitled to a commission of the peace, had no ward divisions, and had a standard-sized council. It is significant that borough councils had right of appointment of its officers such as clerk, treasurer, coroners etc. (Section 58); and also that a magistrate or justice of the peace for a borough was exempt from the property qualifications required of those appointed for a county (Section 101).

15 K.B. Smellie, *A History of Local Government* (London 1968), 25

16 V.D. Lipman, *Local Government Areas 1834–1945* (Oxford 1949), 121–2

17 R.M. and J. Baldwin, *The Baldwins and the Great Experiment* (Toronto 1969), 148

18 Laski, ed., *A Century of Municipal Progress*, 33–4

19 I.P. Ubom, *The Role of Edward Gibbon Wakefield in the Durham Report and British Colonial Policy* (unpublished MA thesis, University of Ottawa, 1963)

20 E.M. Wrong, *Charles Buller and Responsible Government* (Oxford 1926), 78. The only political office Buller held was, significantly, that of Poor Law Commissioner.

21 C.P. Lucas, ed., *Lord Durham's Report* (2 vols., Oxford 1912), II, 287. 'The establishment of a good system of municipal institutions throughout these Provinces is a matter of vital importance ... the power of local assessment, and the application of the funds arising from it, should be entrusted to local management.'

22 J.H. Aitchison, 'The Municipal Corporations Act of 1849,' *Canadian Historical Review*, XXX, 1949, 107–22. The opposition centred apparently on Edward Ellice, a reformer who had been a supporter of Lord John Russel, but who parted company with him after 1832. Ellice had large landed interests in Canada. See *Dictionary of National Biography* (Oxford 1917), VI, 665–6

23 4 & 5 Vic., c 10

24 Baldwin, *Experiment*, 136

25 R. Baldwin to Glenelg, 13 July 1836, printed in *Report of the Public Archives for 1923* (Ottawa 1924), 329

26 Ibid., 335

27 Public Archives of Canada [PAC], Correspondence of the Provincial Secretary's Office [PSO], vol. 248 (1849), no 313, Petition of the Home District Council for amendments in the District Councils Act, 31 Jan. 1849.

28 J.J. Talman, 'The Impact of the Railway on a Pioneer Community,' *Canadian Historical Association, Papers*, 1955, 1–12

29 Toronto Public Library [TPL], Baldwin Papers, A 84, ff 37–8, W.W. Baldwin to R. Baldwin, 5 Aug. 1841

30 Ibid., A 83A, f 113, W.W. Baldwin to R. Baldwin, 22 Aug. 1841

31 Ibid., A 66, ff 1–2, G. Ridout to R. Baldwin, 20 July 1841

32 Ibid., A 85, ff 56–7, W.W. Baldwin to R. Baldwin, 16 Sept. 1843

33 Ibid., A 51, f 2, F. Hincks to R. Baldwin, 15 June 1843

34 Elizabeth Nish, ed., *Debates of the Legislative Assembly of United Canada 1841–67*, I: *1841* (Montreal 1970), 618–25

35 TPL, Baldwin Papers, A 61, f 82, G. McMicking (Chippewa) to R. Baldwin, 24 Oct. 1843

36 Nish, *Debates*, III, 1843, *passim*. The bill to abolish districts passed at third reading on 6 December 1843, that for the Municipal Corporations the following day. The Baldwin-LaFontaine ministry had tendered their resignations on 26 November.

37 9 Vic., c 40

38 *Mirror of Parliament of the Province of Canada*, March 20th to June 9th 1846 (Montreal 1846), 213, col. 1

39 Ontario Archives [OA], Baldwin Papers, MS 88 reel 2, 8 Dec. 1847

40 In 8 Vic., c 7 all townships are listed.

41 C.F.J. Whebell, 'Corridors: a Theory of Urban Systems,' *Annals of the Association of American Geographers*, LIX, 1969, 1–26

42 PAC, PSO, vol. 237 (1848), no 716, Petition of the Warden and Council of the Bathurst District, 6 Oct. 1848

43 Ibid., vol. 254 (1849), no 565, Petition of the inhabitants of Brantford, etc. nd (received in the Provincial Secretary's Office 7 March 1849)

44 Lucas, *Lord Durham's Report*, II, 146

45 OA, Records of the Western District Council, ff 564–5. Date of petition 9 Oct. 1848

46 Weldon Library (University of Western Ontario), Special Collections, Journal of the London District Council, f 200, 6 Oct. 1848

47 Toronto *Globe*, 7 April 1849, 2, cols. 1, 2

48 TPL, Baldwin Papers, A 88, f 19, Petition dated January 1843. A minute, 6 March 1843, in Baldwin's hand notes 'they need be under no apprehension of unnecessary haste.'

49 OA, Records of the Western District Council, ff 542–9. Petition dated 4 Feb. 1848

50 OA, Records of the Johnstown District Council, miscellaneous papers

51 OA, *Journal of the Proceedings of the Municipal Council of the District of Gore*, February Session 1848 (Dundas 1848), Appendix 84–5

52 Montreal *Gazette*, 23 April 1849

53 TPL, Baldwin Papers, A 87, f 96, R. Baldwin to D. Thompson, 1 May 1847

54 Toronto *Globe*, 18 April 1849, 2, col. 3

55 OA, *Minutes of the Proceedings of the Municipal Council for the District of Huron* (Goderich 1848), 27–8. The councillors voting against the petition (ie in favour of division) were Daly, Thompson, Hamilton, McIntyre, and McPherson. Daly appears to have been from Stratford, and it seems probable that the 'noes' represented the group of southern separatists within the district. The petition asking for division came from Stratford and adjacent townships, citing distance from Goderich as a hindrance to local development. PAC, PSO, vol. 247 (1849), no 271. (No petition appeared from the area of Bruce County, as this was at the time almost unpopulated. Provision for separation of this county was doubtless made in anticipation of similar difficulties arising from distance.)

56 Toronto *Globe*, 12 April 1849, 2, col. 3

57 Toronto *Globe*, 25 April 1849, 3, col. 3

58 F.H. Armstrong, *Handbook of Upper Canadian Chronology and Territorial Legislation* (London, Ont. 1967), 195

59 Toronto *Globe*, 7 April 1849, 2, col. 2, speech of Wilson

60 Ibid., speech of Smith of Durham

61 Ibid., 2, speech of R. Baldwin

62 Baldwin's famous letter to Glenelg on responsible government was written while he was in London. See footnote 25 above.

63 Toronto *Globe*, 7 April 1849, 2, col. 3

64 OA, Toronto *City Council Papers*, 13 Feb. 1849, Report of Select Committee appointed to examine the new Municipal Council bill

65 29–30 Vic., c 70

66 Whebell, 'Core Areas,' 100

67 12 Vic., c 29

68 C.F.J. Whebell, 'Some Regional Effects of Transport Innovation: the Case of Grey and Bruce Counties, Ontario,' *High Speed Ground Transportation Journal*, V, 1971, 33–41

Some Aspects of Urbanization in Nineteenth-Century Ontario

J.M.S. Careless

In Canada, the rise of urbanism is popularly seen as a twentieth-century phenom-enon. Yet one of the most notable features of the nineteenth century in Ontario was the steady advance of urbanization; the growth of urban places in number and size through the concentration of population at particular sites. This theme is already the subject of considerable specialized scholarly study. Still, it seems worth-while to try a broader approach: to make a selective, reflective inquiry into major aspects of urbanization in Ontario by way of producing a general, if highly quali-tative, analysis of the process as a whole.

In pursuing this quest, certain points of reference will be utilized, basically derived from Eric Lampard's conceptual article, 'American Historians and the Study of Urbanization,' but varied to fit Canadian circumstances in the well-tried Canadian way of borrowing.[1] He names four primary factors involved in urbani-zation: environment, population, organization, and technology. The process of societal change that builds urban communities is an interplay of environment and concentrating population, mediated by organization and technology. It is a sug-gestive formulation that can cover a great deal; but rather than follow it rigidly, this present venture will use the four terms of factors as categories for examination in turn; and, it is hoped, for some illumination of aspects of urbanization that sig-nificantly shaped nineteenth-century Ontario.

Of course, the physical environment provided the first term for urbanization in Ontario. Land forms and water systems, climate and vegetation, soils, resources and site advantages, all entered into play. Beyond that, they set the underlying conditions for general community development in the whole Ontario region, which first received political definition as the province of Upper Canada in 1791, was reconstituted as Canada West in the province of Canada in 1841, and finally (with subsequent enlargements) as the province of Ontario at Confederation.

The distinctive environment in which this human community took form was preeminently that of the central lakelands, extending downward to the great St

Lawrence waterway. While deep in the continental interior, this region was unlike the western plains of Canada in having a broad and basic artery of water transport bordering its full length, although its more broken and forested land mass was initially harder to penetrate than was western prairie or parkland, and the southern edge of the Shield confined its fertile agricultural lands more narrowly than in the expanses of the West. Then, too, unlike the Maritime region, Ontario's main line of water access was sealed off by winter, whereas on the coasts the wintry Atlantic was hazardous but open all the way to Europe. And unlike Quebec, there was no Appalachian barrier along the southern limits of the Ontario region but the St Lawrence and Great Lakes, which provided ready contact with the neighbouring United States from the very start of Upper Canadian settlement. All these features entered into the urbanizing process as it developed in Ontario.

In the first place, urban communities emerged in a long string along the river and lake fronts in the fertile southern Ontario region below the Shield. They were tied to the waterways. It was only slowly that other centres grew up behind them, up rivers into the land mass, or where early roads like Yonge Street penetrated the terrain. It well may be, as T.F. McIlwraith has demonstrated, that the poor roads of Upper Canada before the railway age were still adequate for the spreading of farm settlement and commercial agriculture.[2] Yet it is clear that no sizeable urban places developed in the interior of the province before railways brought all-weather bulk transport, especially in the quite extensive inland reaches of the western peninsula. Urban Ontario was originally oriented to its trunk water system; and really remained so during the nineteenth century, despite the spread of the railway net, for the main cities on lake fronts tended to hold their lead – the railways themselves being directed to their harbours as major transhipping and distributing points. Thus urban life in nineteenth-century Ontario was strongly shaped by ports, a condition not greatly altered till the coming of the automobile highway in the twentieth century.

The 'water-born' nature of so many primary Ontario towns and cities assuredly deserves emphasis, looking as they did to lake horizons or river courses, whereas later inland centres (as in the plains west) essentially were structured on the railway line. Waterside location shaped Kingston, the province's first commercial centre of importance, as the key transhipment point on the St Lawrence route between lake and river navigation. It founded Toronto, as York in 1793, to be the 'naval arsenal' and seat of the government for the new province of Upper Canada.[3] It supplied prime impetus to Cornwall, Belleville, Niagara, and Hamilton (once Burlington Bay was channeled open in 1832); and even gave Bytown, or the city of Ottawa from 1855, its vast inland lumber empire up the Ottawa river system. Only London, of the earlier emerging concentrations of any size (it was a town by 1848), grew initially as an inland service-centre for prosperous surrounding farming districts. Yet other relatively early inland places, from Peterborough to Brantford to Chatham, flourished first as shipment points on waterways.

Urban growth in Ontario, in the second place, was constantly influenced by close proximity and ease of access to the United States. The same might obviously be said of other regions in Canada; yet there was some significant degree of difference, for many leading Ontario centres from Kingston to Toronto and Hamilton to Windsor were right on the water border, at most a few short hours' passage from American cities across the lakes. Furthermore, the whole southern Ontario peninsula was thrust into the midst of one of the richest and fastest-developing areas of the United States, the Great Lakes basin. Still further, in pre-railway times, the chief answer to Ontario's winter isolation when the lakes and the St Lawrence were shut was travel by ice across to the United States. In short, despite the strong Upper Canadian connection eastward with the St Lawrence outlet to the sea, a pattern of communication and commerce southward was equally inherent, stemming from the very physical position of the region.

The latter pattern was considerably reinforced, in spite of existing tariff hindrances, when the Erie Canal opened water communications between Buffalo and New York in 1825, with feeders subsequently being added directly to Lake Ontario. This man-made feature no less became an environmental force acting on Upper Canada, since much of its grain went out to market via the Erie – especially after the American Drawback Acts of 1845–6 remitted duties on goods in transit between Canada and the United States Atlantic ports. Toronto in particular benefitted from ease of access to the Erie system, for it found itself ideally situated as an entrepôt between American and St Lawrence routes to the sea, able to use both to advantage, or play one off against the other.

Britain's adoption of free trade and repeal of the Navigation Acts from 1846 to 1849 removed the structure of imperial preferences and restrictions that had worked to channel traffic into the St Lawrence route for trade with the British market. The new colonial free-trade environment (for such it might well be termed) further enhanced the pattern of north-south connections for Ontario towns. The establishment of reciprocal free trade in natural products by the treaty of 1854 with the United States was a wholly consistent climax to the development. Quite as significant, however, was the rising demand in the eastern United States for Canadian supplies in lumber and foodstuffs, which made the reciprocity treaty less a cause than a result of mounting north-south traffic between the Ontario region and American urban industrial markets.

The coming of the railway age to Ontario in the 1850s again enlarged north-south traffic, as lines funnelled Canadian commodities southward to the United States: the Bytown and Prescott or Brockville and Ottawa lumber routes; Toronto's Northern Railway; and the Great Western, focussed on Hamilton, provided direct connection between New York rails at the Niagara border and Michigan lines across the Detroit River, Ontario, in fact, became thoroughly tied into the spreading United States railroad net, as a commerce of convenience grew across it between the American mid-west and the Atlantic seaboard. The abrogation of the Reciprocity Treaty in 1866 by no means brought this to an end – although the new 'national environment' of Confederation and subsequently the protective National Policy did add a stronger alternate overlay of east-west connections.

In the whole process, urban centres like Windsor, Sarnia, London, Hamilton, Toronto, and Ottawa gained markedly from the through traffic with the United States, which plainly fostered urbanization at these points. More than this, however, the powerful north-south ties that had been created for Ontario's urban communities also brought American business connections, techniques, and capital for branch plants after the National Policy of 1879. The communications with the south as readily conveyed American books and periodicals in mounting quantity to Canadian towns, touring American road companies and lecturers, American fashions and models to emulate. Granted, the countryside as well as the town felt these influences; but they were strongest in the urban centres that were the foci of traffic with the United States.

Moreover, in the later nineteenth century the north-south pattern grew more extensive, as Americans invested in rising factories in Ontario towns, in rail lines probing further northward for lumber supplies, and, above all, in the new frontiers of development opening in the North – of silver, copper, and nickel mines and pulpwood mills all the way to Lake Superior. The American tie-up, which was conditioned by environment from the start of Ontario's urban development, was thus a far larger factor by the close of the century. In one sense, urbanization and Americanization had proceeded together.

In regard to population, the essential fact prevails that it is the concentrating of people, in whatever environment, which produces an urban centre. This in itself is not enough, of course; a mere crowding together of numbers might constitute a rural slum with no particular urban functions – or a prisoner-of-war camp. Function as well as number is involved. The people must compose a community engaged in services or activities that can be designated as urban: which normally mean those of a commercial, financial, industrial, administrative, cultural, or informational kind, which are not generally part of primary production and are carried on in close contiguity with considerable differentiation of labour. A further point worth noting is that the concentration of population should be seen in relative terms. What matters is the size of the closely populated centre in relation to its whole society; indeed, in regard to the age and kind of society as well. Thus Kingston could be a significant urban concentration in 1817 with 2250 inhabitants in a thinly settled pioneer Upper Canada, whose total population was around 100,000. Likewise, in 1851, in a rural Canada West of some 950,000 people, Toronto could loom fairly large with 30,000 – about the size, incidentally, of the highly important town of Bristol in the English Middle Ages.

To trace this urban population growth in Ontario across the century, one may begin with the estimate (for want of reliable figures) of an average rate of increase of over two percentage points a decade from the 1820s to the fifties, during the period when waves of British immigrants were pouring into Upper Canada, chiefly to settle its agricultural frontiers but stimulating town development as well. By 1851 the urban proportion in Canada West stood at 14 per cent; by 1861 it had reached 18.5, an increase of 4.5 points in the era of the first great railway-building boom. By 1871 the proportion stood at 20.6, a solid 4.1 advance. But in 1881 the urban segment had risen to 27.1, up by 6.5; and in 1891 to 35 per cent: a soaring growth of nearly eight points, reflecting the rapid industrial development of the eighties. Moreover, the increase by 1901 to 40.3 per cent still indicated a continuing rise of 5.3 despite the state of depression during the mid-1890s.[4] Obviously, then, urbanization had taken off in the later nineteenth century in Ontario, although its mid-century growth was substantial, and even its course in the earlier decades was definitely worthy of attention. For it bears noting that in this early era, that is generally treated as a time of frontier and rural settlement, urban centres were nonetheless steadily increasing their proportion in the total provincial community. In this respect, they were growing faster than the populating countryside itself.

Several factors were involved in this early period of urban growth. To begin with, small service centres appeared inland, as immigration pushed out farm frontiers, supplying a tavern, general store and mill, blacksmith's shop, and probably a log church. Concurrently, there was the corresponding advance of older places on the fronts, from crossroad or waterside hamlets to well-settled villages and towns serving a much bigger hinterland, each with several mills, warehouses, stores, and churches, and with lawyers, doctors, clerics, and teachers, and soon little newspaper offices. Thus, as Peterborough emerged in the 1830s in the Otonabee backwoods, Cobourg grew on the lakefront as key to the Otonabee district, or Hamilton as a marketing centre for new hamlets in the Grand River Valley. There was also a 'multiplier effect,' most apparent in the larger towns. Increasing urban activities in variety or size tended to produce additional activities as spin-offs. Timber production at Bytown in time led also to towing companies, shingle mills, and sash factories. In the forties, the growth of wholesaling in Toronto brought the specialization of retail trade out of it for the flourishing local market, while the overall expansion of the city's business community caused the establishment of more newspapers and printing offices. And all this meant more jobs and people in urban centres.

In addition, some of the immigrants themselves did not go to the country but stayed to swell the towns directly. Incoming settlers halted there, while arranging and preparing to take up a farm, and often to find work to pay for stock and supplies. The age saw such a stop as temporary – and certainly transciency was a marked feature of the town population. But often the halt became quite permanent. Some immigrants stayed because they found better prospects in the urban setting; others because they had scant prospects at all. Those best equipped with capital or work skills or those least advantaged with only unskilled labour to offer – and often ill-nourished, sick, or unadaptable besides – either might remain to add to the urban population. The result was the heightening of class differences and a growing urban concentration of poverty. The scale of urban misery, with attendant problems of degradation and disease, alcohol and violence, was nothing like the size it would become in the later century. Still, it began there: Toronto had its slums by the 1840s. But social problems would long be left to private charity or church effort, with little urban community action beyond providing constables and a workhouse: the latter by 1837 for Toronto.

In the mid-century years of the fifties and sixties, immigration declined and agrarian expansion came up against the intractable line of the Shield. A period of intensive more than extensive growth ensued, but there was much to be done in filling in and consolidating. Indeed, this led to greater urban concentration, in the rapid economic development stimulated by the export boom of the fifties in wheat and lumber, by reciprocity, and, above all, by the coming of rail transportation. Railways affected urban centres about as much by their promotion and construction as by their actual operation. They brought land speculation and glittering schemes in towns for each to rule a new transportation empire as well as high wages, free-flowing money, jobs, and hopes of jobs. People poured in. Expensive private and public buildings went up, such as the imposing town hall Cobourg erected in visions of becoming a grand railroad capital. Hamilton's population shot up from 10,300 in 1850 to 27,500 in 1856, London's from 5000 to 15,000. Toronto's property values more than doubled in the period, while present-day landmarks like the St Lawrence Hall, University College, and an enlarged, reconstructed Osgoode Hall rose in the city's lavish building boom.

The railway fever broke in 1857 along with the world depression, leaving a heavy load of civic and private debt, and even declining population in some cities. Hamilton, for example, fell to 19,000 by 1861. But many of the urban gains remained solid, and the new trade boom rising during the American Civil War quickly recovered lost ground. Moreover, towards the close of the sixties, railways were again being promoted, aided by the government of the new province of Ontario established at Confederation in 1867 – which, of course, made Toronto a political capital again. Any setbacks which that city had suffered in depression had more than been made good; indeed, by the seventies it was in the midst of another, still mounting boom. It had expanded its industrial, commercial and financial facilities greatly, founding the Toronto Stock Exchange in 1852, the powerful Bank of Commerce in 1867. It was the principal Ontario educational, publishing, and newspaper centre, with a dominating hold on the shaping of provincial opinion. Consequently, its population had climbed in keeping with this increasing metropolitan stature and diversification of activities: from 30,000 in 1851 to 44,000 in 1861, and 56,000 ten years later.

As for rural Ontario in the period, it had evolved a stable, well-knit agricultural society, still based mainly on an export wheat economy, but with other specializations appearing such as dairying and stock-raising. Accordingly, this was the heyday of the country market-town set in prosperous agrarian surroundings. Outside of cities like Hamilton and Toronto, or in some respects in the lumber world of Ottawa, manufacturing industry was not yet of much significance in Ontario's urban life.

The next period, however, from 1870 to the end of the century, brought the mounting impact of factory industry. Urban population continued to grow for many of the older service-providing reasons, but the main new factor added was that of industrial production. True, the forest frontier went on extending northward, creating new lumber centres from Muskoka to Kenora, and Sudbury was increasingly mining copper from 1887. Nevertheless, major development of the forest and mineral resources of the vast Northern Ontario region was only beginning in the 1890s, and its effects on urban Ontario belong mainly to the twentieth century. In the later nineteenth century, instead, the rising theme in population concentration was industrialization.

Of course, the National Policy's protective tariff of 1879 had much to do with the noteworthy spread of factories and factory towns. Yet industrial enterprise had been growing in Ontario during the seventies, despite depression after 1875. In fact, heavy industry had appeared in the Toronto Rolling Mills in the sixties to meet railway needs for iron rails, in Hamilton's extensive car shops, or Kingston's locomotive works during the fifties. And steam power had been applied at least from the forties in some flour or saw mills where water-power resources were not adequate for rising demands. None the less, the rapid growth of factory industry in the later century was certainly impelled by the size of the markets now available for home manufactures, in a much more populous Ontario, in the Maritimes since Confederation, and in the Canadian West that opened particularly after the completion of the Canadian Pacific in 1885. All these, moreover, existed as protected markets by the eighties.

The consequent growth of industry – in textiles, agricultural machinery, milling and food processing, in clothing, iron ware, wood products, and leather goods –

was much too extensive to be detailed here. Suffice it to say that urban centres were widely affected, and that some in particular emerged as distinctive manufacturing communities producing for much more than merely local hinterland consumption; notably places in western Ontario on good rail communications, like London, Brantford, Galt, Guelph, and Berlin (later Kitchener). Obviously, population concentrated still further at these factory sites, as it did also in Hamilton and Toronto. In fact, as time went on, the workings of economies of scale and the multiplier advantages of the bigger industrial centres – more subsidiary operations, more financial and commercial services at hand, larger pools of labour, broader transportation facilities – tended to enlarge the size of factory operations and again concentrate them more and more in major places. The result could be seen by the 1890s in the decline of small village industries, along with fewer but larger manufacturing units in the chief centres.

One indicative instance of the trend was the movement of the Massey agricultural machinery plant from Newcastle to Toronto in 1879. Another was the fact that Toronto had, in round numbers, 930 industrial establishments in 1881 with 13,200 workers, and in 1891, 2400 units with 26,200 workers.[5] But then over the nineties its number of units became reduced to 847 by 1901, while the much smaller manufacturing centre of Kingston saw a still greater reduction during the decade, from 401 to 42.[6] In general, this consolidation meant more concentration of people at the leading places. It was, in fact, another mark of urbanization – as evidenced in the growth of Hamilton from 35,000 in 1881 to 49,000 in 1891, and Toronto in the same decade from 86,000 to 181,000, then to 208,000 by 1901.[7]

A final mark of urban concentration to be noted for the period was the corresponding emergence of rural de-population. No longer were cities growing chiefly because of immigration from abroad (though there was some revival of it in the eighties) or from the surplus of a still-increasing agrarian society. From this point on, rural society ceased to grow in size, and even began to lose ground to urban population. The movement from the country to the city developed from the 1870s onward, particularly of young females, which would produce a feminine dominance in urban numbers, as well as leave a persisting degree of rural bachelorhood. But farm society, as such, did not decline in size during the later nineteenth century. The loss thus far came mostly in rural non-farm elements – an additional indication of the decline of local village industrial and service occupations, as more and more industry and services were concentrated in the larger towns and cities. This movement out of the country became most evident from the mid-eighties, but its beginnings can be traced back earlier, for many rural areas had reached their population peaks at the census of 1861. Thus Peel County, for example, declined from its maximum numbers in 1861 by 21 per cent in 1901, and its Chinguacousy Township, in which was the rising town of Brampton, fell from 6129 in 1871 to 5476 in 1881, and to 4794 by the end of the century.[8]

In sum, the major effects of modern urban population concentration were manifest in Ontario by the time the nineteenth century had closed, including the social strains and problems produced by people crowding into cities. Indeed, the very size of the complex of problems thus created led in the later century to the framing of provincial and municipal social policies and institutions to cope with baneful urban conditions. But this brings us to another aspect of urbanization – organization.

The human organization of urban centres has so many facets that it is impossible to do more here than select one or two, while leaving out a great many of equally valid interest. Those chosen – municipal framework and social structure – do not include such major considerations as religious and educational institutions, occupational and family patterns, spatial distributions and streetscapes, social and physical services, and much else besides. But they do illustrate distinctive features of Ontario's urban growth, and that is their reason for choice.

Municipal institutions developed slowly and piecemeal in early Upper Canada, an expression of the frontier state of its society and the prevailing conservative context of rule by oligarchy. Though a representative assembly was there from the founding of the province, the fact that administration at the centre was by appointed officials not under popular control was naturally reflected in the localities also. Hence, in spite of the existence of minor locally elected officers in townships, the real power over the countryside was wielded by the appointed district magistrates sitting in Quarter Sessions, from whose authority the incipient urban centres were not excepted, not even the little capital of York.

The growing population of these places, however, and the resulting problems with which they had to deal, did gradually bring them distinctive though limited grants of authority. Some of them secured 'police acts' from their district Quarter Sessions (not the modern connotation of 'police,' but rather the power to regulate) enabling them to deal with street improvements, nuisances, and fire prevention: Kingston first in 1816, York in 1817, Niagara in 1819. But as fuller, more effective powers grew necessary, agitation rose for some form of municipal government in the 1820s. This was largely frustrated by the sharp divisions in the legislature between Reform exponents of popular power and Tory defenders of appointed right. At last a provincial act of 1832 established an elected Board of Police for Brockville, setting a precedent that partly broke through the old control of the appointed magistrates. A number of other police board towns followed all along the front, including Hamilton in 1833, Belleville, Cornwall, and Port Hope in

1834, Cobourg in 1837. But York took a long leap forward, achieving incorporation as the city of Toronto in 1834 under its own elected council and mayor – who was, however, chosen by the council from its members.

The Rebellion of 1837 and the stresses that followed brought a temporary check to the evolution of municipal organization. Still, Kingston, which had sought incorporation since 1828, managed to become an incorporated town in 1838. In any case, the towns' needs were pressing, and the provincial mood was clearly changing by the forties. When the oligarchic power of the Family Compact at the centre was uprooted, the local oligarchies were foredoomed as well. Furthermore, the Reformers' drive for responsible government in the province during the decade also involved the establishing of municipal self-government. Thus the road led naturally from the partially elective District Councils Act of 1841 to the Municipal Corporations Act of 1849, defining a complete series of incorporated, elected rural and urban municipal authorities: on the urban side, from police village to city, the latter being equal to a county in status, but separated from the county's jurisdiction under its own mayor and council.

Even before this general Act, which remained the basis of municipal organization in Ontario until almost the present day, particular enactments had carried individual towns forward. Hamilton and Kingston were both incorporated as cities in 1846. Bytown and Brantford became police board towns in 1847, each, too, with a mayor and council. Moreover, the structure given all these places was modelled on that first developed for Toronto in regard to taxing powers, a rate-payers' franchise, and the like. Consequently, the Act of 1849 simply generalized a pattern that was already being worked out in urban Ontario to fit its needs and attitudes, a pattern set in its fundamentals by the 1850s, and one which would be of lasting significance.

It was a combination of North American circumstances and precepts of British Victorian middle-class liberalism. Based on rule by elected representatives, it by no means went as far as popular democracy. A still engrained conservatism, the set habit of looking to an elite, distaste for party politics in municipal affairs, the fear of 'Yankee' boss rule and corruption, all militated against any further move to full democratization. Though mayors became directly elected from the late fifties, no basic change in the character of Ontario urban political organization occurred through the rest of the century. Hence the structure of public life in the towns, the kind of places they became, continued to differ significantly from American counterparts across the border, in the lesser play of popular power, the greater degree of social control from above – and, one might add, in less evidence of confused and corrupt administration.

The kinds of places that Ontario towns became equally expressed the social structure which they developed during the century. On the one hand, their expanding wealth and economic dominance produced a newly powerful capitalistic and entrepreneurial middle class that was displacing the older urban elite of officials and large resident landholders even in the 1840s. On the other hand, the very concentrating of population shaped a much larger urban working class. The rise of factory industry in the later century added greatly to its mass, while no less adding a strong component of industrialists to the ruling urban element of wholesalers, shippers, railway directors, and bankers. In sum, the old graduated range of social orders in the towns, from unskilled labourers through artisans and shopkeepers to gentlemen, became much more plainly polarized into two main class groups representing either numbers or power. One accordingly could see the indicative organizing forces at work in the establishment of Boards of Trade (in Toronto in 1844), of manufacturers' associations (at Hamilton and Toronto in 1858, and more lastingly in 1871), or in the growth of the labour movement: the Trades Assembly set up at Hamilton in 1863, at Toronto in 1871, and Ottawa the next year, leading to the enduring Trades and Labour Congress founded in 1886.

The degree of class polarization still must not be over-emphasized. At one end of the social scale there continued to be an aristocratic leaven. Originally this had much to do with the presence of officers of the British garrisons, but it lasted particularly in towns like Kingston and London, and to some degree Toronto, supported by the continuing imperial fount of honour and prestige, and the strength of social conservatism and British loyalty. Further down the scale, the still numerous 'respectable' artisans and tradesman elements served to bridge and blur sharper class identification; and they were often quite prominent in civic politics and Orange lodges. Finally, the strong sectarian religious ties that cut across class lines were frequently the more in evidence, particularly when deep-rooted Protestant and Catholic antipathies divided the working class itself.

In ethnic terms, this was a remarkably homogenous urban society, with virtually no non-English-speaking immigrant groups till late in the century, where there was a widespread preponderance of British ancestry, and most were proud of it. It was the result, of course, of the long continued migration from Britain: as late as 1861 more than half the inhabitants of Toronto had been born in the British Isles, and their children would have constituted a large part of the remainder. Nearly every wholesaler in the city of the fifties was a native of the United Kingdom,[9] and at least to the end of the century Toronto's influential business elite came largely from that sort of background: from England, the Gooderhams and Wort's; from Ulster, William McMaster and Timothy Eaton; from Scotland, Robert Hay and John Macdonald. Much the same might be said of the other urban centres, except London. To a less but still highly influential degree their dominant middle-class elements also had a strongly British orientation, in background, outlook and sentiment.

As for the lower classes, the case was not greatly different. In Ottawa, it is true, they were largely Catholic Irish or Catholic French Canadian. Hamilton had a sizeable Catholic Irish minority; one quarter of Toronto was Catholic by the later century – chiefly Irish also. Yet in general the towns were Protestant British in complexion; and with a strong coloration of Ulster Irish, as in Toronto, that was exemplified in the power of the Orange Order in their midst. Moreover, the Catholic Irish stressed religious more than national identity. Hence the towns could well be called focal points for Victorian British attitudes in nineteenth-century Ontario: another important offset, in the realm of organization, to American influences in the urbanizing process.

The significance of technology for urban development is so fundamental and pervasive that once again only a scant selection can be made here from the varied aspects of technological change that bore upon the growth of Ontario centres both from without and within. Yet one particular aspect stands out as obvious for discussion: changes in the technology of transport, from the steamboat to the railway, that so signally affected the nineteenth century everywhere.

The steamboat came to Upper Canada with the launching of the *Frontenac* on Lake Ontario by Kingston enterprise in 1816, and spread rapidly in the next few years, along the lakes and up navigable waterways. Its impact on an embryonic urban society living by water transport was sweeping. It not only made passenger traffic far more swift and sure, but also brought steam towage, whether for timber rafts or barges filled with freight or immigrants. It made coping with rapids on the St Lawrence and the use of new canals far more effective, especially with the introduction of more powerful propeller craft that supplemented the paddle-wheeler in the forties. And it led increasingly in the little Upper Canadian ports to investment in steamboat building or steamboat and harbour companies, one of the first significant developments in local capital accumulation and business organization in these emergent urban places. Finally, it implanted in them a knowledge of steam technology, exemplified in marine machinery works at Niagara or in Kingston's shipyards. Well before the arrival of the railway, Upper Canadian towns could produce boilers and engines, which were applied as well in early 'steam mills.' In many ways, indeed, the steamboat was the harbinger of the nineteenth century for Ontario.

It was, however, still only one part of advances in water transport that quickened the whole pace of economic development for Ontario towns in the first half of the century. There was also the widespread introduction of the lake schooner, that efficient work-horse of the Lakes, or the improvement of harbours and of aids to navigation. Beyond this, there were the canals – and the telling impact of the Erie that has previously been noted. The Welland Canal not only cleared the way to the Upper Lakes; the water power and shipping facilities it offered fostered new urban centres along its course; for example, St Catharines and Thorold (once Stumptown). The Rideau brought lumber traffic down to fatten Kingston at its western entry, and at the other created Bytown, the canal construction head-quarters, which had a single cabin on its site in 1826 and 1500 inhabitants when the work was finished in 1832.[10] As for the chain of St Lawrence canals, finally completed by 1848, the lower shipping rates and heavier imports they engendered widely affected the urban centres of Ontario's commercial life.

In regard to land transport, the earlier part of the century did see some improve-ments with the introduction of macadamized and plank roads that undoubtedly aided towns in acquiring larger or more effectively held rural hinterlands. Thus the Port Dover plank road gave young Hamilton an advantage over nearby rivals like Dundas, while the macadamizing of stretches of the Dundas and Kingston roads or Yonge Street (almost to Lake Simcoe in the thirties) much enhanced the spreading inland dominance of Toronto, which was already 'a fledgeling metro-polis' by the time of the Rebellion of 1837.[11] But the projecting of railways in the 1840s and their implementation in the fifties, led to a transformation in land transport technology that would command the second half of the nineteenth century for urban Ontario: the building of its rail communications net.

The opening of the Great Western in 1854, inspired and backed by Hamilton enterprise, made that city headquarters of one of the most successful early Ontario lines. Moreover, Windsor rose fast as its western junction with the United States, Niagara Falls as its eastern, and London advanced no less rapidly when its rails went through in 1853. Toronto's Northern, opened in 1855, created Collingwood as its port-terminus on Georgian Bay, and gave the Lake Ontario city a much greater northern hinterland, reaching even into the Upper Lakes. Toronto, in fact, became a major lumber port, as timber resources up to Georgian Bay were drained by rail to its harbour, leading in the seventies to the extension of the Northern into Muskoka to exploit its wealth of forests. Other lines served Ottawa or Cobourg, Port Hope or Brantford. But the greatest of all was the Grand Trunk, running westward from Montreal to Toronto by 1856 and on to Sarnia by 1859. Though this transprovincial system became a costly failure for its private investors, a heavy burden on the public purse, and a dire entanglement for governments, it none the less tied the southern Ontario region together with one through, all-weather iron highway, and inevitably had profound influence on urban centres all along its path.

Places in the inland west like Guelph or Berlin were decidedly stimulated by the new line of transport. Port towns along the upper St Lawrence and Lake Ontario, however, were often hit by the rail competition that carried through traffic along behind them but not to their harbours. Kingston, for instance, had no expanding hinterland to tap in its corner of the province, and could not become a sufficient focus of rail traffic to benefit much from the Grand Trunk. In contrast, Toronto certainly gained. It did become a major rail focus, what with its large hinterland, its own Northern, and also the extension of the Great Western from Hamilton – which actually allowed the larger city's interests to penetrate into the southwestern reaches of the province. In consequence, the Grand Trunk to Toronto meant even better access east and west, and more spokes in the railway hub it was building up. Rail technology was completing a metropolitan pattern that could bring the whole Ontario region under the economic dominance of its chief city.

The main outlines of the pattern had been drawn when the first railway-building boom collapsed in 1857. When construction rose again in the early seventies, it largely filled in the pattern further, with more lines across the western peninsula or fanning northward out of Toronto and Hamilton. But by 1880 it was approaching a new phase, entrance into Northern Ontario. The building of the Canadian Pacific Railway from 1881 westward across Northern Ontario provided stimulus for a line to reach it from the south; above all, so that Toronto could tie into the transcontinental traffic, which otherwise would go far above it, eastward to Ottawa and Montreal. Between 1884 and 1886 the Northern and Pacific Junction Railway was built from the Northern rails in Muskoka to reach Callandar, then on to North Bay. By this time the CPR route was fully open from Montreal to Vancouver; and as well the Ontario rail net was linked with it. Furthermore, the Canadian Pacific line itself had brought about the uncovering of the mineral resources at Sudbury, the beginning of western grain shipments from the Lakehead, and the building of a branch completed in 1888, across Algoma to Sault Ste Marie.

By the nineties, then, the railway had begun to raise urban centres in Northern Ontario as well, through conquering its formidable distances and opening up inland resources as nothing could have done before. Meanwhile it had greatly stimulated the manufacturing growth of the south, making Hamilton in particular a city of heavy iron industry, with its first modern blast furnace in 1895; concentrated whole complexes of factories at focal points on the transport network (especially, of course, at Toronto); yet equally had brought decline to many a smaller manufacturing centre from Dundas to Bowmanville. The depression of 1893 was only a brief setback and recovery spread fast from 1896. As the century closed, rail transport was moving on to big new designs: the Ontario government's Temiskaming and Northern Ontario line from North Bay, announced in 1900, and soon two new transcontinentals across the northern Shield.

Moreover, rail technology had now developed a wholly new instrument for affecting the growth of cities, the electric street railway. Electric traction, first displayed in Canada on a little line to Toronto's Exhibition grounds in 1885, came into use in St Catherines in 1887, and spread rapidly in the early nineties in Toronto, Hamilton, and Ottawa. Its effect on the internal organization of Ontario cities was about as profound as the influence of steam traction had been on their external organization within the regional community as a whole. For one thing, it invited urban spatial expansion, or even explosion, since the same period of travelling time could carry the town dweller much further from home to job by way of electric street car than by horse car, or assuredly, by foot. For another, it greatly advanced the sorting-out of residential from business or industrial districts, already under way, as whole new residential districts developed with the tram lines. And still further, electric rail technology notably affected urban land values and land use, just as railways had done, while raising similar issues of privileged, franchised private corporations in contention with public interests in mass transport. Yet the full impact of this latest technological factor to impinge on urbanization in Ontario would not become plain until the early twentieth century, by which time the next great transport revolution, the automotive upheaval, was already in preparation.

Accordingly, it is time to call a halt. Let it merely be said, in conclusion, that the nineteenth century in Ontario had witnessed a multiplicity of developments in technology, as in organization, that intricately affected the relations of population and environment in the urbanizing process. If this examination has only outlined some of the complexity and sweep of that process in nineteenth-century Ontario, that will be accomplishment enough.

NOTES

1 E.E. Lampard, 'American Historians and the Study of Urbanization,' *American Historical Review*, LXVII, Oct. 1961, 49–61
2 T.F. McIlwraith, 'The Adequacy of Rural Roads in the Era before Railways: An Illustration from Upper Canada,' *Canadian Geographer*, XIV, 4, Dec. 1970, 344–58
3 G.P. de T. Glazebrook, *The Story of Toronto* (Toronto 1971), 11
4 L.O. Stone, *Urban Development in Canada* (Ottawa 1967), 19, 29
5 D.C. Masters, *The Rise of Toronto, 1850–1890* (Toronto 1947), 174
6 J. Spelt, *Urban Development in South Central Ontario* (Toronto 1972), 173
7 It has not been thought necessary to give citations throughout for population figures taken directly from published census tables. It should be noted here, however, that Toronto's jump to 181,000 over the eighties was partly due to anexations of suburban areas.
8 S.A. Cudmore, 'Rural Depopulation in Southern Ontario,' *Transactions of the Canadian Institute*, IX (Toronto 1912), 262
9 D. McCalla, 'The Toronto Wholesale Trade in the 1850's' (typescript, Department of History, University of Toronto, 1965), 41–3
10 R.F. Leggett, *Rideau Waterway* (Toronto 1965), 205
11 F.H. Armstrong, 'Metropolitanism and Toronto Re-Examined, 1825–1850,' Canadian Historical Association, *Papers*, 1966, 30

The Rise of London: A Study of Urban Evolution in Nineteenth-Century Southwestern Ontario

Frederick H. Armstrong and Daniel J. Brock

We walked over a rich meadow and at its extremity reached the forks of the river. The Governor wished to examine this situation and its environs, and we therefore stopped here a day. He judged it to be a capital situation, eminently calculated for the metropolis of all Canada. Among many other essentials, it possessed the following advantages: Command of Territory – internal situation – central position – facility of water communication up and down the Thames superior navigation for boats to near its source ... the soil is luxuriously fertile and the land capable of being easily cleared and soon put into a state of agriculture. A Pinery upon an adjacent high knoll, other timber on the height, well calculated for the erection of the public buildings, climate not inferior to any part of Canada.[1]

Take a map of Southwestern Ontario.

In the heart of the triangle, equidistant from Toronto on the east, Windsor on the west and Owen Sound on the north, is the city of London ...

Around the city hub, the land of southwestern Ontario is rolling, rich, productive. Its people are wealthy, complacent, insular. Because the city of London sits squarely in the middle of this beauty, she is immensely rich, prideful, self-sufficient.[2]

The proud capital of the southwestern Ontarian peninsula, as Miller describes London, may be a far cry from Simcoe's metropolis of all Canada. Yet the failure of London to achieve metropolitan status, while still attaining primacy in its own region, reflects upon a most interesting problem in the development of urban North America: why certain cities rose to metropolitan status, while others, seemingly more favoured by natural or political factors, are vanquished in their attempt to develop, and eventually became tributaries to centres which they had once seemed destined to dominate. For Ontario, the examination of the evolution of towns in the south-central region of the province received a careful geographical examination by Jacob Spelt some fifteen years ago,[3] but as yet little has been written on the southwestern peninsula of the province, roughly that section west of the

Niagara escarpment which contains some of the nation's finest agricultural land and is one of its most populous areas.

Southwestern Ontario, for practical political and economic purposes, is now a subsidiary of the Toronto metropolitan area, but it still retains a certain separate identity and boats its own metropolitan centre, the city of London, which has a population of some 225,000 (1971). Today London appears as an unrivalled centre of the region: Windsor is off on the western periphery and for many purposes has become a suburb of Detroit; Hamilton, at the foot of the Niagara escarpment, has never really been an integral part of the western peninsula, even if, along with Dundas and Ancaster, it has been the gateway for much of the trade to the west. Nevertheless, London's dominance was not always an obvious matter and an examination of the factors which led to London's paramountcy may tell us something about urban evolution not only in Ontario, but also on a developing continent.

In evaluating the causes of the rise of cities the initial place must be given to geography, which sets the underlying pattern upon which human events take place. Topography, climate, fertility of the soil – these constitute the framework provided by nature, and the western peninsula of southern Ontario, with its central location in the developing continent, rich lands, and lake communications, was blessed on all counts. Here was an obvious site for the rise of one or more important cities, especially as the territory was originally far enough removed from the growing metropolitan area of York/Toronto to be able to assume something of an identity of its own. Toronto, the provincial capital, with its natural harbour on Lake Ontario, its inland and St Lawrence water connections, was soon able to dominate Hamilton and eventually other Lake Ontario cities, including its early rivals Niagara and Kingston. It could not, however, completely control the southwestern peninsula. In the early days travel was too slow and difficult, and from 1825 an alternative route to the outer world existed via Lake Erie and the Erie Canal. Thus, although the provincial capital might rightly assume the title of the metropolis of the colony, subsidiary, of course, to the commercial rivalry of Montreal and New York City and to the overall primary of London, England, there was still room for a tertiary metropolis to rise further west.

The western counties of southern Ontario thus possessed the capacity for developing their own regional centre, but in what way did physical factors particularly favour London over what are today its subordinate towns in southwestern Ontario? St Thomas, Woodstock, and Stratford are also centrally located. One of these potential rivals, St Thomas, was even closer to Lake Erie and had approximately a ten-year head start. The village of Delaware, now virtually a suburb to the southwest of London, had origins which dated back to the late 1790s.[4] From a purely geographical point of view London originally possessed few significant advantages

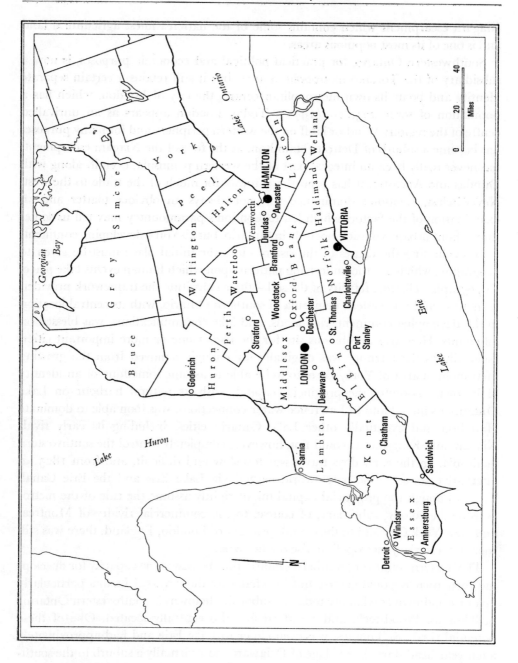

over other future town sites. All possessed the natural qualifications necessary for the growth of an important centre: an ample hinterland, reasonably healthy climate, and a river to provide an adequate water supply, a handy method of waste disposal, and power for mills and other industries. Thus geography provided London with the necessary qualifications of an important centre, but gave it no real advantages over its potential rivals.

A second major factor in the growth of many metropolitan areas is simply *luck*. Certain of the key events that govern the evolution of any metropolis are purely fortuitous. Antioch in Syria believed it was under the personal protection of *Fortuna*, the Goddess of Fortune: London might well make the same case, for from the appointment of Lieutenant-Governor Simcoe in the 1790s onward the city's history has been highlighted by boons granted by a smiling goddess – or possibly a benevolent Church of England deity.

The physical setting and luck are only the first two factors in urban development for it might be argued that another major influence is the human equation, the people whose activities determine the development of a city, whether they are citizens, or those who influence development from the outside. Those who affected London's growth in 'passing by' are best examined in their chronological place; a word, however, should be said about its citizens.

In a pioneer community, undergoing rapid growth, certain individuals are inevitably pushed to the fore, the men of capital and enterprise who are to be found in every town, for a growing metropolis can attract men of ability and give them every opportunity for advancement. In some centres, nevertheless, they possibly display more enterprise than others; often the biographies of a handful of the leading citizens of the first generation, can, *in toto*, provide an insight into the 'why' of much of the political, social, and commercial development of a North American urban nucleus. For London, the active lifespan of the first generation of its citizens was almost equal to the period covered by the rise and consolidation of the city. In the mid-1820s the first settlers had arrived; by 1880 the majority of them had died. At the same time London had grown up from a wilderness, consolidated its position, and obviously had become the 'capital' of southwestern Ontario.

To demonstrate the contribution of the town's early leading citizens and their importance in its growth, a few may be selected as examples and worked into the picture of development. Some arrived as young men with the first wave of settlers and virtually grew up with the city: George Jervis Goodhue, merchant, land speculator, first 'millionaire,' and first village president; Simeon Morrill, tanner and first town mayor; Ellis Walton Hyman, a second tanner, and Benjamin Cronyn, first Anglican bishop, all appeared in the 1820s and early 1830s. Others, such as Elijah Leonard, iron founder, John Birrell, the first large dry goods wholesaler, and Thomas Carling, the brewer, who was the father of Sir John, came after the 1837 Rebellion as the town was solidifying. Still others, for example John K. Labatt, London's other leading brewer, and Charles Hunt, a miller, moved to the town in the boom period of the late 1840s and early 1850s. Most of these men lived through the formative years to see the successful city of the 1870s. A study of their careers is to a large extent the story of the commercial, financial, and municipal evolution of the city, for business and urban government were dominated by the same individuals.

Geographic factors, luck, and the enterprise of individuals may represent the why of urban expansion; however, when examining the growth of a city, it is helpful to have some criteria by which the stages of urban evolution can be identified. In Canada, the favoured theory of metropolitan expansion has been that advanced by an early graduate of the University of Western Ontario, Professor Norman Gras (1884–1956), who went on to head the business school at Harvard. Gras suggested that in the course of its rise to metropolitan status a town passes through four stages: first it becomes a market centre, then a focus of industry, next a hub of communications, and finally a centre of finance. Simultaneously, the expanding urban centre extends its influence over an ever-growing hinterland, with which it is economically interlocked, so that the two form a single interdependent unit.[5]

That this thesis has its uses in the study of Ontarian urban development is demonstrable; at the same time it must not be adopted too rigidly, for Gras based his thesis primarily on a study of London, England, which moved from stage to stage as technological advances took place. For London, Ontario, however, as for most North American cities, such is not the case. By the time Upper Canada was being opened up, the level of technology was such as to make a more or less concurrent development of the first three stages possible. Thus the evolution of a metropolis in the New World necessarily followed a somewhat different course from that of old London: a compression of stages took place which Gras himself noted in the case of Minneapolis and St Paul. Still, the factors that Gras selected provide an extremely useful set of criteria for the examination of the course of urban economic development.[6] At the same time, it must be noted that growing economic hegemony is paralleled by advancing cultural influences and sometimes administrative control.[7] Simultaneously, within the burgeoning city a constant struggle takes place to provide adequate services for the expanding population, a problem vastly complicated in the nineteenth century by the ever-advancing march of technology. Finally, the growth of a city is not the tale of a quiet course of evolution, but rather of spurts of growth interspersed with periods of virtual hibernation, or even drastic setback. Each city has crucial turning-points in its history and establishing these watersheds is one of the most important tasks of the urban historian. Merely to apply dates of importance for the province or nation to the city is to establish a totally false chronology, one which can easily obscure the actual course of development.

In searching for the vital events in London's history particular attention should be paid to two old but very interesting analyses of the rise of the city. The first was formulated by *The Times* of St Thomas on 13 June 1885.[8] In it the editor, in presenting what might be dubbed the case of the defeated rival, stated that there were three turning-points in the rise of London: the decision to locate the regional, or district administration at the forks of the Thames; the stationing of an imperial garrison there after the rebellion of 1837; and the effects of railway development. Sixteen years later, in 1901, Sir John Carling presented the second interpretation when he told the London and Middlesex Historical Society that he believed the two basic reasons for the rise of London were the selection of the site as the district town and the location of the garrison there. He also implied the role of the railways was significant,[9] thus reiterating exactly the same reasons.

As will be demonstrated the dates 1826, 1838, and 1853 are certainty turning-points in the history of the city. To start the story at the beginning, however, long before there were any settlers in the area, when forest and wilderness reigned supreme, the basic factors we have noted of geographical situation, luck and an individual's outlook combined to give the future city an important lead. In 1791 the Province of Upper Canada was formed from the western portion of the old Province of Quebec; John Graves Simcoe, the earliest of the 'passers-by' who played a role in London's evolution, was appointed its first lieutenant-governor through the opportune circumstance of two of his friends holding office in England. Thus, by accident, the province received as governor a man of unusual energy, considerable – if sometimes misplaced – imagination, and the belief that there was a great future for a colony which many saw as merely a backwoods outpost left over after the American Revolution.

The major problem facing the new governor was the potential threat of the United States, especially as the European situation was rapidly degenerating and America might well end up as an ally of France in a future war. A prime necessity was to find a safe site for a capital; another to retain a line of communications from Lake Ontario to Detroit – as yet not ceded to the Americans – and the fur trade posts in the far West. At the same time it was necessary to maintain both economic and political control of the Indians in the western part of the province and to provide a centralized concentration point for the settlement of the region.

A governor with less energy and imagination than Simcoe would not have looked as far west: a governor in the period after the cession of Detroit in 1796 might not have concentrated on a defensive position in the furthest regions of the province. Both man and time were fortunate for London. In his search for a capital location, Simcoe eliminated the temporary headquarters at Newark (Niagara-on-the-Lake) as totally indefensible. Kingston, the chief town of the colony, was also obviously open to attack from Lake Ontario, as was the excellent harbour at Toronto. The site of London, however, was well inland, not only on the way to Detroit, but also at the theoretical head of river navigation at the forks of the river *La Tranche* (which he renamed the Thames). Furthermore, down-stream Chatham, where no settlement would develop until the 1830s, could be designated as the naval depot for the Upper Lakes. Thus, undeterred by the fact that London was far from anywhere and almost inaccessible, Governor Simcoe chose it in 1793 as the ultimate capital, even if Toronto became his immediate 'temporary headquarters.' If Upper Canada was to be the bulwark of the British empire in North America, London was to be the fortress and metropolis of this bastion of civilization.

His selection was, of course, far too premature, and the provincial capital was to become established at Toronto, but the governor took certain steps which later were to play a major role in the evolution of the city. First, after a personal inspection of the site, he proposed, and later began, a road from present-day Dundas at the head of Lake Ontario designed to run to the forks and provide a connection, via the Thames, with the west.[10] Dundas Street may only have reached as far as the site of Paris during his governorship, for he left in 1796, but the route was to mark the beginning of the vital, but still little investigated, Ancaster/Dundas/Hamilton link, which probably played a more important role in the development of London than the Port Stanley connection. It was along this route that such pioneer merchants as Goodhue were to pack their goods in the early 1820s, and the *Gore Gazette* of Ancaster was to carry the first notices of commerce from the London area.

Simcoe's second step was to cause a large tract of land, encompassing the forks of the Thames, to be surveyed and purchased from the Chippewa Indians. Most of this block became the Township of London. A second township, surveyed from previously purchased lands immediately south of the block, was appropriately named Westminster. Within the townships of London and Westminster the governor then set aside some 3850 acres for his proposed provincial capital, a reserve which was to be conveniently utilized later.[11]

As well as the road and the crown reserve, Simcoe left as a legacy the idea that a second London would one day rise at the forks.[12] The appropriate nomenclature for an important centre was continued when in 1800,[13] under a revision of the internal boundaries within Upper Canada, the county comprising the area was renamed Middlesex and a new administrative unit was established for the eastern half of the western peninsula: the District of London.[14]

By that date settlers were firmly, but thinly, established in Delaware Township and from the Long Point area northward to Dundas Street. Thanks mainly to the efforts of Col. Thomas Talbot in the two decades that followed, settlement gradually spread, first along the shore of Lake Erie, west of the Long Point Settlement, and then inland. The village of Delaware and the cluster of hamlets which later became St Thomas grew up as the main centres in the western portion of the London District, although the administrative centre for the district remained in the Long Point Settlement, first within the own plot of Charlotteville at Turkey Point and then slightly inland at Vittoria in Norfolk County. The first of these centres has now disappeared, the second survives as a police village.

Further inland from Lake Erie settlement had begun in the northern part of Westminster Township in 1810 and, with the opening of London Township to settlers in 1818, a rather concentrated population began to develop surrounding Simcoe's reserve.[15] Seven years later the Canada Company was chartered to bring colonists to the tract even further to the north, in the territory that now comprises the northern portion of Middlesex County, as well as the counties of Perth and Huron.

By the 1820s the centre of population had obviously shifted and the location of the district town, or capital, at Vittoria became increasingly inconvenient for most of the inhabitants, many of whom periodically had to visit that centre for either legal or administrative purposes. In November 1825 the court house at Vittoria was ruined by fire, another fortuitous circumstance which paid off immediately to London's advantage. As both *The Times* of St Thomas and Sir John Carling observed, this catastrophe led to the first step in London's rise to power – its selection as district town. Although early plans for St Thomas included a court house square and the magistrates met there to plan the facilities, the actual transfer of the district administration was to the location of Simcoe's old capital reserve. This decision, made by the provincial authorities, was not popular with many of the inhabitants of Middlesex County, who favoured St Thomas, or the Vittoria officials, who were loath to move from the comfortable, long-settled coast to the inland frontier wilds.[16]

The administrative area which London now acquired stretched from just west of Brantford to the present-day Lambton-Kent County borders in the west and north from Lake Erie to Lake Huron and Georgian Bay. Although 'the Forks,' as London was to be popularly called for some time, was then well to the north of settlement, it was obvious that the annual influx of settlers would soon push well north of Simcoe's reserve, especially as the operations of the Canada Company got under way.

The question remains, however, why none of the three other major contenders were chosen – present-day St Thomas, the most serious rival; Dorchester, another of Simcoe's reserves, or the Village of Delaware. In 1825 St Thomas would have been on the best line of east-west land communication, as the famous Talbot Road excelled all others in the district, including Dundas Street. Like Delaware, St

Thomas was a well-established community, but it was hardly much further north than Vittoria and a more central capital was needed. Besides, the Yankee settlers in the village and environs were already gaining an unhealthy reputation for radicalism and opposition to Col. Thomas Talbot who had been responsible for opening up the region. There is a legend that Talbot's right-hand man, Col. Mahlon Burwell, had gained little support from Talbot Road votes in 1824.[17] Although Burwell himself still supported St Thomas as the district town, such radicalism was hardly a quality that would appeal to Simcoe's super-Tory successor, Sir Peregrine Maitland, and his Family Compact advisers at York.

The second possibility, the land reserved for the town plot of Dorchester, some eight miles upstream from the present village of Dorchester at the junction of the south and middle branches of the Thames, had poor navigational connections, being beyond the main forks of the Thames. In addition, it lacked both the potential for expansion and the relatively heavy settlement to be found in the environs of the London reserve.[18]

Delaware was on a road which served as a line of communication from the head of Lake Ontario to Sandwich and Detroit and was the oldest community in the district outside of the Long Point Settlement. It too, however, had radical leanings, having produced a few individuals disloyal to the crown during the War of 1812. More immediately, it would appear that when the commissioners actually entered into negotiations to purchase a proposed location for the court house square and other public lands, the Delaware landowner, Dr Oliver Tiffany, refused to come to reasonable terms of sale.[19] It seemed illogical to buy up private land at high rates in the Village of Delaware when, with the site of London already a crown reserve, there was ample free land available for both an administration centre and for individual grants to compensate those district officials who would have to leave their old homes and move northward. Once the roads to the forks, such as Dundas Street, had been improved, its immediate disadvantage would be overcome. Moreover, it was anticipated that the heavy influx of immigrants, which was beginning to flow from the British Isles to Upper Canada, would make the forks a strong centre of conservatism, thus balancing the radicalism of the region. Future events were to bear testimony to the strength of this argument.

Thus, on 30 January 1826 a statute which provided that the forks would become the administrative and legal centre of the London District[20] received royal assent. During the next few years streets were laid out and the still extant, though much enlarged court house erected to house the district court, the local sessions of the provincial assizes, the magistrates who administered the district through their courts of quarter sessions, and the London Township town meetings. Gradually the district officials began to settle around it, men such as Treasurer John Harris whose 1834 'Eldon House,' now a municipal museum, still stands a short distance to the north. With them came lawyers to plead before the courts, skilled workmen to build the town, the first hotel keepers to provide accommodation, and the first merchants to dispense supplies.[21] St Thomas had been bypassed on the direct route to the northerly Canada Company land, which was just being opened; Delaware had lost out because of its avariciousness, Woodstock was no more than Simcoe's wilderness reserve for the town plot of Oxford, and other possible rivals, such as Stratford, were not as yet on the drawing boards.

In the next few years growth was rapid; as the population of the region grew so did its needs, and the district town became a fount of leavening activity.[22] In July 1834 a local census revealed the population, within the town limits as surveyed in 1826, to be slightly over 1100 souls.[23] Two years later, for the election of 1836, Lieutenant-Governor Sir Francis Bond Head constituted London a separate riding, a decision aided, no doubt, by the fact that he quite correctly assumed it would be a safe Tory seat. London immediately elected Mahlon Burwell. But all the newcomers were not Tories. Among the first merchants was George J. Goodhue, who became postmaster and partner in a store which provided the essentials of life: from liquor, to groceries, to ropes for the public hangings. Later he became the leading mortgage and land speculator in the western peninsula.[24] Simeon Morrill and Ellis W. Hyman, both tanners and, like Goodhue, American emigrants, arrived to set up business, the former in 1829, the latter probably in 1834.[25]

With their arrival Gras' second stage, the growth of industrialization, may be said to have begun, almost simultaneously with his first phase, for, impelled by the rapid growth of agriculture as the surrounding forests were cleared, the lieutenant-governor granted the settlement the right to hold a public market in 1835.[26] A decade later the present site at Covent Garden was in use.[27] London quickly became the trade focus of a rich agricultural area that, even by 1861, was at most only cultivated to a quarter of its growing capacity. At that date, with the coming of the American Civil War, southwestern Ontario ceased to be dependent on wheat economy and became involved in more diversified forms of farming.[28] To cite the London Prototype, the city became 'a place of resort for a wealthy and growing farming community for the disposal of produce and the purchase of necessaries or luxuries, as the case may be.'[29]

Nevertheless, at the same time as commerce and industry were developing rapidly, the administrative hinterland of the village was being reduced. In March 1837 came the first important step in the limitation of the size of the London District, when provision was made for Norfolk County to be separated as the District of Talbot and Oxford County to be detached as the District of Brock. Simcoe and Woodstock respectively became the new district towns.[30] But these counties were fairly settled areas and London retained administrative control of the rapidly growing north until 1841, when the Huron District covering what is now the territory of Huron and Perth counties and the then wilderness to their north, was officially separated. Goderich became the northern administrative centre.[31]

By that time, however administrative control had ceased to be as important as it had been a few years earlier, for London had grown beyond the stage of being merely a legal centre and the village's economic control of the north was to be retained. London merchants remained the wholesalers for the Goderich area and London speculators, such as Goodhue, invested heavily in Huron lands and mortgages. The loss of territory politically thus meant little dimunition of commercial power. Further, even after the district system was abolished in 1849, London was to remain the county seat of Middlesex County, which until 1854 also included Elgin County.[32] It was only at that date that St Thomas, at last, became a territorial capital.

More important, the second major step in the development of London, as *The Times* and Sir John Carling correctly saw it, had already taken place. In 1838, during the troubled post-rebellion times when there was a renewed threat of American invasion, the British government decided to place a garrison in the centre of the peninsula. St Thomas, where a barracks had recently burned, repeated Delaware's mistake of asking too high a price for the required land. Also, possibly, the town had no desire to have unruly soldiers in its midst.[33] Yet London leaped at the chance, probably because the local oligarchy saw the army as a balance to American frontier influences and, until 1869, it remained a British garrison town. True the soldiers were moved out in 1853 because of the Crimean War, but they were back in 1861 in case London needed to be defended against the Americans if the empire became involved in the civil war on the southern side. The troops were soon stationed on what is now Victoria Park, an open space that has survived as a legacy from the British army and not as a fine example of early town planning.[34] Their presence with their dependents naturally meant an increased population, and quite possibly a touch of British culture, but, most important, it also meant defence spending. Not only did the merchants generally prosper, but also some of the first fortunes were made on government contracts. In typical Canadian fashion Ellis W. Hyman, an American, soon received the British army leather contract to help defend British North America against his compatriots. He did not become a British subject until after the annexation crisis in 1849. The prosperity that resulted from the presence of the troups was well demonstrated by the fact that in 1840, almost immediately after the garrison settled there, London was incorporated as a village,[35] with Postmaster Goodhue as first village president.

The next stage in the development of the city, a less spectacular one, was not noted by either *The Times* or Carling, yet it was still economically very important[36] and consistent with the telescoping of Gras' phases. In 1841 the provinces of Upper and Lower Canada were united to form a single Province of Canada to which Britain granted a loan of £1,500,000 for much-needed public works. The commissioner of public works was none other than Hamilton Hartley Killaly,[37] member of the assembly for the Village of London. Thus a man who was basically another 'passer-by' entered the picture. Up to that time London had had poor road communications[38] with both its sources of supply and its hinterland, and suddenly it received its first planked and gravelled roads. Killaly spent almost his entire first appropriation of £100,000 in greatly improving London's communications with Port Stanley, Chatham, Windsor, Sarnia, and Hamilton,[39] and built extensive dock facilities at Port Stanley. Fortune had smiled on London again. A few years later, in 1849, London's road communications network was completed. 'The Proof Line Road Joint Stock Company,' whose shareholders included John K. Labatt and the Carlings, turnpiked the road that ran directly north to connect London with the Canada Company's Huron Tract.[40]

Thus, the basis of Gras' third, or communication stage was firmly laid a dozen years before the railways. Despite the temporary setback of two fires of major proportions, in October 1844 and April 1845, which almost totally destroyed the business section of the village, London's population grew from 2616 to 4584 between 1842 and 1848.[41] This led to its incorporation as a town in 1847.[42] Simeon Morrill became the first town mayor, another recognition of the close links between the business community and municipal politics that was to serve the town so well.

The improved communications system had an immediate expansion effect on industry. Some of the most important London manufacturing firms were founded in the 1840s. Late in 1838 Elijah Leonard had commenced erecting an iron-foundry in London as the result of disagreements in St Thomas and a conviction that London was 'sooner or later to become the hub of Western Canada.' By 1845 he was making steam engines.[43] A year earlier Thomas Carling founded his 'City Brewery.'[44] The McClary brothers began their tin, agricultural implement, and stove warehouse by 1847. These men soon supplied an area which stretched west to Chatham, Windsor, and Sarnia, north to Goderich, St Mary's, and Stratford, east to Ingersoll and Woodstock, and south to St Thomas and Port Stanley.

The same may be said of commerce. For instance, John Birrell, a Scottish emigrant, soon built up a dry goods wholesale business with outlets at St Thomas, Port Stanley, Sarnia, Goderich, and Stratford.[45] Most important, the roads strengthened the London-Ancaster/Dundas/Hamilton axis.[46] The goods that Birrell shipped to Goderich had been originally imported by Isaac Buchanan and Company of Hamilton. So close did the link become that, when the Bank of Hamilton was established in 1872, Ellis W. Hyman, who already had business interests in that city, became the only out-of-town member of the provisional board of directors.

London's third stage of economic development received a further impetus in December 1853 when the first train steamed in from Hamilton on the tracks of the Great Western Railway.[47] The idea had been mooted by the merchants since 1832[48] and the railway was carefully guided through the centre of town by the business interests. Mayor Simeon Morrill himself cast the deciding vote which placed what are now the Canadian National tracks on their present site – running across his lands and adjacent to his tannery.[49] The Hamilton axis was finally consolidated.

The connection with Port Stanley on Lake Erie, via St Thomas, was guaranteed by the completion of a rather local project, the London and Port Stanley Railway, in 1856. It was this line that confirmed London's ascendancy. Instead of developing St Thomas, which had invested heavily in its construction, the London and Port Stanley Railway made it a way station and in a few years its population had declined by 50 per cent. Two years afterward, in 1858, a branch line of the Grand Trunk Railway was opened, linking London to Stratford. Later in 1875 the London, Huron, and Bruce Railway to Wingham joined London to its northern hinterland. It was also pushed forward by the London merchant community: John Birrell was president, Ellis W. Hyman, treasurer.

With the coming of the railways the urban pattern of Canada West/Ontario was set for a century, until the throughways began to supplement them, and London was fixed in its place as the economic hub of southwestern Ontario. It could ship in goods from the outside world to its growing hinterland and could ship out its manufactured products. That the significance of the railway was well appreciated by the old Londoners is demonstrated by the fact that today the first railway train may yet be seen atop the city's coat of arms, its long plume of smoke signifying progress, not pollution.

Other communications developments were taking place simultaneously. In October 1847 the telegraph reached London from Hamilton.[50] The newspaper network that was to cover southwestern Ontario had already begun to evolve in the early 1830s.[51] By the late 1840s the modern papers were appearing: the still-flourishing *London Free Press*, at first called *The Canadian Free Press*, was established in 1849, the London *Advertiser*, which survived until 1936, appeared in 1863. Gras' third stage was thus consolidated; London had its communications and its transportation network, both by road and rail. This consolidation of communications was recognized politically by the proclamation which provided for London's incorporation as a city on 1 January 1855.[52] By way of comparison St Thomas had become only a village in 1852 and did not become a town until 1861 or a city until 1881,[53] nine years after its economy had been somewhat restored by the building of the Canada Southern Railway. Delaware failed to develop at all.

London's status as a city in 1855 was marked by more than a legal change, for the municipal services were evolving rapidly at this period. True, such amenities as a mechanics' institute movement, to provide reading material and lectures, were to be found as early as 1835,[54] but in the prosperity of the mid-1850s changes came rapidly. London received her first, though admittedly inadequate, water and gas system, which included the first street lights in 1854, and both the police force and first permanent hospital appeared in 1855. The provincial government provided postal delivery in 1853 and a customs house the following year.

Economically London had entered a new period of expansion – or overexpansion, part of the boom that spread across the continent in the wake of the iron horse. Around the railway terminals new warehouses sprang up, the grain depots for the still expanding hinterland. The Board of Trade was incorporated in April 1857.[55] New merchants appeared; Charles Hunt of Windsor is a good example, a prosperous, established contractor, produce dealer, and member of the first Windsor village council, who deliberately moved his operations to London because he, like Leonard, saw it as the future commercial hub of the peninsula.[56] There Hunt founded the City Milling Company in 1856, which was to remain in business for over a century. Relatively large scale, but very specialized industries, also appeared, such as the Beltz Hat and Cap Manufactory in 1857 and the Perrin and McCormick biscuit companies in 1856 and 1858 respectively. Speculators sold land at exhorbitant prices throughout the surrounding countryside. The overexpansion of the period is probably best shown by the start of the construction of the Tecumseh House, the largest hotel in British North America, for which the plumbing alone cost $5000.

Boom, however, was followed by bust, as so frequently happens, and with the panic and depression of 1857 such emerging frontier communities as London were particularly severely hit, especially as the wheat economy was so important for the city and both crops and prices failed badly.[57] Land prices were to take nearly half a century to reach their former heights and such astute London merchants as Ellis W. Hyman lost badly on the Tecumseh House, which became 'a deserted barracks.' But the basic economic soundness of the city was shown by its quick recovery and even the economic depression was of advantage to some of London's wealthy speculators, such as George J. Goodhue, who were able to exploit the money shortage by charging 24 per cent on first mortgages.[58] Soon, with the return of prosperity, London was booming again and preparing to take a place of dominance in a new endeavour that was just opening up – the 1861 discovery of oil in Enniskillen Township in Lambton County. Englehart & Co's refinery, the first in London, opened in 1869. On a lesser scale another important business was making its appearance: the processing of tobacco and manufacturing of cigars.[59] The city might have had its troubles, but it had no real rivals, London was obviously commercially and industrially predominant in western Ontario.

Financial ascendancy came next and London in the 1860s began to enter into the fourth stage of Gras' process of evolution. The merchants who again had money to invest began to look beyond land and mortgages – the basis of the Goodhue fortune – to the founding of financial empires. Branches of the leading banks and agents for many insurance companies had long been established in the city.[60] In the 1860s a rash of financial institutions broke out in London as they did in other cities. What was important, though, and what shows the soundness of London's position and the ability of her merchants, was the number which have survived until today. The Huron & Erie Savings and Loan Corporation (the Canada Trust/ Huron and Erie of today) had its origins in 1864, and counted Ellis W. Hyman and John Birrell among its first presidents. The Ontario Loan and Debenture Corporation (now part of The Royal Trust) was incorporated in 1879, and the London Life in 1875. Although some enterpreneurs fell by the wayside – Morrill, for instance, went bankrupt in 1868 – fortunes were still being made. In 1876 *Bradstreet's Reports* estimated the worth of the Carling brothers, who had taken over their father's brewery, at $250-300,000, Hyman's tannery at $200-250,000, and the Birrell business and several other at $100-150,000.[61]

At the same time that financial autonomy was moving ahead, London was consolidating its municipal services. The City Gas Company was re-established in 1864, under the presidency of Charles Hunt, whose sons were later to bring in the first electric company. Two years later the city received its first police magistrate in Lawrence Lawrason, Goodhue's former business partner, and in 1868 the Western Fair became a permanent institution.

The 1870s witnessed equally rapid endeavours of urbanization beginning with the transfer of the Insane Asylum from near Amherstburg, south of Windsor, in 1870. Again London's member of parliament had played a role, for John Carling was responsible. St Joseph's Hospital was founded by the sisters of that order in 1878. In 1873 came the street railway, and in 1875 Blackfriar's bridge was rebuilt as the first steel bridge in the city. By 1879 London had its first telephone exchange. The fact that London, England, also received its first telephone exchange in the same year demonstrates how the spread of technology had equalized the course of metropolitan evolution in widely separated centres. A year earlier, in 1878, when the city finally took action to establish a proper water supply system, the two commissioners, elected on a non-partizan ticket, were John Carling and Ellis Hyman: Tory and Liberal, brewer and tanner, combined to transcend politics for the advancement of commerce. The Springbank Water Works resulted in 1879.[62]

Concurrent with its commercial and financial advance London was gaining the other functions of a minor metropolis. The first suburbs, London East and Petersville, were incorporated in the mid-1870's. Culture too came to the city. In 1866 Hyman bought up a racket court and turned it into what was probably the first permanent theatre;[63] by 1877 the Mechanics' Institute had accumulated 1500 books. Urban comfort was visible with the growth of the suburban estates of the wealthy spreading to the south into rural Westminster Township and northward up from 'Eldon House' along the north branch of the Thames. By the end of the seventies mansions were beginning to rise along Queens Avenue, long the show place of the city.

Meanwhile, ecclesiastical supremacy over the hinterland was assured when the Roman Catholic Diocese of London was established in the city in 1856 and the Anglican Diocese of Huron, with Benjamin Cronyn[64] as first bishop, followed a year later. True, Adolphe Pinsonnault, the first Catholic bishop, was a Frenchman who transferred the see to Sandwich (Windsor) in 1859, but his successor, John Walsh, was a sound Irishman, who moved it back to London with even greater alacrity a decade later. Virtually simultaneously, in 1856, the Kirk of Scotland Presbyterians set up a presbytery in London. The Wesleyan Methodists had had a district there from 1831 and the city was the headquarters of the New Connection Methodists. With the Methodist union of 1874 these two groups joined and a London Conference of the Methodist Church was established which, like the Anglican and Catholic dioceses, covered much of the southwestern peninsula.

Education also developed within the city. The London District Grammar School, transferred to London from Vittoria in October 1837, evolved into the London High School of 1871. School boards first appeared in 1848 and were amalgamated in 1856. By the 1870s there was also the Union School, with several branches, for younger children. The Catholics founded their own school board in 1857 and had at least two schools by the 1870s. In 1863 Bishop Benjamin Cronyn established Huron College to train Church of England priests in low church tenets, and in 1878 his successor, Isaac Hellmuth, obtained a charter for what is now the University of Western Ontario.

By that time most of the first generation of men who had done so much to build the city had passed to their eternal reward: Labatt in 1866; Goodhue in 1870; Cronyn, Morrill, and Hunt in 1871; Birrell in 1875; Hyman in 1878. Their impressive funeral corteges marked the end of an era. The British garrison, having played its role, marched away in 1869. Another generation of enterpreneurs had grown up, however, and London had passed the stage where the military fact was a basic necessity.

When, on 27 August 1874, only half a century after the trees were first felled on Governor Simcoe's reserve, Governor General the Earl of Dufferin arrived to dedicate the site of the old military parade grounds as Victoria Park, he saw a thriving metropolis which was the undisputed capital of the western peninsula. So great were the changes that London-in-the-Bush was having to plant shade trees along its streets.[65] A good physical setting, luck, and the efforts of the founders had combined to establish London's ascendancy. Using Gras' criteria the four stages were complete. Minor rivals, such as Vittoria and Delaware, had become sleepy hamlets; major ones, such as St Thomas, and latecomers, including Woodstock, Stratford, and Goderich, had had to settle for the rank of county seats. Only the long shadow of Toronto, spreading across Hamilton, was there to indicate the limits of London's potential metropolitan growth. In the hierarchy of metropolises the city had attained an important, albeit a tertiary, rank.

NOTES

1 Major Littlehales' account of Simcoe's visit to London, 2 March 1793, in E.A. Cruikshank, ed. *The Correspondence of Lieutenant-Governor John Graves Simcoe* (5 vols., Toronto 1923–31), I, 293
2 Orlo Miller, *A Century of Western Ontario* (Toronto 1949), 7–8
3 Jacob Spelt, *Urban Development in South-Central Ontario* (Assen, The Netherlands 1955), reprinted Carleton Library, no 57 (Toronto 1972)
4 The Rapelje Family, *Reminiscences of Early Settlers and Other Records* (St Thomas 1911), 10–15; *History of the County of Middlesex, Canada* (Toronto 1889), 476
5 Norman S.B. Gras, *An Introduction to Economic History* (New York 1922)
6 Harold A. Innis, 'The Changing Structure of the Canadian Market,' *Essays in Canadian Economic History* (Toronto 1956), 289
7 See J.M.S. Careless, 'Frontierism, Metropolitanism and Canadian History,' *Canadian Historical Review*, xxxv, 1, March 1954, 1–21
8 See reprints in W.C. Miller, *Vignettes of Early St. Thomas* (St Thomas 1967), 54, 60–1
9 John Carling, 'The Pioneers of Middlesex,' London and Middlesex Historical Society [LMHS], *Transactions*, I, 1908, 29–35
10 Cruikshank, ed., *Simcoe Papers*, II and III
11 Daniel J. Brock, 'Richard Talbot, The Tipperary Irish and The Formative Years of London Township: 1818–1826,' (unpublished MA thesis, University of Western Ontario [UWO], 1969), 48–51. Unless otherwise stated, the contents of this paragraph and the succeeding two paragraphs are based upon Daniel J. Brock, 'The Anatomy of the Formation of Two Counties in the Pre-Confederation Era: The Territorial Evolution of Middlesex and Elgin.' (Special Collections, D.B. Weldon Library, UWO)
12 See Patrick C.T. White, ed. *Lord Selkirk's Diary, 1803–1804* (Toronto 1958), 306; The Reminiscences of Mrs George Webster, Seaborn Diaries, London Public Library, Seaborn Collection
13 Cruikshank, ed. *Simcoe Papers*, I, 18
14 Statutes of Upper Canada, 38 Geo. III, c 5 (1798)
15 *History of Middlesex*, 567; *The London Sun* (London, UC), 7 July, 1831, cited in *The Western Mercury* (Hamilton), 14 July 1831; Brock, 'London Township: 1818–1826,' 52, 56–8
16 See *Journal of the Legislative Assembly of the Province of Upper Canada*, Appendix, 1825–26, 10–13; Cl. T. Campbell, 'The Settlement of London,' LMHS, *Transactions*, III, 1911, 9; *History of Middlesex*, 35
17 Campbell, 'The Settlement of London,' 9, citing Edward Ermatinger, *The Life of Colonel Talbot* (St Thomas 1859), 86
18 See Return of Patents Issued in the London District up to 30 June 1820, Middlesex County Municipal Building, London, Treasurer's Office

19 See *History of Middlesex*, 482. Under the caption, Delaware Town Lots, Dr Oliver Tiffany had advertised: 'The Plot consists of a PUBLIC SQUARE, of 5 acres, three sides of which are laid out into Lots of nearly ½ acre each, fronting the square; the other side reserved for the site for a court house, which, whenever the proposed division of the present District shall take effect, will probably be locating there; it being precisely in the center of the new District.' *The Advocate* (York), 7 March 1825

20 Statutes of Upper Canada, 7 Geo. IV, c 13

21 Campbell, 'The Settlement of London,' 9–10

22 The Rev. William Proudfoot wrote on 7 March 1833: '... Mr. John Talbot, school-master ... called. He told me that Mr. Cronyn had returned from York; that the Governor told Mr. Cronyn that Upper Canada will probably be divided and that London will be its capital; that it is his intentions to send respectable loyalist emigrants who may apply to him to this district. He wished Mr. Cronyn to send him a list of unsold land in London and Westminster, that he might be able to direct emigrants where they might find locations. That it is the intention of the government to raise up such a body of persons attached to the Constitution of Great Britain as may counteract the influence of Yankeeism so prevalent about St. Thomas and along the lake shore ...' 'Proudfoot Papers, Part II: Diary of Rev. J. Proudfoot,' LMHS, *Transactions*, VIII, 1917, 23–4

23 *The True Patriot and London District Advertiser* (London, UC), cited in *The Western Mercury*, 31 July 1834

24 Frederick H. Armstrong, 'George Jervis Goodhue: Pioneer Merchant of London, Upper Canada,' *Ontario History*, LXIII, 4, Dec. 1971, 217–32

25 Frederick H. Armstrong, 'Ellis Walton Hyman, (1813–1878)' and Madaline Roddick, 'Simeon Morrill (1793–1871)' in *Dictionary of Canadian Biography* [DCB], X (Toronto 1972), 374–5, 533–4; UC Land Petitions, M-7-129-1832

26 A copy of this proclamation, dated 11 June 1835, is at the University of Western Ontario.

27 The first market was for several years held on the court house square on the site of the present Middlesex County municipal building. In August 1844 the Board of Police ordered that the market house be removed to the block reserved by order-in-council for a market place in the New Survey – bounded by York, Wellington, Bathurst, and Waterloo streets. The old market house was not removed, however, and was destroyed in the great fire of April 1845. By-law 52 provided that the old market house should cease to be used in January 1845 and that the house erected in the fall of 1844 on the new site be opened from 27 January. The inhabitants of the central and western parts of the town, protesting the inconvenience of the new site, donated land on the present site of Covent Garden and erected a market house thereon. They stipulated that they did not wish to disturb the eastern market and offered the building and land as a free gift to the corporation. The president and Board of Police opposed the new Covent Garden Market, which opened on 31 October 1845, and its operators attempted to evade the authority of the board over markets by re-naming it the Covent Garden Bazaar. Individuals were prosecuted for transactions carried out at the Covent Garden, and it was only after the court acquitted them that the president and Board of Police reluctantly agreed by March 1846 to recognize Covent Garden Market as one of the two markets within the town. Between March and May titles to the site and building were obtained gratis by the Board of Police. See [James B. Brown], *Views of Canada and the Colonists* (Edinburgh MDCCXLIV), 104; *The Times* (London, CW), 12 Sept. 1845, 13 March 1846; *The Western Globe* (London, CW), 6 Nov. 1846; *History of Middlesex*, 282–3; Instrument 8520 (1846), City of London Registry Office

28 Miller, *A Century of Western Ontario*, 149

29 *The London Prototype*, 5 March 1861

30 Statutes of Upper Canada, 7 Wm IV, c 33 and 7 Wm IV, c 30

31 Frederick H. Armstrong, *Handbook of Upper Canadian Chronology and Territorial Legislation* (London 1967), 166

32 On 1 January 1852 Middlesex County became the United Counties of Middlesex and Elgin. Work on Elgin's public buildings was completed in 1853, and the county began its separate existence on 1 January 1854. Statutes of Canada, 14 & 15 Vic., c 5; Dissolution of the United Counties of Middlesex and Elgin, *Weekly Dispatch* (St. Thomas), 6 Oct. 1853

33 *A Memoir: The Honorable Elijah Leonard* [London 1894?], 12

34 Describing London in the first issue of the *Sun*, Edward Allen Talbot noted that: 'The town is laid out on the old mathematical plan so servilely copied by the Surveyors of every town in the Province. Streets intersecting each others at right angles – without a square, a crescent or even a spot upon which to erect a market house, or any place of public worship. The streets are also too narrow. Four rods for the streets of a town which will doubtless ere long rival some of the proudest in the Province, is certainly much too little, we know not who is to blame for these defects, but we are surprised that in this enlightened age of the world, there cannot be some person employed to furnish the surveyor general with plans for towns, which without being so strictly mathematical, might combine some of the advantages possessed by our citizen ancestors, when straight lines and right angles were as well understood as they are now.' Cited in *Western Mercury*, 21 July 1831

35 Statutes of Canada, 31 Vic., c 31

36 In a letter to the editor of *The Times* (London, cw), 28 Nov. 1845, 'A Well-Wisher for the Prosperity of the Town of London, cw,' observed: 'Our river not being navigable, is said by some few short sighted persons to be an insuperable obstacle to our future welfare. This assertion only proves the want of reflection in those who make it. The situation of London is a centre, where all the leading roads that intersect the country terminate. Thus, the Eastern road from Montreal, Toronto and Hamilton – the Western from Detroit and Chatham – the Southern Plank Road from Port Stanley – (on Lake Erie) the Turnpiked Road from Port Sarnia and the Northern road from Goderich.'

37 George Mainer, 'Hamilton Hartley Killaly (1800–1874),' dcb, x, 402–6

38 Late in 1828 George Gurnett wrote of London that: 'It is out of the main travelled route, and at present no public road leads to, or through it. If the Governor's road (Dundas Street) were opened throughout from thence to the eastward, and a good road were made from it to the Westminster road, a distance of a little more than a mile, it would soon become a place of thoroughfare, as the distance from the Head of the Lake to Sandwich would be less by this route, than by the one now travelled. But unless this is done, or manufactures of some kind be established, it can never become a place of consequence.' *The Gore Gazette* (Ancaster), 6 Sept. 1828

39 See Freeman Talbot, 'The Fathers of London Township,' lmhs, *Transactions*, vii, 1916, 12–3. Killaly had considered the improvements along the St Lawrence, the Great Lakes, and the waters of the Newcastle District to be public works of the first class. Works of the second class comprised the main provincial highways which at first were conceived to be only two in number. The first of these was the Main Province Road which ran from Quebec to London, where it divided into a southern branch passing through Chatham and Sandwich and terminating at Amherstburg, and a northern branch ending at Sarnia; the second was the Main Northern Road from Lake Ontario at Toronto to Georgian Bay at Penetanguishene. James Hermeston Aitchison, 'The Development of Local Government in Upper Canada, 1783–1850' (unpublished phd thesis, University of Toronto, 1953), 504–6

40 Fred Landon and Orlo Miller, *Up The Proof Line: The Story of a Rural Community* (London 1955), 50

41 *St. Thomas Standard*, 10 Oct. 1844; *London Inquirer*, 11 Oct. 1844, cited in *The British*

Colonist (Toronto), 15 Oct. 1844; *The Times*, Extra, 14, 18 April 1845 as cited in *The Chatham Gleaner*, 22 April 1845; and *The British Colonist*, 18 and 22 April 1845; *The Times*, 25 April 1845; *Appendix to the Journals of the Legislative Assembly for Canada*, 1849, Appendix J. The population for 1842 is based upon a detailed examination by Daniel J. Brock of the manuscript census for the Town of London, 1842

42 Statutes of Canada, 10 & 11 Vic., c 48, was assented to on 28 July 1847

43 He had started on the first engine that he built 'out-and-out' in January and in an advertisement, dated 27 Nov. 1845, stated that he was 'now able to announce that he is manufacturing steam engines, from four to twelve horse-power' and 'also thrashing machines from 2 to 8 horse-power.' *Memoir: The Honorable Elijah Leonard*, 12–13, 17; *The Western Globe*, 27 Nov. 1845 and 27 Feb. 1846

44 *The London Prototype*, 5 March 1861

45 Frederick H. Armstrong, 'John Birrell (1815–1875),' DCB, X, 68

46 '... From 1827 Ancaster was on the stage route to Brantford and London; but in 1833 it was cheaper to send goods from York to London by way of Port Stanley than to send them overland by wagon

Through the 1830's Ancaster was losing trade and local importance to its neighbouring rivals Dundas and Hamilton, now possessed of better access to Lake Ontario. There was a change in the early forties, since the London Road was planked in 1842–43, bringing some revival of the freight traffic ...' Press Release of Department of Public Records & Archives (Historical Branch), Toronto, 23 Sept. 1966, re: Plaque to Commemorate the Founding of Ancaster

47 'The Great Western Railway,' LMHS, *Transactions*, II, 1909, 43, fn d

48 Edward Allen Talbot had initiated agitation for a railroad from London to the head of Lake Ontario through his newspaper the *Sun*. In the 29 March 1832 issue, cited in *The Courier of Upper Canada* (York), 28 April 1832, he wrote that: 'Should we succeed in obtaining a charter for a Railroad to [Lake] Ontario, of which success we have not a doubt, we hesitate not to predict that before 10 years shall have elapsed, London will lay claim to a competition with any town in Upper Canada. It is situated in the heart of the finest and most fertile tract of land in Upper Canada, millions of acres of which are yet unsettled ...' On 22 December a meeting was convened in London 'for the purpose of addressing the Legislature on the subject of a Rail Road between London and the head waters of Lake Ontario ...' *Western Mercury*, 10 Jan. 1833; Emma Harding [Freeman Talbot's Life as Dictated to His Granddaughter], Richard Talbot Papers, typescript copy, Special Collections, UWO, 1900

49 Roddick, 'Morrill,' DCB, 533–4

50 *London Times*, 8 Oct. 1847. '... a line of communication by telegraph is now complete between London and Quebec, a distance of 710 miles.' *The Examiner* (Toronto), 13 Oct. 1847

51 *The London Sun*, the first newspaper printed in Upper Canada west of Ancaster, began its sporadic existence on 7 July 1831. *Colonial Advocate*, 14 July 1831; Daniel J. Brock, 'London's first newspaper,' *The London Free Press*, 3 July 1971, 8-M. See also Miller, *Century of Western Ontario*

52 *The Canada Gazette*, 30 Sept. 1854, for complete text of proclamation

53 *The Canada Gazette*, 27 Sept. 1851, Statutes of Canada, 23 Vic., c 89; Statutes of Ontario, 44 Vic., c 46

54 *Proudfoot Diary*, 11 April 1835; *Journal of the House of Assembly of Upper Canada, 1836*, 177, 178, 230. This institute did not last long, but a successor in 1841 had a relatively prosperous existence.

55 *The London Free Press*, 21 and 23 April 1857

56 Frederick H. Armstrong, 'Charles Hunt (1820–1871),' DCB, X, 372
57 Orlo Miller, 'The Fat Years, and the Lean: London (Canada) in Boom and Depression,' *Ontario History*, LIII, 2, June 1961, 73–80
58 See Instrument 5190, North and East Middlesex County Registry Office, London. Goodhue Papers, Special Collections, UWO
59 Felix Drouillard had established a 'Cigar Manufactory' in London by December 1845. *The Times*, 2 Jan. 1846
60 On 11 June 1835 the Bank of Upper Canada purchased lot 2, west on Ridout Street for the site of their branch in London. From 25 June 1835 to 3 May 1836 Lawrence Lawrason and George J. Goodhue, under the style of Lawrason & Co, put up a large property bond during which time they acted as agents of the Bank of Upper Canada from their general store at the northwest corner of Dundas and Ridout streets. This marks the first banking agency established in London

London's own financial institutions began with the London Benevolent Society, organized on 28 April 1846; the London Building Society, established October 1846; and the London Saving's Bank, established in 1847. See also Instruments 2604 and 2701 (1835), 3970 (1836), City of London Registry Office; *London Times*, 9 Oct. 1846; 14 and 28 May 1847
61 *Bradstreet's Reports of the Dominion of Canada, February 1, 1876* (New York 1876), 242–51
62 E.V. Buchanan, *London's Water Supply: A History* (London 1968), 12
63 In the 7 Dec. 1839 issue of the *London Gazette*, it was noted that: 'We are requested to state that the Garrison Theatre at this place, will be opened on Monday the 16th instant, when the Officers will perform the Comedy of Sweethearts and Wives, and Bombastes Furioso.' This is the earliest known record of plays being performed in London. By October 1842 the military theatre had become known as the Theatre Royal (*London Inquirer*, 7 Oct. 1842). In March 1845 under the caption, 'New Civilian Theatre,' it was noted that a building was contemplated which was to be devoted to drama and under the superintendence of Mr Powell; this became the 'Theatre Little Olympic' by the following month (*The Times*, 14 March and 11 April 1845). A map at the Ontario Archives, believed to have been drawn prior to October 1844, indicates that the site of the theatre was on the southwest corner of Wellington and North (Queens Avenue) streets.
64 James J. Talman, 'Benjamin Cronyn (1802–1871),' DCB, X, 205–9
65 Miller, *Century of Western Ontario*, 92

William Allan
A Pioneer Business Executive

M.L. Magill

William Allan was born in 1770 at The Moss near Huntly in Aberdeenshire, Scotland, one of at least two sons of Alexander Allan.[1] He received a scanty education, probably at the parochial school in Huntly which limited its curriculum to English, writing, and arithmetic,[2] but otherwise nothing whatever is known about his Scottish background. How long he remained in school is also unknown, but by 1788 he was in Canada as a clerk with George Forsyth at Niagara.

There has been some dispute as to when he arrived in this country. The best evidence is his own affidavits attached to various land petitions. In June 1795 he said that he had been in the province '... for these Seven Years Past ...' In March 1797 he said he had lived in the province since 1788;[3] but in still another affidavit in that year, that he had been in the country for twenty years. Why he came to Canada and how is also a matter of conjecture. Most likely it was through a member of the Forsyth family which originated in Huntly, and the arrangement was probably that he should become an articled clerk in Robert Ellice and Company[4] in which firm John Forsyth was then a partner.[5] He may have spent a short time learning the elements of the business in Montreal and then in 1788 come to Niagara as clerk to George Forsyth, who was then the agent of the firm at Niagara.

The Niagara agency was a very important one, not because of the actual trade in furs done there, but because it was the trans-shipment point for all goods going up to, and furs coming down from, the western posts where the actual business of the company was done. It also had a garrison which needed supplies and was a centre for the distribution of the presents to the Indians which were furnished by the company on a contract with the Indian Department. This meant that Allan received an ideal training in matters of great importance to the pioneer merchant. He became thoroughly familiar with what was long the basis of mercantile trade in Upper Canada – the shipment of goods up and down the river between Montreal and the interior. He learned bookkeeping, the handling of bills, and acquired the painstaking accuracy and efficient handling of affairs which were to have an important influence on his later career. Above all he must have impressed his employers, because from the days when he was a clerk at Niagara until his death he was the agent for Forsyth Richardson and Company, and for many of those connected with that firm.

The probability that he was an articled clerk is strengthened by the fact that in 1795, when his seven-year term would have been up, he began preparations to leave the firm and set up on his own account. Instead of locating somewhere in the Niagara district with which he was familiar, and which was the most prosperous region in the western part of the province, he decided to remove to York which Simcoe had tentatively selected as the capital of the province. Just why he made the decision is not known and it was in a way uncharacteristic because it was risky, and Allan had a vast amount of Scots caution. Except for Simcoe no one liked the idea of York as a capital and there was certainly a good chance that the decision would be rescinded, but in 1795 he petitioned for a grant, as an intending settler who had not yet received land, of '... such Quantity of the Waste Lands of the Crown in any of the back concessions of the Township of York ...' and since he intended to live in York '... any Lott [sic] remaining vacant in the town.'[6] The petition was approved and in July he was granted a town lot and two hundred acres.

He did not, however, move to York until 1797. The reason probably was that he had decided to begin business in partnership with one Alexander Wood. Wood was a Scot who was born in Aberdeen and for some time had been associated with another Forsyth. This was a brother of George Forsyth, Joseph, who lived at Kingston where he was the Forsyth Richardson and Company agent. He was also in business for himself and among other things ran a brewery in which Wood seems to have been a partner. There was some dispute between the two and Wood decided to come to York as a merchant where he and Allan joined forces. As part of the arrangements Allan petitioned in June to be allowed to exchange the town lot which had previously been granted to him, but for which he had not yet received a patent, for '... a Front Lot in the Town on land which may hereafter be laid out and annexed thereto.'[7] This was agred to on condition that he not receive a patent for a year and make improvements.

The partnership did not last long; disputes began and it was dissolved amid the mutual recriminations which normally attend such events.[8] Allan and Wood both set up on their own account and both prospered, though Allan in the end became the wealthier of the two. Both dealt in the same general line of goods and like all pioneer merchants sold everything from pins to groceries, from cloth and whiskey to tools and hardware. Because of the actual shortage of currency, which was so bad that except for the official class hardly anyone in the community handled five shillings in cash in six months, most business was done on long-term credit and by barter. The merchant granted credit to his customers and was repaid over long intervals in wheat, potash, pork, beef, or any other saleable product.

These goods in turn were sent to the merchant's agent in Montreal who exported them, used the proceeds to settle the merchant's debts to him, and ordered and shipped his next year's supplies. The prosperity of the upcountry merchant really depended on his relations with his Montreal agent and the competence of that agent. Here Alan was fortunate. Wood and Allan had used Forsyth Richardson and Company and had been their agents in York. When the partnership broke up the agency remained with Allan, and this connection with the greatest mercantile house in the country must have been of great service in his early days.

A second recognised function of the merchant was that, in a community which lacked either banks or trust companies, he performed many of the functions which are now normally a part of their business. As a banker the merchant on occasion lent money; he was in constant touch with merchants across the province, so he could arrange for the collection of accounts from persons scattered all over this area; through his agents in Montreal he could arrange for the purchase and sale of bills of exchange. His trust functions were principally acting as agent for persons living abroad who owned property in the province, and acting as executor of wills. In his capacity as agent he managed and sold lands and remitted and accounted for the proceeds; as an executor he handled estates on behalf of heirs mostly living abroad. All this was done on a commission basis (usually about 10 per cent) and though a useful source of income was not really profitable because of the time involved, but it had a use to Allan over and above this. It got him known in important places. He held dozens of these agencies. He represented W.D. Smith, the surveyor general, and the family of Lieutenant Governor Simcoe; he and Strachan were the executors of Chief Justice Scott and he also acted by himself for a number of other estates. His handling of such matters was meticulous from the point of view of efficiency and integrity and it all helped to bring to public attention that there was more to this poorly educated merchant than an Aberdeen accent.[9]

Another function of the pioneer merchant was that he was the local holder of those minor, ill paid, and thankless offices essential to the functioning of the community. There were, perhaps, two reasons for this. Firstly, the merchant had leisure. It is a mistake to think of the pioneer store as a place crowded with customers from morning to night. The merchant had his desperately busy seasons (a month or so in the spring perhaps), but most of his real trade was done in the winter when the sleighing was good. On a normal day he might serve only two or three customers' leaving him ample time for community affairs. Secondly a merchant was one of the few men who had the necessary business training to enable him to deal with the detail attached to local offices.

As far as Allan is concerned the point is important. It is generally considered that he was an important figure in the Compact right from the beginning, and the evidence cited is the number of local offices he held in York between 1801 and 1828. Now it is true that he held a number of these, perhaps more than usual. But beyond the obvious fact that this indicates that authority thought him politically sound, it means little. In terms of office holding there were dozens of similar men scattered throughout the province at this time, none of whom any one would dream of thinking of as a person of any real importance. Neither at this time was Allan. He was simply an able, conscientious, hard working merchant willing to take on these jobs and in several cases having facilities to do so.

He was customs collector, inspector of pot and pearl ashes, and postmaster of York. Why? Someone had to be; he was willing; and in each case he possessed special facilities. Early in his career at York he had built a commercial wharf on his property at the foot of Frederick Street. Aside from the Government Dock to the west, it was the only one in York and because it was in the commercial centre of the town it was used by lake schooners. The bulk of the customs duties were collected in Lower Canada; the amount of dutiable goods landed at York was small; who better than Allan to collect them? The same was true of his inspectorship and his position as postmaster. Pot and pearl ashes were an important export commodity and the quality had to be mainatined; Allan not only dealt in ashes, but, like many others, he owned a potasherie. What better choice was there for a job no one really wanted? As for the post office, it was a source of endless grief since nothing was more complained of than the postal service. The odd customer who might buy something while collecting his mail was no compensation for the trouble attached to the office.

The same is true of his other offices. He was a member of quarter sessions and a magistrate. Aside from the honour, this meant simply that he was part of a combined town council and magistrates' court. This honour and work was shared at one time or another by dozens of other merchants, including Alexander Wood. He was treasurer of the Home District for years, but as evidence of political influence this is about on par with the fact that he was treasurer of Saint James Church and of almost every other society in York. Why? He was noted for the strictest integrity in money matters[10] and he could keep accounts.

The real cause of his rise to the inner circle of power was the War of 1812. As with every male in the province between the ages of eighteen and sixty, Allan was legally obliged to serve in the Sedentary Militia and was subject to being called out in case of invasion. With most people militia service was either something to be evaded or an excuse for a jollification on muster day. As far as Allan was concerned it was a duty to be taken seriously. He had held a commission since 1795[11] and was promoted to major of the 3rd York Regiment on 15 April 1812.[12]

When the war began he was at once called out and posted to the garrison to command the flank companies in spite of the fact that he was then forty-two years old. On 7 September he was ordered to proceed with these companies to Fort George as part of the force being gathered to protect the Niagara frontier, and on the morning of the battle of Queenston Heights he and his men formed the infantry protection for the battery at Brown's Point. Brock, riding from Fort George to Queenston Heights, paused to order Allan and his men to follow. Proceeding at the double they caught up with him a few minutes before he was mortally wounded and so were 'the brave York volunteers' to whom his last order was given. Push on they did not, but none the less they took part in all the events of the day and were part of the force, led by Sheaffe and the regulars, who finally drove the Americans across the river.

His next experience of action was far from satisfactory. After spending the winter in escorting prisoners of war to Kingston and the prosaic duties of a garrison, he and Lt-Col. J.G. Chewett were the two senior militia officers in the garrison when the Americans attacked York on 27 April 1813. Sheaffe was in overall command and to defend the town he had the militia, a small party of Indians, and a small force of regulars. This force was badly outnumbered and, after some hours of fighting in which the chief casualties were the result of the explosion of the main magazine, Sheaffe decided that further resistance was hopeless, retreated with the regulars toward Kingston, and left Chewett and Allan to surrender the town.

After some hours of troublesome negotiation, a surrender was arranged on terms whereby the militia became prisoners on parole, all government stores and military supplies were to be surrendered, and the lives and property of the civilian population to be secured. These terms were reasonable enough but were not properly carried out because the American commanders failed to control their troops who burned the parliament buildings, looted a number of properties, and in general made nuisances of themselves before, several days later, the whole force sailed away after a most successful raid.

These two events were to have a most important effect on Allan's later career. In the first place, the leaders of the Compact and the members of the party generally looked back on Queenston Heights with almost as much pride as the Athenians did to the Battle of Marathon. They believed that this battle saved Upper Canada and that it had been won, as indeed they held that the whole war had been,[13] by the militia. Allan had not only fought in the battle – he had commanded the force from York. This automatically made him a heroic figure, not in Allan's view, but as part of the general myth about the war. His connection with the capture of York was even more important.

If the Compact as a party looked back on Queenston Heights with pride, they regarded the fall of York with a mixture of shame and rage. The cause of their anger was Sheaffe's decision to order the surrender of the town after first withdrawing the regulars. This it was believed was the cause of the capture of the town. If Sheaffe had remained the militia would, with the aid of the regulars, have beaten off the attack, and might even have done so without them, if Sheaffe had not ordered the surrender of the town. They were outraged at what they considered his supine cowardice and none more so than Allan.[14]

None the less the event had value to him. After arranging the terms of the surrender he spent the night at the fort looking after the wounded, while his store was being plundered, and the next few days trying to have the terms of the surrender observed. In these activities he was joined by the new rector of York, John Strachan, who was at the very beginning of his day as a power in the land. There is no doubt that when some years later he was looking for a man he remembered the militia major.

Once the Americans had left, Allan found himself in a new position as far as the war was concerned. He was a prisoner of war on parole, which meant that, though he was free, he was once again a civilian, bound not to serve again under arms until he had been formally exchanged. This did not mean that he could not continue to serve the war effort, and he did this in two ways, one of which cost him much trouble. The other made him a considerable profit. The first was by acting as what was known as government agent for the Home District. One of the problems that plagued the government was the fact that while the population as a whole was loyal enough, considerable portions of it were not when it came to taking an active part. There was great reluctance to serve in the militia and desertion was rife; much of the population was of direct American origin and believed to be enemy sympathisers; and there is no doubt that there were a number of spies and active collaborators about. The government's solution was to appoint agents in each district to deal with these matters. Allan was appointed for the Home District and if William Dummer Powell is to be believed, was a most successful one. Powell was a judge of the Court of King's Bench, and in June Sir George Prevost asked him for a report, among other matters, on the morale at York, and on the capacity of the civilian officials in the district.

Morale he reported to be bad and only to be strengthened by stationing regulars at York to defend the town in addition to a troop of dragoons to show the flag by periodical excursions through the settlements in the neighbourhood. Officialdom he damned with faint praise, but '... Major Allan of the Militia, although on parole, fulfills with promptitude and decision, the duties of governmental agent in this place.'[15] Now Powell is generally regarded as one of the early leaders of the Compact; by the 1820s his day was over, but he was still a power behind the scenes. When, as suggested, Strachan was looking for a man, and when considering Allan, Powell may have been consulted as leader of one prominent group of shareholders.

The other means by which he served the cause, in this case at a profit, was in his capacity as a merchant. While he was on duty in the garrison the business had been carried on by clerks with such supervision as he could give. He now began to push one of the most profitable trades, sales to the garrison through the Commissary General. Every merchant in York had been engaged in this business since the beginning of the war, and Allan had made some sales, but the bulk of his orders were in 1813 and 1814. The evidence for his dealings is to be found in the Account Books of the Garrison at York.[16] These records show that during the whole course of the war his sales totalled £12,724 in local currency, under which five shillings equalled four English shillings in value. The importance of this is that though this was not all profit it was additional sales, paid for in army bills which were immediately redeemable in drafts on the Treasury in London. This was equivalent to payment in hard coin instead of the trash which passed current in Upper Canada. Just as the war laid the foundation of his political power, so it was the foundation of his later fortune.

After the war Allan returned to his business as a merchant faced with the problem of a decline in trade after the war, a decline aggravated by the withdrawal of the army bills, and the return of the problem which had always plagued the Canadas, the lack of a stable currency adequate to the needs of trade. This matter had been a prime concern for years, and for years the great merchants, such as Forsyth Richardson and Company, had realized that the only solution was the establishment of a bank which, on the basis of the capital it held in gold and silver, could issue promissory notes to serve as money. John Richardson had begun the effort to establish a bank as far back as 1808 but had always failed because the hostility of the Assembly had prevented the granting of a charter. In 1817, therefore, he and a group of associates established the Bank of Montreal as an unincorporated partnership. In 1818 the bank established agencies in Kingston and York and Allan was appointed as agent for York.

Exactly the same problem had been troubling the merchants in Kingston who, since 1808 had been trying to organize a bank, and in 1810 had even got to the stage of trying to set one up.[17] Nothing had come of these efforts, presumably from lack of capital and the threat of war, and the matter was not raised again until January 1817 when Thomas Markland and others petitioned the legislature for an act incorporating the Kingston group as a bank with a capital of £200,000 divided into 8000 shares. In March of the same year a petition was presented from York in the name of John Strachan, Alexander Wood, and others for a charter as The Upper Canada Banking Company to be located at York. Writers on the subject have often used this application as evidence of the determination of the Compact to control any business that looked as if it would prove a source of power, influence, or profit. The real explanation is more prosaic. While it is true that Strachan probably had political motives, the real reason was rivalry between York and Kingston. It was a firm belief, based on American experience, that the possession of a bank gave a town a distinct advantage over a rival which did not have one. It was obvious that the province could support only one bank and it therefore mattered greatly where the bank was located.[18] In the event Kingston won. The Assembly rejected Strachan's scheme and passed an act in favour of the Kingston group conditional on the bank going into operation within two years of the passing of the act, which was reserved for the Royal Assent.

Time dragged on, and when the bill had still not been returned the Kingston group resolved to imitate the Bank of Montreal, and in April 1819 began business as an unchartered partnership under the name of the Bank of Upper Canada. They had hardly opened when the bill was returned approved but quite useless because the time allowed for opening the bank under the act had expired. The Kingston group, sure now that the bill would be approved, applied again to the legislature and at the same time the York group, still backed by Strachan but headed now by William Allan, renewed its application. The Kingston bill was passed by the Assembly, but when it went to the Legislative Council that body demanded a consultation, with the result that the bill was amended by striking out the names of the Kingston incorporators and substituting the names of Allan's group who thus stole the bank for York. At the same time the Kingston group was granted an act incorporating them as the Bank of Kingston and both bills were reserved for the Royal assent.

There is no doubt that the struggle to incorporate the Bank of Upper Canada as a York institution marks the emergence of Allan as a full-fledged member of the Compact – a position he owed to Strachan's influence. Strachan was behind the incorporation of the bank and Allan was his selection to head it. There were many reasons for the choice. What was needed was a man of ability, but above all, someone who could inspire confidence, and here Allan was ideal. His abilities were obvious and strengthened by his practical experience as agent for the Bank of Montreal; whatever else may have been thought of him, his integrity was known, and the personal confidence he inspired would extend to the bank.

Once again there was a long delay but finally in April 1821 the bill came back and, a few days before its proclamation on 21 April 1821, William Allan, Peter Robinson, and Alexander McDonnell gave notice that they had been appointed a committee to receive subscriptions,[19] and the work of organizing the bank was under way. The matter was long and involved. It quickly became obvious that there was no hope of receiving subscriptions for the £50,000, or of raising the £20,000 required by the act before the bank could go into operation. The capital, the amount to be subscribed, and the paid-in capital required were twice reduced, but still it proved impossible to raise the money, and the scheme would certainly have been abandoned if the government had not stepped in. Under the act it had the power to take 5000 shares, but it proved extremely reluctant to do so. Finally, when it was evident that the scheme must collapse otherwise, John Henry Dunn, the receiver general, acting on instructions of the lieutenant governor, signed the subscription list.[20] This done, the rest was relatively smooth sailing and in 1822 the bank opened for business, with Allan as president, an office he was to hold until he resigned in June 1835.

With the opening of the bank Allan changed careers. In 1822 he sold his interest in his store to his brothers-in-law and partners and in July announced that he '... gave up all his concern in trade.'[21] His time hereafter was to be devoted almost entirely to being what would now be called a business executive and, until 1835, his main concern was the bank. Allan was not a banker. He was, like all bank presidents of his time in North America, a merchant who ran a bank. This was a perfectly satisfactory arrangement because the only function of a bank was to serve merchants. Its business was to discount or make loans on what is called 'real paper,' that is, notes and bills of exchange passing between merchants and representing goods actually bought, sold, and delivered. It also bought and sold coin and bullion, occasionally and reluctantly made loans to governments by purchasing debentures, and accepted deposits from customers purely as a courtesy and for safekeeping only, on which it paid no interest. This was Allan's idea of a bank and the Bank of Upper Canada was run on these lines. His duty was to make the shareholders as large a profit as was consistent with safety by operating on strictly mercantile principles and avoiding manufacturers, promoters, and similar 'speculators,' which in his eyes they were. Allan was not a great banker, nor even a particularly knowledgeable one, but zealous attention, caution, and judgment made him a successful one.

Aside from the bank, he was involved in numerous other ventures. In 1825 having invested £250[22] in the new stock of the Welland Canal Company, the amount needed to qualify him for the position, he became a director and in time vice-president of the company. In part his interest was due to his long career as a merchant and his consequent interest in the movement of goods between Montreal and the interior. He belonged to the school which regarded the St Lawrence as the key to the prosperity of Canada. It was the natural artery for the movement of goods from the interior of the continent to the sea, and hence he was much interested in the development of the canal system necessary if that dream was to become a reality. There was also another reason. The province had made its first loan to the company and Allan also represented the government on the board.

In 1829 when the Court of Directors of the Canada Company decided that they had to get rid of John Galt they replaced him by two commissioners. One was Thomas Mercer Jones, who was to be stationed in the Huron Tract, the other was Allan who accepted the position on condition that he continue to reside at York.

Basically this was a political appointment. One of the troubles with Galt had been that he was not able to get on with the powers that be at York and someone was needed who could. Allan, however, was not the court's first choice for the post. Jones was instructed that the first choice was Thomas Markland and that only if he declined was Allan to be approached. In the event Markland refused the offer and Allan accepted. This means that in the eyes of the court Allan was not yet in the first rank of those who ran the province. He probably owed his selection[23] in part to his position as president of the company's Canadian bankers, and in part to the recommendation of Edward Ellice who was a large shareholder. Allan had been his agent in Upper Canada for years and they had known of each other as far back as the old days with Forsyth Richardson. Allan was a good choice. He understood land sales and leases and had an interest in seeing a large immigration from the British Isles. It would improve business and counteract the deplorable influence of the American-born settlers who had caused such trouble during the war and were now providing ammunition for such dangerous nuisances as Gourlay and Mackenzie.

All these activities were more or less connected with government, but he also took an active part in three other ventures. In about 1833 he became interested in a plan to form an insurance company and in 1835 he resigned the presidency of the bank and became the first president of the British North American Insurance Company.[24] About the same time he became a partner along with Samuel Street of Niagara, James Buchanan the British consul at New York, and Lt-Gen. John Murray in a scheme to establish the colony's first subdivision at Niagara Falls. Acting under the name of The City of the Falls the partnership bought a large area of land around Niagara Falls and set to work to create a cottage community. Allan retained his interest in the project to the end of his life. It did not succeed in making the partners a fortune but it did result in the foundation of Clifton, now Niagara Falls.

Finally he became involved in the early attempts to build railways. In the 1830s a Toronto group set to work to organize a company to build a railway from Toronto to Lake Simcoe.[25] Allan was not at first involved in this project, but about 1836 he became vice-president of the company. The project came to nothing, partly because of squabbles about the route and quarrels over whether or not it should extend to Lake Huron, partly because of difficulties in raising money. Finally, because of the depression of 1837, the scheme was abandoned. Allan, however, did not lose interest. He kept the papers and in 1844 revived the scheme as The Toronto and Lake Huron Railway Company. This time his plan seems to have been based on the idea of financing the road in England through the Canada Company. He was no longer a commissioner but still retained connections with it, and the new commissioner, Frederick Widder, was convinced that the best inducement to attract settlers to the Huron Tract was a railway to connect it with Toronto. The Canada Company, therefore, organized an English company to provide the financing, while the Toronto company was to build and operate the road. This too failed for a combination of reasons: the depression of 1847 and the quarrels of the Canadian directors over the terminus of the road – whether it should be at Sarnia, Collingwood, or Goderich. In the end Allan once more put the papers away perhaps hoping the scheme might still be revived. In due time it was, but Allan did not live to see the first train of The Northern Railway pull into Toronto.[26]

Almost every historian who mentions Allan does so on the ground that he was politically a powerful figure and one of the members of the political elite who ran the province. Both statements are true but the matter is oversimplified. It is forgotten that he was actively concerned in politics for only sixteen of his sixty-five years in Canada and that he was a member of the inner circle – the Executive Council – for barely five. Politically he was important, but the true position is that expressed in his somewhat chilly obituary in the *Leader*: '... he managed successfully a large amount of business, and became rich. His name became associated with everything where money was concerned. As a politician Col. Allan had none of those qualities which constitute a political leader, and his position in his party, though sometimes high, was always subordinate ...'[27] Throughout his entire active career in politics Allan was just what he was in his later business career. He was an executive, a man of shrewd judgment, and, as the years went on, of ever increasing experience, but he was not an innovator or an originator of policy. In political matters he was intensely conservative and intensely narrow in his views of both society and government. In part at least this was the result of his Scots background and his limited education. He was born, and received his earliest impressions, at a time and place when men knew their place and realized that for most it was a low one; where Andrew Allan of The Moss was in no sense the equal of the Dukes of Gordon who owned Huntly; where a clerk in Forsyth Richardson was not the equal of a partner. Politically, though like most of the Compact he took no second place to an Englishman, the crown and the constitution as he understood it were sacred. No good would come of tampering with either. All that could result was the wild republicanism that disgraced the Americans across the border. In consequence he set his face against any concession to the Reformers, and in equal consequence was hated by them.

His political career began with his appointment to the Legislative Council in 1824 where he quickly came to have great influence. One reason of course was his practical ability. It was quickly found that his advice was shrewd and to the point, but equally important was his diligence. He was in attendance at the majority of the meetings of the council and over the years acquired a fund of knowledge and experience unequalled by any other member. The result of all this was that the view of 'Mr Allan' in time became the view most often adopted. The real importance of the man came out on his appointment to the Executive Council in 1836. When the members were sworn in Robert Baldwin Sullivan realized that he was the senior member and that should Head become incapacitated he, Sullivan, would become administrator of the province. He declared that in that case he would resign, and it was arranged that if so Allan would be administrator because, as Augustus Baldwin stated, he '... had preferable claims from his age and long standing in society.'[28]

His political career ended in 1840 when Thompson arrived to carry out some part of the terms of Lord Durham's report. Allan regarded the report with horror and was opposed to Thompson's views, though true to the principles of a lifetime he supported his early measures, but clearly his position was impossible. Thompson was reconstituting the Legislative Council and Allan, who was anathema to the Reformers, could not be retained. He himself knew this; he knew a generation had arisen which knew not Moses, and was not surprised when he was not appointed to either the Legislative or Executive councils of the United Province. His day as an active political figure was done but he remained almost to his death a power as a sort of elder statesman among the high Tories.

His active business career came to an end with The Toronto and Lake Huron and thereafter his time was spent looking after his private affairs. This brings up the point how rich was Allen? The answer must be that in the absence of his accounts[29] it is impossible to say. It is probably true that he and Thomas Clark Street of Niagara were the wealthiest men in the province. His major investments were clearly in land and in mortgages. It is known that he owned a great deal of land in Toronto, in East York, in Niagara, and around Ancaster; that he had interests in grist mills, and owned fairly large amounts of provincial debentures. In short he was the rich Mr Allan.

He died on 11 July 1853 in his house at Moss Park, thirty-one years to the day since he announced he had '... given up all his concern in trade.'

NOTES

The author is grateful to the Canada Council for the financial support which made his research possible.

1 E.M. Chadwick, *Ontarian Families* (2 vols., Toronto 1894), I, 79
2 Sir John Sinclair, *The Statistical Account of Scotland* (21 vols., Edinburgh 1791), XI: *The Parish of Huntly*. This is a description of the town in 1790 but it was probably much the same in the 1770s. The school is noted as being bad and was probably so in Allan's time if his abominable handwriting, shaky spelling, and peculiar grammar are evidence of its standards.

3 Ontario Archives [OA], Land Petition Book Upper Canada, bundle A 1–11 and A 2–22
4 Reorganized as Forsyth Richardson and Company in 1790. See R.H. Fleming, *Phyn Ellice and Company of Schenectady* (Toronto 1932)
5 The use of articled clerks was common in the North West Company and was likely taken over from the practice of the firms which made up that company. See G.C. Davidson, *The North West Company* (Berkeley and Los Angeles 1918), 227–8
6 Land Petition Book Upper Canada, bundle A 1–11
7 Land Petition Book Upper Canada, bundle A 3–39
8 Edith Firth, 'Alexander Wood: Merchant of York,' *York Pioneer*, 1958, 5–29
9 John Strachan, the school master and clergyman, had one to the day of his death; so undoubtedly did the ill-educated merchant.
10 Something by no means common among the leading citizens of York.
11 Public Archives of Canada, RG 9, I B I, vol. 21, Allan to Coffin, 17 Dec. 1825
12 RG 9, I B 7, vol. 17
13 It hardly needs saying that this opinion was false. In matters of myth it is not truth which counts but what men believe to be true.
14 Metropolitan Toronto Public Library [MTPL] Papers Relating to the Capitulation of York. Letter signed by Strachan, Allan, et al protesting Sheaffe's conduct.
15 RG 8, 'C' Series 679, Powell to Prevost, 16 June 1813
16 Held in the Library of the Royal Canadian Military Institute
17 The Kingston *Gazette*, 1808 to 1810 *passim.*
18 I hope to discuss these points at some length in a projected study of the Bank of Upper Canada. [Only the first three chapters were drafted at the time of Mr Magill's death: Eds.]
19 The York *Weekly Post*, 19 April 1821
20 RG 19, B I, vol. 19, Dunn to Hillier, 16 Oct. 1821
21 *Upper Canada Gazette*, 11 July 1822
22 This was his own money.
23 There were others equally acceptable to the authorities and of similar abilities.
24 He did not resign from the bank to head the insurance company. He had long been dissatisfied with the quarrels among the members of the bank's board. Several attempts had been made to unseat him and he was glad of an opportunity to leave.
25 For details see F.H. Armstrong, 'Toronto's First Railway Venture, 1834–1838,' *Ontario History*, LVIII, March 1966, 21–41
26 MTPL, William Allan Papers, Toronto and Lake Huron Railway
27 *The Daily Leader*, Toronto, 12 July 1853
28 Public Record Office, CO 42/433–41
29 They are not among his papers at MTPL.

Construction Materials
in Colonial Ontario 1831-61

W.R. Wightman

Interest in the nineteenth-century housing of the province dates back beyond the founding of the Architectural Conservancy of Ontario in 1935.[1] In recent years it has grown, stimulated by general architectural works[2] and by studies of particular styles, buildings in specific communities, and structures in certain rural areas.[3] To date, however, the work has tended to concentrate on the architecture or form of the structure and to rely heavily for source materials on those old buildings which have survived to the present day.[4] Thus, attention has wandered away from the more general topic addressed here: the study both of those forces which converted the province from pioneer log homes to dwellings in other materials and of the comparative emphasis placed on the use of log, frame, brick, and stone in different parts of the province over the century.

In addition to contemporary documents, some statistical information on the problem is available for several decades prior to Confederation, a fortunate situation that does not occur again until the closing decade of the century.[5] Before mid-century some details of construction materials appear in the assessment summaries and later more are to be found in the census reports of 1851 and 1861.[6] The assessment summaries give yearly information by township on all non-log structures, but only the taxable log dwellings. While frame, brick, and stone are listed, they are lumped in varied combination by storey so that the only useful figure to be derived is an aggregate for all non-log in the township, a feature which severely curtails the utility of this record. The two census reports provide full information on log, brick, frame, and stone. Neither the summaries nor the reports, however, deal adequately with urban centres. The assessment records separate these only sporadically from their township figures in most cases. The census, because of the Municipal Corporations Act, lists many more urban centres in 1861 than are given separately a decade earlier when the act had just come into force. As a result, in some of the following analysis, which concentrates primarily on trends and tendencies in the period 1831 to 1861, such centres, even where they are separated out statistically, must be included with their township figures for practical comparability. Where necessary,

TABLE 1

Total housing

CLASS	1831	PER CENT TOTAL CHANGE	1841	PER CENT TOTAL CHANGE	1851	PER CENT TOTAL CHANGE	1861	TOTAL CHANGE
Non-log	9477	19	29,781	32	63,262	49	115,134	105,675
Log	33,380	22	48,950	48	82,694	30	103,565	70,185
Total	42,857*	20	78,731†	39	145,956	41	218,699	175,742

*Figure taken from J. McGregor, *British America* (2nd ed., London 1863)
†Figure taken from the summary of the Census of 1841–2 in *Canada Census for 1871*, Vol. 4, 292–8

these will be distinguished as urban-centred as opposed to rural townships. Only in the final year of the period will the urban places be treated as separate entities.

GENERAL TRENDS 1831-61

In contrast to the laggardly economic and demographic development and the poor land administration of the province, which by 1831 resulted in a population of scarcely 200,000 spread thinly and unevenly over about 260 townships,[7] the next three decades were marked by dramatic growth and prosperity. With rising immigration, the population climbed to over a million. New settlers filled old townships, which had long lain partially empty, and began colonization in an additional 130 townships which were surveyed during these years. Urban centres, frequently born in the twenties, grew rapidly on a resultant wave of agrarian prosperity. Despite revolt, recession, and major market disruption, these were the early years of the take-off which was to lead the province out of its economic adolescence by the late decades of the century.

Commensurate with this take-off went a building boom, which by 1861 had produced about 70,000 new log dwellings and more than 105,000 of other materials – an increase of two- and eleven-fold respectively over the number erected during the prior half century (see Table 1). Of this increase, the proportion of non-log additions had accelerated in each decade – almost half of the total being added in the last ten years. Log followed suit into the forties, after which its rate of increase fell sharply. Thus, while in 1831 only one in every five houses was built of frame, brick, or stone, by 1861 log dwellings were out-numbered for the first time by those erected in other materials. Involved here were two major geographical trends. The one was expansive from the older centres of settlement, increasing the rural portion of the province where non-log housing was becoming prominent because of rising agrarian wealth. The other was concentrative, adding to the number of non-log dwellings built in urban centres as a result of rapidly generated commercial and professional income. Together these trends brought about a remarkable change during these thirty years, but they were still strongly evident at Confederation when the balance between the materials in use remained far from that achieved by the close of the century.

THE EXPANSIVE TREND

Expansive development resulted from two basic forces which were continually in play in the rural scene. The first was that of colonization, producing log homes in both recently opened townships and on formerly unoccupied properties in older areas.[8] The second was that of the replacement of these log pioneer homes with structures of other materials as the property or the township gained in economic maturity. The situation was described by 'Tiger' Dunlop, Warden of the Forests for the Canada Company, when he noted, 'Most of the houses, more particularly of recent settlers, are built of log. When a man gets on a little in the world, he builds a frame house, weather-board outside and lathed and plastered within; and in travelling along the road, you can form a pretty accurate estimate of the time a man has been settled by the house he inhabits; indeed, in some instances, you may read the whole history of his settlement in the buildings about his farmyard.'[9] Even today the truth of this last statement can be confirmed visually on the occasional rural property.

The operation of these forces can be considered to have caused each township to pass through a series of stages in the evolution of its housing. In the first, buildings were almost exclusively of log with frequent new ones being added as colonization proceeded. In the second, log buildings remained prevalent, but their numerical increase dwindled as the township filled. Replacement on older properties, meanwhile, raised the non-log component to more than 20 per cent, a figure which continued to accelerate.[10] In the third, buildings erected in other materials made up more than 50 per cent of the total and continuing replacement forced log into an absolute decline which pointed towards its eventual disappearance. Undoubtedly, the length of each stage and its detailed characteristics varied with each township, making the actual operation of the process much more complex than this simple description would suggest.[11]

The lack of log statistics at the township level before mid-century prevents early classification by these stages and masks much of what might be learned about their early operation. By 1851, however, a total of seventy-eight townships were dominantly non-log and an additional ninety-nine were in the second phase of their development (see Table 2). Most of these would appear to have entered upon their current stage during the prior decade. Only about a fifth of the former townships

TABLE 2

Total housing by developmental stage

DEVELOPMENTAL STAGE	NO TOWNSHIPS	LOG HOUSES	PROPORTION OF TOTAL	NON-LOG HOUSES	PROPORTION OF TOTAL
		1851 Census			
Stage 3	78	20,845	26%	43,522	69%
Stage 2	99	30,050	36%	16,111	25%
Stage 1	181	31,799	38%	3629	6%
Total	358	82,694	100%	63,262	100%
		1861 Census			
Stage 3	133	29,439	28%	92,427	80%
Stage 2	107	39,172	38%	18,873	16%
Stage 1	152	34,955	34%	3,834	4%
Total	392	103,565	100%	115,134	100%

and a third of the latter had non-log values in excess of 75 and 35 per cent respectively. Some, if not all of these, may have held their status from some date prior to 1841, but not necessarily from before the opening of the period.[12]

By 1851, with the exception of minor isolated parcels in both east and west, those townships in which non-log prevailed formed a nearly continuous core extending from Kingston to the heart of Oxford and Elgin counties (see Figure 1). Townships in the second stage, with a few exceptions, were interspersed in the core, prolonged it in both east and west, or formed a moderately continuous band along its northern fringe. Just as few townships may have been dominantly non-log in the thirties, so, given the inadequate land policy of earlier years and the time required for its correction, the proportion of the townships open for settlement but remaining in the first or second stage of development may have been larger in prior decades. Similarly, the core in earlier years was probably less continuous – a series of small sub-cores bounded by townships in the second phase – as indeed the case remained in 1851, both along the St Lawrence and in the extreme southwest.[13] The less developed isolates, as at Goderich or in the Lake Simcoe area, would appear in this light as the first stage of a repetitive process of separate sub-core formation, usually focused on a newer urban centre, which sub-core through growth would eventually coalesce with the major concentration. In spite of this, however, the more common tendency in expansion would appear to have been the stadial development of the townships contiguous to the major core.

Over the subsequent decade the number of townships in each stage changed in response to continuing building, which in this decade was particularly rapid (see Table 2). While those townships in the third stage sharply increased in number, the losses so incurred in the second were only just exceeded by the addition of town-

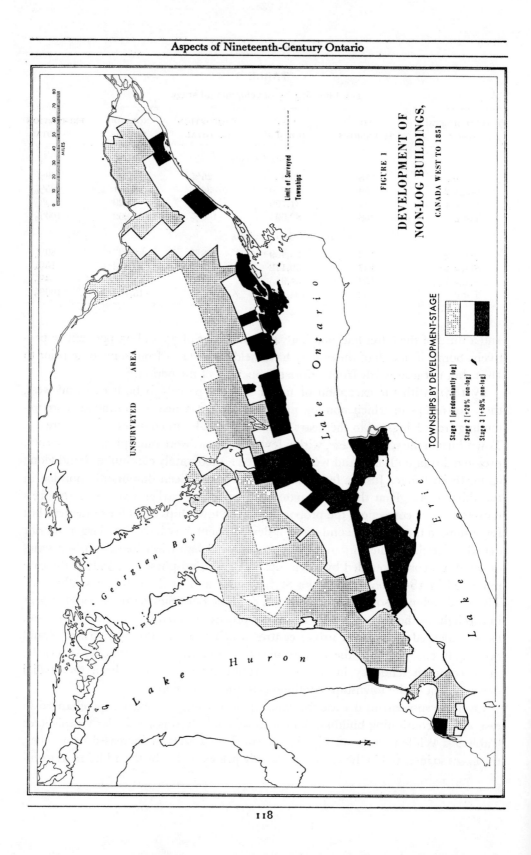

FIGURE 1

DEVELOPMENT OF NON-LOG BUILDINGS,

CANADA WEST TO 1851

Limit of Surveyed Townships ----------

TOWNSHIPS BY DEVELOPMENT-STAGE

Stage 1 (predominantly log)

Stage 2 (+20% non-log)

Stage 3 (+50% non-log)

Lake Ontario

Lake Erie

Lake Huron

Georgian Bay

UNSURVEYED AREA

MILES

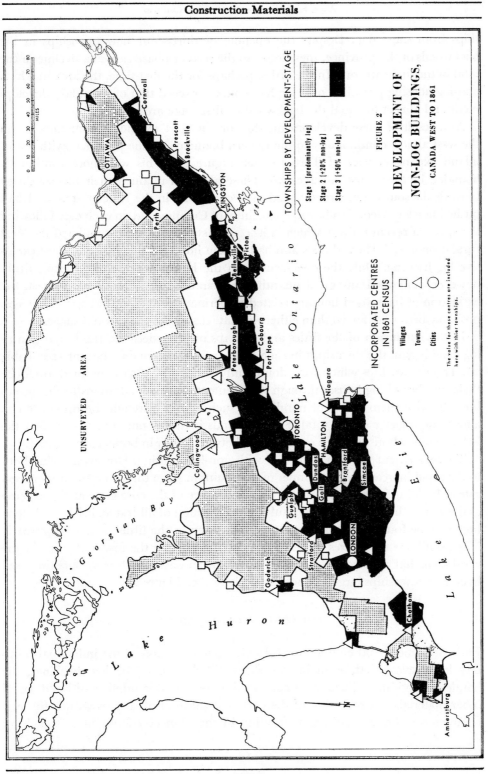

TOWNSHIPS BY DEVELOPMENT-STAGE

Stage 1 (predominantly log)

Stage 2 (+20% non-log)

Stage 3 (+50% non-log)

FIGURE 2

DEVELOPMENT OF
NON-LOG BUILDINGS,
CANADA WEST TO 1861

INCORPORATED CENTRES
IN 1861 CENSUS

Villages

Towns

Cities

The value for these centres are included
here with thier township.

UNSURVEYED

AREA

Lake Ontario

Lake Erie

Georgian Bay

Lake Huron

Cornwall
Prescott
Brockville
OTTAWA
Perth
KINGSTON
Belleville
Picton
Peterborough
Cobourg
Port Hope
Niagara
TORONTO
HAMILTON
Dundas
Galt
Brantford
Guelph
Simcoe
Collingwood
Stratford
Goderich
LONDON
Chatham
Amherstburg

ships from stage one. Despite the opening of thirty-four new townships in the backwoods of the province, these losses to the second phase caused a decline in the total in the first category. In the fifties, perhaps for the first time, the area in which non-log housing prevailed over log had come to exceed that of secondary development and almost to equal the backwood or first stage area.

As a result of these developments the core in 1861 extended from London on the west almost continuously to the eastern boundary of the province, with major inland expansion west of Toronto (see Figure 2). This was more continually bounded by townships in stage two. These also had retained their former thrust towards the southwest, strengthened their continuity in the Rideau area, and had pushed north to Georgian Bay in the vicinity of Collingwood, in each case following the axis of a recent railway which in its construction may have stimulated the local rural economy.[14] These thrusts also had broken into cells the area of almost exclusive log housing. Only the one focused on the Huron Tract and Queen's Bush, however, contained any great quantity of desirable land. Elsewhere, at least, the extinction of backwood housing related to permanent agricultural settlement was probably better advanced than either the statistics or the map would suggest.

In this expansion of the fifties and perhaps in prior decades, the proportion of log dwellings in the townships in each stage tended to remain constant (see Table 2). Those townships which were dominantly non-log in 1851 continued to reduce their number of log houses through replacement, but new additions to this group brought with them sufficient numbers of such homes to retain the proportion at about one quarter of the total. Similar trends in stages one and two caused the balance of log housing to be roughly split between them in both census years.

To some extent the same was true with non-log housing. However, owing both to the rapid increase in the number of townships in stage three and to an increased rate of building in these townships, the importance of the core grew at the expense of the rest of the province. As a result, the proportion of all frame, brick, and stone houses to be found in stage three townships, even in the fifties, seems surprisingly large, until one recognizes that this not only stems from the forces at work in the rural scene but also from the concentrative urban ones which were superimposed in certain townships largely concentrated here (see Figure 2).

THE CONCENTRATIVE TREND

Early assessment and enumerator rolls giving information at the individual property level reveal that, even in townships still dominated by log dwellings, the hamlet or budding village often contained a considerable number of buildings of other materials – a reflection of the earlier acquisition of surplus wealth through commerce rather than through farming in the pioneer community. If such an urban place failed to grow significantly, as was true in the majority of cases, improvement in its rural surroundings soon overcame any nascent concentrative tendencies. If it became a large village, town, or city, however,[15] the number of new frame, brick, and stone structures added in the process exceeded, often by several times, the growth that was possible in the surroundings township even through the replacement of all log farm dwellings. Under these circumstances, the urban centre became a separate major contributor to the building boom.

At the opening of the period there were no cities and few communities of town size in the province. Many centres, including both London and Bytown (Ottawa), which were cities in 1861, were in 1831 raw villages less than ten years of age. By the close, five cities, thirty-four towns, and almost fifty incorporated villages dotted the map (see Figure 2). These were situated primarily in those townships where non-log structures dominated the rural scene. As hamlets they may have begun to replace their log buildings earlier than did their townships and, as they grew, often to have built in other materials from the first. But in 1851 all those listed separately (with the exception of Kingston), continued to have some log structures within their bounds. In some, such as Amherstburg, Galt, and Bytown, log still made up more than a quarter of the total – a feature also common to most of the villages and younger towns which appeared first in 1861. Most of the large centres at mid-century, however, were less than 10 per cent log and some lost their last buildings of this material over the subsequent decade – a feat not even the most advanced township was able to match. Most townships continued to contain at least 20 per cent of their housing in log at the close of the period.

Of the more than 70 per cent of all non-log housing which in both census years was lodged in townships in the third phase, less than a third was contributed by rural townships. (Even here, the contribution of the unincorporated commercial centre may have influenced the figure considerably.) The balance came from those townships which contained at least an incorporated village in 1861 (see Table 3). Those with the cities of Bytown, Kingston, Toronto, Hamilton and London accounted for about twenty per cent, those with the more numerous towns an additional twenty-four per cent and those with villages only about twelve per cent. These urban proportions of total non-log were curiously constant over prior decades (see Table 3). Although the rural contribution in urban-centred townships may have been of some importance in this situation in earlier years, as it continued to be in those townships with villages in 1861, a constant relationship in the rate of building would appear to have been generally maintained between urban and rural townships. The exact contribution of the former, however, cannot be determined except at the close of the period. At that time the cities of the core accounted for 16 per cent, the towns, 12, and the villages 5 per cent of all non-log housing in the province, or about 30 per cent in aggregate, leaving more than 40 per cent of

TABLE 3

Stage three townships: urban/rural 1831–61

STAGE THREE TOWNSHIPS (1861)	1831		1841		1851		1861	
	PROPORTION OF TOTAL	NO HOUSES	PROPORTION OF TOTAL	NO HOUSES	PROPORTION OF TOTAL	NO HOUSES	PROPORTION OF TOTAL	NO HOUSES
Rural townships	35%	3388	26%	7600	30%	18,886	27%	31,444
*Urban townships	55%	5186	51%	15,179	57%	35,891	53%	60,983
City-centred	17%	1378	16%	4765	19%	12,206	18%	20,846
Town-centred	24%	2317	24%	7251	26%	16,684	24%	28,047
Village-centred	14%	1491	11%	3163	12%	7001	11%	12,090

*The urban centred townships of the second stage of development which are not included in the textual analysis only added a total of 3865 dwellings to the total in 1861.

all non-log housing to those rural townships which were in the third stage of their development.[16]

The available documentary sources would suggest that, if such a relationship between urban and rural building was maintained through the period, this was done despite marked variations in the timing and the intensity of urban construction from centre to centre. In the thirties, Rolph and others, while impressing upon their readers the rapid growth of urbanism in the province, noted in particular the speedy construction of substantial housing in such communities as Brockville, Belleville, Cobourg, Dundas, and Brantford.[17] Writing in a similar vein a decade later, Smith was impressed by the rate of building in Perth, Port Hope, Guelph, and Galt.[18] He also commented on the near stagnant condition of Cornwall and Amherstburg,[19] the tawdry appearance of the housing in both Goderich and Stratford,[20] and the recency of the building boom in Chatham and Simcoe.[21] Both authors also confirm conclusions about the centres to be drawn from an examination of the sporadic urban statistics of the assessment summaries. While Hamilton and Toronto built steadily through the thirty years and London and Bytown at comparatively higher rates, Kingston suffered no marked boom except in the early forties, the years of its political prominence. Conversely, while building briskly in the early thirties, Niagara became nearly static after 1841 as it fell further within the commercial sphere of St Catharines. In the fifties Kingston increased but slowly, while the cities of Toronto and Hamilton, Bytown and London continued their previous trends. Other towns, such as Brockville, Picton, Dundas, Niagara, and Amherstburg built little and Cornwall, Prescott, and Cobourg added few new structures. However, newer centres, primarily in the central and western part of the province, including Perth, Peterborough, Port Hope, Galt, Guelph, Chatham, and Goderich, followed the rapid spiral of Bytown and London with rates of addition greatly in excess of the provincial average. From this it would appear that continuous building, sometimes very rapid, was characteristic of all cities or 'regional capitals' through these years except for Kingston with its unique lack of agrarian base and peculiar economic reliance on the varied trade of the Rideau and St Lawrence waterways. Among the towns, however, booming construction was more periodic. Those building most rapidly in the fifties were probably doing so in response to the increasing economic maturity of their rural hinterlands, as presumably their older fellows had done when similarly stimulated in earlier years.

TRENDS IN NON-LOG CONSTRUCTION MATERIALS

In 1851 85 per cent of all the non-log housing in the province was of frame with the balance almost equally divided between brick and stone (see Table 4). Despite the particularly pronounced increase in non-log construction over the ensuing

TABLE 4

Total non-log material by type

DATE	FRAME			BRICK			STONE	
	NO	PER CENT*		NO	PER CENT*		NO	PER CENT*
1851	53,917	85		5133	8		4213	7
1861	95,002	82		12,755	11		7377	7
1901†	267,210	70		103,719	27		10,732	3

*In each case this is a percentage of total non-log in the province.
†In these figures a special category of the census, termed Composite, has not been included, since no comparable category was listed in earlier years.

decade, more than 80 per cent remained frame in 1861, although brick increased slightly in provincial proportion and stone maintained its share. Frame may have been an even more prominent alternate to log in earlier years. Although apparently preferred even over the snug squared log home, however, certain reservations were held about frame houses during the period. They were recognized to be both highly inflammable and frequently cold and draughty owing to construction in local lumber which had been ill-cured and poorly dressed.[22] Some contemporary writers suggested that such homes were almost as expensive to build in simple style as ones of either stone or brick.[23] It seems quite probable in the light of this information that the intensive use of frame at mid-century stemmed primarily from the local availability of lumber from an early stage in the development of every township rather than from any aura of tradition as has sometimes been claimed.[24]

Yet in many instances the frame dwelling was but a passing phase on the property. In time, like the log structure before it, as wealth continued to increase, it was replaced in brick or stone, materials not only warmer and more durable but more prestigious. Again, as Dunlop described, 'the original shanty, or log hovel which sheltered the family when they first arrived on their wild lot, still remains, but has been degraded to a piggery; the more substantial log house, which held out the weather during the first years of their sojourn, has, with the increase in their wealth, become a chapel of ease to the stable or cowhouse; and the glaring and staring bright red brick house is brought forward close to the road, that the frame dwelling, which at one time the proprietor looked upon as the very acme of his ambitions, may at once serve as the kitchen to, and be concealed by, its more aspiring and aristocratic successor.'[25] As is evident in the modern scene, however, the early frame home frequently remained the permanent dwelling, and this additional cycle of replacement incomplete. (Alternatively, there is no reason to assume that every brick or stone house had frame antecedents, particularly in the rapidly developing urban centres.) Nevertheless, in spite of a large increase in the number of structures,

TABLE 5

Stage three non-log material, by type, urban/rural

DATE	STATUS	FRAME		BRICK		STONE	
		NO	PER CENT*	NO	PER CENT*	NO	PER CENT*
1851 {	Rural	11,159	93	544	5	294	2
	Urban†	25,753	82	3,784	12	1,988	6
1861 {	Rural	27,991	89	2,321	8	1,177	3
	Urban	48,300	79	8,563	14	4,075	7

*The percentage is of total rural or urban non-log in stage three units of each category.
†Urban centres in stage two units are not included here. As noted previously, these added only insignificantly to the urban figure.

by the end of the century replacement and preference for other materials had reduced the proportion of frame in the townships under discussion to about 70 per cent in circumstances which saw much heavier emphasis on brick, a decline in the importance of stone, but the near disappearance of log buildings in much of the area (see Table 4).

Beneath these general figures, marked differences in emphasis on different non-log construction materials existed, both between urban and rural areas and between different parts of the province. In the rural area of the core in both 1851 and 1861, although there was a slight decline, frame structures continued to make up about 90 per cent of all non-log housing (see Table 5), and this proportion was even higher among townships in stages one and two. Brick increased its total slightly, this increase being largely, but not totally, among the core townships, while the percentage of stone remained roughly unchanged. Although frame replacement must have been going on for some decades as rural areas gained further in economic maturity, as yet the process had not gained the momentum in the countryside which it was to gather in later decades of the century.

Such replacement was also tempered by the local availability of alternate materials; brick, the result of local manufacture from suitable clays; stone, the product of quarry or farm-field where it was to be found locally. These circumstances combined to create varied rural regional emphasis in construction materials across the province – emphasis which was not entirely limited to the townships of the core, especially in the case of stone. This material, while occurrent in small quantities over much of the province, was in considerable use only east of Kingston and in the middle Grand River Valley where it was particularly abundant and accessible. Except around Hamilton, however, its employment was curiously limited in townships along the Niagara escarpment (see Figure 3).

Brick, in comparison, was in most pronounced use west of the Toronto area,

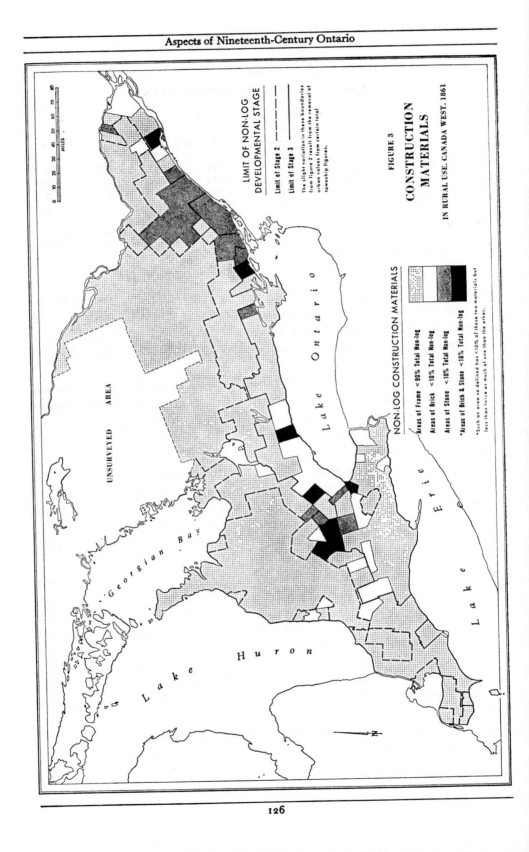

FIGURE 3

CONSTRUCTION MATERIALS

IN RURAL USE, CANADA WEST, 1861

although also employed in smaller quantities elsewhere. It showed a remarkable tendency to be a significant building material in townships which focused upon larger urban centres such as Goderich, London, Woodstock, St Catharines, and the vicinity of Toronto. This would appear to reflect an urban orientation of brick-yards in 1861, although it may also be indicative of peculiar rural wealth generated by proximity to local urban markets. In certain areas where both brick and stone were available, as in Waterloo County and around Hamilton, Whitby, Kingston, and Cornwall, these materials would appear to have been in significant preferential competition for use in construction.

Nevertheless, frame was still the ubiquitous alternative to log, regardless of the stage of development achieved by each township of the province in 1861. In no instance was a township less than 70 per cent frame in its non-log component and many, even in the core, were more than 90 per cent frame in their non-log value. This was especially true in the counties of Elgin, Norfolk, and Welland where often log was almost the only alternate to frame at this time. Most frame structures were of less than two storeys.[26] Many were of mortise and tenon construction, based on beams pegged together (as in many barns still standing) rather than the then recently developed balloon frame with which we are familiar today.[27] They were most frequently of a simple (vernacular) style familiar to a local builder, a style which varied little across the province.[28] Most were sheathed in plain weather-board, although vertical board-and-batten siding was coming into vogue.[29] Many were probably unpainted or painted infrequently.[30] Although not unknown in the rural scene, painted frame, like more pretentious architecture and structures of two storeys or more in any material, seemingly remained primarily a feature of the towns and cities.

In contrast to the rural area of the province at mid-century and a decade later, the urban-centred townships of the core were already somewhat less prevalently frame (about 80 per cent of the non-log) and had commensurately larger components of brick and stone (see Table 5). While both of these prestigious alternates to frame would appear to have come into substantial urban use more rapidly than in the rural countryside, there is some reason to believe that stone may have been the earlier of the two to be put to frequent use. Although Kingston, like other older communities on the St Lawrence, commenced extensive construction in local stone at as early a date as the supply of immigrant masons would allow,[31] York (Toronto), with no such local resource, remained a frame town with only three brick structures at least as late as 1820[32] – a situation which would appear to have been paralleled elsewhere. By the thirties, however, Rolph and other travellers indicated not only that brick was becoming more common in the capital but also was being put to use in such new communities as London, as well as in centres like Belleville where stone was also available.[33] In the forties Smith revealed the further employment of brick as well as the continuing use of stone not only in eastern communities but also in new western towns such as Galt and Guelph.[34] This apparent tardy development of a formal brick industry supported by yards remains curious and unexplained, but by the fifties, and probably a decade earlier, the urban oriented brickyard at least was a common feature in the province.[35] Production from these by about mid-century was in the millions of bricks per year and yellow brick, although twice as expensive per thousand as red, was the more popular and was produced from Goderich to Cornwall.[36] The popularity of yellow, however, would appear to have been most pronounced west of Toronto where brick was most prominent both in urban and rural use.

As in the rural scene in 1861, the urban centres showed regional emphasis in construction materials (see Figure 4). While urban stone, with the exception of its significant appearance at Amherstburg, St Mary's, and St Catharines, followed the same pattern as the rural, brick was more broadly distributed. In the core area only Perth, Prescott, and Ottawa failed to contain some, although both brick and stone were absent or insignificant in such centres as Collingwood and Barrie outside the core. With few exceptions, however, brick was commonest west of Kingston where it was competitive with stone in such centres as Belleville and Hamilton or was the primary alternate to frame as in Toronto, Brantford, and London. As previously pointed out, log had disappeared or was on the verge of doing so in many centres of the core area in 1861, although still of considerable importance in the newer communities in the zone of secondary development such as Owen Sound and Lindsay.

This relatively frequent use of brick and, where available, stone as building materials in the towns and cities would appear likely to reflect more than simple wealth, the availability of these materials, or the presence of craftsmen to employ them with taste and style. While prestige was a factor, there may have been a more practical consideration as well. Most of these communities had had to renew some portion of themselves after a major conflagration during the thirties, forties, or fifties and often then chose to do so in more fireproof brick or stone rather than in inflammable frame.[37] Thus fear of fire under the congested conditions of the urban area was also involved. This was reflected in local bylaws which listed the fire precautions expected of each householder and often prohibited the erection of wooden structures in areas of the business section.[38] Also, it may have reflected a reaction either to the high cost of or inability to secure fire insurance on frame buildings. Such problems, given urban housing densities and the rudimentary fire protection offered by most communities at the time, must have prevailed in residential areas as elsewhere. Although all these factors may have been at work behind the urban housing scene to promote the use of brick and stone, however, no urban centre,

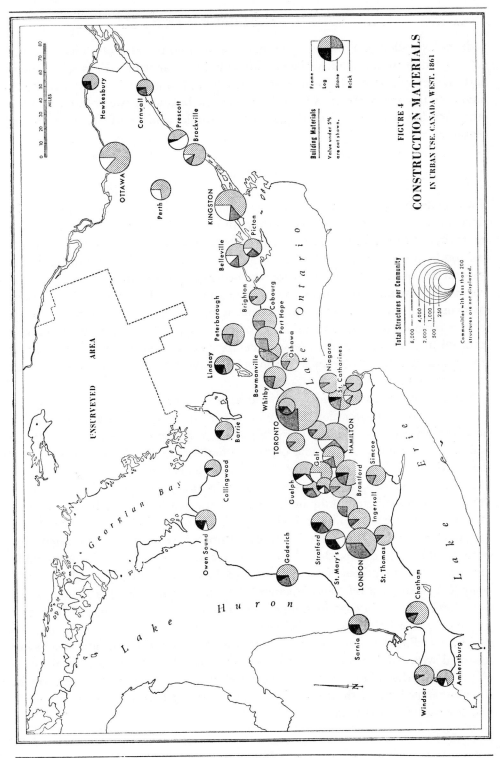

FIGURE 4

CONSTRUCTION MATERIALS

IN URBAN USE, CANADA WEST, 1861

Building Materials

Value under 5%
are not shown.

Frame
Log
Stone
Brick

Total Structures per Community

8,000
4,000
2,000
1,000
500
250

Communities with less than 200
structures are not displayed.

with the exception of Prescott, as yet had less than 60 per cent of all its buildings constructed of wood. Thus, while considerably in advance of their rural counterparts in the replacement of log and, to some extent, frame buildings by Confederation, even the urban centres were still far from the balance between frame and the other non-log building materials which they would achieve by the close of the century.

CONCLUSIONS

The decades from about 1830 to 1900 were those of economic take-off in the province, during which it was converted from an ill-settled landscape where log housing prevailed to one in which such structures were almost absent from both town and southern countryside and where brick, next to frame, was the most common construction material. This conversion was accomplished through processes of rural expansion, township by township, based upon gradual economic maturation, involving the slow and orderly replacement of log and, later, frame structures with more prestigious dwellings. In urban areas it sprang from concentrative processes involved in the speedy growth of such centres where more rapid profits derived from maturing rural hinterlands were quickly converted into homes and buildings of some architectural pretension.

These processes had already produced a predominance of non-log housing in the province by Confederation, but about 80 per cent of this was frame, with brick quite limited and only slightly more important than stone. The expansive trend had produced a nearly continuous core of predominantly non-log townships across the province, this area containing the greatest percentage of all such housing, although a large proportion was actually in its urban centres which over prior decades had contributed to the building boom at a particularly high and constant rate. These centres frequently had replaced all, or nearly all, of their log structures, and, in response to both wealth and threat of fire, contained somewhat larger proportions of brick and stone than did their rural counterparts in which considerable log and larger quantities of frame remained to be replaced by the close of the century. Despite their relatively advanced state in the conversion process, however, even these centres still contained much larger proportions of frame buildings than future decades would reveal. In both urban and certain rural areas, however, the rapidly receding log and the ubiquitous frame countryside already was being leavened with varying amounts of brick and stone, depending upon local availability and perhaps in some instances on preference. Certain regional patterns in the pronounced use of these materials were beginning to appear – patterns with which we are familiar today.

NOTES

1 Interest was also created by such studies as E.R. Arthur, *Small Houses of the Late Eighteenth and Early Nineteenth Century in Ontario* (Toronto 1927), and 'Early Architecture in Ontario,' Ontario Historical Society, *Papers and Records*, XXVII, 1932, 150–4, as well as E. Nobbs, 'Canadian Architecture,' in A. Shortt and A.G. Doughty, eds., *Canada and its Provinces* (Toronto 1913), XII, 671–5. In this same period a major contribution was made by C.S. Buck in a thesis, which has subsequently been updated and enlarged by him, 'The Origins and Character of the Early Architecture and Practical Arts of Ontario to 1850' (unpublished MA thesis, University of Western Ontario, 1930).

2 See A. Gowan, *Looking at Architecture in Canada* (Toronto 1958) and A. Gowan, *Building Canada: An Architectural History of Canadian Life* (Toronto 1967); also M. MacRae, *The Ancestral Roof: Domestic Architecture of Upper Canada* (Toronto 1963). Other works important here include: V.B. Blake and R. Greenhill, *Rural Ontario* (Toronto 1969); J.A.S. Evans, 'The Classical Tradition in Ontario,' *Canadian Geographical Journal*, LXIV, Feb. 1962, 60–9; M. Jukes, *New Life in Old Houses* (Toronto 1966), and Royal Architectural Institute of Canada, *Historic Architecture of Canada* (Ottawa 1966)

3 See M. Angus, *The Old Stones of Kingston before 1867* (Toronto 1966); J.I. Rempel, 'History and Development of Early Building Forms in Ontario,' *Ontario History*, LII, 1960, 235–44; LII, 1961, 1–35; and C.F.J. Whebell, 'Pre-Confederation Housing in Norfolk County,' *Ontario History*, LVII, 1966, 225–35. Other recent studies of this type include E. Gillespie, A. Cortes, and I. Smith, *Caledonia's Century Homes* (Caledonia 1967); J. Kinloch, 'Perth – Solidity and Style,' *Canadian Geographical Journal*, LXXIX, Aug. 1969, 40–51; P.J. Stokes, *Old Niagara on the Lake* (Toronto 1971); and A.G. McKay, G. Simmons, A.W. Wallace, eds., *Victorian Architecture in Hamilton* (Hamilton 1967).

4 Little seems to have been published on technical details and problems of construction in the century except for J.I. Rempel, *Building with Wood, and Other Aspects of Nineteenth Century Building in Ontario* (Toronto 1967), and to some extent P.J. Stokes, *Early Architecture of the Town and Township of Niagara* (1967).

5 *Canada Census 1891* (Ottawa 1893), I, 36–72 and *Canada Census 1901* (Ottawa 1906), IV, 336–42. The areal units used here are not the townships and the information listed does not always use the same categories as in earlier years, making detailed comparison of this record impossible.

6 These statistics are to be found in the *Appendices to the Journal of the Legislative Assembly of Upper Canada* after 1826, the *Census Report of the Canadas, 1851–2* (Quebec 1853), II, 403–31, and the *Census Report of the Canadas, 1860–1* (Quebec 1864), II, 288–317. On occasion in 1831 only district figures are given. Under these circumstances, the author sought out the statistics for the first subsequent year when these townships returned separately, determined the proportion of the district's total non-log accounted for by each township at that time, and applied these proportions to the district total in 1831 to obtain an approximate township value for that year. Like the assessment statistics, there are some discrepancies from decade to decade apparent in the eastern townships, particularly in the returns for Prescott and Russell. Also it should be remembered that, while frame, brick, and stone were the major materials, others such as plaster over log or frame (Blake and Greenhill, *Rural Ontario*, 28, 34) and the cobble construction around Paris and in Sydney Township (D.A. Smith, *At the Forks of the Grand* (Paris 1967), 40) were also in use by this date and are presumably included here, although in the case of plastered dwellings it is hard to imagine where.

7 All references to township surveys and to townships open to settlement are taken from *The List of Subdivided Townships in the Province of Ontario with Dates and Systems of Survey* (Toronto nd).

8 Many properties of course hosted a sequence of log structures beginning with a shanty and sometimes concluding with a substantial house of squared timber before building in other materials. See Malcolm Ross, ed., *Tiger Dunlop's Upper Canada* (Toronto 1967), 131

9 Ibid, 130

10 This figure of 20 per cent is arbitrary, taken as a reasonable break between the two stages in the absence of any definitive information as to when the replacement process began significant acceleration in the average township.

11 While some contemporary commentators suggested that an industrious colonist could build a home in frame on wealth generated from less than a decade's occupation (W. Catermole, *Emigration: The Advantages of Emigration to the Canadas* (London 1831), 133, and E.A. Talbot, *Five Years Residence in the Canadas* (London 1824), 103), Arthur has suggested that on the average it may have taken the better part of a generation (E.R. Arthur, *The Early Buildings of Ontario* (Toronto 1938), 9). In preparation of this paper, the writer attempted to determine the average time spent in each stage of development by comparing the individual township percentages for non-log in both 1851 and 1861 with the dates of their first settlement recorded in the *Ontario Agricultural Commission Report* (Toronto 1881, Appendix B, Vol. 2. The results were too varied to be incorporated in the text, but it would appear that something in the order of thirty years was often involved in stage one and an additional twenty years in stage two. Something then in the order of half a century frequently passed before more than half the housing was built in materials other than log, suggesting that Arthur may have been closer to the general truth than either of the more optimistic contemporaries.

12 Only about twenty townships in the province had as many as 100 non-log houses in 1831, most of these containing urban centres or budding urban places to complicate the picture of the rural scene. One wonders under the circumstances if more than a very few rural townships at that date were dominated by non-log housing. The literature is of little help on this point, but by 1841 the number of townships with 100 or more such dwellings had increased by three times and many of these additions were truly rural.

13 If those townships with more than 100 non-log structures are mapped for 1831 and 1841, this suggested earlier pattern is very evident as is that of discrete sub-core formation and coalescence subsequently discussed. While no absolute number of non-log houses can be considered critical in the movement of a township from one stage to another, it would seem likely that what is evident in one pattern is likely to be generally characteristic in the other.

14 The dramatic changes which railways often brought to the pioneer township is thoroughly discussed in J.J. Talman, 'The Impact of Railway Development on the Pioneer Community,' *Canadian Historical Association, Report*, 1955, 1–12.

15 The consideration of the urban scene raises an interesting issue of definition concerning structures included under housing. In the larger urban centres in the census, religious, collegiate, and other public institutional land is specifically included, but were they always covered elsewhere? In the assessment rolls, because such property was tax exempt, the answer may well be no. In the same light, were all business structures of the town included where they did not have resident owners or tenants? At least in the assessment records they appear to have been, but this, while likely, is difficult to determine for the census, although the author is of the opinion that all such buildings were covered in these figures.

16 This then makes the rural gradient in 1861, exclusive of urban considerations, as follows: 70 per cent in stage three, 25 per cent in stage two, and 5 per cent in stage one on the basis of 77,306 truly rural non-log houses at that date.

17 A.B. Jameson, *Winter Sudies and Summer Rambles in Canada* (Toronto 1823), 78 and T. Rolph, *A brief account, together with observations made during a visit to the West Indies, and a tour through the United States of America in part of the year 1832–3;*

together with a statistical account of Upper Canada (London 1836), 147, 157, 219

18 W.H. Smith, *The Canadian Gazetteer* (Toronto 1846), 62, 144, 150, and W.H. Smith, *Canada, Past, Present and Future* (Toronto 1850), I, 244; II, 104, 322

19 Ibid, I, 25; II, 387

20 Ibid, II, 172, 176

21 Ibid, I, 16, 122

22 J. Pickering, *Inquiries of an Emigrant* (London 1832), 74 and G.W. Warr, *Canada as it is; the emigrant's friend and guide to Upper Canada* (2nd ed., London 1847), 94–5

23 Ross, *Tiger Dunlop's Upper Canada*, 131 and Warr, *Canada as it is*, 95

24 Nobbs, 'Canadian Architecture,' 671

25 Ross, ed., *Tiger Dunlop's Upper Canada*, 131

26 In the census report for 1861, housing is given both by construction material and by the number of storeys, and the urban/rural dichotomy in the latter is very noticeable. Since taxation was partially based on the number of storeys, rural frugality may have been a factor here, but in urban areas the ability to pay this extra tax was a common element of status (Blake and Greenhill, *Rural Ontario*, 25) and the two or more storeyed house was more common, although many one storey houses were also to be found.

27 Although balloon frame was first used in Chicago in the early thirties, it is difficult to determine when it came into common use in Ontario. Rempel, *Building in Wood*, 114–27

28 Nobbs, 'Canadian Architecture,' 665–71 and Gowan, *Building Canada*, 40–7

29 Blake and Greenhill, *Rural Ontario*, 34

30 The evidence for the use of exterior paint in the rural countryside is somewhat conflicting. Some writers, summarized by MacRae (*Ancestral Roof*, 25-48) would suggest it was fairly common at least on the homes of wealthier rural persons. Alternately, several sources dealing perhaps with the 'everyman' of the period (C. Haight, *Country Life in Canada Fifty Years Ago* (Toronto 1885), 88, 112; W.H.G. Kingston, *Western Wanderings, or a Pleasure Tour in the Canadas* (London 1856), II, 17; and Smith, *Canada, Past, Present and Future*, I, 220-3) would imply that paint was used sparingly, if at all, by most settlers of British extraction, although possibly more commonly employed by other cultural groups. Considering the trouble required to gather together the basic materials to make paint and also to create the colourant in the home (for interesting insight into just what was involved see A.W. Chase, *Dr. Chase's Receipts* (10th ed., Ann Arbor 1867) as well as the superb weathering qualities of first growth timber (see E. Sloane, *Our Vanishing Landscape* (New York 1955), 9) our frugal ancestors may have regarded paint as unnecessary and costly decoration and may have discounted any preservative qualities it might have, as indeed do some authorities even today (see R. Roberts, *Your Engineered House* (New York 1964), 22–3). The author is very much in the debt of Mr T. Hinckley for many leads and much help in researching this topic

31 In addition to comments made by Angus, *Old Stones of Kingston*, 34 on this matter are those of A.M. Machar, *The Story of Old Kingston* (Toronto 1908), 90, 99

32 G.M. Adam, *History of the County of York* (Toronto 1885), I, 229

33 Jameson, *Winter Studies*, 94 and Rolph, *Brief Account*, 157, 238

34 Smith, *Canada, Past, Present and Future*, I, 244; II, 104

35 MacRae would suggest that brick was available from an early date from brickyards (MacRae, *Ancestral Roof*, 17) but the author has found little evidence of this. At the outset, at least, brick often was made under contract by an itinerant craftsman from clay 'found' on the property. Later brick-making may have been a seasonal farm occupation (see R. McKenzie, *Leeds and Grenville: the First Two Centuries* (Toronto 1967), 180–1). Even as late as the forties and early fifties (see Rempel, *Building with Wood*, 229–37) unburned brick, a highly mooted but relatively crude material, was in use in rural areas. By the fifties, however, there were more than forty brickyards in the province and the

largest, supplying Toronto, appears to have been near Yorkville (Smith, *Canada, Past, Present and Future*, II, 19)

36 *The Geological Survey of Canada; a Report of Progress from its Commencement to 1863* (Montreal 1863), 801

37 This is well documented, for example, at Bytown in 1836 (L. Brault, *Ottawa Old and New* (Ottawa 1946), 118–19), at London in 1845 (Smith, *Canada, Past, Present and Future*, II, 91), at Toronto in 1849 (F.H. Armstrong, 'The Rebuilding of Toronto after the Great Fire of 1849,' *Ontario History*, LIII, 1961, 234–49), at Port Hope about 1856 (W.A. Craik, *Port Hope: Historical Sketches* (Port Hope 1901), 124), and at Galt during the fifties (G.G. Monroe, ed., *Picturesque Canada* (Toronto 1883) II, 464).

38 The early bylaws of the town and city of London are an excellent example of this. *History of the County of Middlesex* (London 1889), 261

The Security of Land:
Mortgaging in Toronto Gore Township
1835-95

David P. Gagan

The history of nineteenth-century Ontario can be written, from one perspective, in terms of the continuing experience of successive generations of rural families who were the essential instruments in the forging of a society whose social, economic, cultural, and demographic characteristics, and hence the region's identity, remained fundamentally agrarian until well into the twentieth century. The historian intent on documenting the evolution of this society's identifying characteristics must examine the economic circumstances of these rural families. Their economic condition in point of time, over time, and in comparison to that of their neighbours or to the lot of preceding and subsequent generations reveals much about the environment which shaped their experience, about the relative quality of life they enjoyed, and the factors which determined their ability at best to move up the social scale, at worst merely to survive. Among the indices of a rural society's economic condition the extent of its indebtedness, particularly debt incurred by borrowing capital on the security of real property, affords the historian a useful avenue of approach to the problems of rural society, to the question of the relative security and stability of rural life, and to the social ramifications of economic behaviour.

We are accustomed to think of the nineteenth-century agriculturist as having no security beyond his equity in his land and the sweat of his brow, and therefore as perennially dependent on capital borrowed from institutional lenders on the security of his land at high interest rates and unfavorable terms; or, worse, unable to borrow at any price or under any conditions because of the high risk and low profits involved in farm mortgaging, and the general unavailability of long-term investment capital. Perpetually in debt, or in search of credit, and a poor manager to boot, the 'average' yeoman apparently fought a losing battle with his economic environment until he or his sons escaped, at the first opportunity, to a new rural or urban frontier.[1] Whether or not this is, in broad outline, an accurate reflection of the economic circumstances of nineteenth-century rural Ontarians remains to be seen, for as yet no comprehensive analysis of rural indebtedness in the province has been undertaken, comparable, for example, to Allan C. Bogue's study of a similar phenomenon in an American community.[2] Where the problem has received consideration has usually been from the institutional lenders' viewpoint, or as a footnote to the larger question of banking, fiscal, and monetary regulation.[3]

This essay represents an attempt to shed some light on the problem of rural indebtedness by inquiring into one nineteenth-century farming community's record of debt incurred through mortgages secured by land. It should be stated at the outset that the methodology employed in this study conforms to the methodological requirements of a larger project aimed at reconstituting from routinely generated records the nineteenth-century population of Peel County in order to document the evolution of its social, economic, demographic, and cultural characteristics. This involves collecting all of the surviving records of resident families at regular decennial intervals, linking them over time, and subjecting them to quantitative analysis. Thus, the mortgage records employed here do not represent all of the indentures available, but rather those still in force, or coming into force, at the beginning of each decade. The sample does include, however, the records of mortgage indebtedness of the whole population of the township at each survey point. The statistics cited are derived from analyses of these indentures in point of time and longitudinally across the period 1841–91. The chronological limits of the study reflect the absence of reliable data in the preceding and following time periods.[4]

How many landholders mortgaged their property, how frequently, and for what purposes? What was the extent of the community's, and individual, indebtedness? What was the cost of borrowed capital, and did those costs include, for the debtor, the probability of losing his property and the prospect of having to uproot his family? Was there a hard core of perennial mortgagors? What sources of capital were available and on what terms? To whom did the agriculturist customarily indenture himself? Finally, do the patterns of mortgage indebtedness in this community reflect the influence of economic developments taking place in the broader context of the region and the nation? The answer to these and other questions have been sought among the mortgage records of Toronto Gore Township.

The smallest of Peel County's five township, 'the Gore,' as its name implies, is a wedge-shaped tract of land encompassing approximately 19,000 acres on the eastern edge of the county. Today much of the township consists of suburban housing and commercial developments, but in the nineteenth century it represented the best agricultural land in the county, consistently producing the highest yields of the area's most valuable export commodity, wheat. As a result, it was also the most extensively cultivated township in a period when uncultivated land went untaxed.[5] Settled later than the other townships of Peel, but linked from the beginning to major markets or transhipment centres by good roads, by mid-century the township had developed a thriving agricultural economy and a production record which sent land values soaring in the 1850s. By 1860 an acre of Toronto Gore land cost about $48, an increase of nearly 300 per cent over 1851. Thereafter, with the exception of the 1860s when land value declined somewhat, land in the township continued to be inordinately expensive and in high demand, considering the fact that cheaper, vacant land was available elsewhere in the county right through the 1870s. It is also worth noting that there seems to have been a relative absence of the practice of subdividing land through sales or inheritance, with the result that farms tended to be substantial both in size and price.[6] Finally, because of its advanced state of agricultural development Toronto Gore township was also more vulnerable to external economic influences than isolated, 'backwoods' communities such as Caledon Township. Whether it is possible, or even desirable, to attempt to generalize from the economic experience of Toronto Gore's landholders is, however, quite another matter.

Contrary to expectation, mortgages against property were not as common among the landholders of Toronto Gore as might have been expected given the excessive costs of land acquisition, concentration on a single, extremely vulnerable crop, and the persistence of unfavourable market conditions for half the timespan of this study. The mortgaged population of the township does not include all, most, or even a bare majority of proprietors in any decade. Indeed, indentured owners never represent more than 37 per cent of the total in any decade (the 1870s accounted for this peak), and throughout the period 1831–91 they constitute substantially less than a third of all landholders. Moreover, of those proprietors who did encumber their land nearly three-fifths did so on one occasion only, and one-fifth acquired two mortgages. Plainly, this was not a society of chronic debtors.

On the other hand, 20 per cent of the mortgagors acquired a minimum of three and as many as ten indentures in the course of a lifetime. For example, the McGees, James and James, jr who occupied lot 14 concession 7 north were never without mortgages, usually two at a time between 1851 and 1881. Their mortgages each involved an average debt of $500 and, though they invariably discharged them, both father and son seem to have been constantly in need of capital. Similarly, Edward Kelly and his wife (later widow) Margaret of lot 14 concession 10 north were indentured, through numerous small mortgages, for better than $1600 in every decade. Both the Kellys and the McGees appear to have been chronic debtors who had to borrow to survive. Conversely, Joseph Figg who sometimes carried as many as three mortgages, and John Gardhouse who successfully amortized ten very substantial mortgages between 1861 and 1881, fall into quite another category. Figg regularly loaned money to his neighbours, while Gardhouse's mortgages were the means by which he bought out his neighbours and established himself as one of the townships great proprietors. There was, then, a hard core of multiple mortgagors, but it consisted of no particular stratum of society exclusively, cutting across class lines in an altogether inconsistent fashion.

Similarly, categorizing mortgagors by occupation yields little evidence that any occupational group was mortgaged disproportionately in relation to any other. In this township which contained no towns or villages of consequence and no large manufacturing or processing establishments beyond a grist mill and tannery, yeomen and gentlemen farmers together comprise more than two-thirds of the mortgagors. The remaining third represent more than a dozen occupations consisting primarily of artisans and mechanics who supplied the agricultural population with goods and services. Merchants, blacksmiths, and, for some reason, publicans seemed, however, to require capital more frequently than other businessmen. In any event, it is evident 1) that mortgaging of real estate, for whatever purposes, was a practice common only to a small, but nevertheless consistent, percentage of the township's landowners; and 2) that these mortgagors did not collectively constitute a significant class of perpetually indentured proprietors.

This general impression of extreme moderation in both the extent and the frequency of mortgaging among the landholders of Toronto Gore must be tempered, however, by the record of indebtedness compiled by those who did indenture their property. Their needs apparently were great, for in only one decade, the 1860s, does the indebtedness of the typical mortgagor fall below roughly 80 per cent of the market value of an average farm.[7] In fact, in the early decades of settlement, the 1830s and 1840s, average individual indebtedness considerably exceeded the value of a mortgaged farm, a reflection of the disparity between the costs of acquiring land and the expenses involved in settling, clearing, and cultivating it. Perhaps more to the point, between 1831 and 1861 the number of mortgagors increased absolutely by 400 per cent and by 16 per cent in relation to the total number of proprietors. Thereafter, both the number and the percentage of mortgagors remained virtually constant except for a slight increase in the 1870s. At the same time, the average number of mortgages per mortgagee held constant while the percentage of multiple mortgagors remained the same or was significantly less than the 1841 total in every decade but the 1880s. Yet the total mortgaged debt of the community increased, with only a slight reprieve in the 1860s, in every decade until by 1891 it stood at 850 per cent above the 1841 figure. In 1891 a typical mortgagor was in debt to the tune of $3,180.00, triple the average debt of 1841; and the $216,247.00 represented by the outstanding mortgages in 1891 was equivalent to a debt of more than $1000.00 for every proprietor in the community, as opposed to $220.00 in 1841. The inevitable conclusion is that the indentured minority were mortgaged, as the saying goes, 'to the hilt' from beginning to end.

Perhaps the pattern was inevitable, for each decade brought with it a new reason to borrow capital. In the thirties and forties men borrowed to put new land into production. In the fifties they borrowed to expand production in anticipation of new markets, then borrowed again to keep their heads above water when the bubble burst in 1857. The early sixties were more settled, but as the decade pro-

TABLE 1

Mortgagors, mortgages, and indebtedness Toronto Gore Township 1841–91

YEAR	NO PROPRIETORS	NO MORTGAGORS	NO MULTIPLE MORTGAGORS	NO MORTGAGES	TOTAL DEBT	AVERAGE DEBT	AVERAGE VALUE OF A FARM
1841	103	17 (16.5%)	5	24	£5764	£240.3.0	£176.5.0
1851	160	39 (24.4%)	12	53	$ 52,600.00	$1348.72	$1110.00
1861	193	62 (32.1%)	18	87	$161,484.00	$2604.58	$2779.00
1871	201	65 (32.3%)	12	78	$112,196.00	$1726.09	$2785.00
1881	213	77 (26.2%)	19	108	$210,952.00	$2739.64	$3502.00
1891	209	68 (32.5%)	24	97	$216,247.00	$3180.00	$4046.00

gressed the trend toward farm modernization sustained the need for capital. The seventies, of course, produced both widespread economic depression and a series of bad harvests, and with them a staggering increase in mortgaged debt in Toronto Gore. The next decade brought no measurable reprieve.[8] Yet through all this, the great majority of the township's proprietors were able to avoid indenturing their land, or chose not to employ capital borrowed on the security of their land. Perhaps they had access to other sources of capital,[9] or were sufficiently affluent to avoid borrowing entirely. Their true circumstances remain a mystery. All that can be said with certainty is that those who did resort to mortgage financing used the security represented by their land to the fullest possible extent.

Within the context of these general patterns of mortgaging in Toronto Gore it is possible to distinguish, in a broad sense, among some of the reasons for encumbering land. That is to say, the available records permit the historian to segregate primary mortgages acquired to capitalize the purchase of new or additional land from secondary mortgages intended for purposes other than land acquisition. It is not possible, unfortunately, to elaborate on the uses to which secondary financing was put, although its possible uses are endless: to underwrite capital improvements to the farm, to acquire modern machinery, to purchase livestock, to tide the borrower over until his harvest was marketed, or merely to see him through a period of personal hardship.

For whatever purpose they were intended, secondary mortgages account for the majority of the indentures entered into by the residents of Toronto Gore, more than 54 per cent of the total. At the same time however, they represent only 42 per cent of the community's total indebtedness between 1841 and 1891. The discrepancy is probably a reflection of the need for more frequent, but at the same time more limited borrowing associated with the need for constant improvement and short-term financing of capital intensive projects. For example, a secondary mortgage averaged only 47 per cent of the value of a farm, as compared with an average of nearly 80 per cent for primary mortgages. Similarly, a typical secondary mortgage might represent about 57 per cent of the value of an average primary mortgage. In short, a man might borrow a large sum of money once to acquire his land, and several smaller amounts subsequently to improve, or protect, his original investment. This inference is supported by the data on primary mortgages which account for less than half (45.5 per cent) of the Toronto Gore mortgages, but for nearly 58 per cent of their total value. On balance, then, it would seem that maintaining a farm or other property was the principal cause of indebtedness in the community while acquiring land produced the most burdensome debts.

These generalizations ignore, however, periodic deviations from the general patterns of mortgage use, deviations which seem to reflect accurately contemporary economic conditions. In two decades, the 1830s and the 1850s, secondary mortgages represent not only the greatest number of indentures but also the greatest share of the community's mortgaged debt. This seems to support, in the former case, the assumption that during the period of settlement the costs of settling, clearing, and putting land into production involved heavier charges than did the acquisition of land itself.[10] In the next decade, the 1840s, rapidly increasing land values and a poorer class of immigrants apparently combined to reverse the situation, since primary mortgages in this decade account for the largest percentage of both indentures and indebtedness. These conditions ought to have persisted through the 1850s as well given the now skyrocketing price of land in Toronto Gore. Between 1850 and 1860 the amount of money involved in an average real estate transaction increased by 70 per cent, while the average amount of land involved in a transaction declined by more than 20 per cent. Nevertheless, new landowners seemed to have little difficulty underwriting their purchases from their savings. Only 22 per cent of them acquired mortgages as part of a transaction, and primary mortgages account for substantially less than 40 per cent of mortgaged debts in this decade. The impetus for both new and established proprietors to capitalize improvements and increased production existed in the spirit of optimism engendered by the 1854 reciprocity treaty and the wheat boom created by the Crimean War. When optimism turned to despair with the collapse of 1857, many had to borrow to keep the wolf from the door.[11] Thus, by 1861 secondary mortgages acounted for 71 per cent of the township's indentures, and for more than 60 per cent of their value.

In the 1860s secondary mortgages rapidly declined as a factor in mortgage indebtedness in Toronto Gore, accounting for less than 25 per cent of the mortgaged debt. Conversely, more than 60 per cent of the mortgagors and their mortgages, and in excess of 75 per cent of mortgaged indebtedness represent real estate transactions. Among the reasons that might be invoked to explain this change the most convincing is that land and debts acquired in the 1850s in a rash of speculation proved to be the undoing of many proprietors who were forced to sell out, often at a loss, within a few years. The land records for the township indicate, for example, that more than half the sixty-six real estate transactions which took place in the 1860s involved indentured proprietors whose debts had not been discharged when the sale of their land took place. Interestingly enough, nearly half of these 'failures' were non-resident proprietors representing almost 80 per cent of all the absentee owners. In any event, it seems evident that incoming, and less affluent proprietors acquired both the land and the debts of the vacating owners in the form of primary mortgages, while the established owners assiduously avoided new commitments.

The purposes of borrowing closely conform, in the 1870s and 1880s, to the broad outlines previously described, though with two qualifications. The first is

TABLE 2

Primary and secondary mortgages

Year	PRIMARY MORTGAGES			SECONDARY MORTGAGES		
	% of mortgages	% of mortgagors	% of total value	% of mortgages	% of mortgagors	% of total value
1841	40.0	50.0	46.5	60.0	50.0	53.5
1851	55.8	59.6	61.0	44.2	40.4	39.0
1861	28.7	31.0	37.8	71.3	69.0	62.2
1871	60.3	60.3	75.5	39.7	39.7	24.5
1881	39.3	48.2	60.4	60.7	51.8	39.6
1891	49.5	49.3	65.1	50.5	50.7	34.9
Averages	45.6	49.7	57.7	54.4	50.3	42.3

Table includes new mortgages only, in each decade.

that the depression of 1873, which brought with it a rapid increase in land turn-over, in the use of property mortgages, and in the extent of the community's indebtedness, produced what appears to be a curiously anomalous situation. The number of primary mortgagors remained virtually unchanged from the previous decade, as did the number of mortgages for which they were responsible, although the value of their mortgages increased by nearly 12 per cent. On the other hand, the number of secondary mortgagors increased by 60 per cent, secondary mortgages by more than 100 per cent and their value by 200 per cent. Yet, in relation to each other, primary mortgagors continued to account for more than 60 per cent of the mortgaged debt in 1881 but less than 40 per cent of the mortgages, while secondary mortgagors were responsible for more than 60 per cent of the mortgages but less than 40 per cent of the debt. Tight money, as might be expected, simply forced more proprietors to borrow more frequently in smaller amounts; and new owners, lacking ready cash but anxious to buy a good farm at any price ($51.00 an acre in 1880 as opposed to $36.00 in 1870) were forced to borow, on the average, up to 85 per cent of the value of their land. The next decade seems to have brought some relief, particularly in the availability of capital for land acquisition,[12] since the average value of a primary mortgage decreased while the number and total value of primary mortgages increased substantially.

The second qualification is that from about the time of Confederation onward, indentures to underwrite the acquisition of family-owned land become a significant factor in the record of mortgage indebtedness in Toronto Gore township, account-ing for an ever increasing percentage of both primary and secondary mortgages. Indeed, the indentures for Toronto Gore suggest that for every son who acquired his patrimony in return for one dollar and his 'filial love and devotion,' another and sometimes two more paid full market value. Moreover, the indentures arising out of most of these intra-familial transactions often had far reaching social and economic consequences for the families and the individuals involved. Consequently, they deserve special treatment here.

Many of these indentures are mortgages in name only. In fact they are performance bonds posted by a son who, in return for his father's land, guaranteed his parents security in their old age. The mortgages are therefore open-ended, and their 'cost' to a mortgagor depended very much on the length of time that his parents survived. For example, when Christopher Burrell indentured himself to his father, Thomas, in return for the family homestead, he did so for a minimum of £500 calculated on the basis of the following conditions: that he provide a home for his parents, supply them with food and all the other necessities of life, have their clothes laundered weekly and give them £5 a year in pocket money. Failing this he was to pay his parents £60 *per annum* while they both lived and £30 annually to the surviving parent.[13] Similarly, John O'Donnell acquired his stepfather's land for an annuity of £100, but in addition guaranteed his stepsister's dowry of £400.[14]

If the indentures in respect of annuities represented the old age security of the farmer who was land rich but money poor, indentures arising out of wills were, for the same individual, a means of guaranteeing his family's survival after his death. Of the ninety-six estates of deceased Toronto Gore residents probated between 1851 and 1812, nearly 30 per cent oblige principal heirs, as a condition of inheriting land, to discharge direct monetary bequests and annuities to surviving spouses, children, and relatives. A.R.M. Lower has called this the English-Canadian system of inheritance[15] and its effect on those who experienced it was to start life burdened with the debts of a well-intentioned but impecunious parent, legacies which averaged more than two thousand dollars for those estates so devised. Almost invariably the inheritor of the deceased's lands under these conditions could be found encumbering his patrimony shortly after probate. George Bailey, for example, inherited his father's farm in 1880 on condition that he commence payment, at the end of five years, on bequests totalling $6200 and annuities of $100. The 1891 mortgage records indicate that George Bailey owed two mortgages representing $8300.[16] The list might go on to include nearly 5 per cent of all the Toronto Gore mortgages contracted between 1861 and 1892, mortgages representing more than 4 per cent of the community's mortgaged debt in the same period.

Here again one generation of the rural family presumed to make its successor responsible for the immediate and future well-being of the family, frequently defined in terms of all those who survive. Thus some heirs, of whom John Lawrence and Michael Dougherty are good examples,[17] found themselves saddled with an annuity to be paid to their mother, dowries for their sisters, monetary gifts to their brothers, the costs of educating nieces and nephews, gifts of land or money to their own minor children, and even perpetual care of an infirm or invalid relative – all for the gift of a farm into which they had already ploughed many years of hard labour. If the nineteenth-century family farm was, as the Rowell-Sirois commissioners argued, 'a mutual welfare association,' it was an association defined in the broadest sense of kinship whose welfare often depended on the willingness of the younger generation to mortgage its future. As T.W. Magrath remarked to his British correspondent several years earlier, children indeed represented the 'riches' of the Canadian farmer.[18]

The extent to which the level of mortgage indebtedness, for whatever purpose, in Toronto Gore reflects the relative availability of capital to be loaned on the security of real estate is a question that must go begging. There does seem to be some agreement among scholars, at least by inference, that farm mortgages would have been more common in nineteenth-century Ontario had greater supplies of domestic long-term investment capital been available.[19] All that can be documented with certainty here is the availability of capital as the mortgagors of Toronto Gore found it, and the conditions under which it was loaned to them.

Broadly speaking, two sources of mortgage funds were available to nineteenth-century Ontarians, institutional and private lenders. The former included the province's chartered banks, savings and loan companies, building societies, insurance companies, charitable and educational institutions, as well as foreign mortgage companies. The proprietors of Toronto Gore tapped all of these sources; but as might be expected building societies (the Canada Permanent Building Society is the best example) and the trust and loan companies, both of which appeared in force about mid-century in response to the growing demand for mortgage capital, attracted most of the business that mortgagors conducted with institutional lenders. In fact, building societies and trust companies together held more than three-quarters of the mortgages underwritten by institutions between 1841 and 1891. Chartered banks, conversely, accounted for 16 per cent of the institutionally held mortgages but less than 9 per cent of the borrowed capital, compared with more than 85 per cent for the building societies and loan companies. As expected, banks in fact cease to be represented among institutional lenders in Toronto Gore after 1861, having been forbidden by statute to lend money on the security of real estate after they overextended themselves in the speculative climate of the 1850s.[20] Thereafter, building societies dominate the institutional field.

The fact nevertheless remains that these institutional lenders represent the least significant source of mortgage funds for the residents of Toronto Gore. Even at the peak of their activities in the township in the 1850s the institutional lenders never captured more than 17 per cent of the mortgage market, and thereafter they steadily decline in importance until, by 1891, they account for only 1 per cent of the value of outstanding mortgage loans. Assessing this trend in 1876, the president of one foreign mortgage company opined that the farmers of Ontario were so affluent that soon they would have no further need of mortgage capital.[21] This was clearly not the case in Toronto Gore where, as we have already seen, mortgage indebtedness increased, unabated, in every decade save one after 1841. What was happening was that the institutions' already minimal share of the market was steadily being assimilated by the private lenders who were, always had been, and remained the principal source of mortgage capital for Toronto Gore's proprietors.

In this respect, Toronto Gore fails to conform to the situation which seems to have existed generally throughout the province, a situation characterized by a shortage of domestic capital which was available in limited amounts at very high rates of interest. Yet private lenders never account for less than 83 per cent of the total value of extant mortgages in Toronto Gore, and in all but two decades, the 1840s and 1850s, they account for more than 90 per cent of the borrowed capital, reaching a peak of nearly 99 per cent in 1891. Nor is there any evidence that the terms exacted by these private lenders were more onerous than those of the institutions. Indeed, with the exception of the briefly inflated interest rates of 1857-60, private lenders behaved as though they too were bound (as they were not) by the laws against usury.[22] Perhaps this is some indication that competition for business was keen even among the private lenders, competition which the institutional lenders could not weather. For whatever reason, the mortgagors of Toronto Gore indentured themselves most frequently not merely to private lenders, but moreover to individuals whose social and economic standing were comparable to their own, individuals who in all probability were friends and neighbours as well.

This conclusion emerges most forcefully from a comparative analysis of the geographical location of private lenders and their occupational distribution. For the purposes of this analysis, mortgagees have been segregated into two groups, residents and non-residents, and the latter category has ben subdivided according to place of residence – specifically, elsewhere in Peel County, other Ontario counties, and the city of Toronto.

With minor fluctuations, the mortgage market represented by Toronto Gore township was dominated, in the period under study, by non-resident private lenders. The exceptional decades were the 1840s and 1850s when borrowers looked increasingly to institutional lenders and to their immediate neighbours and relatives for capital. Nevertheless, non-resident private mortgagees never account for less than 49 per cent of the capital borrowed in any decade, and in three decades for more than 70 per cent of it, reaching a peak of nearly 80 per cent in the 1880s. Significantly, residents of Toronto provided the bulk of these private loans in the 1830s and 1840s, further evidence of the Queen City's economic influence on its immediate hinterland. After 1861, however, a perceptible shift takes places as the numbers of Toronto-based lenders rapidly decline, to be replaced by residents of the other townships, towns and village of Peel County. By 1861 residents of Toronto

TABLE 3
Sources of rural credit
Toronto Gore Township, Peel County, Ontario 1841–81

Year	RESIDENT LENDERS			INSTITUTIONAL LENDERS			NON-RESIDENT LENDERS		
	% of lenders	% of mortgages	% of total value	% of lenders	% of mortgages	% of total value	% of lenders	% of mortgages	% of total value
1841	31.57	25.0	32.66	5.26	4.16	8.67	63.15	70.83	58.65
1851	31.91	28.3	29.26	12.76	22.64	17.0	55.31	49.05	53.74
1861	40.32	34.48	38.11	8.06	13.79	16.71	51.61	51.72	45.16
1871	23.80	19.23	26.31	1.58	5.13	4.19	74.60	70.51	69.47
1881	22.97	15.74	16.94	4.05	5.60	3.39	72.97	78.70	79.65

held only 42 per cent of all Toronto Gore indentures compared with 70 per cent in 1841; and by 1881 their loans accounted for about 16 per cent of the extant mortgages. Meanwhile, residents of Peel County, who were not represented among mortgagors in 1841, held notes representing more than half the mortgages owed to non-resident lenders in 1881. Equally important is the fact that by 1881 more than 40 per cent of the Peel County mortgagees were residents of Brampton. This seems to suggest that Brampton, which was little more than a crossroads in 1851, swiftly developed as a new focus of regional economic activity partially supplanting some of the functions and services formerly provided by the metropolis.

An equally vital source of capital for the proprietors of Toronto Gore were rural residents of neighbouring counties, especially York. Although these individuals never account for more than 30 per cent of the extant mortgages, they invariably capitalized more than 20 per cent of them in any decade. Since the great majority of these mortgagors resided in the townships of York immediately adjacent to Toronto Gore and were in reality close neighbours of their clients, there is again striking evidence of the extent to which some forms of economic activity were localized, and becoming increasingly so, as the nineteenth century wore on. This raises a question, of course, about the role played by resident mortgagees who decline in importance as a source of capital between 1841 and 1881. One obvious reason for their dwindling involvement is that the township and hence the population, especially those with money to lend, was a comparatively narrow field for credit of any sort. Not surprisingly, then, the bulk of the mortgages held by residents are those taken back as part of a land transactions involving either newcomers or family members. In any event, it may be quite misleading to distinguish, in the long run, among those mortgagees who are residents of Toronto Gore, those who live elsewhere in Peel, and those who live in other counties. As the foregoing sug-

TABLE 4

Private non-resident lenders 1841–81

Year	PEEL COUNTY		TORONTO CITY		OTHER COUNTIES	
	% of lenders	% of mortgages	% of lenders	% of mortgages	% of lenders	% of mortgages
1841			66.66	70.58	25.0	23.52
1851	26.92	26.92	34.61	34.61	30.76	30.76
1861	31.25	24.44	25.00	42.22	31.25	22.22
1871	40.44	38.18	36.17	40.00	21.27	20.00
1881	46.29	51.76	14.81	16.47	38.88	30.58

This table does not include categories for non-resident lenders living outside the province or in other countries.

gests, they were all part of a single rural community defined both in geographical and in economic terms. The fact that more than 3 per cent of the mortgages stipulate that no interest will be charged by the mortgagees, and the fact that many of the Brampton and York County mortgagees can be identified as either retired relatives or neighbours of their clients, are evidence that this 'community' extended well beyond the concession lines of Toronto Gore township in a social context as well.

The occupations of these private lenders, resident and non-resident alike, indicate that all classes of society, though not necessarily with equal intensity, had capital to lend on good security. The list of mortgagees who held indentures of Toronto Gore land includes students, labourers, photographers, carpenters, chairmakers, school teachers, innkeepers, clergymen, spinsters, housewives, millers, blacksmiths, merchants, and, of course, farmers. Merchants, the traditional source of rural credit,[23] fall well down the list behind widows, housewives, gentlemen, and farmers. These five groups, however, together account for more than 80 per cent of the private lenders, with the remaining 20 per cent distributed almost evenly across the other occupations noted. Unquestionably, though, when a yeoman of the Gore required capital he normally sought it among men of his own vocation. Farmers and 'gentlemen,' usually retired farmers, constitute more than two-thirds of the total number of private mortgagees, nearly two-thirds of the non-resident private lenders and almost 80 per cent of the resident private mortgagees.

These figures attest, perhaps, to the relative affluence of area farmers who, from the very beginning, were able to capitalize their own operations and to meet their neighbours' demands for capital as well from time to time. For every yeoman who needed capital, in short, there was another to supply it, and as many more 'local' residents with investment capital to lend as demand required.

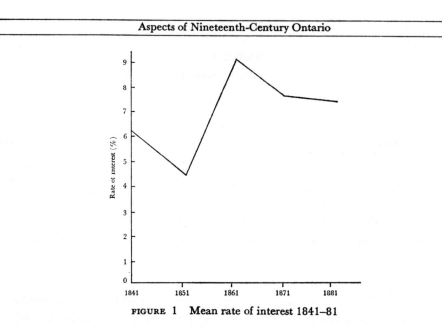

FIGURE 1   Mean rate of interest 1841–81

For the potential mortgagor then, as now, two factors apart from availability undoubtedly determined the extent to which he was willing and able to borrow capital: the cost of borrowing and the terms of amortization. It is traditional wisdom that the farmer sought moderate rates of interest and long-term financing.[24] As to the former, the editor of the *Farmer's Advocate* ventured the opinion, in 1872, that Ontario's institutional lenders operated 'a lot of shaving shops,' while the smaller fry ran 'robbing dens.'[25] Yet the mortgagors of Toronto Gore do not seem to have been the victims of usurious interest charges. Between 1841 and 1881 the average rate of interest sustained by their loans exceeded 7½ per cent in only one decade, the 1850s, when the average rate rose to 9.2 per cent. This increase was due almost exclusively to the effects of the depression of 1857 which briefly produced interest rates as high as 16 per cent and an average rate, for the years 1858–61, of 11½ per cent. Thereafter, although interest rates did not fall to their pre-depression levels of 4–5 per cent, they stabilized at a mean rate of about 7½ per cent for two decades, then gradually declined to 7 per cent or less toward the end of the century. In this respect, at least, Toronto Gore mortgagors were considerably better off than the average Ontario farmer who might expect to pay anywhere from 2 to 5 per cent more than the rates which prevailed in this township.[26]

Undoubtedly the comparative moderation of the rates charged to Toronto Gore borrowers has much to do with the predominance of local, private lenders who evidently did not take advantage of the laws against usury which gave individuals complete laissez-faire to charge whatever the traffic would bear. Whether these moderate rates were the result of competition or good will is, however, a matter for speculation.

The only discrimination in rates that the borrower was likely to encounter relates to the purposes for which the borrowed funds were to be used. A survey of 100 primary, and 144 secondary mortgages reveals that the mean rate of interest on the former was 7.3 per cent, while the latter yielded an average rate of 8.4 per cent. More to the point, perhaps, the most common rate of interest on primary mortgages was 6 per cent and for junior mortgages 8 per cent. The 2 per cent differential may reflect the private lenders' assumption that secondary financing involved greater risk. Whereas institutional lenders scrupulously inspected applicants' properties and refused to accept encumbered land as security,[27] the private lenders appear to have had no such qualms (as evidenced by the number of mortgagees with multiple debts); but the price they exacted was a higher interest rate. As well, because secondary mortgages were often intended to underwrite such capital intensive projects as mechanization, barn building, or improved housing which produced little measurable increase in the actual value of a farm and required only limited, short term capital, lenders undoubtedly charged higher rates of interest as a reflection of the greater risk involved in unproductive borrowing and to increase their return over the short span of the loan.

In this regard, although ten, fifteen, and twenty year mortgages were not uncommon in Toronto Gore, especially toward the end of the century, most of the mortgages, in fact nearly 87 per cent of them, stipulated amortization over six years or less. The reasons for the persistence of short-term borrowing are not clear. Capital for long-term investment in farm mortgages was not generally available, according to most sources, until the last two decades of the nineteenth century. On the other hand, the government of Canada introduced and enacted legislation in 1880, presumably at the behest of borrowers, guaranteeing mortgagors of real property the freedom to discharge their obligations of longer than five years' duration at the end of five years on payment of three months' penalty interest.[28] This would appear to offer some evidence of a preference among mortgagors for shorter terms, or at least for less restrictive conditions, to acommodate suddenly improved circumstances. One thing is apparent: through good times and bad, whether their debts were great or small, the mortgagors of Toronto Gore rarely encumbered their lands beyond the immediate and foreseeable future. And since they managed, for the most part, to discharge their obligations on time without apparent hardship (without acquiring another mortgage, that is), it must be assumed that they were both able and willing to accommodate the costs and the terms of their indentures. Indeed, if their wills are any indication of their condition, many of the mortgagors of Toronto Gore seem to have been quite sophisticated in their use of mortgaged debt, using short-term and relatively inexpensive capital to underwrite improvements while their own savings were securely invested in stocks, bonds, and – mortgages.

The question that remains to be answered is whether mortgaged indebtedness was the cause of any measurable degree of social and economic dislocation in this community. Unfortunately, the most reliable gauge of the burdens of indebtedness, foreclosures, cannot be documented from available sources. Similarly, the absence of discharge dates in the registry records is less likely to be evidence of bad debts than of an absent-minded clerk. What can be documented, however, are instances of mortgagors disposing of their property with undischarged mortgages still to be paid off. By eliminating, with the aid of wills, transactions that occur as the result of deaths and, from the land records, transactions related to retirement within families, it may be possible to isolate with some qualifications those mortgagors who succumbed to the burden of their debts, bearing in mind that nineteenth-century land law differed in one vital respect from modern practice. The mortgagor, in the act of indenturing himself, in fact conveyed full title to his property until the mortgage was successfully discharged. The mortgagor became, in short, the mortgagee's tenant for the duration of the indenture. This undoubtedly helps to account for both the obvious restraint exercised by the farmers of the Gore in indenturing their land, and the short terms of their indentures; and it lends some credence to the argument that the disposal of mortgaged land may imply hardship on the part of mortgagors.

In the half century under study, approximately 44 per cent of the indentured proprietors of Toronto Gore sold their land before they had discharged their mortgages. As might be expected, there are significant fluctuations in the 'failure rate' from decade to decade. In the period of settlement, the 1830s, more than 47 per cent of the mortgaged proprietors disposed of their land while still in debt. The 1950s similarly exacted a high toll as the rate of turnover among mortgagors reached 58 per cent of the total number and nearly all of the non-resident owner-debtors. Thereafter, the number of 'failures' declined to 38 per cent, increasing slightly during the years of depression after 1873. This surprisingly high rate of turnover among mortgaged landowners, never less than a third of the total in any decade, suggests that even amid the general prosperity characteristic of economic conditions in this township mortgage debt may have been a prime cause of dislocation in the best of times and, for the imprudent borrower, an invitation to disaster in periods of rapid economic change. To underscore the point, those mortgagors who appear to have 'failed' never account for less than one-third of the community's *total* outstanding mortgage debts, and in the 1850s for more than 62 per cent of it.

Given the essentially quantitative character of the foregoing discussion it may be an instructive diversion, in closing, to focus attention briefly on a single individual, William Cawthra, 'capitalist.'[29] Cawthra was a resident of Toronto whose family owned extensive property, as did other leading Toronto families, in the exclusive lake fronting ranges of Toronto Township in Peel County. He alone held more than 5 per cent of all the Toronto Gore indentures transacted between 1851 and 1880, indentures representing almost 8 per cent of the community's total mortgaged debt in the same period. Cawthra's interest rates normally exceeded the average rate by at least 1½ per cent, and he usually managed to increase his immediate yield by selling his mortgages at a discount. On those mortgages which he retained until they were discharged it would appear, on the basis of an admittedly simplistic reconstruction of an amortization schedule, that Cawthra realized a minimum profit of 50 per cent on capital invested, on the average, for five years. One can only surmise the ultimate magnitude of his investments and profits assuming that his dealings in Toronto Gore, the smallest township in Central Ontario, represent a mere fraction of his involvement in the mortgage field. Cawthra stands alone among our mortgagees, however, as the only private banker whose services were consistently sought out by the residents of the township.

According to the editor of the *Farmers' Advocate* there was 'no accommodation' for the farmer who required the use of capital for less than ten years at moderate rates of interest, an ideal situation in his opinion.[30] According to one of his correspondents, on the other hand, ease of borrowing was too great a temptation for the farmer who might 'gain independence sooner' by borrowing wisely, but was more likely to 'lose all.' 'So the surest and safest way,' he concluded, 'is not to borrow at all.'[31] The proprietors of Toronto Gore historically fall between these two poles of opinion. Most did not need, or did not choose, to mortgage their land and remained secure in their possession of it either as a home and a vocation, or, if they did not occupy it, as a source of income. Those who did indenture themselves seem to have encountered little difficulty in obtaining capital on conditions suited to their economic circumstances, nor did they, for the most part, mortgage themselves in a reckless and irresponsible fashion. For both groups, mortgagors and non-borrowers alike, land was good security.

Unquestionably, a minority of Toronto Gore's proprietors lived with the burden of mortgaged debt year in and year out. Many of them succumbed, and were forced to move on not, apparently, by the threat of foreclosure which was clearly to the mortgagee's disadvantage, but rather to minimize their losses and to start anew elsewhere. Whether they drifted to the cities or to the new agricultural frontiers cannot be documented. One thing is certain, however; they did not join the ranks of a visible movement of agrarian discontent, in Ontario at least. If Toronto Gore Township offers an even remotely accurate reflection of rural economic conditions in the better farming areas of southern Ontario generally, those who faltered under the weight of their mortgaged debts were too few in number and could scarcely identify their friends and neighbours as the sources of their misfortunes.

NOTES

The data on which this essay is based were collected with the assistance of Herbert Mays and Robert Leitch whose help I gratefully acknowledge. I am also indebted to the Canada Council for its support of the Peel County History Project.

1 See, for example, W.T. Easterbrook and Hugh G.J. Aitken, *Canadian Economic History* (Toronto 1965), 507–9; E.P. Neufeld, *The Financial System of Canada* (Toronto 1972), 79; A.R.M. Lower, *Canadian in the Making,* (Toronto 1969), 336–41; W.T. Easterbrook, *Farm Credit in Canada* (Toronto 1938), especially Chapter II

3 Allen C. Bogue, *Money at Interest: The Farm Mortgage on the Middle Border* (New York 1968); also Paul W. Gates, *The Farmers Age: Agriculture 1815–1860.* The Economic History of the United States, Vol. III (New York 1962), 92, 403–11, and Merle Curti, *The Making of An American Community* (Stanford 1969), 157–61

3 Neufeld, *Financial System*; and R. Craig McIvor, *Canadian Monetary Banking and Fiscal Development* (Toronto 1958)

4 Unless otherwise indicated, the data employed has been taken from the Abstracts of Deeds and Copy Books of Deeds for Peel County, Ontario, Toronto Gore Township, Abstracts 1826–65, 1865–1950; Copy Books, 1826–81 (4 vols.), Ontario Archives [*OA*], microfilm.

5 John Lynch, 'Agricultural Report on the County of Peel, 1852,' *Journal and Transactions of the Board of Agriculture for Upper Canada,* 1 (Oct. 1855), 349–51; *Census of the Canadas, 1851–1852* (Quebec 1855), II, 40–1; *Census of the Canadas, 1861–1862* (Quebec 1864), II, 54–5; *Census of Canada, 1870–71* (Ottawa 1875), III, 32–3; *Census of Canada, 1880–81* (Ottawa 1882), III, 92–3

6 Data on land ownership and values have been calculated for each decade of the period under study, from registry office records.

7 In computing the market value of farms, where sales are recorded in pounds sterling, we have used a conversion rate of $4.00 = £1.0.0, the rate used by mortgagees in the 1850s.

8 For agricultural conditions in the province of Canada 1841–90 see Robert L. Jones, *History of Agriculture in Ontario, 1613–1880* (Toronto 1946), 189–205, 246, 325

9 Easterbrook, *Farm Credit,* 33–5 suggests, for example, that country merchants remained an important source of credit throughout the depression years.

10 One settler in Peel County estimated the expenses involved in starting up a farm as triple the cost of land. T.W. Magrath, *Authentic Letters from Upper Canada* (Toronto 1967), 5

11 Jones, *History of Agriculture,* 202–4

12 Easterbrook, *Farm Credit,* 37

13 Copy Books of Deeds, Toronto Gore Township, Vol. I, Instrument no 1382

14 Ibid., Instrument no 4459

15 Lower, *Canadian in the Making,* 336

16 Peel County, Surrogate Court Records, Wills, Vol. II (1876–81), Will no 616

17 Ibid., Vol. I, Will no 131 and no 95

18 *Canada, Report of the Royal Commission on Dominion-Provincial Relations* (Ottawa 1940), I, 27; Magrath, *Letters,* 8

19 Neufeld, *Financial System,* 179; Easterbrook and Aitken, *Canadian Economic History,* 507–8

20 Neufeld, *Financial System,* 88

21 Cited in ibid., 205

22 See the discussion of interest rates below
23 Easterbrook, *Farm Credit*, 34
24 Neufeld, *Financial System*, 179
25 *Farmer's Advocate*, VII, March 1872, 34 (editorial)
26 Neufeld, *Financial System*, 559 indicates that the average rate of interest on mortgages in Canada never fell below 11 per cent between 1850 and 1880
27 Neufeld, *Financial System*, 196
28 Vic. 1880, c 42
29 See W.S. Wallace, ed., *The Macmillan Dictionary of Canadian Biography* (Toronto 1963), 125
30 *Farmers' Advocate*, VII, March 1872, 34
31 Ibid., April 1872, 54

The Common Man in the Era of the Rebellion in Upper Canada

Fred Landon

The purpose of this paper is to look in upon the common man of the era of 1837 in Upper Canada, who, in the crisis of the year, marched out with Mackenzie or Duncombe, or rallied to the side of Sir Francis Head, or, as was more generally the case, stayed at home and mended his fences. The term 'common man' must not be interpreted to mean any inferior group in the province; it includes those who farmed and worked at trades or kept shop; those who attended horse races or wrestling matches as well as those who attended revival meetings; those who came from the United States as well as those from the British Isles; the stage-driver, the inn-keeper, the doctor, the missionary, the postmaster, the editor of the local paper; the Anglican, Methodist, Presbyterian, or Quaker; the people of whom Abraham Lincoln said that God must have loved them because he made so many of them. Most of these people had some point of view upon the main issues of 1837 and in the mass they must have had some influence upon those issues. We have studied intensively the policies and activities in this period of the Colonial Office and the Upper Canada assembly and legislative council. But how much do we know, for example, concerning the point of view of the Yarmouth Quakers or the Lobo Township Scotch or the London Township Orangemen? Here were three groups within a comparatively few miles of each other who, in December 1837, took quite different attitudes towards the troubles of the day. How much do we know about the miniature Family Compacts which were to be found here and there throughout the province, adept at feathering their nests, basking in the sunshine of official favour, and in some cases contributing quite as much to local discontent as anything that was done by the more famous group which surrounded the lieutenant-governor at the capital.

The ordinary reader still tends to interpret the words 'Rebellion of 1837' as referring to certain military events at the city of Toronto where an attempt to overturn the provincial government was thwarted by the action of certain loyal people who did not wish to see the government overturned, at least not by Mackenzie. This version of events persists because it offers a simple explanation of what is really complex and because it also provides an interesting villain. But is it really so simple as that? We know that the period of the thirties witnessed important demo-cratic movements in Great Britain and on the continent, while in the United States, more close at hand, there was a transformation of society that affected not only government but almost every other phase of human thought and activity. To these American changes has been given the name Jacksonian Democracy, though every student of American history would recognize that Jackson was the product rather than the creator of the new democratic spirit and that he 'rode into power on a tide of forces that had been gathering strength for more than a decade and which he had done little or nothing to bring into being.'

In Upper Canada William Lyon Mackenzie was the most prominent figure in the agitations that coincided with Jackson's presidency in the United States and the Mackenzie uprising took place in the year in which Jackson retired from office. In the case of Mackenzie, just as in the case of Jackson, there has been a tendency to make him the creator of conditions of which he was actually rather the reflection. In the United States a new party arose in Jackson's time, made up of diverse elements but having one common bond, hatred of the president. In Upper Canada the Family Compact lost no time in fixing upon Mackenzie the responsibility for the rebellion, knowing how much easier it is to place blame upon an individual than upon a group. Mackenzie's subsequent absurdities, at Niagara and in the United States, strengthened the idea that he was chiefly responsible for the Upper Canada troubles and this tradition has come down to our own day.

The correct estimate of Mackenzie would be that he was first and last an agitator. He cannot be credited with leadership in any of the more prominent issues before 1837. That leadership was assumed by Gourlay, Ryerson, the Bidwells, Robert Baldwin, and lesser figures. But Mackenzie was adept at seizing other people's ideas and promulgating them as his own, though his great weakness was that he could place evils in no order of importance. Ryerson said of him that 'every evil which he discerned was in his estimation truly an evil and all evils were about of equal magnitude ... He felt a longing desire to right the wrongs which he saw everywhere around him. This, therefore, constituted, as he believed, his mission as a public man in Canada.'[1]

The source of Mackenzie's basic political theories and ideas has been given careful investigation by Professor R. A. MacKay, who points out that from the year 1824 Mackenzie became more North American in his point of view and that the reforms which he thereafter urged were those which had already been achieved in many of the states and were being agitated for in others. In addition to his read-ing of American periodicals, Mackenzie made personal contact with the United States by an extended visit in the summer of 1829. During this visit he met many public men, including President Jackson, and was 'highly impressed with economic conditions and with the apparent simplicity and cheapness of government.'[2] There has been a tendency of late to discount the influence of Jacksonian democracy upon developments in Upper Canada during the thirties, but it is not at all necessary that there should be in Mackenzie's political theories an analogy with American political theory in order to connect these concurrent North American movements towards greater democracy. So far as Upper Canada was concerned, it was not Washington and the White House that exerted the influence but the newer states of the West. Indeed, throughout the thirties and forties the agency of the national government at Washington was reduced to a minimum. The charter of the Bank of the United States was allowed to expire in 1836. Jackson vetoed legislation for internal improvements and thereby stopped such development under national auspices. Even the tariff, though it continued protective in character, was a compromise between sectional interests rather than a well thought out plan for developing industry.[3] Since the national government failed to meet their demands, the people turned, where it was possible, to the state governments which throughout this period were the scene of great activity in debate and in legislation. Ohio, Illinois, Indiana, and the other states of the West were dealing with the very subjects that were of greatest interest to the common man in Upper Canada: non-sectarian common schools, roads and bridges, solemnization of marriage, the franchise and elections, tenure of office, and freedom of religion. It was the state, not the national government at Washington, which was legislating in those fields which most closely touched the life of the individual, and though the common man in Upper Canada may not have known much of the reign of King Andrew the First at the White House, he had only to spend an evening at the nearest tavern or inn to learn from some American immigrant or traveller what was going on in the neighbouring states.

Here we have indicated one of the means by which the spread of ideas took place. Today we are subjected to the influence of such agencies as the press and radio, public assembly, and easy facilities of travel. None of these, except public assembly, was common in the thirties. The part played by the press is particularly possible of exaggeration. Though there were more than a score of newspapers published in the province in the early thirties, they were all weeklies, most of them with but a limited local circulation and not all of them attempting any serious comment upon the public affairs of the province. The majority of the people of the province did not see a newspaper of any kind regularly and even those who had access to newspapers sometimes found their days so occupied with other tasks that they could give little time to this occupation. The Rev. William Proudfoot, an educated and intelligent man, records more than once in his diary that he had not read a newspaper in some time, simply because he was otherwise busily occupied.

A continuous and effective agency in the spread of ideas was the tavern or inn. The erection of a school-house generally preceded that of a church or chapel in

Upper Canada but earlier than either came the mill and the tavern. The school-house usually touched only the children, the church influenced a settled group, but the tavern, open frequently on Sundays as well as week days, saw a steady procession of newcomers, few of them remaining more than a night but all of them bringing some tidings of the outside world, to be retailed again and again by the inn-keeper who, in many cases, would be found to be an American. In the records of travel of the thirties there are constant references to the inns and to conversation with strangers, and also mention of evenings spent about the fireside with much debate and discussion.

A similar source of ideas was the constant addition to the community of new-comers from the British Isles and from the United States, part of the large immigration of the period. In proportion to the number of settlers at the beginning of the decade, the number of immigrants was large. The opportunities for contact with people from the outside world were numerous and in time of starved social life these contacts were more appreciated than they would be today.

One of the most effective agencies for disseminating ideas, however, was the public assembly of the people, of whatever type this might be. The religious service and the revivals, the militia muster, the temperance society, the bee, the agricultural fair, the meeting of the court of quarter sessions, all these occasions brought people together and gave just such opportunity for interchange of news and ideas as similar gatherings do even in our own day. Despite the scarcity of ministers of religion, there were numerous religious assemblies held in school-houses, in homes, and not infrequently in barns. Political gatherings were less numerous than at a later period but frequently became riotous in character as bitterness of political feeling increased.

The moral conditions of Upper Canada in the era of the rebellion were the subject of special comment at the time, since church leaders of the day placed much of the blame for the outbreak upon the lack of religious agencies within the province, or, more maliciously, placed the blame upon the fanatical doctrines of their competitors in the field. Extreme views with regard to the morals of Upper Canada are likely to be unsafe. The traditional piety of the forefathers, so often dwelt upon at anniversary gatherings, requires qualifications. A contrasting picture of Upper Canada in terms of traditional frontier life would be equally inaccurate. It would be a safe judgment to say that the morals of Upper Canada a hundred years ago were in general about the same as they are today, with this difference, that for the more primitive sins which were then more conspicuous we have managed to find some new forms of digression from the straight and narrow path.

Doctor Thomas Rolph published in 1836 a statement of criminal statistics for the years 1830-5. The trials included 47 murder, 20 manslaughter, 10 rape, 53 felony, 13 arson, 25 forgery, 17 perjury, 266 larceny, and 28 horse-stealing. The number of murder charges appears large but the others are not abnormal.[4] Offences such as assault and battery, which were very numerous, were dealt with by the courts of quarter sessions.

Every denominational group which was active in Upper Canada dwelt in its reports upon the religious destitution of the province, but this rather generally referred to the lack of church buildings and the absence of formal congregational organization. More remote parts of the province might not see a preacher or missionary of any denomination for months at a time, but this was not true of the more settled portions and in the towns there were frequently three, four, or even more separate congregations. School-houses were often utilized for meeting places and there were even instances of union church buildings.

The lack of Sabbath observance shocked the ministers and also shocked many of the newcomers from the British Isles who had been accustomed to see the day decently observed. In 1819 John Goldie, then visiting Canada, wrote: 'It must give uneasiness to any person who has any regard for religion to witness the general inattention to even the external duties of the Sabbath, both in the States and in Canada. Instead of preserving a tolerably decent behaviour on that day, it is commonly spent in drinking, shooting, fishing, or some such amusement, and that even by many who consider themselves to have good moral character. Any person newly arrived would not recognize the Sabbath at all. No doubt there are many people who behave otherwise, but they certainly are in the minority.'[5]

The Rev. William Proudfoot was in York on Good Friday of 1833 and though the shops were closed, which he attributed to the influence of the Episcopal Church, the day was one of feasting and sport. Yet it was much quieter, he observed, than the preceding Sabbath when there was much loitering and disorderly conduct on the streets. 'The Canadians grudge the observance of the Sabbath,' was his comment. A few days before, in Elgin County, he had noted in his diary that he had never in his life seen a Sabbath less observed as it ought to be.[6]

Writing shortly after the rebellion year, John R. Godley said of conditions in Upper Canada: 'There is much to lament in the religious conditions of most of the rural districts, as must always be the case where the population is much scattered, and allowed to outgrow the supply of ecclesiastical administration. From never having the subject forced upon them, they begin to forget it, gradually neglect the observance of the Lord's Day, or else employ it as a day simply of bodily relaxation and amusement, omit to have their children baptized, and end by living as though they had no religion at all.'[7]

The prevalence of drinking and the evils that grew out of drinking in this period are well known. At such assemblages of people as bees and militia musters, drinking was carried to great excess. When the Rev. William Proudfoot raised a barn on his little farm in Middlesex County in 1833 he had the assistance of the people of his community, who spent three days on the job. Of the first day he says: 'The people wrought very well in the morning, but after dinner they did very little.' Of the second day's operations he writes: 'There were more today than yesterday, yet they did far less work, owing to their having had too much whiskey, I suppose. There were many who came for no other purpose than to drink whiskey.' At the end of the third day he recorded in his diary: 'And now that the raising is over, I am able to form my own opinion of these bees. From first to last there have been at this raising the work of ninety men for one day, which was the very least about two thirds more than was necessary ... Many of the people came for the sole purpose of drinking, and never once assisted in lifting a log. Many of them got drunk. There was such a quantity of swearing and low buffoonery that the whole thing was very painful. Upon the whole I would never again make a bee if I could help it.'

The wide-spread use of hard liquor was accompanied by much fighting and other disorderly practices. W.H. Merritt, promoter of the Welland Canal, said of conditions: 'At every bee, every militia training, even at our dances, swearing, cursing, quarreling, figthing, biting and even gouging was of common occurrence.'[8]

The efforts of organized religion to combat such evils as have been described and to aid the isolated settlers form an appealing phase of the early religious history of the province. At the same time, however, a most distracting and dividing conflict was under way between the several denominations over such questions as clergy reserves, clerical control of education, the solemnization of marriage, and, after 1837, over the nice question of loyalty. It is not a pretty picture that presents itself.

The most spectacular quarrel was that between the Church of England and the Methodist, or, perhaps more accurately, between John Strachan and Egerton Ryerson as the doughty champions of those two bodies. A century of repetition has built up the tradition of a bold and courageous Ryerson storming the Strachan castle of privilege and eventually breaking down its walls. That tradition may gain added strength with the recent appearance of a highly documented life of Ryerson because the other side of the story has yet to be adequately presented.

There is good reason to believe that the Church of England in Canada would have been much more democratic in its policy in this earlier period had it been less dependent upon, and less under the control of, the Society for the Propagation of the Gospel. The SPG at this time was in close harmony in its religious policies with the political policies of the Colonial Ofice. The Society greatly influenced the church policies in Upper Canada and to have run counter to it would have been to risk the financial support which it gave. The late Professor A.H. Young believed that domination from London, a truly 'baneful domination' in this instance, was responsible for many things that were done by Archdeacon Strachan which at the time and since excited criticism. It is greatly to be regretted that Professor Young did not live to write the life of John Strachan to which he devoted so many years.

Had we this biography to place beside that of Egerton Ryerson, we would approach the study of the period with greater confidence. Departing from more generally acepted judgments, Professor Young believed that there was a distinct strain of democracy in Strachan but that powerful external influences forced him into positions in which he seemed to be the very personification of special privilege.

That some at least of the clergy of the Church of England believed that a more democratic organization would better suit the conditions of Upper Canada is recorded by the Rev. Isaac Fidler, rector of Thornhill. 'Many of the Episcopal ministers of Canada,' he wrote, 'think favorably of the American church, and imagine that, if their own were made to approximate more clearly to it in church government, they would find it become more flourishing and interest more warmly the lay members of its body. More energy would, they thought, be thereby infused into it, and its measures invigorated.'[9]

Religious controversy weakened, and to some degree tended to discredit the representatives of the denominations which were engaged in it but there was another phase of denominational rivalry which was equally unpleasant. This was the unholy delight shown by the clergy of one denomination in adding to their number strollers from other folds. Both the practice and the apparent gratification that arise therefrom have persisted into our own day, but in an era when large sections of the province were without regular religious ministrations these proselytizing efforts appear particularly obnoxious. Yet the effort was, in many cases, actuated by a sincere belief that to snatch the erring one from the doctrines which he professed was to save him from destruction. 'I deeply lament,' wrote the Rev. William Proudfoot, an earnest Presbyterian, 'the ascendancy which Methodists have acquired in this country. Their doctrines are frightfully in opposition to the grand, the glorious doctrines of the Gospel.'[10] He was shocked to find that a Presbyterian church in York permitted Methodists to come to communion and still more shocked when he was informed that at least one Methodist had been at the table when he assisted the resident minister. On the effects of Methodism he writes:

I have fancied that in every place where I have preached where Methodism prevails, that the people are exceedingly careless in hearing the Word, whether it is because I have not given them the highly seasoned food which they are accustomed to, because they care not for scriptural statements, I know not, but the fact is as I have stated it. The Methodists have had almost no opposition the whole of the people in the Townships, on the lake side, and the majority of the people do not even profess religion and these are the men who are said to have done good, and who tell of the good they have done. Something must be done to dislodge these pretenders, these so distant preachers. The country will never become Christian till these fellows be dislodged.[11]

We must recognize, however, that there was another side to the picture. This same dour old Scot, with all his bigotry and narrowness of mind, possessed the spirit of the true misisonary and it is a most engaging picture that he has left us of the first administration of the Sacrament to his little congregation in the village of London:

June 1st, 1833. When I went into London, the meeting house was full and many outside. It was judged proper to have the service outside. The people in a twinkling made a pulpit outside – boards laid upon two casks – seats were placed all around and the audience all comfortably seated. Preached from Luke 23:33, 'And they crucified Him.' The sermon went off well. I fenced the tables also out of doors ... After the fencings we went into the meeting house. There were four table services. I also gave an address after the service was over. The place was not very convenient for the service, but I never saw a Sacrament conducted with more external decorum. I was much afraid of disorderly behaviour at the outdoor service, but was happily disappointed. I did not give an evening sermon lest I should weary the people, I had already spoken for six hours.

A pleasant picture of a Sunday service in the backwoods in 1834 is given by D. Wilkie in his *Sketches of a Summer Trip*: 'The farmers as they arrived, some from many miles distance, threw the bridles of their horses over a convenient stump or branch at the door, quaffed a bowl of water from a pailful placed at the roadside, on the root of a fallen tree, and then, Bible in hand, slipped into their places with all the unobtrusive simplicity of the Covenanters of old. When the solemn chant of the unsophisticated Psalmody rose from the lips of the little flock, it presented a vivid and pleasant picture of the primitive Church of Scotland in the olden time.'[12]

And where may one find a more living picture of the church militant than that left by John Carroll describing the closing scene of a conference of Methodist preachers:

Anticipating the time when the Bishop would announce their appointments, the preachers came to the church with their horses and saddle-bags, ready to start for their homes as soon as they should learn their destination. The larger number of them were on horseback; and forming near the church in regular order, two abreast, they slowly moved away over the hill and out of sight, soon to separate, however, and disperse to their several fields of labour, probably never all to meet again.

Our equipage for the battle field was a portmanteau and valise; in them we stored our wearing apparel, Bible and what other books we were able to get, and but a few dollars in our pockets. Our outward dress and appearance when mounted gave us the name of the Methodist cavalry.[13]

In any analysis of the causes of unrest in Upper Canada in the period before 1837, emphasis is properly laid upon the constitutional aspects of the situation because the faults of the constitution had ramifications which extended even to the daily life of the humble settler in remote districts. The land question seemed to be ever present in one form or another. The clergy reserves, the crown reserves, and the large blocks of land allotted to friends of the government interfered with the life of the small farmer who paid taxes and did road work, from both of which some other people seemed to be absolved. The land policy of Upper Canada abounded in mistakes, the chief of which was the lavish alienation, so that in the end a large area was held by absentee owners who did nothing to improve their holdings, but merely held it for speculative purposes. Benedict Arnold, of American Revolutionary War fame, received 5000 acres in Gwillimbury North and East as a retired colonel, with an additional grant of 8400 acres in Elmsley Township in the names of his wife and children. Two sons also received 2000 acres each, so that the total amount received by the traitor to the American colonial cause was 15,400 acres. In the Talbot Settlement on the north shore of Lake Erie, the eccentric Colonel Talbot long kept two fine townships almost entirely out of settlement, holding them back for his own profit and sending applicants for land off to other sections. When called to account from time to time, his device was to secure intervention on his behalf by influential friends in England, a method which was invariably successful. It is not without significance that Doctor Dunscombe's force in 1837 was recruited almost entirely from the area over which Colonel Thomas Talbot held sway.

Land speculation had made its appearance in Upper Canada in the first decade of the province's history when the executive council had to refuse applications from many people who did not intend to be settlers. But even with such care as was exercised, abuses soon began to creep in, among them some which had official sanction from London. In the end Upper Canada became a paradise for the land speculators who were eventually able to enlist the help of government servants at York. 'A half pay officer in Canada,' writing in the *United Service Journal* of January 1839, declared that it was notorious in Canada that every clerk in every public office was speculating in public lands in the name of some friend. This was the reason that so little land seemed to be available for the ordinary settler. Writing again in the February 1839 issue he drew attention to the enormous number of United Empire Loyalist rights being granted. 'The number of claims of this nature established within the last few years is truly miraculous,' he said, adding that when new surveys were made the best lots were gone at once under UEL rights and immigrants had no choice. Speculators merely held the lands for a rise in value.

When the public departments at York were investigated in the year after the rebellion, reference was made in the report to the 'system of partiality, favoritism and corruption' in the surveyor-general's department, 'begun at an early date and continued, with but few interruptions, up to the present time.'[14] J.G. Chewett, of the surveyor-general's department, in his statement said: 'The system upon which the lands have been granted was the greatest prostitution of the sovereign's bounty ever practiced in any country. The intentions of the sovereign's will evidently appear, from the instructions given for the settlement of the country, wise and guarded – but the system pursued was corrupt; actual settlement was required upon the grants, but the influence of interest obtained for individuals whose claim could not exceed 200 acres large grants to themselves and their families, dead parents as well as infants who never lived to walk out of their cradles had orders-in-council passed in their names and their families eventually obtained the lands.'[15] Of the operations of the chief clerk in the office of the commissioner of crown lands it was stated that 'his policy has secured for him a numerous band of partizans, as the list of names he was able to command when soliciting ... the appointment of Surveyor-General sufficiently testifies.'[16]

During the years after 1830 the speculative land fever rapidly spread, despite the fact that many settlers were in deplorable economic conditions. Travellers reported that small settlers were offering their holdings at prices that were sometimes lower than the upset price at the public sales. Patrick Shirreff had much to say concerning the situation as he found it in 1833.

To the system of disposing of land by credit much of the wretchedness and poverty of the present Canadian landholders may be justly attributed. The experience of the United States government demonstrated this, and a law was passed to abolish credit on the price of land.

Much land is held by absentee proprietors, or the members of the party who sway the councils of the province. It is commonly in the hands of agents empowered to sell. The prices are generally higher than crown lands and credit unlimited ... There is never any hesitation in selling land to a man without capital, as the rights are withheld. Every tree which is cut down enhances the value of the property which is unproductive while they are standing. When a settler absconds after some years residence, a case by no means rare, the proprietor derives great advantage from his operations ... In almost every district people are found anxious to sell land, and small farms may be bought on cheaper terms than land belonging to the Crown, Canada Company, or large proprietors, more especially if cash is paid. Indeed the necessities of many people are so urgent, and credit so general, that an individual with cash in his pocket may drive a good bargain at all times ... The whole system of settling land in Canada has been bad for many years.[17]

Shirreff had much more to say upon the abuses in the government's land policies but the above will serve to illustrate his criticisms. Some of the accompaniments of modern land booms were present in this era in Upper Canada. John Howison reported that in embryo towns in Upper Canada he had been shown sites for universities, hospitals, and churches before even a hotel had been erected. Evidence could be multiplied to show the prevalence of land speculation. Some of the fever was caught from the Western States where a wild orgy was in progress, soon to be given a disastrous check by Jackson's 'specie circular' in the summer of 1836. Another factor was the disproportionate idea held by settlers as to the actual value of land. In Upper Canada the immigrant from the British Isles, hitherto a servant, once he had acquired land felt that he had become a proprietor, equal to his former master. Land was therefore viewed as a sort of deity capable of raising the poor to a better station. In this respect it was not unlike the populist deification of silver in the Western States forty-five years ago. Behind the religious agitation concerning the disposal of the clergy reserves, there was doubtless also much land jobbing influence, just as behind the Populist's free silver demands lay the personal interests of the Western silver producers.

A special grievance in connection with the disposal of public lands was aired in the St Thomas *Liberal* in the summer of 1833. The *Liberal* stated that a sale of lands in Oxford County had been announced to take place at Hamilton and that to this sale there had come prospective purchasers from points fifty and sixty miles distant, only to find the auction postponed from day to day until they were forced to leave. Afterwards a group of half-pay officers who could afford to lounge around until the coast was clear obtained at a low rate a large portion of the lands that had been announced for sale. 'No class of individuals,' said the *Liberal*, 'profit so much by this grand humbug of "Lands sold at public auction" as the military officers who have retired to the province on half pay ... The land granting system in this province has ever been a subject of loud complaint; it is well-known to have hitherto been one of the strongest holds of corruption and to have developed more fully the operations, extent and objects of government favoritism than perhaps any other of the very many prolific sources of partial, illiberal legislation.'

Grievances, whether of the land or of whatever origin, would have contributed less to unrest had there not been the widespread feeling of frustration which is reflected so often in the comment of the times. Mackenzie and his friends felt that they were opposed by an entrenched enemy when they criticized the Family Compact. But there were miniature Family Compacts, or shall we say, branches of the Family Compact in communities quite other than the provincial capital. The St. Thomas *Liberal*, already quoted from, said in 1833:

The county of Middlesex, from its first settlement up to this moment, has been controlled by two distinguished individuals, as absolutely and despotically as is the petty sovereignty of a German despot. This they have been enabled to do through the immense influence their high official stations give them. Magistrates, officers of the excise, surveyors, militia officers, commissioners to carry the appropriations of public money into effect, all are appointed through the recommendations and influence of these sages of the District – thus forming a host of worthies who are ever at the beck of their Patrons. We assert without fear of contradiction, that the Hon. Colonel Talbot rules with a more absolute sway, and his power is infinitely more to be dreaded than that of the King of Great Britain ... It is the fear of this Iron rule that has controlled our former elections – except at the elections of Messrs Rolph and Matthews, then the people aroused from their lethargy and braved the power that had so long oppressed them.[18]

Frustration may easily become the prelude to violence, which is excellently illustrated by the fact that in 1836 the Talbot Settlement was a hotbed of unrest and one of the most seriously disturbed portions of the province in the time of the uprising. Encumbered with the débris of worn-out institutions, the people of Upper Canada were restricted in the actual practice of citizenship. We hear much in these days of education for citizenship, but the only real and effective education for citizenship lies in its actual practice. One of the early fruits of the English Reform Bill of 1832 was the remodelling of the ancient corporations by the Municipal Reform Act, whereby in place of the old governing bodies, based on very narrow franchises, town councils were established, elected by all the ratepayers. In Upper Canada one of the greatest of Sydenham's reforms was the establishment of local self-government, though this was opposed by the reactionary Tories of the day as a dangerous concession to 'republican principles.' The new district councils took over many powers and functions of the old courts of quarter sessions, which since the beginning of the province had been both legal and municipal agencies. At once opportunity was given for training men in local administration, and through that schooling they received preparation for political activities in larger fields. But this was after the rebellion was over. Prior to the rebellion the courts of quarter sessions, appointed by the government and therefore in general sympathetic to government policies, formed little strongholds of Toryism that held back the rising tide of democratic feeling. This lack of opportunity for actual participation in local government meant a lack of opportunity for that orderly clash of opinion and eventual compromise which distinguishes English-speaking communities in general today. There was lack of opportunity for coming into the open and uttering what the old Greeks called the 'word said into the middle'; what Milton meant when he said:

> That is true liberty, when free-born men
> Having to advise the public may speak free.[19]

In place of open expression of opinion there developed the practice of violence in dealing with political opponents, an evil practice which brought dire results in the Canadas as late as 1849. In the election of 1836 it was conspicuous, though it might properly be claimed that no wilder demagogue appeared in that election than the representative of the crown, Sir Francis Bond Head. His appeals to prejudice, suspicion, and fear were of the boldest character. He openly spread the idea that an enemy was about to attack the province. 'In the name of every regiment of militia in Upper Canada I publicly promulgate – Let them come if they dare.'[20] A writer of this period has aptly said: 'The method of Sir Francis Head, that of appealing to the people, was itself a great tribute to the power of democracy and a presage of its victory.'[21]

The turbulence of the election of 1836 may be illustrated by the events in the village of London, of which there remains a fairly extensive record. The disorder at London may not have been typical of the province at large, but it serves to illustrate the bitterness which had developed in this particular community and for which there were probably counterparts elsewhere. We have this picturesque description of the election preserved for us in a contemporary journal:

The magistrates ceased to do their duty and a general riot ensued every day that the polls were open. I attended the election on Saturday, the last day ... A procession headed by a Negro with a national standard waving it, and at the same time shouting an offer of five pounds for any Liberal heads. This procession turned out to be an Orange mob who commenced beating a number of Liberals who were taken up for dead. Two hours before the polls closed Member Parke had to be rescued by a guard and marched to a place of safety and Member Moore had to make his escape out of town for home. The Liberal poll was secured by two clerks who made their escape into the jail for protection and were locked up.[22]

Statements similar to the above are contained in Doctor Charles Duncombe's petition to the British House of Commons. He declared that at the 1836 election he went to London on the last day and that a mile and a half from the village he met Mr Moore, the former Reform member, escaping from the Orangemen, who he claimed, had threatened his life. He told Doctor Duncombe that the Orangemen were driving the Reformers from the polls with clubs and beating them wherever they found them, and that the officers of the government 'with Mr. Cronyn, a clergyman of the Church of England who had been recently inducted into the rectory of that place, were constantly hurrahing and cheering on the Orangemen who were seen running through the streets, intoxicated, with clubs, threatening the Reformers with instant death if they shouted Reform.' Doctor Duncombe stated further that in the earlier part of the election, when the rioting commenced, Edward Allen Talbot and John Scatcherd, magistrates, swore in twenty special constables to keep the peace, but Mr Wilson, returning officer, forbade the magistrates from interfering with the rioters during the election, and when Mr Talbot insisted on his rights as a magistrate to keep the peace, at any place not immediately about the hustings, the returning officer threatened to commit him to prison.[23]

When the Duncombe charges were referred to a select committee of the assembly, the Rev. Benjamin Cronyn appeared on 21 December 1836. He denied that he had been hurrahing on the Orangemen and said that he had often seen more fighting on a training day than during the whole election. In his evidence he stated that the 'loyal party,' as he termed them, numbering several hundred, advanced upon the hustings after the Reformers had occupied it for several hours, and made an entrance for themselves through the Reformers. He charged that a Radical had torn the Union Jack from the staff (presumably the Orangemen's flag) and had dragged it through the mud at the tail of a wagon, then torn it into pieces and thrown it into the river. The Rev. Wiliam Proudfoot made this brief comment upon the election: 'July 2, 1836. Went into the village ... to see the election which was a scene.' A week earlier he had written: 'Everybody wholly occupied with the approaching elections, party spirit runs high. Parson Cronyn has been all over the township electioneering.'

All this hubbub concerned the casting of sixty-four votes, Mahlon Burwell, the Tory candidate receiving thirty-seven while his Reform opponent, John Scatcherd, received twenty-seven. Shortly after the election both John Scatcherd and Edward Allen Talbot were dropped from the list of magistrates.

One other reference to the disorder prevailing in 1836 may be cited. Recalling the election of that year, W.H. Merritt said: 'The election occurred on the 1st of July 1836 and the author, who was present, has for remembrance a gathering which, for riot and drunkenness, though his own village could get up no mean display, exceeded everything he had ever seen before, and challenges the world to beat the Grand River roarers in their peculiar line.'[24]

The rowdyism and violence that was present in the election of 1836 found a larger stage in 1837 and in the name of loyalty and patriotism there was abundant opportunity for paying off old grudges. The descent of Colonel MacNab's force upon the Quaker settlement at Norwich after the collapse of Duncombe's abortive enterprise was purely revengeful. There had been unrest and agitation in this community, but few Quaker families were concerned in it. The inhabitants of Norwich district, however, were of American origin and the Quakers had taken their traditional attitude toward military service. MacNab's force was quartered upon the community for three days, 'for the purpose of scowering the very hot bed of treason,' it was stated. The 'march through Norwich' was not forgotten for many a day. Writing in the Oxford *Star* a decade later, 'An old settler' said: 'When that part of the late rebellion which was more intimately connected with our county comes to be written and well understood, the name of Duncombe himself will lie under lighter and less general execration than some who early made themselves hoarse with cursing the rebels and crying "God save the Queen," who swore and swaggered in front of raw recruits and led raids into Norwich in which some scores of Quakers' farmyards were reduced, as many pig pens carried by storm, and bleaching yards sacked and rased.'

MacNab, in his zeal to arrest the fugitives from Duncombe's army, made use of the Six Nation Indians who, with painted faces, were sent into the woods to cut off escape. When Colonial Secretary Lord Glenelg heard of this he expressed his deep repugnance to such action. 'It is scarcely possible,' he wrote, 'to conceive any necessity which would justify it and nothing would in my opinion tend more to alienate the inhabitants of Upper Canada and to irritate the people of the United States than the attempt to let loose on the assailants of the government the horrors of savage warfare.'[25]

It would be unfair to blame the administration at Toronto for all the petty persecutions that followed. The miniature Family Compacts, formerly subjects of criticism and attack by the radicals of their community, now had the satisfaction of clapping their critics into jail and subjecting them to lengthy examination. The Rev. Mr Proudfoot records in his diary on 17 December 1837: 'Preached ... to about forty persons. The whole town taken up with catching the Radicals so that nobody had time to attend meeting for the worship of God. Such a scene I never witnessed.'

Looking back at the events of a century ago, we can see that all possibility of a rebellion succeeding was doomed when Head in 1836 raised the 'devastating factor' of anti-American prejudice. 'I publicly promulgate – Let them come if they dare' was a challenge addressed to some hostile force or influence that was threatening the province, and with the War of 1812 less than a quarter of a century in the background popular imagination pictured but one enemy. The echoes of Head's challenge drew many men to his side who were little in sympathy with his actions in office.

A rumour which spread at the very time of the uprising, and which had visible effect, is mentioned by Egerton Ryerson in a letter to Sir James Stephen, the permanent undersecretary of the Colonial Office, written after the rebellion: 'I was in Cobourg, Newcastle District, when the volunteers rallied from all parts and the report was there that Rolph and Bidwell were under arms in defence of the city against Mackenzie. You may judge of the effect of this report throughout the province – it doubled the number of volunteers in defence of the government.'[26]

The business of history is to get at the thoughts, passions, endeavours, and failures of mankind and of individual men and women in the past. That is the definition of a great English historian, George Macaulay Trevelyan. But true history, as Croce teaches, must be contemporary history, contemporary in the sense that, however remote in time, it lives in the historian's mind with the urgency of the present. It is this present interest that moves him to attack it. Narratives and memorials apparently dead thus become living documents, and one problem of the past after another is drawn out of sleep and into the second life of history.

It is more than the mere observance of a centenary that prompts our interest in the events of 1837. A new democracy was being born a hundred years ago; democracy today is concerned with the problem of its continued survival. What part did the common man have in the struggles of the earlier period; what part does he have in the struggle of today? If there are leaders there must be followers, and leaders, then and now, must adapt the length of their steps to the capacities of those who will follow them. There is much yet to be learned about the thoughts and the passions, the endeavours and the failures of the common folk of 1837. Not until we know more intimately the nature of conditions and events in many communities of that era will we have right understanding of the rebellion. There is here the argument for wider study of local history. It was not one rebellion but many rebellions, and to generalize may be an acknowledgement of insufficient evidence. Ulrich B. Phillips has put it this way:

A cartographer 'generalizes' a river course if its meanders are not known in detail or if they are too small to be shown in his reduction. A merchant generalizes his customers when he prints an advertisement, and a physician when classing his patients as cases of pneumonia, measles or smallpox. The practice is not merely convenient but necessary. On the other hand a lover generalizes his lady, to be startled by her individualism after marriage ... The past, however, may remind us on occasion that its people were not lay figures but men, women and children of flesh and blood, thought and feeling, habits and eccentricities, in the grip of circumstance and struggling more or less to break it. Traditions are simple, conditions were complex; and to get into the records is to get away from the stereotypes.[27]

NOTES

Reprinted from Canadian Historical Association, *Report*, 1937, 76–91

1 Egerton Ryerson, *Story of My Life* (Toronto 1884), 186–7
2 'The Political Ideas of William Lyon Mackenzie,' *Canadian Journal of Economics and Political Science*, Feb. 1937, 12–3
3 C.R. Fish, *The Rise of the Common Man, 1830–1850* (New York 1927), 34–5
4 Thomas Rolph, *A Brief Account together with Observations, made during a Visit in the West Indies, and a Tour through the United States of America, in Parts of the Years 1832–33; together with a Statistical Account of Upper Canada* (Dundas 1836), Appendix
5 John Goldie, *Diary of a Journey through Upper Canada and Some of the New England*

States, 1819 (Toronto 1897), 55

6 Garland, M.A., ed., 'The Proudfoot Papers,' entries of 24 March and 5 April, Ontario Historical Society, *Papers and Records*, XXVI, 1930, 512, 522

7 John R. Godley, *Letters from America* (2 vols., London 1844), I, 174–5

8 J.P. Merritt, *Biography of the Hon. W.H. Merritt* (St Catharines 1875), 268

9 Isaac Fidler, *Observations on Professions, Literature, Manners and Emigrations in the United States and Canada made during Residence there in 1832* (London 1833), 426–7. Archdeacon Strachan's point of view on the limitations caused by the close connection of church and state given by Fidler is as follows: 'The Archdeacon of York, in Upper Canada, was of the opinion that the system of church government, which connects church and state so closely together as to admit of no trifling alterations being made without the intervention of Parliament, is untenable by scripture, and hurtful to the interests of the church itself. The Church of England, he remarked, is the only religious community which does not possess inherent rights to regulate its own affairs. There are no synods of its clergy, no unity of counsels and proceedings, like what were possessed originally by the christian church, or like what are adopted by other denominations of the present day. The national church ought to be so modelled, as to be able to conform itself, in its outward ceremonies, to the improvements of the age' (p. 427)

10 'The Proudfoot Papers,' 22 April 1833, 532

11 Ibid., 24 March 1883, 512

12 D. Wilkie, *Sketches of a Summer Trip to New York and the Canadas* (Edinburgh 1837), 163

13 John Carroll, *Case and his Cotemporaries or Canadian Itinerants' Memorial* (Toronto 1869–74), II, 157, 319

14 Report on public departments, 5th Session, 13th Parliament, 1840, 233

15 Ibid., 247. The Cobourg *Reformer* said: 'Whenever he [a settler] buys his land, whether from the Crown or The Canada Company, more or less fraud is mixed up with, or flows from the transaction' (quoted in St Thomas *Liberal*, 8 Aug. 1833)

16 Ibid., 20

17 Patrick Shirreff, *A Tour through North America, together with a Comprehensive View of the Canadas and United States as adapted for Agricultural Emigration* (Edinburgh 1835), 362-5

18 St Thomas *Liberal*, 25 July 1833. (Middlesex then included Elgin, but not the northern townships of the present county. The second individual was probably Col. Mahlon Burwell.)

19 See Ernest Barker, 'Education for Citizenship,' University of London, Institute of Education, *Studies and Reports*, X (London 1936), 12–3

20 Reply to the address of the electors of the home district.

21 Aileen Dunham, *Political Unrest in Upper Canada 1815–36* (London 1927), 188

22 MSS of Elijah Woodman. Thomas Parke and Elias Moore were the members from Middlesex between 1834 and 1836. London received its first seat in that year.

23 Appendix to *Journals of the House of Assembly of Upper Canada*, Session 1836–7, no 5, 3–4

24 Merritt, *Biography of the Hon. W.H. Merritt*, 161

25 Public Archives of Canada, *Series* Q, 425A, 52 and 109. The Rev. Richard Flood, who was the Church of England missionary at Delaware, wrote on 27 December 1837: 'Our Indians have been mercifully spared, amidst the late revolutionary movements from being called out by the Lieutenant-Governor to aid the loyalists – as under these circumstances they would have been entirely thrown back – and would probably have resorted to all those horrid barbarities of scalping and burning which they practiced (mild as they are) in the revolutionary war of old, when fighting against the enemies of Great Britain.' W.J.D. Waddilove, *The Stewart Missions* (London 1838), 182

26 C.B. Sissons, *Egerton Ryerson, his Life and Letters* (Toronto 1937), I, 427

27 Ulrich B. Phillips, *Life and Labor in the Old South* (Boston 1929), Preface, viii

Pioneer Drinking Habits and the Rise of the Temperance Agitation in Upper Canada Prior to 1840

M.A. Garland and J.J. Talman

The latter part of the eighteenth and the first half of the nineteenth centuries saw the birth of many very interesting movements. The common man, during this period, achieved a larger measure of civil and political liberty than he had ever enjoyed before. This aspect of the period has been well explored and quite fully explained by the historians but they have not delved with the same fervor into the moral and humanitarian endeavours of the era. The humanitarian and moral endeavours were influential particularly in the countries which were inhabited by English-speaking peoples, namely Great Britain and her dependencies and the United States.

Liberalizing and humanitarian movements were reflected in the United States by the growth of the abolitionist and temperance agitations, by the interest in education, by the founding of homes for the deaf, blind, and insane, by improving conditions in the prisons. The rise of peace societies was symptomatic in the Republic and the Province of Nova Scotia of a wider interest in humanity. The people of the British Isles, too, expressed some interest in humanity through the growth of missionary societies, the formation of a peace movement, the abolition of slavery, and improved conditions in penal institutions.

In Upper Canada prior to 1840, scarcely more than one-half of the inhabitants had been living in the country for over a decade. A group of people separated by thousands of miles from the old area of culture, Western Europe, and backwoodsmen who were struggling heroically to carve out economic independence from a forest could hardly be expected to display a lively interest in humanity. Nevertheless, humanitarian impulses of a type were not lacking. These impulses received their outlet in part in the treatment of the escaped slave. Though the interest in the Negro was more marked between 1840 and 1860, nevertheless evidence exists which demonstrates that at an earlier date the Negro found in Upper Canada a haven of refuge from the wrath of the southern planter. A yet more striking example of the growth of the humanitarian movement, which was being expressed in other parts of the world in various ways, was revealed in this province in the efforts to combat the glaring growth of intemperance.

A vast amount of evidence points to an excessive consumption of alcoholic liquors in Upper Canada; but no estimate can be made of the annual output of the distilleries, the amount of liquor imported or retailed, or the average quantity consumed per person. A general idea can be gained of the amount of liquor consumed in a locality by the number of distilleries and taverns in operation. In 1836, the Bathurst District alone, which had a population of approximately 30,000, contained thirty-five shops that sold liquor, six distilleries, and sixty-five inns.[1]

The distilleries varied in output. Some distilleries produced forty gallons a day, while others were capable of an output of sixty or eighty gallons a day.[2] If the distilleries were in operation for only 300 days a year, and if their average output was sixty gallons a day, the production was rather formidable for a district of 30,000 population, many of whom were children.

Taverns were plentiful, especially along the stage roads. From Hamilton to York, a distance of roughly forty miles, there were in 1833 twenty taverns.[3] Yonge Street running northward from York and many of the other main roads had a still higher percentage.[4] Mrs Jameson states that there were in London seven taverns and a population of about thirteen hundred people. Besides these taverns there was a number of little grocery stores, which were, in fact, drinking houses.[5] In Goderich, in 1833, there were about forty houses and three taverns.[6] The poor roads and correspondingly short distances it was possible to travel in a day led to the building of many taverns, which seem to have averaged about one to a mile in Upper Canada before the building of the railroads.

Inns served not only as places where travellers might secure a lodging but also as gathering centres for the settlers. Here it was that they discussed the larger issues of the day, the best means of logging, or of curing a balky horse or recalcitrant ox, or where they boasted of their feats of axemanship or strength. Meetings of all kinds were held at taverns and it was at these places that the executives for agricultural societies, the British Constitutional Society, the St George's Society, and many other organizations met.[7] Practically all the dances, banquets, and similar functions took place in inns.[8] It was at these places that circuses stopped and at Ancaster and Toronto, plays were acted. Advertisements generally contained the information that posters could be seen and tickets procured at some inn. Mrs Jameson went so far as to say that 'taverns and low drinking houses' were practically the only places of assembly or amusement.[9]

Other uses of inns were infinite; elections were held commonly in the neighbourhood of an inn, and the first religious service held at Port Burwell,[10] and probably in many other places, was conducted in an inn. The prevalence of taverns and their continuous use as community centres have played a marked part in the development of the province.

The existence of numerous taverns and distilleries does not always prove conclusively that liquor was consumed in an excessive manner by the pioneers or that drunkenness was prevalent. Some of the diaries of the period,[11] the travellers' accounts, and the findings of the coroners' inquests show that drunkenness was widespread. An anonymous writer calling himself 'ex-settler' summed up the prevailing opinion of most travellers: 'In travelling through the country, you will see every inn, tavern and beer shop filled at all hours with drunken, brawling fellows; and the quantity of ardent spirits consumed by them will truly astonish you.'[12] The commonest remark in all the letters sent to England from a group of Sussex settlers who came to Canada in 1831 was the cheapness of the liquor and the amount drunk.[13]

The Rev. Isaac Fidler, who spent some time at Thornhill on Yonge Street in the early thirties, did not agree with the usual accounts, for he said: 'I never saw but one man intoxicated, and he was an Englishman returning to England.' But he admitted that intemperance existed 'to a great extent' in the province.[14]

Liquor was a very common commodity in many of the homes of the province. The distiller often lacked ready cash and the settler exchanged his grain for whiskey. The settler in turn sold the whiskey to the innkeeper. In many families, whiskey was served to each member of the household every morning, and thus from infancy the children were accustomed to its taste. Whiskey or cider was usually offered guests or visitors and liquor[15] was served with the meals at many of the inns and on all the boats.[16] The hired help, also, received their portion of the stimulant.[17] Then, as now, liquor was considered by some to be a preventive of colds and a stimulus to more energetic work.

During the pioneer period the constant consumption of alcoholic stimulants was widespread among all classes of the inhabitants. Some of the clergy partook too freely of the beverage, and set an example which others were not slow to follow.[18] Magistrates, who were responsible for enforcing the laws and for granting licenses to distilleries, were in some instances interested in the sale of liquor or engaged in the manufacture of it.[19] The magistrates were even known to drink a portion of the tavern keepers' beverages whilst they were administering justice.[20] The court was held frequently in a tavern because it was the only accessible building. A civil court, the first in Dundas County, showed its earliest expense account (1790) charges for 'Liker for the gentlemen of the grant jury' and for decanters broken.[21]

Men of position and influence were often incapable of performing their duties after a certain hour of the day because they were drunk. It was reported that Colonel Thomas Talbot during the latter years of his sojourn at Port Talbot was frequently the worse of liquor by 3 PM when he was rude and insulting.[22]

Why was excessive drinking prevalent among the pioneers? The immigrant sometimes brought the taste for intoxicating liquor with him from the motherland. Many of the backwoodsmen were mere boys who at an early age were freed from parental control. They took up land frequently some distance from home and the restraining influences of society. William Garland, the grandfather of one of the writers of this paper, for example, set out from his father's home in the Ottawa Valley at the age of twenty to procure and clear a farm in Bruce County which was then, in 1850, almost solid bush. The young backwoodsmen were consequently sometimes exposed to the influence of settlers who had failed to establish economic independence and had turned to drink in order to forget their misfortunes. The 'gentleman settlers' found life in the backwoods very trying. Frequently this type of settler invested all his savings in a bush lot, and eventually lost everything because he was unfitted to meet the hardships demanded of pioneers. Many of these settlers turned to whiskey as an antidote and many perished through over-indulgence.[23] The young settler, wishing to appear self-reliant, joined these broken-down gentlemen in their cups, falsely imagining he would thereby be considered an excellent backwoodsman.[24]

The war of 1812 played its part in lowering the morals of the inhabitants of the province. The American army committed excesses and their example was followed by some Canadians. Many of the inhabitants were forced to abandon their farms to repel the invader. Some of the settlers were impoverished through the loss of their buildings and crops and were mentally unfitted to face once more the hardship necessary to secure economic independence. Thus bereft of possessions and hope they sank into habits of intemperance.[25]

The 'treating system' in vogue in Upper Canada was another cause of the prevailing drunkenness. Under this system a number of persons came to the bar and one bought liquor for the group. Others in a similar manner would treat their companions. Later they might saunter to another tavern and repeat the performance.[26] Liquor was plentiful and a strange custom grew up. The decanter containing the beverage was placed on the bar and everyone was free for three or four coppers to dash into the tumbler as much of the stimulant as he desired. This custom was particularly harmful to the individual when he had cultivated a taste for stimulants and when he had had already partaken freely.[27]

Drunkenness was ascribed usually to the cheapness of the liquor,[28] but had distilleries not been numerous this would not have been the case. The distilleries themselves were the expression of conditions as it was preferable to take grain to distilleries rather than have it rot – a likely event when it was impossible to sell it or provide suitable storage. One bushel of grain made three or three and a half gallons and the distiller usually kept half of the product.[29] When liquor was sold at the inn the usual price was three pence halfpenny a gill, that is a quarter pint,[30] but many bought it by the gallon, when according to some writers it cost two shillings and sixpence or half a dollar.[31]

Life in the bush had a tendency to demoralize the settlers. Many of the newcomers, for example, were almost penniless. The task of clearing his land, erecting buildings, and providing the necessities of life was a hard and monotonous one. The pioneer was surrounded by many dangers. Fire sometimes destroyed the work of years. Disease swept off those whom he respected. The new settlement presented a drab appearance. All the trees were cut down as a matter of safety. Charred stumps stood on every side and a flower garden was so rare that it was quickly noted by the traveller.[32] The poor means of communication, lack of books, libraries, music, and other restraining influences were in part responsible for the harshness which grew up. The pioneer, lacking the mental and moral poise which comes from social contacts, was guilty of drunkenness, swearing and fighting. One of the first obligations which many religious denominations took upon themselves was the restraining of these obvious faults. The Methodist church met part of this need by the camp meeting but more systematically through the agency of the class meeting. The Presbyterian church used their elder system to combat the worst forms of vice noticeable in the pioneers. The diary of the Rev. William Proudfoot had numerous references in which the elders who report sins of commission are advised to talk to the guilty party. Following is a characteristic example: 'James Fraser told me that Archie McFarlane at a bee had sworn profanely – but that he was not in drink. I told James Fraser to talk with him on the subject.'[33]

The social structure of the backwoods was of a type that increased the temptation to drink. The backwoodsman was forced to rely on his neighbours for their aid in clearing his land and erecting his buildings. Usually wherever the pioneers gathered liquor would be found. Numerous instances are recorded of the prevalence of whiskey at the logging bees or at the 'raising bees' called for the purpose of erecting houses or barns. Indeed, the most important man on these occasions was the whiskey boss or the individual responsible for the serving of liquid refreshments to the thirsty workers. Apparently some attended the bees for no other purpose than to partake of the refreshments. The bee was the only logical method by which the heavy work of the period could have been performed but it sometimes proved an uneconomical one. The Rev. William Proudfoot of London, an opponent of temperance societies, perceived the weakness of the system of bees when he raised his log house, in the year 1833. The task occupied three days and ninety men were engaged in the work though not all on the same day. His ideas of thriftiness were somewhat outraged for he records: 'Had I to give them their victuals and drink the raising would have cost an outlay more than a frame house. Many of the people came for the sole purpose of drinking and never once assisted in lifting a log. Many got drunk.'[34] The Rev. William Proudfoot was not called upon to provide meals and drink either because of his profession or more likely because much of the work was being performed by members of his congregation.

The men were often difficult to control on these occasion and fatalities sometimes occurred. Different methods were employed to retain the services of the men from one day to the next. One man found it necessary to procure the services of a fiddler in order to hold the men for the following day. J. Thomson, a settler in Medonte township, wrote in 1834 that on the second evening of a bee, one man was killed during 'a half-playful scuffle' in the kitchen. During this bee, which lasted three days only, and at which no more than thirty men were present on any one day, the men consumed fifteen gallons of whiskey, a barrel of flour, a barrel of pork, besides tea, sugar, etc.[35]

Pioneer weddings provided many opportunities for festivity, although some of the amusements were harmless. For example, the Highland Scotch often celebrated the occasion by the playing of the bagpipes. The dancing and drinking which often accompanied the festivity, however, were often not quite as harmless.

The descendants of the pioneers still recount some of the stories told by their forefathers of the hilarious occasions which attended the wakes of the period. So hilarious did the participants become at times that the corpse was offered a share of the beverage. The practice of supplying liquor to the mourners and friends of the deceased was widespread. In 1817 a Mrs Hewit was buried in the Niagara peninsula. The cost of digging the grave and for the seven different kinds of liquor was £12.4.0.[36] Written or verbal notices were forwarded to the neighbours and friends and the funerals of the era were largely attended. Very often the rooms were too small to contain the crowd and the surplus remained outside, where trays of cake and wine were distributed.[37]

June 4 of each year was set aside in many of the districts as a day for the training of the militia. Many writers who had viewed these parades drew ludicrous pictures of the equipment and the manœuvres. The accounts agree in telling of the drinking which enlivened the proceedings. The only point of disagreement was as to how much drill was attempted before the horse racing and drinking began. During a debate in the House of Assembly[37] in February, 1828, according to William Lyon Mackenzie, Captain Mathews enquired, 'What good effects had arisen from militia trainings – the people assembled from various part of the country, and on reaching the ground, a spectator would find beer kegs, and whiskey kegs, and the people drinking and stimulating themselves with ardent spirits; the officers and men often make fools of themselves, going through a few manœuvres they know very little about. Then comes whiskey again.'[38] Joseph Pickering, an observant writer, dismissed the whole thing as merely a frolic for the youngsters.[39]

The officers continued the consumption of liquor at the mess held the same evening which always followed the parades. In 1833 the Rev. William Proudfoot attended the officers' mess held in London. He departed after the king's, queen's, governor's, and his lady's health were drunk.[40] He remained evidently for a longer period the following year for he notes that one of the toasts proposed by an officer was 'to the memory of the Duke of Wellington,'[41] who did not die till eighteen years later.

Other writers recorded the distribution of liquors and other refreshments in abundance at elections, with the result that some became 'frolicsome and others mischievous, some danced and sang, others swore and threatened,' and before evening, 'several bloody battles' were usually fought.[42] The close of an election was made the occasion for a final outburst. At Perth, in 1820, William Morris was 'chaired' in a handsome manner and a procession paraded the streets for several hours. The procession and crowd stopped at various places and were 'regaled with wines and other liquor, which soon made them forget all their hardships and difficulties of a new settlement.'[43] Artificial stimulation must have been liberal to keep such a programme interesting in a village two years old and of about 300 inhabitants.

The religious meetings, especially the camp meetings, served as a splendid place for the vendor to dispose of his wares. Beer and cider were sometimes sold outside the camp grounds[44] and liquor was brought by some even within the area of the grounds. Rowdies and intoxicated men were often present at the meetings.[45] This state of affairs casts no sinister reflections upon the leaders of the religious meetings or the sincere worshippers, but serves as evidence to prove that liquor flowed freely wherever and whenever men gathered in the pioneer era.

Much of the liquor drunk was of the poorest quality, being described by MacTaggart as little better than fire and brimstone, 'made of frosty potatoes, hemlock, pumpkins and black mouldy rye.'[46] Sir Richard Bonnycastle, writing in 1846, noted that whiskey, with very atrocious brandy, was the only beverage excepting water that could be procured along the country roads of Canada.[47] Liquors of various kinds were kept on board the Canadian steamers. Whiskey, rum, port, and sherry, the two latter as fiery as brandy, were all kept on board. It was customary for the passengers to call for a pint of wine while they were at dinner, or for a bottle, according to the size of the party.[48] Cider was to be found in many of the homes of the province, especially in the older settlements. This beverage was sold at from 5 shillings and 6 pence to 9 shillings per barrel. The customary charge for making cider was one-half the product, the farmer providing the barrels and the apples.[49] Joseph Pickering noted that beer was coming into use in 1826.[50] The inhabitants had developed a taste for alcoholic stimulants and were not particular as to the kind offered or sold. The ease with which liquor could be procured, combined with the mental attitude of the backwoodsman who lived a drab and colourless life, made drinking a natural effort to escape from the realization of surroundings and to attain some measure of forgetfulness.

Authentic accounts are rarely given of the amount consumed daily or even yearly by the individual. One man believed that he had consumed forty gallons a year before joining a temperance society.[51] The description of carousals and the drunkenness contained in the old diaries indicate the quantity must have been great though one hesitates to accept the estimate of forty gallons a year.

Considerable emphasis was placed by temperance advocates upon the numerous deaths caused by the excessive drinking. John Rolph, an exponent of temperance societies, said in a speech at the Union Chapel, Ancaster, 23 October 1829, that eleven of the thirteen deaths in the Ancaster region had been directly or indirectly traced to intemperance at coroner John Burwell's inquiries. In the district of Bathurst, in 1828, there were twenty inquests at each of which the cause of death was traced to the use of ardent spirits.[52] Other writers give gruesome details of suicides committed while people were under the influence of liquor or narrate numerous instances of individuals who perished because of drink.[53] The most common crimes in the province were those of offences against the person or assault, many of which could be traced to the influence of intoxicating drinks.[54]

Drunkenness, amongst the aboriginal Indians, was very prevalent during the pioneer era. The practice of giving liquor to the Indians was not a new or peculiar one to the period, rather it had been a problem for some centuries. The intense rivalry of the English and French traders found part of its expression in the struggle of rum and brandy. The English trader enticed the Indian with rum while his competitor endeavoured to beguile the red man with brandy. Brandy was of a much better quality than rum but the Indian was not concerned so much with quality as with quantity. The result, however, was always the same, namely the debauchery of the Indian. Political and economic considerations were more powerful than humanitarian impulses until 1840. However, one of the greatest governors of New France, Count of Frontenac, was recalled in 1682 because of his stand on the liquor question. His recall was brought about chiefly through the influence of the powerful Bishop Francois de Laval. While Laval's influence was sufficient to bring about the recall of a governor, it was not powerful enough to end the traffic. The French traders claimed that a cessation of the practice would have thrown all the fur trade to the English.

After the fall of New France, liquor was still used in the Indian trade; national rivalry giving way to a struggle for profit. The fur traders sought every opportunity of leading the Indians into habits of intemperance and thereby procuring their furs in a fraudulent manner.[55] They fed the red man whiskey and endeavoured to keep him under its influence while they were trading with him.[56] Various devices were tried if the Indian refused to partake peaceably of the beverage offered. Some traders offered cider, not telling the red man that whiskey had been placed in the cider.[57] One of the traders brought a barrel of rum into an Indian village and after placing a straw in it, invited everyone to take a suck through the straw gratis.[58] The unscrupulous dealer even resorted to physical force and poured liquor down the throats of the resisting Indians.[59]

For many years the government included a supply of rum among their annual presents to the Indian. On some reserves this practice was discontinued by 1827.[60] Too often the annual presents, blankets, guns, knives, and tomahawks were bartered by the Indians immediately for a little whiskey.[61] An Act was passed in 1840 forbidding anyone to give, sell, barter, or exchange liquor with the Indians. This Act was the result of an Indian petition which came from the reserves at Muncey, Grand River, and other places.[62]

The entry of the farmer drove many of the fur-traders northward and removed from the Indian one source of temptation. The red man, however, did not gain from the advent of the tiller of the soil. His hunting grounds were curtailed and the villages which grew up, though providing some benefits to the Indian, also offered increased facilities for procuring alcoholic stimulants.[63] Drinking was the besetting weakness of the Indian and frequently he lay by the roadside drunk, or around the shops kept by the whites.[64]

What were the effects of the heavy consumption of liquor? A number of the Indians suffered violent deaths. Some shot themselves,[65] some were burned or frozen to death while they were intoxicated. The Rev. James Evans, the Methodist missionary, Rapids Mission, on the St Clair, records the death of thirty-nine adults at that place because of the use of ardent spirits. This survey covered the years 1834–8, the four years previous to the introduction of the Gospel.[66]

The temperance movement, like all other great movements in history, began not with the crowd but with the lone call or the few voices in the wilderness. Dr Rush, who had signed the Declaration of Independence, endeavoured to arouse the thoughts of the people of the United States to the physical evils of drunkenness, during the closing years of the eighteenth and beginning of the nineteenth centuries. The Rev. Lyman Beecher and a few others made an effort in the first quarter of the nineteenth century to arouse further the inhabitants of the Republic. This latter group stressed the moral, physical, and spiritual evils of the traffic.

The heralds of this movement went forth into a world where the habitual use of liquor was customary. Some men, undoubtedly, perceived the evils of the traffic, especially if carried to excess. Because the after world was continually stressed by the theologians others were apprehensive of the future punishment that would fall on those who abused liquor. The apprehension arose not from the thought that there was anything inherently wrong in drinking liquor, but from observation of the evil effects of excessive drinking. The parent might disagree with the individual who had become a slave to liquor, but he still partook of it, and gave it to his child, sometimes cautioning him not to take too much. Some attempt was made to build up the ideal of self-control, but the environment was of such a type the teaching was difficult to put into practice. Pioneer life has never been noted for the ideal of self-control. The backwoodsman of Upper Canada and the frontiersman of the United States often ate too much, swore profanely, or fought at the least provocation. Eventually some men thought that the habits were in need of reformation. Under the prevailing system, men who were licensed to sell liquor to the public frequently made drunkards and helped to bury them, and sometimes seized their property for debt.

The men interested in organized reform took what was regarded as an eccentric step for their day in renouncing the use of strong liquors. They formed themselves into little groups or temperance societies for mutual encouragement and the propagation of their ideas. A society was formed in Virginia in 1807, and another in Massachusetts in 1821. A rather remarkable society was organized in New Jersey, not far from Morristown, having the following pledge: 'That no member should be able to drink more than a pint of liquor in one day.'[67] This was finally reduced to one half-pint a day.

In 1826 a simultaneous effort was commenced by the philanthropists of America to remove intemperance. On the 10 January of this year a meeting was held in Boston, an agent sent out, and a committee appointed to prepare a constitution for the society.[68] The movement, thus begun, gathered momentum through the years and eventually spread throughout the Republic.

It is rather difficult to estimate the influence of the United States upon the beginning of the temperance movement in Upper Canada. At this period temperance societies were arising in many different sections of the Republic and in their origins these societies were not connected with one another. The same may be true of Upper Canada. The feeling toward temperance was growing in the public mind and a society could have arisen in the province without any special American influence. The early educational efforts of Dr Rush and the Rev. Lyman Beecher should not be forgotten, however, in a study of the question. Though it is impossible to prove conclusively any direct American influence in the formation of temperance societies in the province, still there would seem to be some foundation for this belief because of the influence of American thought in other fields. The religious phenomena of the one were revealed in the other and the movements passed rapidly from one country to the other. Camp meetings and protracted meetings originated in the Republic and quickly made their appearance in the province. Colonel Thomas Talbot and others condemned the temperance movement partly because they believed that it was tinged with 'Yankeeism.' Some men believed that the first temperance society formed at Aylmer was organized by some Yankees of strong anti-British tendencies.[69]

Evidence is quite conclusive that the American influence was very marked in Upper Canada in the thirties. This influence came, chiefly, from the State of New York, which was a strong temperance centre at this date. Mr T. Turner, the organizer of the New York State Temperance Society, visited and lectured in the province in 1835. He was invited to deliver an address at the quarterly temperance meeting of the Thorold society on 20 November.[70] During the autumn of 1835, he visited twenty-one places in the province and delivered addresses. The *St. Catharines Journal* records that more than five hundred pledged abstinence from all intoxicating liquors. In Hamilton, one hundred persons became members of the temperance institution, 75 per cent of whom pledged total abstinence from all intoxicating stimulants.[71]

Humanitarian impulses in both countries gained a great impetus from the speeches and writings of the Revival preachers. To us in the twentieth century the theology of the Revivalist seems harsh and crude. The theology did stress the value of human life, though it developed also a spirit of intolerance toward other individuals and their opinions. The audience of these clergy must also be kept in mind. They were addressing a people who were living close to nature, whose passions were primitive and whose minds and emotions were best stirred by harsh words. One of these ministers, the Rev. Charles Finney, influenced a number of men, particularly Theodore Dwight Weld, a man who became a leader in humanitarian enterprises.

Another factor which throws some light upon the subject is revealed in the attitude of the various churches and their leaders. Churches which depended upon the United States for a supply of clergy were invariably ardent supporters of the temperance movement. The American Presbyterian, Methodist Episcopal, and some sections of the Baptists turned to the Republic for some of their leaders. Many of the clergy and members of the American Presbyterian church were favourable to temperance societies. Indeed, one church of this denomination was founded at Hamilton in 1833 'in which none were received or retained as members who make, vend or use as a drink, ardent spirits.'[72] The minister of this church, the Rev. Edward Marsh, was an American by birth. The members of this denomination were pledging themselves to a stricter abstinence than was customary in temperance societies in Upper Canada and the discipline was more exacting than that in force in the Methodist Episcopal church. According to the discipline of the latter body the preacher in charge was to proceed against a member if he sold or gave spirituous liquors or if anything disorderly took place under his roof on that account.[73]

The Methodist Episcopal church which was of American origin revealed an early interest in the temperance movement. Many of the circuit riders had been influenced directly by the revival preachers of the Republic or had imbibed the sentiment from the older men of the body. As early as 1830, the Rev. William Case commended temperance societies to the conference. He stressed the point that 'It is the design of our discipline, and it has ever been our aim, to make our church emphatically a temperance society.'[74] He noted that the aim of the body was to make every follower a member of a temperance society, as well as to place ardent spirits on the shelves of apothecary shops, to be used only for medicinal purposes upon the advice of a physician. The conference passed a resolution, the first unanimous record in this direction, though individual churches had expressed sentiments favourable to this course as early as 1830.

The Baptists, in the tenth annual meeting of the Western Baptist Association, passed a resolution 'that we cordially recommend the Temperance cause to the consideration and patronage of the churches which we represent and the associations with which we correspond.'[75]

What was the attitude of the bodies which were begun by missionaries from the British Isles? These denominations as a whole did not take an active part on either side of the question. Individual members, however, expressed their opinions. The Rev. William Clarke, of London, a clergyman of the Congregationalist church, was very active in promoting the work of the societies. He joined a society in Toronto in July 1839. The Rev. Egerton Ryerson, editor of the *Christian Guardian*, gave in his allegiance at the same meeting.[76]

The Rev. William Proudfoot, a minister of the United Secession church (Presbyterian), opposed temperance societies because he felt that they did not rest upon the Word of God.[77] He was not in sympathy with unrestricted or excessive drinking and apparently believed that the solution of the problem lay in the building up of self-control in the individual. He perceived the evil of the habit and notes the abuse of liquor at bees and military training. On one occasion he asked a tavern keeper to close his bar on Sunday.[78] The Rev. William Fraser, a Canadian belonging to the same denomination, was an ardent teetotaler who spoke at some temperance meetings.[79] The Rev. George Cheyne of Amherstburg, Rev. William Smart of Brockville, and the Rev. William Harris of Toronto were Presbyterians of other sections of the body which supported the movement.

The clergy of the Church of England were probably the most united in their opposition. Part of the opposition might be classed as indifference. The feeling that these societies were of American origin made some of the clergy distrustful. Then again some took a similar stand as that of the Rev. William Proudfoot or felt that the supporters of the temperance movement were mixing the principle of temperance and prohibition. Certain of the clergy were in sympathy with the impulse. Bishop Stewart of Quebec in 1836 attended a temperance meeting at Saratoga and asked leave to speak.[80] Some of the delegates at the conference were somewhat perturbed at the request because they thought that he shared the aversion so often displayed by his clergy. His speech, however, was a helpful one in the cause of temperance. The Rev. Richard Flood, the Church of England missionary at Delaware and to the Indians of the neighbourhood, formed a temperance society among the Indians of that place. After taking down the names of the Indians who desired to join he prayed for a blessing on the good work. The oath taken by a number of the chiefs is rather interesting: 'That we believe that the fire-water (spirits) of the white man is very bad for our bodies and souls, and that we and our people will strive to be sober, and to obey our father (ie, me) in all he tells us, that the Great Spirit has spoken in His Book.'[81]

Temperance writers and workers believed that the indifference of the Church of England was also reflected by the officials in high positions in the country. One quotation from an account by James S. Buckingham, probably written in 1839, will serve to show this. He wrote: 'There is a Temperance Society here (Toronto), on the principle of total abstinence from all that can intoxicate, but their members are few, the higher classes of society, and the Episcopal clergy, withholding their patronage and support. During one of the evenings of my stay here, I delivered a public address on the subject of Temperance in the Wesleyan Methodist Church, but though it was very numerously attended, there were very few of the leading families among the auditory; and the only members of the clergy present were a congregational minister and a Roman Catholic priest.' The writer went on to say that the absence of all the heads of the community on the occasion could only be attributed to their 'indifference or unwillingness to countenance or uphold the cause of temperance' because on all other occasions when he gave lectures on Egypt and Palestine the church was crowded to excess. The lieutenant-governor, the chief justice, and other official dignitaries of the province and city attended all lectures but that on temperance.[82] In Kingston, he also found that the Temperance Society was not countenanced by the higher classes.[83]

The Quakers were friendly to the cause of temperance. Their views of discipline and ecclesiastical policy, however, tended to discourage the formation of societies amongst their people.[84] Their influence was exerted in an effort to restrain their members from drinking at bees and offering others liquor.

The Rev. Isaac Fidler, writing in 1832, stated that there were no temperance societies in Canada but that, if those in the United States were a success, they would be adopted.[85] At that time, contrary to Fidler's opinion, there were several societies in Canada. Evidence is quite conclusive that the first temperance society in Canada was formed in Montreal. A meeting was held in St Andrew's church, St Peter's Street, on the evening of 9 June 1828. After some statements on the subject of intemperance by the Rev. J. Christmas, the following preamble was submitted and signed by twenty-nine persons of different religious denominations.

PREAMBLE

We the subscribers, in view of the many evils resulting from the use of distilled spirits, do hereby promise, that we will entirely abstain from their use, except as medicine, that we will banish them from our families, that we will not give them to persons employed by us; and that we will use our influence in discouraging their use among our friends.[86]

The city of Montreal may seem to be outside the range of our topic, but Montreal was the great temperance centre of the pioneer period. The societies in that city had a very large membership. A newspaper, the *Canada Temperance Advocate*, was published there and circulated through Upper Canada as well as the other colonies. The societies in Montreal were very active since they sent forth numerous organizers to spread their doctrines.

The first temperance society organized in Upper Canada was formed in Bastard Township, in Leeds county, on 10 June 1828.[87] The movement spread over Upper Canada rapidly. In 1829, societies were organized at Beverley, Ancaster, and Stoney Creek.[88] By 1830 the *Canadian Watchman* was able to announce that 'temperance has commenced its glorious and irresistible march.'[89] R.D. Wadsworth, the corresponding secretary of the Montreal Temperance Society, reported that by 1832 there were about 100 societies in Upper Canada, with a membership of 10,000 persons, and that twelve newspapers lent their aid to the advance of temperance principles.[90] He gives a list containing the names of some of the places which had temperance organizations prior to 1832. This includes towns and townships from almost every section of Upper Canada.[91]

The organization of the societies was entirely local and they belonged, at first, to no larger provincial or American body. The meetings, usually annual, though occasionally semi-annual or quarterly, were simple. They were begun with prayer and the minutes of the previous meeting. An address or sermon on the evils of intemperance followed. After the sermon, if it was not a 'teetotal' society, a discussion usually took place on the merits of total or partial abstinence. Occasionally no special speaker was heard, but any members of the organization who wished to do so aired their opinions. At other times, the meeting was given up to passing, after suitable discussion, resolutions which had been previously prepared. These resolutions were directed against the 'crying evils of intemperance.' Periodically they contained clauses of congratulation to other societies on their formation, and expressions of gratification at the spread of the movement. Constructive suggestions advocating a more unified organization were not neglected.[92] It was not uncommon for the annual sermon to be published in the form of a pamphlet for distribution.

The constitution of the local society was usually introduced with a preamble similar in thought to that signed by the members of the Montreal society. In some societies each member paid a small fee. Officers were elected and usually a provision was placed in the constitution requiring a two-thirds vote of the members present at the general meeting to bring about a change.

Some attempts were made to build up district and provincial organizations. The Bastard Township, in 1830, recommended a union of all local bodies and offered to provide the first executive but, although other societies endorsed the proposal, there is no record of any such organization.[93] Bathurst District, however, did achieve some kind of unity. The *Bathurst Courier* announced a meeting to be held at Carleton Place on 23 February 1836 for delegates and officers of all societies in the district, at which secretaries were expected to present reports.[94] There was no evidence that this was more than a meeting for discussion. A temperance convention was held in the Presbyterian church, St Catharines, on 30 August 1836. Representatives were present from Thorold, Lundy's Lane, Pelham, Smithsville, Beamsville, Grantham, Gainsborough, Niagara, Allanburgh, and St Catharines.[95]

The first Provincial Temperance Convention for Lower Canada was held on 26 February 1834. The first attempt made to form a provincial society in Upper Canada was in the year 1836. The meeting was held at Toronto the 28th of September of that year. Delegates were present from thirteen societies. A resolution was passed to form a Provincial Society,[96] and a number of interesting resolutions were passed. One asked the government to restrain the manufacture and sale of liquor. Another noted the superabundance of public houses and their condition. Other resolutions considered the advisability of establishing stores and inns on temperance principles and advised the clergy to inculate in the youth the principles of temperance.[97]

A rather interesting phase of the tendency toward wider organization was the attendance of delegates from Upper and Lower Canada at the convention held at Saratoga Springs, New York, in 1837.[98] The American Society was reorganized and the name changed to the American Temperance Union, in order that any society on the continent might become an auxiliary.

Almost from the first the societies were divided on the merits of the 'old' and 'new pledge.' The old pledge was taken against the use of spirituous liquors, but with the use of wine and beer allowed. The new pledge was for total abstinence from all acoholic beverages, except for medicinal purposes. This distinction made for three classes of societies, those devoted to total abstinence, those allowing the use of wine and beer, and combination societies with both pledges. A part of the annual meeting in the two latter types was devoted to admitting new members and to changing the pledges of those who wished to become teetotalers. The first total abstinence society in Canada was formed at St Catharines, in the Niagara District, 15 June 1835, when almost forty signatures were obtained.[99] The leaders in the temperance movement early reached the conclusion that only total abstinence societies could succeed,[100] and by 1840 that type was general.

The leaders of the movement spread their doctrines in many ways. A favourite method was to approach one of the recognized leaders of the community and having gained his support use his name for its influence in the district in which he lived. For example, John Bostwick of Port Stanley was approached and gave his support to the formation of a society in that village. A delegate of the Toronto society waited upon the Lieut.-Governor and won his influence.[101] A similar method was adopted in the framing of the constitution of the local society. Some of the leading men of the district were asked to move the resolution to form the society or the laws which governed its business meeting. Some of the distillers and retailers were allowed to sell their stock on hand if they would join the society. Sermons were often preached by those favourable to the cause in the locality.[102]

Some of the societies, particularly the first one organized in Montreal, sent out organizers to speak and to form new branches. The clergy and other suitable men often undertook long and arduous journeys to further the cause. The Rev. W. Clarke of London acted at times in the capacity of organizer as did Mr R.D. Wadsworth of Montreal. The clergy formed societies without the aid of an organizer.[103]

Attempts were made to have mercantile houses stop the sale of liquor. Some of these firms did abandon the trade in intoxicating liquors.[104] In Alophustown the members pledged themselves 'not to furnish drink for raisings, bees, and harvest work.'[105] In some townships the societies were strong enough to prevent the use of liquor at bees. Whiskey was never used at a raising in Oro Township, where a temperance society came with the first settlers.[106] Temperance taverns or houses were opened in some localities. The proprietors advertised these houses in the newspapers which favoured the temperance cause. Charles Marsh, of Chippawa, opened a house of this type in 1836. He set forth the advantages of his house by explaining that 'Every exertion will be made to render the Establishment in reality the "Travellers Home" undisturbed by the noise and turmoil incident to those places more or less where spirituous liquors are sold.'[107]

Different types of societies were formed. Separate groups were organized among young people,[108] women, and soldiers. The Negro was not forgotten, for an African Temperance Society had been formed at St Catharines by 1835.[109]

An appeal was made to the children. Their pledge took the form of a doggerel verse.

This little band   To turn our home
Do with our hand   Into a hell,
The pledge now sign,   Where none could dwell,
To drink no wine,   Whence peace would fly,
Nor brandy red   Where hope would die,
To turn our head,   And love expire,
Nor whiskey hot,   Mid such a fire:
That makes the sot,   So here we pledge perpetual hate
Nor fiery rum   To all that can intoxicate.[110]

The temperance meetings were well attended by the pioneers. This attendance was gained in part by the skilful use of songs and hymns. The backwoodsman stood in need of an outlet for his emotions, an outlet which was furnished to some extent by the opportunity provided to express himself in verse. Many new hymns and hymnals were published in the era. Temperance sentiment was fostered and its doctrines taught by the verse. The following verses were composed to mark the first annual meeting of the Pelham Youths' Temperance Society:

Now wilt thou condescend to bless
    The Temperance cause, we pray,
And over-rule us all on this
    Our annual meeting day

Direct us by the word of truth
    Instruct us as thine own,
That we may spend our days of youth
    To Thee and Thee alone.

It is a cause of peace and love
    In which we have begun;
And without blessings from above
    The work cannot go on.

Let drunkenness with all its woes,
    From day to day decline,
'Till we shall see no more of those
    Who tarry long at wine.

May total abstinence prevail,
    And take its royal stand;
O may its banners never fail
    To wave through Pelham's land.

From sea to sea – from clime to clime –
Soon may it spread its way,
And hasten on that blessed time –
The bright millenial day.[111]

The hymns which were usually set to a lively tune not only drew crowds to the meetings but served to inspire to greater efforts those who had already joined the movement, a necessary action if the movement was to meet with any success. Unfortunately, the exponents of abstinence principles too often drew the implication that all who differed in thought were wrong, unrighteous, or in the language of some of the theologians were sinners.

After the Rebellion of 1837, which retarded the movement, the press was set to work to a greater extent than hitherto. In 1839 the price of the *Advocate* was reduced one-half and its circulation doubled, and copies were sent free for about five years to the clergy and schoolteachers of the province. Other newspapers, notably the *Temperance Record*, were founded for the purpose of disseminating temperance principles. This paper was published in March 1836, and continued for about two years. It was under the supervision of the Toronto society.[112]

Upon the union of the provinces in 1841 the Montreal committee resolved to call a convention of all the societies in the united province to ascertain their present strength; to supply at a very low price every society, and through them every magistrate, member of parliament, clergyman, and schoolteacher with a copy of the pamplet 'Anti-Bacchus'; and to send lecturing agents to visit every township in the land, with the view to reviving old societies and forming new ones.[113]

It is impossible to judge what success in checking intemperance resulted from these efforts. The societies were opposed and certain interests took cognizance of their existence. Colonel Thomas Talbot characterized the societies as 'Damned cold water drinking societies.'[114] No doubt some felt that they would be losing respect by joining such organizations. The *Canadian Watchman* published in all seriousness, yet withal gleefully, an 'awful warning,' telling how the president of an 'intemperance society' formed in Camden Township, following the organization of the temperance society there, had been murdered by the secretary, who in turn was hanged.[115] The inkeepers of Peterborough took notice of a local society, displaying, if not an appreciation of the organization, at least a sense of humour, when they published as an advertisement a 'notice extraordinary, to teetotalers,' which stated: 'It is particularly requested that all our old friends previous to joining the Total Abstinence Society, will have the honesty to abstain from leaving their Tavern Bills unpaid, and thus prove that tho' inimical to *ardent liquors*, they possess a *quantum suff* of the proper spirit.' It was signed the 'Tavern Keepers.'[116]

Many reports of progress were confined to statements that many drunkards 'had been reclaimed' or that there had been no 'instances of apostasy.' These records are not of great historical value as proofs because they contain no definite information. Examples of progress may, however, be noted. At the sixth anniversary of the commencement of the Welland Canal no alcoholic beverages were drunk.[117] William Hamilton Merrit, who had identified himself at an early date with the temperance movement, was responsible, no doubt, for the absence of liquor on this occasion. At Glasgow, River St Clair, two of the stores did not sell liquor, and in the same district some accounts stated that no liquor was used at many of the bees.[118] Temperance societies had some effect in checking crime. Men qualified to judge concede this, but facts and figures are not available on which to base any conclusions. The *Bathurst Courier*, which gave reports of meetings and generally encouraged the temperance movement, was of the opinion that the effect of the movement was not very great.[119]

The forces working toward the goal of total abstinence made some important gains. Prohibition had been forced upon the province during the war of 1812–14 by the scarcity of wheat for food. The sixth provincial parliament called by Sir Roger Hale Sheaffe and sitting from 25 February to 13 March 1813 passed an act authorizing the person administering the government of the province to prohibit the exportation of grain and to restrain the distillation of spirituous liquors from grain. This proclamation was revoked, but after a supply of liquor was distilled for the troops another proclamation was issued forbidding until 1 March 1814 the distillation of grain. After this date prohibition was permitted to lapse.[120] Though this measure was only meant by the authorities to be a temporary one still it it more or less set the goal for the temperance workers. Some men cherished the ideal of prohibition by law at this period and looked to the political field to settle moral problems. The Rev. John Roaf, a congregationalist minister of Toronto, an unflinching teetotaler, was anxious to raise up in Upper Canada a temperance party which he hoped would embrace all the others. A bill with prohibition as its ideal was introduced in the legislature but this was defeated.[121] Upper Canada was probably fortunate in this respect because such laws were reversed in New Brunswick and in several States of the Union. The people were not prepared for drastic legislation of this type and more was gained by a slower and more educational policy. However, some laws which dealt with the control of liquor were enacted. The practice of giving or selling liquor to the Indians was discontinued. The laws governing the granting of licenses were strengthened and the condition of many of the inns improved.

The Rebellion of 1837 and the falling away of many from the societies proved conclusively that numbers did not count nearly so much as quality. At that time the members were fairly united in their belief of the value of the total abstinence form of society. Temperance literature was placed before the public, leaders were trained, and a foundation laid for the greater activities of the forties.

There is but little doubt that some families were benefitted by the movement. Men were awakened to the needs of their fellowmen not only in this field but in others. The great value of the meetings was that they provided an outlet for the emotions and met in part the need for social life. Sometimes the meetings took the form of a free debate. For example, a clergyman at Sandwich rose to protest against the doctrines of the societies. He was answered by the president and another clergyman.[122] This type of meeting provided excitement which the pioneer demanded and which he otherwise secured by fighting or jostling. Occasionally the speaker at a meeting advised rather drastic methods and rather overstated his case. The Rev. John Ryerson, in a speech delivered in the Union Chapel, Ancaster, at a public meeting called for the purpose of forming a society for the suppression of intemperance, advised the female section of the community to turn their backs on all tipplers and all who were in the habit of drinking.[123] We have no record to prove that this advice was followed and the conclusion could be safely drawn that it was disregarded. However frank, if inapplicable, advice like this would help to provide some amusement in an atmosphere that was too often gloomy and disheartening.

NOTES

Reprinted from Ontario Historical Society, *Papers and Records*, XXVII, 1931, 341–60, by kind permission of the society. An extended bibliography which followed has been omitted.

 1 *Bathurst Courier*, 5 Feb. 1836
 2 Joseph Pickering, *Inquiries of an Emigrant* (London 1831), 111
 3 Rev William Proudfoot, *Diary*, 30 March 1833
 4 W.L. Smith, *Pioneers of Old Ontario* (Toronto 1923), 295
 5 Mrs Anna Jameson, *Winter Studies and Summer Rambles* (New York 1839), I, 316–17; cf *Canadian Christian Examiner*, IV, 100
 6 Rev. William Proudfoot, *Papers* (London 1922). Published in the London and Middlesex Historical Society, *Transactions*, Part XI, 85
 7 *The Palladium*, 4 April 1833. Robinson Papers, Ontario Archives [OA], package 25, no 3
 8 *Gore Gazette*, 14 June 1828
 9 Jameson, *Winter Studies*, I, 293
10 W.J.D. Waddilove, *The Stewart Missions* (London 1838), 184
11 Henry John Jones, Diary, published in *Willisons Monthly*, IV, 10, 20 Feb. 1837, 11, 7 Feb., 13, 27 May, 31 July, 2 Sept. 1837
12 *Canada in the years 1832, 1833, and 1834* (Dublin 1835), 25; John Howison, *Sketches of Upper Canada* (Edinburgh 1825), 222, 224; David Wilkie, *Sketches of a Summer Trip to New York and the Canadas* (Edinburgh 1837), 151; Patrick Shirreff, *A Tour through North America* (Edinburgh 1835), 103, 94; Jameson, *Winter Studies*, I, 317; *Canada Temperance Advocate* (Montreal), IV, 85; VI, 12
13 *Emigration, Letters from Sussex Emigrants* (Petworth 1833), 6, 11, 33

14 Rev. Isaac Fidler, *Observations on Professions* (London 1833), 269, 387; John T. McNeill, *Religious and Moral Conditions among the Canadian Pioneers* (New York 1928), published in the papers of the American Society of Church History, VIII, 84
15 Canniff Haight, *Country Life in Canada fifty years ago* (Toronto 1885) 26
16 *Canada Temperance Advocate*, II, Sept. 1837
17 Jameson, *Winter Studies*, I, 214; Proudfoot Diary, 29 April 1833
18 Proudfoot Diary, 10 Nov. 1835; Jameson, *Winter Studies*, I, 214
19 *Canada Temperance Advocate*, II, June 1840
20 Ibid, IV, 43
21 James Croil, *Dundas* (Montreal 1861), 145
22 Proudfoot Diary, 1 Sept. 1834
23 Mrs Susanna Moodie, *Life in the Clearings* (New York), viii, 57–9; Major C.M. Strickland, *Twenty-seven years in Canada West* (London 1853), 140–1
24 Moodie, *Life in the Clearings*, vii
25 Howison, *Sketches of Upper Canada*, 79 ff
26 Proudfoot, *Papers*, 1915, VI, 62
27 Rev. Henry Christmas, *Immigrant Churchman*, London, 1849, I, p. 105
28 Edward Allen Talbot, *Five years residence in the Canadas* (London 1824), II, 57–8; Francis A. Evans, *The Emigrant's Directory* (Dublin 1833); Jameson, *Winter Studies*, I, 62; Fidler, *Observations*, 390
29 Pickering, *Inquiries*, 55
30 Ibid, 73
31 Rev. William Bell, *Hints to Emigrants* (Edinburgh 1824), 181; A.C. Buchanan, *Emigration practically considered* (London 1828), 94
32 Charles Daubeny, *Journal, tour through United States and Canada*, 1837–1838 (Oxford 1843), 40
33 Proudfoot Diary, 22 June 1834
34 Ibid, 12 June 1833. Cf Mrs Catharine Parr Traill, *Backwoods of Canada* (London 1836), 135; Pickering, *Inquiries*, 160
35 J. Thomson, Diary, 19 to 24 April 1834, OA
36 Niagara Historical Society Publications, XXXII–XXXVI, 32
37 *U.E. Loyalist*, 30 Sept. 1826; *Upper Canada Herald*, 5 July 1825
38 W.L. Mackenzie, *Sketches of Canada and the United States* (London 1833), 276
39 Pickering, *Inquiries*, 56
40 Proudfoot Diary, 4 June 1833
41 Ibid, 4 June 1834
42 Bell, *Hints*, 148; cf Pickering, *Inquiries*, 151
43 Ibid, 148
44 *Canadian Christian Examiner*, 1837, 363
45 Ibid, 364
46 John MacTaggart, *Three Years in Canada* (London 1829), I, 200
47 Sir Richard Henry Bonnycastle, *Canada and the Canadians, in 1846* (London 1901), I, 124
48 Ibid, 101–2
49 Pickering, *Inquiries*, 97
50 Ibid, 96
51 *Christian Guardian*, 3 Feb. 1830
52 Ibid, 2 Jan. 1830
53 Proudfoot Diary, 27 July 1834; Jameson, *Winter Studies*, I, 244; Rev. J. Abbot, *Philip Musgrave* (London 1850), 134–5; J.H. Hilts, *Experiences of a backwoods preacher* (Toronto 1887), 228ff; Strickland, *Twenty-seven Years*, 36ff; Traill, *Backwoods of Canada*, 94

54 James B. Brown, *Views of Canada and the Colonists* (Edinburgh 1851), 162–3
55 *S.P.G. Report*, 1827–8, 174; *Missionary Report of Methodist Episcopal Church*, 1837, 11
56 Strickland, *Twenty-seven Years*, 34–5
57 Jameson, *Winter Studies*, II, 53
58 Ibid, 46
59 *Christian Guardian*, 26 Dec. 1829
60 Rev. Peter Jones, *Journal of Rev. Peter Jones* (Toronto 1860), 38–9, 166
61 Pickering, *Inquiries*, 95
62 Ruth Elizabeth Spence, *Prohibition in Canada* (Toronto nd), 28–31
63 Ernest Hawkins, *Annals of Colonial Church, Diocese of Toronto* (London 1848), 69; Jameson, *Winter Studies*, II, 45
64 *S.P.G. Report*, 1827–8, 174; *Canadian Christian Examiner*, 1837, 363; John Carroll, *Case and his Contemporaries* (Toronto 1871), II, 358
65 Egerton Ryerson, *Story of my life* (Toronto 1883), 65
66 *Report of missionary society of the Methodist Episcopal Church*, 1838, 11
67 R.D. Wadsworth, *Temperance Manual* (Montreal 1847), I, 18
68 Ibid, 20. The drinking habits in the United States are given in John A. Krout, *Origins of Prohibition* (New York 1925). The growth of the temperance movement is discussed in John G. Wooley and William Johnson, *Temperance progress in the nineteenth century*.
69 *Reminiscences of early settlers*, Elgin Historical and Scientific Institute (St Thomas 1911), 44
70 *St. Catharines Journal*, Public Archives of Canada, 5 and 19 Nov., 1835. The material procured from the Archives was copied for the writers by Professor Fred Landon, University of Western Ontario.
71 Ibid, 17 Dec. 1835
72 William Gregg, *History of the Presbyterian Church in Canada* (Toronto 1885), 538
73 *Doctrine and Discipline of Methodist Episcopal Church in Canada*, 1829, 84
74 *Minutes of the Annual Conference of the Wesleyan-Methodist Church in Canada, from 1824–1845 inclusive*, 39
75 *Canada Baptist Magazine* (Montreal), CXI, 284
76 *St. Catharines Journal*, 25 July 1839
77 Proudfoot, *Papers*, XI, 32
78 Proudfoot Diary, 7 Aug. 1833
79 William Fraser, Diary, 13 Jan. 1835
80 Ernest Hawkins, *Annals of Colonial Church, Diocese of Quebec* (London 1849), 374
81 Waddilove, *Stewart Missions*, 133
82 James S. Buckingham, *Canada, Nova Scotia, New Brunswick, and other British provinces of North America* (London 1839), 26. (The writers of the article are indebted to Professor A.H. Young for this reference).
83 Ibid, 79
84 Wadsworth, *Temperance Manual*, XI, 31
85 Fidler, *Observations*, 391
86 Wadsworth, *Temperance Manual*, XI, 4–5
87 Ibid; *Canadian Watchman*, 17 Sept. 1830; 7 Jan. 1831
88 Wadsworth, *Temperance Manual*, II, 5
89 *Canadian Watchman*, 13 Aug. 1830
90 Wadsworth, *Temperance Manual*, II, 6–7
91 1830 Glandford, Trafalgar, Belleville, Toronto, Hamilton, Clinton, Ancaster, Thorold, Adolphustown, Cavan, Merrickville, Pelham, Nissouri, London, Ernest Town, Hallowell, Ottawa, Port Hope, Consecon, Kitley, Queen Street, Newmarket, Colborne, Wellington, North Gower, Sidney, Cornwall, Malahide, Union-Street,

Howard, Reach, Smithville, London Village, Whitby, Blenheim and Burford, Ameliasburgh, Oxford, Esquesing, Churchville, Albion, North Gwillimbury, Pickering, Nelson and York.

1831 Dunnville, Matilda, Richmond Hill, Queenston, Sombra and Don, Humber, Yonge Street, Saltfleet, Guelph, Streetsville, Millbrook, Simcoe, Gosfield, Richmond, Peterborough, Middlesex County, Camden, Blenheim and Wilmot, Cobourg, Grafton, Yonge Street, Smith's Falls, Kingston, Murray, Mississippi, Esquesing and Erin Union, Mount Pleasant, Grimsby Gore.

1832 Darlington, Elizabethtown, Scarboro', Perth, Norwich, East Flamborough, Eramosa, Elizabethtown Union.

Wadsworth, Temperance Manual, xi, 5–6

92 *Canadian Watchman,* 17 Sept., 1, 29 Oct. 1830; *Bathurst Courier,* 2 Oct. 1835

93 *Canadian Watchman,* 17 Sept., 29 Oct. 1830

94 *Bathurst Courier,* 5 Feb. 1836

95 *St. Catharines Journal,* 1 Dec. 1836

96 Wadsworth, *Temperance Manual,* II, 11

97 *Canada Temperance Advocate,* Nov. 1836

98 Krout, *Origins of Prohibition,* 153

99 Wadsworth, *Temperance Manual,* xi, 9

100 *Canadian Watchman,* 29 Oct. 1830; *Bathurst Courier,* 2 Oct. 1835

101 *Canada Temperance Advocate,* xi, 11

102 Rev. Anson Green, *Life and Times of Anson Green* (Toronto 1877), 154

103 Carroll, *Case,* IV, 255

104 Wadsworth, *Temperance Manual,* xi, 11

105 McNeill, *Canadian Pioneers,* 86

106 Ibid., 311; W.L. Smith, *Pioneers of Old Ontario* (Toronto 1923), 301

107 *St. Catharines Journal,* 2 June 1836

108 Spence, *Prohibition in Canada,* 43; *St. Catharines Journal,* 16 June 1836

109 *St. Catharines Journal,* 16 June 1836

110 Wadsworth, *Temperance Manual,* II, 9

111 *St. Catharines Journal,* 16 June 1836; cf *The Canadian Ministrel* (Montreal 1842)

112 Wadsworth, *Temperance Manual,* II, 8–9

113 Ibid., 15–16

114 C.O. Ermatinger, *Talbot Regime* (St Thomas 1914), 167

115 *Canadian Watchman,* 17 Sept. 1830

116 *Backwoodsman and Peterboro Sentinel,* 3 June 1840

117 *Canadian Watchman,* 17 Dec. 1830

118 *Bathurst Courier,* 13 Nov. 1835

119 Ibid., 20 March 1835. Some of the leaders, apparently changed their opinions, as the years passed. For example, Rev. Egerton Ryerson imported liquor in 1858. Fred Landon, *Extracts from Old Harris Diary,* published in the London *Free Press* between 14 July and 17 November 1928.

120 Hon. W.R. Riddell, 'First Canadian War-Time Prohibition Measure,' *Canadian Historical Review,* I, 2, 1920, 187–90

121 Wooley and Johnson, *Temperance Progress,* 251

122 *Canada Temperance Advocate,* cxi, 62

123 *Christian Guardian,* 26 Dec. 1829

Old Ontario and the Emergence of a National Frame of Mind

Allan Smith

That Ontario played a leading role in promoting the national idea in post-Confederation Canada is well known. Canada First drew most of its members from that province, much of the literature which attempted to delineate the character of the new nation was produced there, and the principal Canadian support for such agencies as the Royal Society of Canada and the Royal Canadian Academy was provided by its inhabitants. If, however, the fact that the national idea after 1867 was largely Ontario-created is hardly new, less widely broadcast has been the circumstance that as early as the 1820s Upper Canadians had begun to think of their province, and the larger British North American society of which it was a part, as potentially a great nation within the empire. Upper Canada, they thought, was to be understood not simply as an extension of British civilization in an imperial province but as a community with a character and experience of its own. It was this conviction which, within forty years, matured into a belief that the territory Upper Canadians inhabited might function as the centre of a British North American civilization ripe for union into one political framework.

I

Through the first half of the century Upper Canadians became steadily more preoccupied with the business of creating cultural agencies that would expand their knowledge of themselves. Imported culture, many of them felt, could not do the whole job involved in educating Canadians. If they were to learn from, and about, those things close at hand, only a local culture, generated within the framework of local agencies, would suffice.

The important role to be played by educational institutions in acquainting people with their society and training them to function in it was early realized. By 1818 Robert Gourlay could notice the concern of 'gentlemen of competent means' to have their children educated 'without sending them abroad for the purpose.'[1] It was true, of course, that much of the concern felt by Upper Canadians in the 1820s and 1830s over the presence of American teachers and American texts in their schools grew out of anxiety that it would weaken the imperial orientation of their pupils. By the 1840s, however, there was a growing conviction that the schools should be used to encourage a sense of local patriotism as well. As that decade began the first edition of Alexander Davidson's *The Canada Spelling Book* took note of the peculiar importance spelling-books had in heightening their users' awareness of the objects to which the words in them referred, an attribute which allowed them to play an important role in the formation of community conscious- ness. The great variety of books in use in Upper Canada prevented them from playing that role, nor was the situation helped by the fact that most of those books came from Britain or the United States. All of this, Davidson asserted, must be a cause of concern to 'every individual possessed of any degree of *true* patri- otism.'[2] It was the object of his spelling-book to change it, and in so doing to help make the schools agencies of assimilation to a way of life rooted in the community of which they were a part. Egerton Ryerson, sharing this concern, argued in 1841 that the school system of Canada West must be 'not only *British*, but *Canadian*.'[3] Four years later, Alexander Macnab, assistant superintendent of education for Canada West, could lament the fact that the books used in Canadian schools were not suited to the circumstances of Canadian youth.[4] And in 1849 Thomas Hig- ginson, superintendent of common schools for the Ottawa District, similarly in- sisted upon the importance of textbooks which focussed on the peculiarities of the community which would make use of them:

It may be proper to urge upon the Board of Education the necessity of preparing a Geography and a History of Canada for the use of the Schools. It is a matter of regret, that while we can learn from our Text-books something of almost every other country, we can learn nothing of our own; and it is deeply to be regretted that some person of talent has not, ere this, prepared such a work, – pointing out our country's advantages, natural, social, and political. Such a work would be a secure basis whereon our young people could and would rest their loyalty and patriotism; such a work would develope [sic] events and circumstances around which the associations of heart and memory might cluster, as around a common centre, making us what we should be, what we require to be, and what we have never yet been, – a united, a prosperous, and a contented people.[5]

The important role locally produced texts might play in the educational system was fully appreciated by the officials charged with the responsibility of passing judgment on Egerton Ryerson's recommendation that the Irish National Series of textbooks be introduced into the schools of Canada West. In accepting that recommendation they made clear their conviction that there should be no inter- ference with the 'few isolated School-Books ... published in the Province.'[6] These reflected its character in a way no imported material could, and must not be deprived of their place. By the 1850s this concern with the bias and content of text-books and the curriculum had clearly shown results. Normal School students in Toronto, for example, were examined in Canadian history and geography,[7] and, at the end of the decade, J.G. Hodgins' *The Geography and History of British America and of the Other Colonies of the Empire* was in use in the city's schools.[8] In 1866 it was joined by Hodgins' *A History of Canada; and of the other Provinces in British North America*, and in 1865 the Toronto publisher James Campbell issued the first of a projected series of volumes for use throughout the provinces. A geography text, its national character came in for special mention. No longer, noted the publisher, should British North Americans have to rely on books published beyond their borders, which invariably reflected the interests and character of the country in which they were produced. What was needed was a book 'intended especially for the use of Schools [sic] in the British North American Provinces.'[9] It was now available.

If the manner in which Upper Canadian educational authorities viewed their educational system revealed them to be thinking of their community as one which possessed characteristics of its own, the way in which some of their fellow citizens approached the problem of periodical literature showed them to possess similar convictions. *Barker's Canadian Magazine*, founded in 1846 for the avowed purpose of informing Canadians about their community, professed itself especially concerned with the encouragement of Canadian writing.[10] *The Maple Leaf or Canadian Annual* of Toronto, appearing in 1847, 1848, and 1849, similarly set itself the task of acquainting Canadians with their country. Only Canadians, it announced, would be permitted to contribute to its columns.[11] By the 1860s *The Canadian Quarterly Review and Family Magazine* could be founded at Hamilton, in the words of its prospectus, to enhance understanding of 'national politics and interesting family literature. It will review and advocate, aside from party interests, those leading questions that affect the moral, political and mutual well-being of Canadians; and afford original and selected prose and poetry of a choice and useful character.'[12] The *British American Magazine*, published at Toronto in 1863–4, was very much concerned to enlarge its readers' frame of reference by acquainting them with the affairs of British North America as a whole. A three-part article appearing in 1863 urged Canadians to seize the Northwest before Manifest Destiny triumphed there.[13] Others attempted to acquaint them with the Maritimes[14] or to introduce them to important figures in their past.[15]

Newspapers played an even more central role in developing a Canadian frame of reference. As the University of Toronto's Daniel Wilson noted in 1860, they had a 'great influence' in shaping the outlook of those exposed to them.[16] That influence was especially evident in certain areas. So concerned were they with politics, an observer reported, that 'the smallest farmer' was able to have a newspaper suitable to his political views.[17] That fact made them invaluable in heightening awareness on the part of Canadians that they lived in a separate political jurisdiction. Nor was the influence of the newspaper confined to reinforcing the sense that Canadians lived in an emerging polity with characteristics uniquely its own. As Henry Morgan observed in 1867, reading newspapers played a role in the rise of literary sensibility as well. 'The morning journal,' he noted, 'may be said to be as much a literary as it is a political organ ...'[18]

By the late 1850s Upper Canadian newspapermen were sufficiently cognizant of their role in creating a sense of community and self-consciousness to form an association for the purpose of helping overcome the tendencies towards division which seemed so clearly to threaten the future of their province. This special anxiety was hardly inhibited by the fact that those tendencies were in some ways most pronounced in the world of Canadian journalism itself. Many leading newspapermen were in politics, and factionalism was rife among the others. The desire to overcome these internal divisions was one of the considerations motivating the founders of the Canadian Press Association. When, therefore, the association was formed at Kingston in September 1859, it was highly conscious of its role as a unifying agent and anxious to make itself effective as such.[19] Five years after its formation, it took note of the movement towards British North American union in a manner which, if jocular and light-hearted, also indicated clearly that it appreciated the significance of what was taking place. The people of the five provinces, noted the association's president at its 1864 meeting in Belleville, should be encouraged in their efforts to unite:

> Dreaming we could be a nation,
> By a great confederation ...
> Urging that a five-fold mingle
> Stouter far than is a single;
> That one foot on the Pacific
> Should excite no thought terrific,
> And the other on th'Atlantic,
> Ought to drive no neighbour frantic.[20]

By 1867 a number of resolutions had been introduced calling for members of the Quebec and Maritime press to join the association, and in that year David Wylie, a former president, suggested changing its name from the Canadian to the British North American Press Association.[21] That it might spread outwards from Ontario into the whole of British North America was a prospect welcomed by D'Arcy McGee. Such a move, he thought, would not only raise standards and professionalize the business of running a newspaper but also aid in the distribution of news and therefore heighten the national sense.[22]

While journalism and the treatment given contemporary events assumed for some Canadians a role of importance in the making of a Canadian sensibility, others worked towards the same end by offering encouragement to the idea that theirs was a society bound together by a common and meaningful past. In 1823 Charles Fothergill of York projected a 'Canadian Annual Register' which, besides examining recent events, would include material on the early history of Canada.[23] Before many years had passed, the War of 1812 had become a staple of Canadian historical writing. Canadians, much of it argued, had been compelled to resist a common threat and as a consequence had become a self-conscious people determined to preserve its collective existence. Given equal emphasis with the necessity of maintaining the link with Britain was the role Canadians themselves had played in securing their land from invasion. David Thompson's *History of the Late War between Great Britain and the United States* (1832), John Richardson's *War of 1812* (1842), and G. Auchinleck's *A History of the War between Great Britain and the United States* (1855) argued that the bulk of the fighting had been done by the locally-raised militia valiantly rising to the defence of their homeland. Canadians, then, were fully capable of uniting in support of a common cause. That, in fact, was one of the principal points Montreal's *Literary Garland* thought Richardson's book to contain.[24]

That the impulse behind the writing of Canadian history should be a nationalist one was a point made explicitly by the *Anglo-American Magazine* in 1852. Discussing a proposal for yet another history of the War of 1812, it suggested that its purpose should be 'the setting before Canadians, in a modest though spirited manner, the achievements of their fathers ... and the awakening the memory of their own past struggle in defense of the loved land of their adoption ... such a review will, nay must, tend to foster in our day the same national feeling which at that time impelled every colonist to fly to arms to repel the hated invasion of their republican neighbours ... the real object of our undertaking [must be] the exposition of the loyalty, courage and energies of the brave yeomanry of Canada.'[25]

In the 1860s Upper Canadians sought especially to contribute their share of heroes to the nationalist pantheon. Charles Lindsey's *The Life and Times of William Lyon Mackenzie,* published at Toronto in 1862, only marginally met this criterion, for Lindsey was critical of Mackenzie's tendency towards precipitate action and thought the justified grievances of the farmers might have been met without the necessity for rebellion, but Henry J. Morgan's *Sketches of Celebrated Canadians and Persons Connected with Canada* (1862) was clearly intended to mark out the manner in which Canadians had worked together to create a common tradition. Morgan's object, he explained, was to show that 'we have had and do possess men as truly great, talented and devotedly loyal as any other kingdom, not excepting the mother country herself. We may also be able to convince the youth of this rising nation, that their sires, grandsires, and great grandsires, had names associated with great deeds and glorious efforts in the cause of freedom and loyalty ... A just pride, an intense love of our native country, and an ardent hope and desire for its future greatness, have alone enabled and prevailed on us to go through a task of great mental labor, yet to us one of love.'[26] Four years later he expanded his work in order to intensify the pride and sense of accomplishment British North Americans as a whole must feel in their society. *The Place British Americans Have Won in History* (1866) rested upon the earlier volume but included the great men of all the provinces.

Few of those concerned to encourage the development of a national frame of reference failed to appreciate the role literature might play in their enterprise. In conformity with the dictates of romanticism, Upper Canadians regularly pointed to their past as the repository of material that would illuminate the Canadian experience and provide an abundance of material for Canadian literary men. War, primitive peoples, and the tribulations of the pioneer combined to produce a mine of readily exploitable material. 'The sufferings of the United Empire Loyalists,' proclaimed York's *Canadian Literary Magazine* in 1833, '– the privations of those who sank beneath the gnawings of Famine in Hungry Bay, – the adventures of the Hunter, especially if he possessed the romantic spirit of Lord Edward Fitzgerald, – the Guerilla-like achievements of the late War, – the past and present condition of the aborigines, – are subjects equally interesting to the Canadians and to him who has adopted Canada for his country.'[27] The *Canadian Literary Magazine* took the exploration of these themes as its central task, hoping throughout that in so doing it would 'receive the support of every individual who feels a desire that Canada should possess a literature of its own ...'[28] Another journal, based in the same city, thought much had already been accomplished. *The Roseharp*, in fact, professed to see Upper Canada's cultural life on the threshold of a great breakthrough: 'This Province has now arrived at such a state of improvement in population and wealth, that we already see the dawning of the Arts and Sciences; but genius in a young country requires the fostering care of the community at large to bring it forward to the world ... The object ... is to encourage and diffuse sentiments of loyal patriotism – a taste for literature and the fine arts; and by exciting emulation, give energy, and rouse into action, the dormant seeds of genius.'[29]

By the middle of the century, calls for a native literature were frequently made. A resident of Williamstown, Canada West, writing in 1848 on 'Our literature, Present and Prospective,' recommended greater devotion to native historical writing and national songs.[30] The year following, Egerton Ryerson looked forward 'to the day when [school] libraries will be increased and enriched by Canadian contributions and publications.'[31] In 1855 Daniel Wilson called for a Canadian literature 'which shall embrace independent representatives in each department of knowledge.'[32] The *Wesleyan Repository and Literary Record* argued in 1860 that 'even if unexceptionable literature could be obtained from other lands, it is nevertheless, highly desirable that we should cultivate a national literature of our own.'[33] And in 1863 Hamilton's *Canadian Illustrated News* pronounced poetry to be 'as much an element of healthy national life as commerce or manufactures.'[34]

Poets, responding to these pleas, continued in the 1860s to write with their accustomed vigour of the virtue and importance of dealing in verse with their own society. 'Let me hear the tales, and stories,' wrote George Washington Johnson, unabashed by the echoes of Longfellow which resounded throughout his 1864 poem 'Manitoulin,'

> Ballads, songs, and wild traditions,
> And Canadian, Indian legends,
> That are woven with our history ...
> Let it not appear a puzzle
> That the song that first I sing you
> Is about my native country.[35]

A new and significant note was struck in that decade by the fact that Canadian poetry began to be anthologized. This operation was designed to show by bringing it together in one place that a body of Canadian literature existed. In that sense it was artificial and lacked spontaneity. The attempt, moreover, was clearly designed to stimulate an all too obviously weak interest in Canadian literature. Yet the fact that it could be made at all indicates, as its makers intended it should, that there was now in existence a body of literature reflective of, and based upon, the Canadian experience.

For E.H. Dewart, the very act of bringing this material together was a nationalist undertaking. It confirmed the existence of a separate and distinct Canadian national life. 'A national literature,' he wrote, introducing the anthology to which many Upper Canadians had contributed, 'is an essential element in the formation of national character. It is not merely the record of a country's mental progress: it is the expression of its intellectual life, the bond of national unity, and the guide of national energy.'[36]

This idealist vision of the role literature might play in reflecting, integrating, and directing the national experience formed the core of H.J. Morgan's *Bibliotheca Canadensis*, published in 1867. A catalogue of his country's literature, its avowed purpose was to demonstrate that Canadians had for some time possessed a sense of their country as a distinct and special place, one to the comprehension of whose character they had devoted much energy.

The existence of a body of national literature provided critics with the opportunity to assess not only the success with which Canadians had articulated their national tradition but also the depth and richness of the tradition itself. The development of a Canadian tradition, and of a literature embodying it, had been retarded, thought one, by Canada's lack of a mythic and heroic past. Much progress had, however, been made in the land since its discovery. The journey Canadians had undertaken through time was a kind of odyssey of the human spirit, demonstrating the great works of which man was capable. A substantial literature might be built around the exploration of that epic theme. Canadians, then, could overlook the fact that the mists of antiquity had not yet cast 'their picturesque and mystic spells'[37] over the land. The materials for a national literature might be drawn from other sources. Canada must, in fact, 'congratulate herself on the poets she already possesses ...' They had made a distinct and important contribution to her self-knowledge. 'A nation's best benefactors,' concluded the critic on a note of transcendental ecstasy, 'are its poets, for it is their office to refine and exalt material progress by evolving from it that divine life and thought without which it is but a body without a soul.'[38]

Science, like education and literature, was conscientiously promoted as a nationalist tool. It would, its partisans claimed, at once heighten self-consciousness and enhance national strength. Where history deepened a people's sense of themselves in time, science broadened it through space. By isolating a country's geographical, climatic, and geological attributes, the scientists made it better known and so expanded the frame of reference within which their fellow citizens operated. And by locating its riches they helped provide it with the sinews of national strength.

Anxious to know the face of the land on which they came to live, Upper Canadians early sought to explore and catalogue its features. In 1806 the Upper Canadian assembly appropriated a small sum of money for the purchase of scientific equipment.[39] By 1830 the conviction that the British North American provinces had unique and special features deserving of systematic scientific description had grown strong enough for Charles Fothergill to propose a three-year scientific expedition to the Pacific coast. It would, he hoped, include a geologist, botanist, mineralogist, and astronomer and have as its double object an examination of the natural resources of the west and an assessment of the possibilities for settlement there.[40]

Increasing interest in the province's geological character and natural history led the York Literary and Philosophical Society to request a grant from the legislature in 1832. Seeking, it informed the legislature, to do everything necessary to promote acquaintance with the character of the country, it proposed to use any funds received for the purpose of investigating the geology, mineralogy, and natural history of the province 'thoroughly and scientifically.'[41] Four years later William Lyon Mackenzie proposed the appointment of a select committee of the legislature to prepare a 'plan for the Geological Survey or examination' of this province.[42] Finally, in 1841, the legislature of the newly formed Province of Canada appropriated £1500 for a geological survey.[43] Canadians were brought into contact with the knowledge yielded by the survey's activities in a number of ways. Reports of its work were published annually by the middle-1850s. The college museums of Canada West – Victoria College in Cobourg, Queen's College in Kingston, and Trinity College, Toronto – contained samples of Canadian minerals, while the museum of the Canadian Institute in Toronto displayed geological and other specimens from both Canada and the Maritimes.[44]

That this activity was to serve an embryonic nationalist purpose is plain from the motives of those who engaged in it. Fothergill made it clear in the 1830s that his proposal to encourage natural history was founded on the proposition that a large part of the 'power' and 'high character' of nations depends upon their pursuit of science and especially their having accurate knowledge of their own natural resources.[45] The *Canadian Literary Magazine*, drawing attention to the fact that scientific activity augmented the wealth of nations, pointed in 1833 to the richness of the harvest awaiting the scientific investigator. 'The subterranean riches of this favored continent,' it noted, 'are, as yet, but very imperfectly developed: the depths of the lakes, and the recesses of the forests, are teeming with treasures ... which no pen has yet accounted for.'[46] In 1855 William E. Logan, head of the Geological Survey since 1842, made explicit the link between science, development, and his 'country's' future. The purpose of the Survey, he pointed out, 'is to ascertain the mineral resources of the Country, and this is kept steadily in view. What new scientific facts have resulted from it, have come out in the course of what I conceive to be economic researches carried out in a scientific way ... Economics leads to science and science to economics.'[47] Canadian periodicals interested in science were especially concerned with its national relevance. Upper Canada's leading scientific magazine was conscious in the extreme of its community obligations. 'A form of local pride,' a student of it has noted, 'incipient source of national aspirations, colours the scientific pursuits of the *Canadian Journal*.'[48]

The sense that British North America was a unified society possessing characteristics binding it together and capable of being analyzed in a systematic and ordered way was heightened by the appearance in 1863 of a summary treatment of the work done by the Geological Survey over the previous twenty years. A large volume of over 900 pages, it was accompanied by an atlas containing a geological map of British North America embracing Canada, the Maritimes, and adjacent parts of the United States.[49] The next year E.J. Chapman, professor of mineralogy at the University of Toronto, wrote the first Canadian textbook on geology. Entitled *A Popular and Practical Exposition of the Minerals and Geology of Canada*, it was designed to have more than a narrowly educational utility.[50] The national relevance of this kind of work, suggested the *Canadian Illustrated News*, gave it its greatest value. That journal itself proposed to publish articles on the geology of

Canada in order to 'give Canadians a better idea of the land they live in.' It discerned a close connection between geology, self-knowledge, and the nation's future, for the study of the country's land and resources involved its future character 'in all the phases of industrial, social and national development.'[51]

That old Ontario was coming to see itself as a society with its own character, needs, and identity was, perhaps, made most clear by its concern to have government participate in the process by which that sense of identity could be clarified and communicated to an ever wider audience. Government, it was argued, had a responsibility to help the community know itself. And the playing of a central role in establishing an educational system was but one way in which it might fulfil this responsibility: there were other steps that might be taken to promote the idea that the society over whose affairs it presided possessed a character and experience of its own. Only in an atmosphere of cultural vitality could a Canadian culture bloom effectively. Priority might therefore be given to the general encouragement of cultural activity. In 1824, accordingly, the government of Upper Canada voted to spend £124 annually for the purchase of books and texts to be distributed throughout the province.[52] By the early 1830s the first attempts at passing copyright legislation for the purpose of protecting Upper Canadian authors were being made.[53] By the 1850s public authorities could claim much of the credit for the fact that parts of the province enjoyed access to at least some of the masterworks of western culture. Many of the books available throughout the province, noted a government official, would have been unknown 'had they not been introduced by the agency of a public department.'[54]

The government's particular concern with fostering cultural activities which would amplify the sense that Upper Canada was a unique and special community soon became manifest. Major John Richardson's request for government aid, originally put to the governor general in 1841 and later, in revised form, to the legislature, saw him seek government support on the ground that he was 'generally known and acknowledged as the only Author this country has produced, or who has attempted to infuse into it a spirit of literature.'[55] That request was met in 1842 with a grant of £250 to assist in the publication of his work on the War of 1812.[56]

The failure of Richardson's project did not prevent the government from coming to the assistance of others. In 1851 the committee charged with responsibility for implementing the legislature's policy of encouraging literary activity announced that 'In furtherance of the encouragement usually extended by the Provincial Legislature to literary enterprise in *Canada*, the Committee have entertained several applications which have been made to them by parties engaged in various literary undertakings for assistance on behalf their several publications.'[57] In its operations the committee tried carefully to maintain standards and at the same time insure that no worthwhile Canadian project went without some form of an agreement to purchase a specified number of the books produced in order to insure, at the least, that costs of publication would be recovered. In 1852 some requests were refused on the ground that 'no proof has been adduced of their special merit or value ... it is not thought advisable to encourage indiscriminate applications of this nature, or to make applications on their behalf, unless in the case of works of special excellence or utility.'[58] But once the committee was satisfied that work before it did meet these standards, its 'desire to foster native talent'[59] might come into play.

II

In time, it was easy enough for Upper Canadians to distinguish their society from those on the other side of the Atlantic. A part of the New World, it differed elementally from the Old. In its midst man might be remade and lifted to a new and unprecedented eminence. Even an anglophile such as Henry Scadding could write in the early 1830s that

> Glory belongs, I ween, fair West, to thee –
> Westward was aye her cause, and still shall be:
> When one great empire fell, in river hurl'd,
> Still westward rose another on the world.[60]

The *Colonial Advocate* informed its readers in 1830 that they had been cast by Providence 'in a highly favoured land,' whose natural splendours – 'luxuriant harvests' and a 'healthful climate' – allowed them to contrast their situation most favorably with that of Europe. Free from the class tensions of that 'opulent' continent, theirs was not a society riven by the 'unbounded' wealth of one class and the 'degrading' poverty of another.[61] For Samuel Strickland Upper Canada was, quite simply, a 'Garden of Eden.'[62]

Having placed their community firmly in a New World context, many Canadians then took it as their task to indicate in what ways it differed from those other countries who could claim this distinction. There was in particular a marked interest in delineating its character in a manner which would show that for all it shared with the United States it was, in the end, a better and more perfect society.

Two things allowed this distinction: its British heritage and its location in the hemisphere's northern latitudes. Institutions and climate acted in combination to insure that the New World genius would produce in Canada the best of all possible communities. Canada participated in the character of the New World, wrote Susannah Moodie, and could therefore alter fundamentally the status and even the nature of those who crossed her borders. The immigrant, released into the beneficient atmosphere of the New World, was to be likened to 'one awaken'd from the dead.' It was in the West, 'beyond the wave,' where freedom made its home. But in Canada the New World's magic had a kind of material to work with not present elsewhere. The Canadian, heir to British liberty and freedom, along with the principal institutions in which they were contained, was 'no child of bondage' but one who had inherited 'all thy British mother's spirit.'[63] The prospects for the realization of the perfect community were thus brighter in his society than elsewhere.

William Kirby's *The UE*, composed in 1846 but unpublished until 1859, similarly drew attention to the fact that Canada was endowed with the values, traditions, and at least some of the institutions of the homeland. Established in the north by the Loyalists, their presence insured that Canadians would not be victimized by republican excess.[64]

The Loyalists themselves began to attract much interest in the 1850s precisely because they had introduced a specific set of ideas, principles, and institutions to Canada. The passing of the Loyalist generation in the 1840s and 1850s combined with the growing self-consciousness of the Canadians to heighten interest in the men and women increasingly to be regarded as the initiators of a national tradition. It was the death of his father in 1854, noted Egerton Ryerson, that had set him thinking about writing the history of the Loyalists. He wished 'to vindicate their character as a body, [and] to exhibit their principles and patriotism.'[65]

If Canadians were heir to a tradition which, by conferring upon them a particular set of institutions, ensured that in their land the elixir of the New World would not turn brackish and impure, the existence of slavery in the United States could be used to make the point with telling effect. Here, clearly, was an institution which perverted all that the New World stood for. And – this, for many Canadians, was the real point – it was an institution from which Canada was mercifully free. The argument that Canada was the true home of liberty could thus be powerfully reinforced with the assertion that

> The clank of chains, the sighs, and slavery's tears
> Shall never pain Canadians' loyal ears –[66]

To a Canadian, regularly reminded of the great controversy pulling at the vitals of his southern neighbour, this thought must have been the source of convincing proof indeed that he and his society were especially blessed. For Evan McColl, 'The Lake of the Thousand Isles' was infinitely preferable to the Missouri or the Ohio rivers. No matter how majestic their flow or bountiful the land through which they passed, they were irreversibly tainted with the curse of slavery.[67] Canada then, was envisioned as a society in which, paradoxically, the presence of British attitudes toward liberty and freedom insured that the egalitarianism of the New World was not qualified in any way. Its air was rent by 'no heavy clank of servile chains.' On its soil any man,

> ... no matter what his skin may be,
> Can stand erect, and proudly say, I'm FREE.[68]

To many observers Canada's happy mixture of the old and the new was its chief distinction. In 1824 William Lyon Mackenzie suggested that their New World location gave Canadians a rich soil and favourable climate which, in conjunction with their tie to the 'land of intellectual grandeur,' conferred upon them a uniquely favoured position.[69] Many travellers appraised Canadian society in similar terms. As G.M. Craig points out, they often found Canadians to have 'the best of both worlds: British stability and tradition, without the encrustations of outworn institutions and the terrible problem of surplus population, from which Britain suffered; and the illimitable resources and opportunities of the New World, without the curses of mob rule and slavery which made life in the United States so unattractive.'[70]

If Canada's institutional heritage helped it maintain a purer form of New World civilization, its climate was held to reinforce the manner in which those institutions operated. The clear, bright, invigorating air of the north stimulated what was best in men and so encouraged the emergence of those qualities essential if a life of freedom were to be sustained. It was, therefore, in the north that true liberty was to be found. The slave who would enjoy it must, accordingly, direct his footsteps there. Until he could do so it was his unfortunate lot to 'envy every little bird that takes its northward flight.' Canada, in fact, served those slaves awaiting freedom in the same manner the North Star served mariners:

> As to the Polar Star they turn
> Who brave a pathless sea, –
> So the oppressed in secret yearn,
> Dear native land for thee![71]

Typical of this style of appreciating the country were the contents of the 1848 *Maple Leaf Annual*. A selection of poems – 'The Trapper,' 'A Canadian Christmas Carol,' 'The Indian on Revisiting an Old Encampment,' and stories – 'A First Day in the Bush,' and 'A Chapter on Canadian Scenery,' were included with the object of making Canadians generally more familiar with their country. But the volume also offered its readers poems such as 'The Emigrants' Bride,' containing references to 'the North Countrie' and 'our romantic North,' or 'A Canadian Winter Night,' heavily laden with extravagant imagery concerning the travels of the 'Queen of Night' through snow-covered, ice-encased Canada.[72]

Some observers saw the whole of British North America in possession of characteristics which, while clearly in evidence at the time of writing, were, hopefully, transitory phenomena soon to be replaced by others more true and lasting. William Lyon Mackenzie had no doubt that British America in the 1820s was characterized by a kind of cultural pluralism. But to him this engendered not so much mutual tolerance as unpleasant division. Just as the people of Britain had overcome their national differences and joined to form one great people, so must those of the New World. As it was in Britain 'So let it be with British America – let every national Distinction cease from among us – let not the native Canadian look upon his Irish or Scottish neighbour as an intruder, nor the native of the British Isles taunt the other about stupidity and incapacity: Rather let them become as one race, and may the only strife among us be a praiseworthy emulation as to who shall attain the honour of conferring the greatest Benefits on the country of our birth – or the land of our choice.'[73] J.R. Godley, a traveller from England, found pluralism to be a fact of Upper Canadian life. Its population, he noted, was 'exceedingly heterogeneous and exotic, [a characteristic] much more remarkable here than in the United States.'[74] This circumstance, he thought, was attributable to the small size of the native-born population coupled with its failure to develop a definite character to which immigrants might be assimilated. Taken together, these things made it difficult to 'absorb and remodel ... the newcomers.' All of this stood in marked contrast to the United States, where immigrants did 'amalgamate to a certain extent with the native-born population, or at least are swallowed up in it.' Nonetheless, Godley thought, there was 'a national character in process of formation ...'[75] though he scrupulously refrained from detailing the elements which composed it.

By 1860, contended one Upper Canadian, it was possible to isolate a Canadian type and Canadian interests with which immigrants must identify. 'Every person,' wrote the Reverend Wellington Jeffers, 'expecting to stay in Canada and expecting his children to have their inheritance here, whether he was born in England, Ireland or Scotland, ought to feel himself to be a Canadian; he ought to feel for the character and glory of Canada, and to be devoted to its interests.'[76]

Although Jeffers thus saw his idea of the nation as a device that might be used to integrate its different parts into a unified and self-conscious whole (and so gave evidence of his belief that Canada could not be conceived of merely as an extension of another society, however strong the formal ties that bound the two together), he was no more capable than his predecessors of giving that idea an exact formulation. So difficult was this problem, found some Upper Canadians, that it could best be met by avoiding it altogether. Their solution, accordingly, lay not in exposition but in symbol. To comprehend their society's attributes in a single striking image would be to show that it possessed the most compact and tangible of identities. Functioning as a tool for the integration of the collective experience, the symbol would overcome any tendency towards incoherence and division and obviate the need for an elaborate and detailed description of the national character.

The maple leaf, a product of Canadian soil which knew neither Europe, nor (save for its northernmost parts) the United States, was singled out by the 1840s as an especially appropriate symbolic device. It became the title of a new literary magazine published in the last year of that decade, whose editors, having decided that 'no flowers, however lovely, should be twined with "the maple leaf," but those that had blossomed amidst her forests,'[77] sought to give point to their determination that the magazine be unreservedly Canadian. Its peculiar association with Canada and the fact that it came out of the liberty-giving Canadian forest allowed Alexander McLachlan to suggest in 1858 that it was in 'the maple dells where freedom dwells.'[78] Another Canadian poet found in its fresh, green, unspoiled beauty a suitable representation of his country's hopes for the future:

> In her fair and budding beauty,
> A fitting emblem she
> Of this land of promise,
> Of hope, of liberty.[79]

By the 1860s the tendency to epitomize the Canadian experience in symbolic terms was sufficiently widespread to arouse concern on the part of those who felt that it inspired a mode of thinking at once simplistic and overzealous. Symbol, argued some critics, had degenerated into stereotype. A truly sensitive and feeling reaction to the land ought to inform the best writing about Canada. Instead, noted the *Saturday Reader* in 1865, many authors had failed to be 'national in the true sense of the word' and attempted 'to satisfy our mental cravings with a dish of beaver, stewed in maple leaves.'[80]

Interest in the elucidation of Canadian themes came in time to be accompanied by a concern to articulate those themes in a manner and style appropriate to them. To be concerned with content remained vital; but form now seemed no less important. It too might locate art in, and help express, a national tradition.

The Canadian environment, it was argued, imposed an obligation on the architect to design his buildings in a way that not only allowed them to function in, but also harmonized with the difficult Canadian winter. 'Though we can scarcely hope to see,' wrote William Hay, a Toronto architect, in 1853, '... a distinct style of pure architecture formed on the primitive log hut, something may be done to lead the taste of the Province into a direction which may tend to give a local character to our Canadian edifices.'[81] Such a style might rest upon the old English architecture with its use of wood and its steeply pitched roofs, thereby drawing on an abundant Canadian resource and meeting the difficulties posed by the heavy Canadian snowfall.

Canadian critics and literary men were especially preoccupied with the problem of style. The belief that Canadian subjects should be explored remained essential and the mark of a national poet; but increasingly it was argued that those subjects could not be handled adequately by employing the diction and imagery developed by another society in the course of giving expression to its special character. Charles Sangster was, accordingly, brought under critical fire by Daniel Wilson in 1858 for his tendency, even in the course of exploring Canadian themes, to repeat 'old-world music and song.' In much of what he wrote there was 'nothing that would betray its new world parentage.' The Canadian poet must be mindful of language and style: 'However much taste and refinement may be displayed in such echoes [as Sangster's] of the old thought and fancy of Europe, the path to success lies not in this direction for the poet of the new world.'[82] Sangster was especially lax in his stylistic treatment of that quintessential North American figure, the Indian. 'At best,' wrote Wilson, 'it is no true Indian, but only the white man dressed up in his attire; strip him of his paint and feathers, and it is our old-world acquaintance.'[83]

As the century unfolded Upper Canadians came increasingly to encompass all of British North America in their vision of the national future. By the 1860s the entire region might be comprehended in the vision of change and development witnessed by those for whom the most accurate index to a country's state and nature remained the degree to which its progress could be measured. The record, though largely written in Canada West, must embrace all of the provinces. In 1863 H.Y. Hind and his collaborators therefore proposed to lay before their readers the *Eighty Years Progress of British North America*. Progress, they pointed out, was a fact of the industrial age; nowhere was its triumph more marked than in North America; and in North America the British provinces were proving themselves at least as capable of it as the United States. Enough, in fact, had been accomplished to suggest a rate of progress that 'shall place the provinces, within the day of many now living, on a level with Great Britain herself, in population, in wealth, and in power.'[84]

Other Upper Canadians, sharing this frame of reference, argued that since the provinces possessed a unity of spirit, character, and interests, they should come together in a formal way. John Beverly Robinson and John Strachan were only the first among a long line of Upper Canadians to propose a British North American union. Their concern to advance alternatives to the union of the two Canadas projected in the early 1820s led each of them to prepare a lengthy document arguing the case for a more comprehensive undertaking. Such a scheme was practicable, Robinson thought, because it would involve the uniting of a people bound together by their common loyalty to the crown and their shared antipathy to republican institutions. The sense of community was, of course, not yet strong. One of his scheme's objects, accordingly, was to strengthen it by bringing British North

Americans together within a common political framework. This would, he hoped, cause them to develop a greater sense of 'community of interest and feeling among themselves.'[85]

Strachan thought a general union no more difficult to effect than a union of the two Canadas, while its fruits would be far greater. Its formation would, in particular, do much to insure that no 'rival power' took possession of the provinces. 'What glory,' he wrote, 'may be expected to redound to the statesman who gives a free constitution to all the British North American colonies and by consolidating them into one territory or kingdom exalts them to a nation acting in unity and under the protection of the British Empire ...'[86]

By 1846 the Toronto *Globe* could point to the Hudson's Bay Territories to the west as the proper legacy of Canadians. Consciousness of that vast unopened region was heightened by the tours of Paul Kane with their harvest of dramatic paintings. Expeditions such as that undertaken by Henry Youle Hind in the 1850s furthered the work of making the west known to central Canada. George Brown's ambitions for the territory grew through the 1850s, with the *Globe* providing a powerful instrument for the promotion of the cause in whose direction those ambitions led. And this generation of Upper Canadians not only looked west; their frame of reference, like Robinson's and Strachan's, embraced the lands to the east as well. Those territories too could be comprehended in the same expansive vision. Thus might George Washington Johnson write in the early 1860s that British North America, possessing the same quality of freedom throughout its length and breadth, was free from the blight of slavery 'from Erie's shore to Old Atlantic's waves.'[87] The Maritime provinces, no less than Canada itself, participated in the same essential character.

III

Considered as a nationalist phenomenon, the frame of mind which had emerged in Canada West by the 1860s was as remarkable for its deficiencies as for the fact that it had taken shape at all. Far from involving a highly articulated vision of British North American independence and sovereignty, it supposed a Canadian future within the imperial system. British North American union, insisted its partisans, was to be supported precisely because it offered the only means by which such a future could be guaranteed. 'Our connection with the Mother Country,' Alexander Campbell of Cataraqui told the Legislative Council, 'cannot be maintained for any great length of time without such a union.'[88] The ambiguity produced by a commitment on the part of those who would make a nation to continuing subordination within the empire was dissolved by the fact that British power was held essential to the maintenance of British North America, while a unified British North America might use its imperial situation to make a place for itself in the world at large. The essential harmony between this nationalism and the brand of imperial sentiment which was its partner did not, however, always appear clearly, a fact that would produce confusion in the years to come.[89]

Nor was this pattern of thought conceptually adequate. Often tentative and the result of half-formed convictions, its most serious flaw was its failure to contain a systematized and comprehensive idea of the national character. Whatever kind of British North American nationality the statesmen may have found it practically necessary to build, at the level of conceptualization the national future envisioned by many of the poets, writers, educators, and scientists of Upper Canada was an English-speaking one in which the French-speaking inhabitants of British North America had hardly a place. A truncated and incomplete vision of the new nationality might command the allegiance of those whose sensibilities it did embrace but it could hardly win the enthusiasm of those whose character and ideals it neglected. Framing a conceptualization that would overcome this considerable difficulty became the most taxing and complex problem facing the theoreticians of the new nationality.[90]

Finally, how deeply the national idea penetrated into the life of Upper Canadian society cannot with assurance be known. It was, of course, the possession of men who had the talent, the interest, and the opportunity to promote its diffusion among their fellows. They controlled the agencies through which opinion in their society was formulated and broadcast. Yet, in the last analysis, how widespread or influential these ideas were can be no more than the subject of an informed speculation.

Granting the problematical nature of this phenomenon is not, however, the equivalent of saying that it was without significance. It had, in fact, a great significance, amply demonstrated during the Confederation Debates. Because of it Macdonald could invite, and even assume, the consent of his audience to the proposition that British North America already formed, in some important sense, a union. In this way he was to get past a difficult stage in the argument by treating it as something that did not have to be argued at all. Thus might he tell the chamber, and through it the province beyond, how appropriate and unexceptionable it was that British North Americans, 'belonging, as they do, to the same nation,' and having 'a like feeling of ardent attachment for this, our common country,' should come together in a clear and formal way.[91]

The Upper Canadian Fathers, indeed, were able to finesse much of the debate by proceeding on the assumption that their audience possessed a common vision of a collective British North American future even then in process of realization. George Brown contended that the achievement of a great national destiny, far from being a project that must begin from nothing, would rest from the outset on substantial foundations. The British North American provinces, more populous and wealthy than the United States at the moment of their birth, might already be compared to the great states of Europe. How, then, could it be doubted that the child of their union would be a 'future empire' of truly remarkable proportions?[92] Walter McCrea, elected to the Legislative Council for the Western District, pronounced the scheme's opponents guilty of a kind of disloyalty, no less real for the fact that its object as yet existed only in men's minds. 'Had a union of all these provinces existed in fact as it has existed in the minds of statesmen since the commencement of the present century,' he suggested, 'the man who, in the face of our present critical position ... [proposed] to dissolve that union and scatter us again into disjointed fragments, would be looked upon as an enemy to his Queen and a traitor to his country.'[93]

The House, it was regularly told, could in conscience act with despatch. There had been ample opportunity to consider what was proposed. The confederation scheme, far from injecting a new element into the life and politics of British North America, found its place in an old and familiar tradition. 'The question,' said McCrea, 'has been propounded by eminent statesmen both in the old country and on this side of the Atlantic time and again since the commencement of the present century, and has been in the minds of the people ever since.'[94] Brown recalled at length that the idea of a general union had been before Upper Canadians for years.[95] A plain-speaking Macdonald reminded his audience simply that 'this subject ... is not a new one.'[96]

Neither the idea that British North America formed a country nor the proposition that it become a state were, then, the Fathers continually emphasized, new. What was novel and unprecedented was the rightness of the time. The conjunction of circumstance created by deadlock in Canada, civil war in the United States, and a changing view of empire in Britain gave the project a special urgency. It provided, in fact, an opportunity that must not be missed. Confederation, said McCrea, owed its sudden eminence to the fact that 'no opportunity has ever presented itself like the present. [In these circumstances it] had but to be mentioned to take complete possession of the minds of the people.'[97] The 'ripeness of public opinion' thus created must, Brown argued, settle the matter, for who knew when the circumstances producing it would come again?[98] Macdonald similarly stressed the matter of timing. If this great and long-standing objective was to be accomplished, it was imperative that the 'happy concurrence of circumstances' urging the provinces towards it be properly met. 'If we do not embrace this opportunity, the present favourable time will pass away and we may never have it again.'[99]

Old Ontario's national sense, these arguments reveal, at once allowed the creation of, and itself became, an ideology which rationalized that province's thrust towards dominance in British North America. By producing a group of nationally-minded Upper Canadians inclined to see British North America as a unity, it helped to insure that confederation would be viewed, in their province at least, not simply as an expedient for the resolution of important and pressing problems, but as the means of realizing a national destiny. Invested with this weighty significance, it could not help but find its passage easier.[100]

Succeeding generations of Ontario men, building upon this foundation, played a leading role in defining the national idea and constructing the agencies required to sustain and amplify it. Their vision of the national character, like its parent fired in the crucible of the Ontario experience, similarly reflected that province's perspective and interest. By turns centralizing and provincialist, it was carried, thanks to the strength of its sustaining apparatus, to all parts of the country. Those who challenged it with their own sense of the manner in which the country should be understood very often found themselves on the defensive. Thus sure that its influence in defining the terms of debate concerning the national future would be primary, Ontario acquired a powerful instrument for the maintenance of its central position in the nation's affairs. In this way its early sense of the nation at once augmented its power and retained its utility.[101]

NOTES

1 Cited in H.Y. Hind, T.C. Keefer, J.G. Hodgins, Charles Robb, M.H. Perley, Rev. William Murray, *Eighty Years Progress of British North America* (Toronto 1863), 387
2 Alexander Davidson, *The Canada Spelling Book* (Toronto 1848), 'Preface'
3 Egerton Ryerson, 1841 Address, Ryerson Letters, 1840–6, Victoria College Archives. Cited in J. Donald Wilson, Robert M. Stamp, and Louis-Philippe Audet, *Canadian Education: A History* (Scarborough 1970), 218
4 Province of Canada, Assembly, *Journals*, 1846, Appendix P: 'Annual Report of the Assistant Superintendent of Education, on the State of Common Schools Throughout Canada West for the year 1844,' submitted by Alexander Macnab, Cobourg, 1 August 1845
5 Ibid., 1850, Appendix xx, 'Annual Report of the Normal, Model, and Common Schools in Upper Canada for the year 1849,' part I, section XII, extracts from the reports of district superintendents, Thomas Higginson, superintendent of common schools for the Ottawa District
6 Cited in W.R. Riddell, 'The First Copyrighted Book in the Province of Canada,' Ontario Historical Society, *Papers and Records*, XXV, 409
7 Province of Canada, Assembly, *Journals*, 1852–3, Appendix J J, 'Annual Report of the Normal, Model, and Common Schools, in Upper Canada, for the year 1851: with appendices,' by the chief superintendent of schools, E. Ryerson, 27 April 1852, sub-appendix D, Documents Relating to the Normal School, Toronto
8 J.E. Middleton, *The Municipality of Toronto: A History* (3 vols., Toronto 1923), I, 542
9 Toronto Public Library, Campbell's British American Series of School Books, *Modern School Geography and Atlas Prepared for the Use of Schools in the British Provinces –* Specimen (Montreal and Toronto 1865), Preface. Bound with *Canadian Booksellers' Catalogues*, volume II, 1856–74
10 E.J. Barker, 'Editor's Table,' *Barker's Canadian Magazine*, I, 2, June 1846, 112
11 A.R.M. Lower, *Canadians in the Making* (Toronto 1958), 233
12 *Canadian Illustrated News*, II, 19, 26 Sept. 1863, 218

13 'Northwest British America,' *British American Magazine*, I, May 1863, 1–11; I, June 1863, 167–78; I, July 1863, 268–72

14 'The St. Lawrence Route – A Tour to the Lower Provinces,' ibid., II, March 1864, 505–10; II, April 1864, 598–605

15 'Personal Sketches; or, Reminiscences of Public Men in Canada,' ibid., II, Jan. 1864, 225–38

16 Daniel Wilson, 'Family Herald,' *Canadian Journal*, ns, V, 1860, 57. Cited in Carl Ballstadt, 'The Quest for Canadian Identity in Pre-Confederation English-Canadian Literary Criticism' (unpublished MA thesis, University of Western Ontario, 1959), 141–2

17 J.B. Brown, *Views of Canada and the Colonists* (Edinburgh 1851), 161–2, cited in S.D. Clark, *The Social Development of Canada: An Introductory Study with Select Documents* (Toronto 1942), 283

18 Henry J. Morgan, *Bibliotheca Canadensis* (Ottawa 1867), 18, cited in Ballstadt, 'Quest for Canadian Identity,' 142

19 A.H. Colquhoun, 'The Canadian Press Association,' in *A History of Canadian Journalism in the Several Portions of the Dominion with a sketch of the Canadian Press Association 1850–1908*, edited by a committee of the association (Toronto 1908), 1–4

20 Ibid., 48

21 Ibid., 56

22 D'Arcy McGee, 'The Mental Outfit of the New Dominion,' *Montreal Gazette*, 5 Nov. 1867

23 J.L. Baillie, jr, 'Charles Fothergill,' *Canadian Historical Review*, XXV, 4, Dec. 1944, 383–4

24 *Literary Garland*, IV, 10, Sept. 1842, 484

25 *Anglo-American Magazine*, I, 6, Dec. 1852, 553–4

26 H.J. Morgan, *Sketches of Celebrated Canadians and Persons Connected with Canada* (Quebec 1862), vii–viii

27 *Canadian Literary Magazine*, I, 1, April 1833, 1–2

28 Ibid., 2

29 *The Roseharp*, I Jan. 1835, 1

30 *Literary Garland*, ns, VI, 5, May 1848, 246

31 Province of Canada, Assembly, *Journals*, 1850, Appendix N, 'Correspondence Relating to Education in Upper Canada, part VIII: 'Remarks and Recommendations with a view to the Introduction of School Libraries into Upper Canada,' E. Ryerson to James Leslie, secretary of the province, 16 July 1849

32 'Preliminary Address,' *Canadian Journal*, I, 1, Jan. 1856, 3

33 Cited in Lower, *Canadians in the Making*, 285

34 *Canadian Illustrated News*, II, 26, 14 Nov. 1863, 330

35 George Washington Johnson, 'Manitoulin,' *Maple Leaves* (Hamilton 1864), cited in Ballstadt, 'Quest for Canadian Identity,' 167

36 Edward Hartley Dewart, *Selections from Canadian Poets* (Montreal 1864), ix

37 'Canadian Poetry and Poets,' *British American Magazine*, I, Aug. 1863, 418

38 Ibid.

39 Upper Canada, Assembly, *Journals*, 1806, 28 Feb.

40 Baillie, 'Charles Fothergill,' 386

41 Upper Canada, Assembly, *Journals*, 1832–3, 7, 10 Dec.

42 Ibid., 1836, 3 Feb.

43 F.J. Alcock, 'Geology,' in W.S. Wallace, ed., *The Royal Canadian Institute Centennial Volume, 1849–1949* (Toronto 1949), 63

44 Hind, *et al*, *Eighty Years' Progress*, 474

45 Upper Canada, Assembly, *Journals*, 1836–7, Appendix, volume 1, no 30, 'Report of the Select Committee on the Petition of Charles Fothergill, Esquire,' 20 Jan. 1837

46 *Canadian Literary Magazine*, I, 1, April 1833, 2

47 Province of Canada, Assembly, *Report of the Select Committee on the Geological Survey* (Quebec 1855), 38–9. Cited in L.S. Fallis, jr, 'The Idea of Progress in the Province of Canada 1841–1867' (unpublished PHD thesis, University of Michigan, 1966), 109

48 Robert L. McDougall, 'A Study of Canadian Periodical Literature of the Nineteenth Century' (unpublished PHD thesis, University of Toronto, 1950), 101

49 Frank Dawson Adams, 'The History of Geology in Canada,' in H.M. Tory, ed., *A History of Science in Canada* (Toronto 1939), 12

50 Ibid., 18

51 'Sir William Logan,' *Canadian Illustrated News*, II, 12, 1 Aug. 1863, 133

52 A provision of the Common School Act of 1824 (4 Geo. IV, c 8)

53 Upper Canada, Assembly, *Journals*, 1833–4, 10 Dec.

54 'Reply to Objections Which Have Been Made to the Introduction of Libraries in Upper Canada by the Educational Department' (extract from the annual report of the chief superintendent for 1854, 9–13). Cited in *A General Catalogue of Books in Every Department of Literature, for Public School Libraries in Upper Canada* (Toronto 1857), 246

55 Public Archives of Canada, MG 20, volume 4, no 415, Major John Richardson to Lord Sydenham, 20 July 1841. Cited in D. Pacey, 'A Colonial Romantic: Major John Richardson, Soldier and Novelist, part II, 'Return to America,' *Canadian Literature*, no 3, winter 1960, 49

56 Province of Canada, Assembly, *Journals*, 1842, 8 Oct., 117

57 Ibid., 1851, 18 Aug., 292–4

58 Ibid., 1852–3, 13 April, 714

59 Ibid., 13 June, 1077

60 Henry Scadding, 'Emigration,' *Canadian Literary Magazine*, I, 1832. Cited in Ballstadt, 'Quest for Canadian Identity,' 56–7

61 *Colonial Advocate*, 9 Sept. 1830. Cited in Margaret Fairley, ed., *The Selected Writings of William Lyon Mackenzie, 1824–1837* (Toronto 1960), 183

62 Samuel Strickland, *27 Years in Canada West* (London 1833), I, 65. Cited in Fallis, 'The Idea of Progress,' 8

63 Susannah Moodie, 'Canada,' *Victoria Magazine*, I, 1847–8, 3. Cited in Ballstadt, 'Quest for Canadian Identity,' 97–8

64 William Kirby, *The UE: A Tale of Upper Canada in XII Cantos* (Niagara 1859). See also Carl Berger, *The Sense of Power: Studies in the Ideas of Canadian Imperialism 1867–1914* (Toronto 1970), 92–3

65 Egerton Ryerson, *The Loyalists of America and their Times* (2 vols., Toronto 1880), II, 191. Cited in Berger, *The Sense of Power*, 92

66 George Washington Johnson, 'No Despot – No Slave,' *Maple Leaves* (Hamilton 1864). Cited in Ballstadt, 'Quest for Canadian Identity,' 169

67 Evan McColl, 'The Lake of the Thousand Isles,' in Dewart, *Selections from Canadian Poets*, 118

68 Pamela S. Vining, 'Canada,' in ibid., 105

69 *Colonial Advocate*, 18 May 1824. Cited in Fairley, *William Lyon Mackenzie*, 109

70 G.M. Craig, ed., *Early Travellers in the Canadas, 1791–1867* (Toronto 1955), xxxv

71 Helen M. Johnson, 'Our Native Land,' in Dewart, *Selections from Canadian Poets*, 82

72 *The Maple Leaf or Canadian Annual*, 1848

73 *Colonial Advocate*, 30 March 1826. Cited in Fairley, *William Lyon Mackenzie*, 112

74 J.R. Godley, *Letters from America* (2 vols., London 1844), I, 200. Cited in Craig, *Early Travellers in the Canadas*, 143

75 Ibid., 144

76 *Christian Guardian*, 29 Aug. 1860. Cited in Lower, *Canadians in the Making*, 284

77 *The Maple Leaf or Canadian Annual*, 1847, Preface

78 Alexander McLachlan, 'The Genius of Canada,' in his *Lyrics* (Toronto 1858)

79 Rev. H.F. Darnell, 'The Maple,' in Dewart, *Selections from Canadian Poets*, 114

80 'Canadian Literature. On What Has Been Done in it,' *Saturday Reader*, I, 2, 16 Sept. 1865, 20

81 William Hay, 'Architecture for the Meridian of Canada,' *Anglo-American Magazine*, II, March 1853, 253

82 D.W., 'Reviews,' *Canadian Journal*, ns, Jan. 1858, III, 13, 18, 19, 20

83 Ibid., 19–20

84 Hind, *et al*, *Eighty Years' Progress*, 4

85 *General Union of All the British Provinces of North America* (London 1824), 40. Cited in Craig, ed., *Early Travellers*, 104

86 John Strachan, 'Observations on a Bill for Uniting the Legislative Councils and Assemblies,' 25 May 1824. Cited in J.L.H. Henderson, ed., *John Strachan: Documents and Opinions* (Toronto 1969), 170

87 Johnson, 'No Despot – No Slave'

88 *Parliamentary Debates on the Confederation of the British North American Provinces* (Queen's Printer 1865), 295

89 For the thought of the imperialists, see Berger, *The Sense of Power*

90 For some of the difficulties see Allan Smith, 'Metaphor and Nationality in North America,' *Canadian Historical Review*, II, 3, Sept. 1970, 247–75

91 *Parliamentary Debates on Confederation*, 27–8

92 Ibid., 86, 84

93 Ibid., 173

94 Ibid., 169

95 Ibid., 110–15

96 Ibid., 25

97 Ibid., 169

98 Ibid., 114

99 Ibid., 45, 31–2

100 For an introductory statement on the nature of ideology and persuasive belief, see John Plamenatz, 'Ideology as Persuasive Belief and Theory,' in his *Ideology* (London and Toronto 1970), 72–92.

101 In a celebrated 1946 article, W.L. Morton underscored the role centralizing versions of the national experience might play in helping the region whose influence they emphasized maintain its hegemony in the nation's affairs. That the centre's concern to enhance its position did not, however, limit its inhabitants to the promotion of an understanding of the national experience framed in these terms is illustrated by the vision of their country offered the people of Canada by two of Ontario's most prominent premiers. Oliver Mowat rested his case against Ottawa on a vision of the country at once decentralist and explicitly rooted in Ontario's interest. His province, he explained in 1884, had every right to resist attempts to weaken and confine its authority. Indeed, a strong Ontario, acting through its government to limit the power of the Dominion and augment its own, was functioning in a manner entirely consistent with the nation's character and needs. 'It is,' he argued, 'in the interest of the Dominion, as well as of the provinces composing the Dominion, that the limits of Ontario should not be restricted. Ontario is, in fact, the "back-bone" of the Dominion; and we desire that it should continue to be the position of our province ...' The provinces at large, mindful of their pressing needs and not yet aware of the implications a decentralized federal system containing no agency capable of checking the power of the large provinces would have for them, responded with enthusiasm to Mowat's doctrine. By the 1930s some of them were prepared to question an understanding of the nation and its politics which, in the changed circumstances of that decade,

seemed all too clearly to serve the interests of Ontario and the wealthier provinces alone. Their support for a new kind of centralism was, however, complicated by the fact that for so long they had built their case for a more equitable union on its opposite. It was, therefore, almost too easy for Mitchell Hepburn to place those who opposed his criticism of the Rowell-Sirois Report at a tactical disadvantage by founding that criticism on a conception of the national character which for decades they had taken as orthodoxy. Having thus disarmed his opponents at the level of argument, he found his victory the more assured. Again Ontario's interest was rationalized by a non-centralist vision of the national character. See W.L. Morton, 'Clio in Canada: The Interpretation of Canadian History,' *University of Toronto Quarterly*, xv, 3, April 1946, 227–34. Mowat's remarks are quoted in C.R.W. Biggar, *Sir Oliver Mowat: A Biographical Sketch* (2 vols., Toronto 1905), I, 428. For Hepburn's case against the Rowell-Sirois Report, see Neil McKenty, *Mitch Hepburn* (Toronto 1967), 228–30

The Teacher in Early Ontario

J. Donald Wilson

There is probably no better place than a schoolroom to judge of the character of a people, or to find an explanation of their national peculiarities. Whatever faults or weaknesses may be entailed upon them, will show themselves there without the hypocrisy of an advanced age, and whatever future they may possess is reflected without admixture of vice and corruption. In so humble a place as a schoolroom may be read the commentaries on the past, and the history of the future development of a nation.[1]

The foregoing statement made in 1837 by Francis J. Grund, a German-born American author, points up the importance of formal education in the Western world in the past century and a half. One of the ways to understand truly a nation or a people is to turn to the system of education that society erects in order to ac-culturate its young. Once the importance of schools in nation-building is accepted, it follows that those elements contributing to the functioning of the school are worthy of analysis. Foremost among these, perhaps, is the teacher. Thus, in order to know Ontario society one must take into account the sort of schools it created, and the role and status assigned to the teacher in those schools.

The first schools in what was eventually to become Ontario used French as the language of instruction. The earliest was established at Fort Frontenac in 1676, and in 1786 Abbé Dufaux opened a school in his parish of Sandwich. It was staffed by two women sent from Quebec by Coadjutor Bishop Hubert. English-language schools began to appear before the creation of Upper Canada in 1791 – indeed from the very time of arrival of the United Empire Loyalists in the previous decade. In fact, one of the first Upper Canadian Loyalist petitions to Lord Dorchester, the governor general of British North America, concerned the matter of education. Sponsored in 1787 by Richard Cartwright, a prominent Kingston merchant, it lamented the deplorable state of education for the children of Loyalists and re-quested 'a school in each district ... for the purpose of teaching English, Latin, Arithmetic and Mathematics.'[2] Similarly, a two-man committee appointed by Lord Dorchester to investigate the situation reported that those who came to Canada counted on enjoying the same 'expectancies' to which they were accustomed in the Thirteen Colonies. These included the tradition of the common school maintained by the community.[3]

Failure to have their petition granted led those Loyalists who upheld the value of schooling to support the opening of a number of privately operated schools, beginning with that of the Rev. John Stuart in Kingston in 1786. The first Loyalist school in Leeds and Grenville was located in a log building within the old French fortification at Pointe au Baril (Maitland).[4] Before the turn of the century similar schools sprang up in Fredericksburg, Napanee, Hay Bay, York, Dundas, Port Rowan, Newark (Niagara-on-the Lake), Ancaster, Adolphustown, St Catharines, Belleville, and Port Hope. One observer estimates that there were twenty-two private schools before 1800.[5] An early visitor to the colony found time, though his stay was brief, to comment on the schools around Kingston in 1795: 'In this district there are some schools, but they are few in number. The children are instructed in reading and writing, and pay each a dollar a month.'[6]

The teachers of these schools were for the most part clergymen. The early garrison schools at Kingston and Newark were conducted by army chaplains. Church of England clergymen, like the Rev. Robert Addison at Newark, and Presbyterian clergymen, like the Rev. John Burns, his successor as garrison chaplain, predominated. But there were outstanding lay teachers as well. W.W. Baldwin, father of the more famous Robert, opened a classical school at York in 1802. Richard Cockrell, English-born but American-influenced through a stay in the United States, opened a school in Newark in 1796 and then moved to Ancaster to establish another school before turning his hand to publishing a newspaper. Cockrell's ability received praise from no less a critic than John Strachan who described his school as 'an excellent mathematical school.'[7] Among Cockrell's first students was William Hamilton Merritt, whose father was satisfied enough to send his son to Ancaster to continue his schooling with him. Cockrell was also responsible for writing an interesting pamphlet on education entitled *Thoughts on the Education of Youth*. According to J.J. Talman, this pamphlet, published in Newark in 1795, was the first non-governmental publication in Upper Canada, preceded only by Simcoe's speech at the opening of the first Parliament and the laws passed by the first and second sessions of that Parliament.[8]

Most of the early schools were day schools restricted to teaching the rudiments of the 'three R s.' Boarding schools could be found in Kingston and Newark, the early centres of population.[9] Although a few schools taught the classics and higher mathematics – Stuart's at Kingston, Strachan's at Cornwall, and Baldwin's at York – the typical curriculum was confined to 'the art of spelling – reading – writing and arithmetic.'[10]

From the colony's earliest days a great concern was registered about the need to exclude American teachers from Upper Canada. By 1799 it was government policy 'to exclude schoolmasters from the States lest they should instill Republicanism into the tender minds of the youth of the Province.'[11] A commission was established to examine and license teachers, and insure that they were British subjects or had taken the oath of allegiance. The *Upper Canada Gazette* considered this measure a worthy innovation, one that would prevent the entry into the classroom of 'itinerant characters [presumably Americans], who preferred that to a more laborious way of getting through life.'[12] As later evidence will bear out, this policy presumably had little effect on the employment of American teachers.

The sorry state of teachers in the colony prior to the War of 1812 was underlined in a letter to the editor of the *Kingston Gazette* in 1811. The writer welcomed the recent establishment of district schools throughout the province in the conviction that they would be presided over by 'well educated teachers.' 'They will ultimately preclude,' the letter continued, 'the admission and employment of itinerant and illiterate pedagogues, who to the disgrace of our country and the injury of our youth, impose themselves as teachers on the community.'[13] Such sentiments about the itinerancy of teachers at this time were further amplified by another statement in the same newspaper that 'in every township, a teacher of twelve months standing is a prodigy; one of as many weeks the most common.'[14] Another observer declared that teachers 'in this part of the country ... are either strolling vagabonds or so illiterate that they cannot without great difficulty read a passage in the Old and New Testament with any degree of accuracy.'[15]

One of the most devastating critiques of the dangers of American teachers and textbooks at this time was to be found in a series of letters written under the pen name of 'Palemon' and appearing in the *Kingston Gazette* in the autumn of 1815.[16] Books imported from the United States, he began, 'are all intended in every page to raise the merit of their own country, Laws and Constitution at the expense of Great Britain ...' 'Thus,' he continued, 'our children in the Canadas ... are taught as if they were within the jurisdiction of the United States ... The unavoidable consequence of all this is, that in the course of time we shall be American citizens in sentiment and customs, and nothing but strong self-interest and force will keep us in subjection to the venerable British Constitution.' Instead of American books, 'the books we put in the hands of our children should be calculated to furnish their minds with correct ideas on Religion, Morality, the Customs, Manners and Laws, of our own country.' But herein lay the problem: there was no demand for British books 'because there is not a sufficient number of good British Teachers through the country to recommend them, and to refuse all others.' Palemon's solution was simple: 'the Provincial Legislature should make some regulations respecting both imported school books and imported teachers, especially in the schools that are supported by the government.'

It is significant that just such measures were taken respecting teachers in the

Common School Act of 1816 and respecting books in the Act of 1824. The former ruled that a teacher must henceforth be a British subject by birth or naturalization or have taken the oath of allegiance.[17] But American teachers continued to be common in Upper Canada schools. Father Alexander Macdonell, later to become first Catholic bishop in Ontario, commented to Bathurst, undoubtedly exaggerating the point, that 'with the exception of 8 District Grammar Schools, which are principally taught by Clergymen of the Established Church, the education of youth of both sexes in Upper Canada is exclusively entrusted to American Teachers.'[18]

In 1820 Lieutenant-Governor Sir Peregrine Maitland tried to counteract the 'mischief' of American schoolmasters by establishing a system of National Schools headed by Church of England teachers. These schools, whose common name was derived from the English 'National Society for the Promotion of the Education of the Poor in the Principles of the Established Church throughout England and Wales,' were to be monitorial schools functioning under the Dr Andrew Bell system based on the teaching of Church of England doctrine.[19] Maitland believed the system would 'instruct all the youth of the province to the exclusion, not only of American masters, but of their republican apparatus of Grammars and Lesson books.'[20] Despite Maitland's grandiose plans for a National School in every town in the colony,[21] they proved a singular failure. The continuing concern about American teachers led to the inclusion in the Common School Act of 1824[22] of a clause requiring teachers to obtain certification of qualifications from a more central and better qualified body than local trustees – better qualified, in Strachan's opinion, because they were selected by district boards which were appointed by the lieutenant-governor.[23]

In spite of Maitland's reservations, some American teachers were competent men. One of them, a man named Forsyth, was the first teacher in Brant County. He gained a favourable reputation although he used American textbooks exclusively.[24] About the same time Captain Owen, a settler on Yonge Street, wrote to Lieutenant-Governor Gore in praise of 'a young man, an American, [who] is seated near us as a schoolmaster, whose system of education in my opinion does him credit.'[25] Another American by the name of Hoag, who taught near Hamilton around 1820, is credited with having 'taught many a young girl's and boy's budding ideas to shoot forth.'[26] At St Catharines there was another exemplary teacher, one John Huston Clendennan, a native of Pennsylvania. His obituary notice records that he was actively engaged for twenty-five years in conducting an English school. 'The successful issue of his indefatigable exertions in his vocation, is apparent in the advancement of many of his pupils to the Magistracy of this district, and other offices under Government, and in their otherwise becoming influential members of the community.'[27]

Despite these few examples of excellent American teachers, the majority were incompetent. School boards often found that transient Americans were the only ones willing to take on a job which paid so poorly. The Act of 1816 provided for a basic salary of £25 a year for the common school teacher; four years later that was halved and by 1833 a select committee of the House of Assembly could report that in some districts no more than £4 or £5 was being given to any one teacher from the government grant.[28] By that time, in contrast, even an ordinary artisan could earn £75 a year.[29]

Because of the low wages, it is not surprising that those least capable often took up teaching. One report referred to them as 'worthless scum ... more alive to ... the stipend than to the advancement of the education of those placed under their care.'[30] Another spoke of the country schoolmaster as 'an insignificant contemptible being, a mere cipher in society ... no man has ever, within the sphere of my acquaintance educated his son, unless he were a dunce and consequently good for nothing else, to be a schoolmaster. Our schoolmasters are, therefore, composed of untaught boys; or of dunces that are unfit for business and too lazy to live by the "sweat of their face." No wonder then that the profession is reduced to the utmost contempt.'[31] Anna Jameson, wife of the vice-chancellor of Upper Canada, in observing in 1838 that a number of wayside schools between Port Talbot and Chatham were closed for lack of schoolmasters (many of them may have been implicated in the Rebellion), queried: 'Who that could earn a subsistence in any other way would be a schoolmaster in the wilds of Upper Canada? Ill-fed, ill-clothed, ill-paid, or not paid at all – boarded at the houses of the different farmers in turn – I found indeed some few men, poor creatures! always either Scotch or Americans – and totally unfit for the office they had undertaken.'[32]

Certainly the status of a teacher in Upper Canada remained low. As late as 1835, it could be noted that in Toronto, 'the profession of schoolmaster bars all association with Aristocracy of the city. This unique distinction is doubtless borrowed from ... neighbour Jonathan who respects his [schoolmaster] just as much as one bear does his hunters, or another the fine arts.'[33] One of the most biting commentaries on the lowly state of teaching and the involvement of Americans was made by William Cosgrave, a trustee in the Western District. He complained about the pittance paid to teachers which provided little incentive to men of talent. Instead, common school teachers were generally disabled persons unable to labour or old men, usually veterans or half-pay soldiers, with only a limited education. 'The result of this system is that a great number of these schools are conducted by persons from the United States who are unacquainted with the principles of the British Constitution or its jurisprudence, & who inculcate on their pupils a greater love for a republican Government than that of a monarchy & these youths advance in life with the seeds of Republicanism thus sown in their minds to the disadvantage of the British Government.'[34] Concern about the presence of Americans in the schools of the Western District reached the point where an enraged reader of *The Canadian Emigrant* in Sandwich demanded in a letter to the editor an explanation of why the District Board of Education should pay the salary of an American teacher 'who is opposed to Sir John Colborne and the present administration, who supports Mr Mackenzie's grievance petition and who reads and recommends the *Colonial Advocate*?'[35]

In the fall of 1835 the Assembly established a three-man committee headed by Dr Charles Duncombe, a Burford Township (Brant County) doctor, to go to the United States to observe and report on the systems of education to be found there. Duncombe, the only commissioner to go to the States, returned with three reports – one on lunatic asylums, one on prisons and penitentiaries, and one on education. The last called for substantial changes in the education system of Upper Canada.[36]

A special feature of the report was its support for both female education and female teachers. Duncombe detected an important change in attitudes towards women; 'instead of the fainting, weeping, vapid, pretty plaything, once the model of female loveliness, those qualities of the head and heart that best qualify a woman for her duties are demanded and admired.'[37] Not only should young women be educated in schools just as young men were but they should also be prepared as teachers. Since men were attracted to other professions with more prestige and money, it would be wise, Duncombe argued, in view of the increased need for teachers, to turn to women. Fortunately the very education 'necessary to fit a woman to be a teacher is exactly the one that best fits her for that domestic relation she is primarily designed to fill.'[38] Because of economic necessity, then, Duncombe was prepared to promote the idea of female teachers while at the same time expecting those very women to follow a traditional domestic role.

In 1836 Duncombe proposed a common school bill based on his report. Among the many features of the bill was provision for proper teacher training. He had asserted in his report, 'schools will be like their teachers. Hence the necessity of having the teachers well prepared for their arduous responsible office.'[39] His bill proposed the establishment of four normal schools – three for men and one for women.[40] The determined opposition of the Legislative Council, however, resulted, for other reasons, in the bill's rejection.

In the wake of the Rebellion and its ensuing border troubles, Lieutenant-Governor Sir George Arthur in 1839 appointed a committee to investigate the state of education in the province. Headed by Dr John McCaul, the principal of Upper Canada College, the committee heard many witnesses before completing its report which, among other things, once more pointed up the evils of permitting American textbooks to be used in the schools and allowing students to go to the

United States to complete their studies.[41] The weakest link of the common school system, however, according to the report, was the teacher. The committee complained that many teachers were largely 'unfit' for their 'responsible station' because of their 'want either of literacy or moral qualification.'[42] The cause of the 'unfitness' was held to be the 'inadequate remuneration.' 'In this country,' the report continued, 'the wages of the working classes are so high that few undertake the office of schoolmaster except those who are unable to do anything else.'[43]

Private individuals made similar observations about the state of teaching in the province. A contemporary 'Memorandum on Common Schools' also linked inferior teaching with the low remuneration granted the teachers. 'The teachers ... are generally speaking either uneducated lads or persons physically or morally disqualified for any occupation. Of the few respectable persons here and there to be found, the greater part are men whom a delicate constitution or some bodily injury has unfitted for the more profitable employment of their time in manual labour. The majority are persons as unfit as can be conceived. A school indeed seems to be the last refuge of the idle and worthless.'[44] No improvement could be expected, the memorialist argued, until qualified schoolmasters were hired. For this to happen the salary of a teacher must at least match that of an artisan, namely £75 currency per annum,[45] or approximately double the current salaries for common school teachers. Even at that, a common dodge used by school boards to save money on salaries was the practice of 'boarding round,' hardly a practice likely to prove attractive to a refined and cultured man.[46]

About the same time the prominent Perth Presbyterian minister, the Rev. William Bell,[47] wrote a lengthy article on education in the *Christian Examiner and Presbyterian Review* in which he touched on some of these same points.[48] He contrasted the progress made in Europe and the United States with his contention that 'scarcely anything has been done here, to improve the state of our common schools.' He too singled out the importance of improving the calibre of teachers by paying them more money. 'The first improvement necessary,' he stated, 'is a more liberal support' for teachers, because at the moment only 'the lame and the lazy' are attracted. Bell then went on to make special commendation of David Stow's Training System.

Stow, a Glasgow merchant, became concerned about providing some sort of education for his city's poor children. His experience convinced him of the importance of trained teachers, but he did not share the popular enthusiasm for the Bell and Lancasterian monitorial methods. His efforts to devise a new system of teacher training resulted in the founding by the Glasgow Educational Society of the Glasgow Normal School in 1837 and culminated in the publication of a book, *The Training System*, setting forth his approach.[49] The essence of his 'method' may be summarized as: 'the sympathy of numbers' – the learning stimulus that students might gain from one another – and 'activity centred teaching,' as opposed to the rote learning common in that day.[50]

Both Bell and Campbell in their high praise of Stow's system and the Glasgow Normal School make clear that his fame had reached the ears of some Upper Canadians. However, too few Canadians knew of Stow's work to suit Bell, who lamented the fact that Upper Canada 'knows less about the Training System than New South Wales and Van Dieman's Land.'[51] To improve common school education in the colony Bell advised that trained teachers be recruited from the Glasgow Normal School;[52] that young men should be sent to Glasgow at public expense to learn the training system; and that efforts be made to disseminate the principles of the system by purchasing for distribution at public expense copies of Stow's *Training System*.

For its part the McCaul Committee had several proposals for improving the calibre of common school teachers: an average salary of £50 per annum; the establishment of a normal school at Toronto and, ultimately, four such schools throughout the province; and a model school for each township.[53] In support of these recommendations, the normal schools of New York State and Prussia were cited: the former with its eight schools and 374 students; Prussia with its fifty-two schools and 2000 students hoping to be teachers.[54] A check should be placed, it continued, on the calibre of teaching through systematic inspection of all schools under the direction of an inspector general and a provincial Board of Commissioners. The substantial recommendations of the McCaul Committee might have been expected to lead directly to improvements in Upper Canada's educational system. However, in the aftermath of the rebellion and the troubles which followed, jails, court houses, and roads continued to receive primary consideration when it came to appropriating public funds. Then, too, the Act of Union in 1840, following hard on the heels of the committee's report, played a part in postponing implementation of its recommendations.

The union of the two Canadas in 1841 necessitated the passage of a new education act. The Schools Act of that year attempted to play its part in effecting a cultural union of the new province. Although the act had provided for a single superintendent, the government finally settled on two assistant superintendents, one each for Canada West and East. The Rev. Robert Murray, a Presbyterian minister from Oakville, became assistant superintendent for Canada West from April 1842, and continued in that post until replaced by Egerton Ryerson in September 1844.[55]

The School Act of 1841 was not well received. Assistant Superintendent Murray left no doubt about its unacceptability by stating that 'it is acknowledged on all hands that the present school bill does not work well.'[56] The teachers and school commissioners of Cavan, southwest of Peterborough, called the act 'complex, mystical, overbearing, tyrannical and unprecedented in Legislation.'[57] Moreover, according to a Markham teacher, the bill did not succeed in improving school attendance: 'out of upward of 80 between the ages of 5 and 16, which are in the school District, not more than 24 attended during the last quarter.'[58] One scholar suggests that 'instead of improving either the quality or the quantity of schooling, [the act] made things worse than they had been in 1840.'[59]

One of the biggest problems with the 1841 Act concerned the payment of teachers. There seemed to be a lack of clarity as to who was responsible for their payment. One teacher complained, 'the Commissioners ... tell us that they are not in any way responsible for our salaries; nor can the[y] tell us who is, more than they refer us to the government.'[60] In the eighteen months of the act's existence a remarkable number of letters were sent to Murray; those from trustees complained about the lack of money to pay teachers;[61] those from teachers at not being paid.[62] More specifically teachers complained not only about a lack of sufficient remuneration on which to live, but also that their income was spotty because of their dependence on student fees to supplement the government grant and local property tax. This state of affairs was made even worse by irregular attendance on the part of the students. In Toronto Township teachers were even forced to collect fees from parents by themselves, since no money was forthcoming from school commissioners.[63]

Murray was the recipient of many letters outlining teachers' destitute state. One or two bear repeating to enable the reader to savour the general tone of grievance. Nicholas Wilson, a Cobourg teacher, wrote almost pathetically: 'I am really ashamed to walk out in the streets of Cobourg, lest I should meet one or more of these persons whom I should have paid long ago, it grieves me very much to think that it is not in my power to act, decently, and respectably, with every person.'[64] Another teacher in Warwick Township (Lambton County) underlined the difficulties of transportation and communications in this pre-railway era. Murray had called a meeting for district common school teachers in Sandwich as part of his tour of the western end of the province. But for the Warwick teachers, 'being men of families, it would be hard for us to leave our homes and go a distance of 150 miles [return] at this season of the year, besides we have not the means to go, never having received any recompense for our labours either from the Parents of the children under our respective charges or yet from the funds appropriated by Government.'[65] Murray could only conclude that many teachers 'appear, from their correspondence, to be in a state little short of starvation.'[66] Bearing out the reality of all the trials of a common school teacher, a Port Hope teacher confessed to Murray he wanted out and sought the latter's intervention on his behalf, because 'I am so heartily tired of the Life of a Schoolteacher.'[67]

It seems that Murray was himself sincerely concerned about improving the status of teachers.[68] In a letter to the Teachers' Society of Johnstown District, he stated: 'Be assured that my greatest earthly ambition is to make Teachers respectable, efficient & independent ... Much of the civil & religious peace of this great country must depend on the education of the young, and therefore every effort I make to advance the status of the Teachers of youth is tending directly to advance the Standard of Education, and the best interests both civil & religious of this Province.'[69] Certainly the 1841 Act had proven no panacea. Murray was quoted as stating that during 1842 nearly half the school districts were without teachers.[70] Whole townships went through the year without a single school in operation.[71] Early the next year the situation was still desperate; there were 124 vacancies reported in the Home District, 82 in Niagara District, 40 in Brock District, 46 in Wellington District, and 129 in London District.[72]

Improvement of teacher status was dependent upon two elements, according to Murray: a substantial increase in teachers' salaries and 'increasing the protection afforded to Teachers.'[73] The 'subscribers and teachers in Esquesing' echoed Murray's view by stating that most teachers sought 'a competent income, and the prospect of permanency in the situation.' The cases of Scotland and Prussia were cited as models of generous support of teachers with the former providing each teacher with a house, a garden, 'and an arable field, sufficient for the pasture of a cow,' as well as life tenure, and Prussia providing its teachers with a pension at superannuation.[74]

Even prior to his appointment as superintendent of schools, Murray had pointed up the precarious nature of the teacher's position and the lack of protection afforded his job. In a letter to the McCaul Committee in December 1839, he put the case: 'The power of ejecting School Masters vested in three Trustees, or Superintendents, subjects the Teachers to the whim and caprice of every child attending the school; the Teacher is thus left at the mercy of the public, who, presumably, have no conscience, and his situation is rendered more precarious and more degraded than that of a shoeblack.'[75] Job tenure was too esoteric a question to rouse much public interest at this point, but teachers' salaries presented a problem demanding immediate attention.

One way to provide more money for qualified teachers was to curb the proliferation of schools. Murray was of the opinion that there were too many school districts and was pleased to note that municipal councils operating under the new Municipal Act were beginning to reduce the number. Such a measure resulted in larger schools with a corresponding augmentation of teachers' salaries.[76] He was not averse, however, to suggesting greater teacher workloads as a solution. Teachers could be put to work on a shift basis whereby they could teach in one school in the morning and another school in the afternoon.[77] If he could have had his way, Murray would have limited a twelve-mile square township to four schools instead of the from twenty to twenty-six found in a few townships. The cause of this needless proliferation of schools was simple: 'Every kind parent wishes a school at his door.' Murray was adamant that no government could support such a system of education; the cost of 'qualified' teachers for all these schools would be prohibitive.[78]

Moreover, teachers must be relieved of bothersome, unprofessional tasks, such as arriving at school early to light fires to heat the school. Murray argued that one would not expect a clergyman to tend to the fires in his church, nor likewise the Speakers in the Legislative Council and House of Assembly. So, 'Commissioners who would lay such a duty upon the Teacher in order to save the School District the paltry sum which would be required to pay for a person to attend to it, shew that they have yet to learn the value of education.'[79]

A growing concern about professionalism was also apparent among teachers themselves. Rather suddenly from the early 1840s evidence appears among the incoming correspondence to the Education Office, Canada West, of groups of teachers, rather than just individual teachers, expressing cogent and well-reasoned opinions about public schooling. The previously isolated individual cut off from his fellows seems to be increasingly replaced by associations of teachers based on geographical location. The contrast with pre-Union days is all the more startling because of the intelligent tone of the recommendations being proposed, indicating that the teachers themselves must have had more than the usual rudimentary education common in earlier days. There is also reason to believe that as their numbers grew they were becoming increasingly aware of their status in society. Who led these associations, why they emerged just at this time, whether or not they had drawn up professional codes of ethics – these and other questions remain shrouded in mystery. The lack of an Education Office as such in the period before 1841 helps to explain the absence of the sort of documentation essential to answer such questions.

Teachers' groups expressed their opinions on many subjects. For example, they were highly critical of the school commissioners' competence to judge educational matters. One group from Brock District found it hard to understand 'why teachers should be made mere passive tools in the hands of Commissioners and it be left with the latter to the exclusion of the former to frame rules for the conduct of schools.' They concluded that commissioners must be assumed 'to be (in general) more competent than teachers,' whereas 'truth constrains us to say that the reverse will (in general) be found to be the case.'[80] The solution was obvious: teachers must have a greater share in the determination of educational policy, for 'since it is to the teacher that the parents naturally look for the improvement of their children, it is only reasonable that he should have a share in the formation of those rules which he himself is to carry into execution.'[81]

Another group of teachers from Gore District made a specific demand that since teachers knew what was best for education they should compose the district boards of education. Other professions governed their own actions; why not teachers? The plea was carefully reasoned and revealed a highly developed concept of professionalism: '... as teachers alone can give effect to any system of education, they and they alone should regulate the course of study to be adopted, the books to be used, and the various means to be applied, in order to promote the advancement of common school training on a uniform and efficient plan. The branches of duty we have just enumerated belong legitimately to teachers, they cannot be so well understood, or so efficiently performed, by either District Councils, or Boards of Commissioners.'[82] District councils and boards of commissioners would, they conceded, retain all duties not relating directly to the educative process.

If teachers were to act as true professionals they would have to be prepared to police their own ranks. This necessity the Brock District teachers were quick to acknowledge. If they were granted the share of the decision-making powers they sought, teachers would naturally be 'most interested in maintaining their own respectability' and would consequently have some influence in excluding 'immoral and otherwise disqualified characters' from their ranks. Among 'otherwise disqualified characters' the Brock teachers included aliens, especially Americans. The latter, they asserted, 'are persons whose political opinions are diametrically opposed to monarchial institutions and are generally imbued with a morbid zeal for proselytizing to their own principles.'[83] Although they did not include female teachers in the classification of 'disqualified characters,' the Brock teachers opposed the hiring of women at salaries equal to male teachers. Such a practice, they were convinced, was a retrograde step destined to retard education's 'progressive improvement': 'There is no department of business, save that of teaching, in which females receive the same ratio of remuneration as men do, and the consequence is that schoolmasters in general, experience a mortified feeling of degradation, very injurious to the beneficial exercise of this calling.'[84]

There was no denying the presence of numbers of female teachers, a firm indication that Duncombe's recommendation in 1836 was indeed timely. In fact, the feminization of the profession dates from this period. In 1843 more than half the children of the town of Hamilton were learning under female teachers.[85] A Picton resident reported that in one township alone out of twenty-one school divisions sixteen were held by female teachers, 'and I am prepared to say and prove not more than one of the sixteen is in any way qualified to teach correctly even the first principles of Education.'[86] Female teachers were popular with school commissioners, however, because 'having no pretensions to Education,' they were satisfied to accept less money than demanded by male teachers.[87] In 1847, the first year in which male and female teachers were reported separately, about one of every five common school teachers was female.[88]

A common suggestion to improve the calibre of teachers, both male and female, was to erect normal schools and model schools throughout the province.[89] Teachers properly trained at such schools would obviate the situation where 'a Board composed of illiterate men (as must often occur) ... judge the qualifications of teachers.'[90]

The need to erect a uniform and centralized system was widely recognized before Ryerson became superintendent. Some venturesome individuals and groups of teachers even proposed the introduction of compulsion in both taxation and school attendance. Murray himself was committed to a centralized system and saw the disruptive, almost chaotic results of having the power so much divided among the township commissioners. He was realistic enough to admit, however, the 'deep rooted jealousy' in certain quarters 'of such a power being committed to one man.'[91] Murray received many letters from teachers pointing out the need for and benefit deriving from a 'uniform system.'[92] The Brock District (Oxford County) teachers, for example, favoured compulsory taxation, unpopular as such a measure might be.[93] Leaving property assessment optional to the municipal councils, as in the 1841 Act, was bound to be met with non-compliance, they argued. Likewise, those inhabitants who had no families to educate would 'object to contribute any sum however small to build schoolhouses or pay teachers for educating other people's children.' The only way to overcome this 'mere selfishness' would be to make the collection of taxes obligatory on all citizens.[94] Incidentally, Ryerson used the same reasoning when he prepared the original draft of his 1846 bill which included a clause authorizing local assessment on all inhabitants according to property.[95]

Foreign cases were even cited to emphasize the value of compulsory education. One group of 'subscribers and teachers' drew to Murray's attention that in the states of southern Germany, especially Württemberg, parents were compelled to send their children to school from the age of six to fourteen. To help enforce this provision it was declared illegal 'to employ any person, in any capacity, under twenty-one, without a formal certificate that he has attended at school the appointed number of years.' The memorialists agreed such provisions might be unrealistic to expect in Canada West but urged serious consideration of legislation exacting school fees for every child between the ages of six and sixteen years whether that child should attend school or not.[96]

By the time that Ryerson assumed the mantle of office as assistant superintendent in 1844, teachers were beginning to develop a corporate sense, to take the first shaky steps up the rocky road to teacher professionalism. Their opinions on questions such as remuneration, female teachers, tenure, and teacher-trustee relations reveal a more highly developed sense of professionalism than is usually conceded for the time. They were also ready to express opinions, though often conflicting ones, on such controversial topics of the day as compulsory property assessment and free education – innovations which historians have given Ryerson credit for making into lively political issues. On the whole, teachers at this time favoured increased state involvement in public schooling.

By mid-century Ryerson could speak of his Common School Act of 1850 as 'the Great Charter of Common School Teachers in Upper Canada': 'It stamps their profession with new importance, and throws over their interests and character the shield of a new protection. I can now say truly, that I know of no state, where a Popular School System exists, in which the rights and interests of Teachers are so effectually protected.'[97] He now felt prepared to hold up the teaching profession 'as a comfortable, as well as respectable and useful employment for life.'[98] Thus the status of teaching had come a long way from being universally condemned as 'the last refuge of the idle and worthless.'

NOTES

The author would like to express his appreciation to Professor M. Elizabeth Arthur, Department of History, Lakehead University, and Professors R.D. Gidney and J.D. Purdy of Althouse College, University of Western Ontario, who offered many helpful comments on an earlier draft of this paper.

1 Used as frontispiece to Ruth Miller Elson, *Guardians of Tradition* (Lincoln 1964)
2 Petition of Western Loyalists to Lord Dorchester, 15 April 1787. A. Shortt and A.G. Doughty, eds., *Documents Relating to the Constitutional History of Canada* (3 vols., Ottawa 1907), I, 648
3 W.D. Powell and John Collins to Lord Dorchester, 18 Aug. 1787 in R.A. Preston, ed., *Kingston Before the War of 1812* (Toronto 1959), 122–4
4 Ruth McKenzie, *Leeds and Grenville: Their First Two Hundred Years* (Toronto 1967), 94
5 W.E. Macpherson, 'The Ontario Grammar Schools,' *Bulletin of the Department of History and Political and Economic Science,* Queen's University, no 21 (Oct. 1916), 2
6 Duke de la Rochefoucauld-Liancourt, *Travels through the United States of America and Upper Canada* (2 vols., London 1799), I, 286
7 *Christian Recorder,* April 1819. Cited in J.G. Hodgins, ed. *Documentary History of Education in Upper Canada, 1792–1876* (28 vols., Toronto 1893–1904), I, 155. Hereafter referred to as DHE
8 Richard Cockrel [sic], *Thoughts on the Education of Youth* (Newark 1795). Reproduced by the Bibliographical Society of Canada (Toronto 1949)
9 *Upper Canada Gazette,* 8 March 1797, 2

10 Toronto Central Library, Baldwin Room, Articles of Agreement between Alexander William Carson, schoolmaster, and several citizens of York, 30 April 1805

11 Michael Smith, *A Geographical View of the Province of Upper Canada and Promiscuous Remarks Upon the Government* (Philadelphia 1813), 44

12 *Upper Canada Gazette,* 13 July 1799

13 *Kingston Gazette,* 12 Feb. 1811

14 J.M. Flindall, 'Essay on Education in Upper Canada,' *Kingston Gazette,* 1818. In DHE, I, 133

15 Ontario Archives [OA], Hodgins Collection, letter signed 'Seth' addressed to Mr Miles [editor], *Kingston Gazette,* dated Fredericksburgh, 29 Nov. 1815. An example of the near 'illiterate' schoolmaster can be found in an advertisement in the *Kingston Gazette* of 29 Jan. 1811, as follows: 'You will also send books and pens and ink and a pennife, as I alway larne skolars to make their own pens, but you need not send pens to them that you don't want to rite, nor books to them that you dont want to read, which they can do without them.'

16 The letters, first published in the Montreal *Herald,* appeared in the *Kingston Gazette* on successive weeks between 22 August and 9 September 1815

17 56 Geo. III c 36

18 Macdonell to Bathurst, 10 Jan. 1817. In J.G. Hodgins, ed., *Historical Educational Papers and Documents of Ontario* (6 vols., Toronto 1911–12), I, 10–11

19 The other system of monitorial schools common in that day followed a form devised by Joseph Lancaster. For the main distinctions between the Bell and Lancasterian systems, see J. Donald Wilson, R.M. Stamp, and L.-P. Audet, eds., *Canadian Education: A History* (Scarborough 1970), 35

20 OA, CO 42/366. Maitland to Bathurst, 4 Jan. 1821, 3

21 OA, Minutes, General Board of Education, extract of despatch from Maitland to Bathurst [enclosed under letter to General Board from Major Hillier], 13 May 1823

22 4 Geo. IV, c 8

23 Public Archives of Canada [PAC], Upper Canada Sundries [UCS], Strachan to Hillier, undated, 1824 (Nov.–Dec. Box)

24 Charles and James C. Thomas, 'Reminiscences of the First Settlers in the County of Brant,' Ontario Historical Society, *Papers and Records,* XII, 1914, 68

25 PAC, UCS, Captain W.F. Owen to Gore, 2 April 1816

26 Charles Durand, *Reminiscences of Charles Durand, Barrister* (Toronto 1897), 106

27 *St. Catharines Journal,* 5 May 1836

28 Assembly, Select Committee, 1833. Mahlon Burwell, chairman. In DHE, II, 109. Tuition fees would, of course, supplement that sum at an average of 10s per quarter year per student.

29 PAC, Educational Papers, P.C. Campbell, 'Memorandum on Common Schools,' Brockville, 4 Sept. 1839. Abridged and edited version by J. Donald Wilson in *Journal of Education* (UBC), no 15, April 1969, 63–73. Same point made by John Strachan in OA, Minutes, General Board of Education, 5 Feb. 1829, 66

30 William Crooks, Grimsby, in Robert Gourlay, *Statistical Account of Upper Canada, Compiled with a View to a Grand System of Emigration,* (2 vols., London, 1822), I, 434

31 'Palemon,' Letter no 1, *Kingston Gazette,* 22 Aug. 1815. A later observer has concluded that in those days 'a teaching post was commonly regarded as the last refuge of the incompetent, the inept, the unreliable.' J.G. Althouse, *The Ontario Teacher, 1800–1910* (Toronto 1967), 6

32 Anna Jameson, *Winter Studies and Summer Rambles in Canada* (3 vols., London, 1838), II, 23. A similar report from the other end of the province was more restrained: 'Teachers generally speaking are not men of good or liberal education.' PAC, Educational

Papers, Report of Common School Trustees, Eastern District, 9 Dec. 1828

33 Adam Fergusson, *Practical Notes Made during a Tour in Canada and a Portion of the United States in* MDCCCXXXI (Edinburgh 1833), 76

34 PAC, Educational Papers, William Cosgrave to Colborne, 15 Dec. 1828

35 *Canadian Emigrant* (Sandwich), 19 May 1832

36 Charles Duncombe, *Report upon the Subject of Education* (Toronto, 1836). Reprinted by Johnson Reprint Corporation, 1966

37 Ibid. (Johnson reprint), 42. An eloquent appeal for female education, typical of the new regard for women, appeared in the *Christian Guardian* a few years later. 'And shall women be uneducated? No! Every heart that is worth calling by that name, proclaims with emphasis, No! Let the treasures of science be unlocked and poured at her feet. Let her be educated to be the friend and companion of man! Let her be educated for usefulness. Let her be prized, not for the flowers, or drapery, or jewels which decorate her person, but for the riches that adorn her mind. LET HER BE EDUCATED!' *Christian Guardian*, 8 Dec. 1841

38 Duncombe, *Report*, 55

39 Ibid., 71

40 DHE, II, 322

41 *Report of the Committee of Commissioners on Education in Upper Canada* [McCaul Committee]. DHE, III, 250; PAC, Educational Papers, R.C. Horne to Hon. John Macaulay, inspector general, 6 April 1839

42 In a memorandum to Lieutenant-Governor Sir George Arthur, a member of the Board of Education for the Johnstown District painted a vivid picture of the lack of moral qualifications of many teachers of his district. 'Drunkenness with all its train of vices, is constantly prevalent and I am certain that notwithstanding the exertions and examples made by us during the last two years, no small proportion of the Government allowance is spent on liquor in the town, on the day of distribution. We have now two Schoolmasters in jail on charges of forgery.' PAC, Educational Papers, P.C. Campbell to Arthur, 4 Sept. 1839. Edited and annotated version by J. Donald Wilson of same memorandum published in *Journal of Education* (UBC), no 15, April 1969, 63–73

43 Report of McCaul Commission, 1839, DHE, III, 248–9

44 Campbell memo in Wilson edition, 66

45 The McCaul Report recommended the average salary for a common school teacher be fixed at £50 per annum.

46 Campell memo in Wilson edition, 65–6

47 For Bell's biography see Isabel Skelton, *A Man Austere: William Bell, Parson and Pioneer* (Toronto 1947). Bell had been the first schoolmaster in Perth, opening a village school in 1817. Jean S. McGill, *A Pioneer History of the County of Lanark* (Toronto 1968), 175

48 *Canadian Christian Examiner and Presbyterian Review*, 24 March 1838. Original copies lodged at United Church Archives, Victoria University, Toronto.

49 David Stow, *The Training System* (Glasgow, Blackie and Son, 1845). See also Marjorie Cruikshank, 'David Stow, Scottish Pioneer of Teacher Training in Britain,' *British Journal of Educational Studies*, XIV, 2, 1966, 205–15

50 Quoted in W.B. Hamilton, 'The British Heritage,' in Wilson *et al.*, *Canadian Education: A History*, 38

51 *Presbyterian Review*, 24 March 1838

52 Campbell made the same suggestion, memo in Wilson edition, 69

53 In the next decade provision was made for a normal school in the School Act of 1846. The first Normal School was opened in Toronto on 1 November 1847 in temporary quarters. Steps were taken to erect permanent quarters in 1849. The cornerstone for the

new building designed by Frederic Cumberland – the architect of St James Cathedral, the 1850s remodeling of Osgoode Hall, and University College, Toronto – was laid by Lord Elgin on 2 July 1851.

54 Upper Canada, *Journal of Assembly,* 1840, Appendix B, 338
55 For interesting details surrounding Murray's appointment, see R.D. Gidney, 'The Rev. Robert Murray: Ontario's First Superintendent of Schools,' *Ontario History,* LXIII, 4, Dec. 1971, 191–204
56 OA, Education Office, Letterbook A, Murray to Thomas Alexander, 24 Feb. 1843
57 Ibid., Incoming General Correspondence, Samuel Armour, chairman, school commissioners, to Murray, 17 Dec. 1843
58 Ibid., 'A.B.' (teacher) Markham, to Murray, 4 Feb. 1843
59 Gidney, 'The Rev. Robert Murray,' 198
60 OA, Education Office, Incoming General Correspondence, 'A.B.' (teacher) to Murray, 4 Feb. 1843
61 For example, James Strang, Galt, chairman, common school commissioners, to Murray, 14 Sept. 1842; David Thorburn, warden, District of Niagara, to Murray, 31 Dec. 1842
62 For example, ibid., John Unsworth, Talbot Road w, 15 Oct. 1842; D.R. Macleod, Vaughan Township, 24 Nov. 1842; Johnston Neilson, Smith Falls, 28 Nov. 1842; Nicholas Wilson, Cobourg, 26 Dec. 1842; 'A.B.,' Markham, 5 Feb. 1843 (note apparent need for anonymity); David Walker, Milton/Trafalgar, 13 March 1843; John Rogerson, Nottawasaga, 15 April 1843; Henry Livesley, Simcoe, 27 May 1843. Regular payment of teachers remained a problem even after the Common School Act of 1843. See *Christian Guardian,* 13 March 1844
63 Ibid., John Tilt to Murray, 19 April 1843
64 Ibid., Wilson to Murray, 26 Dec. 1842
65 Ibid., Warwick Township teachers to chairman, School Committee, Warwick. Enclosed in letter to Murray, 12 Oct. 1842. Reasons of distance, bad roads, and 'rather straightened circumstances' also accounted for absence of Walter Thomson, a teacher in Raleigh Township, from the same meeting. Ibid., Thomson to Murray, 14 Oct. 1842
66 OA, Education Office, Letterbook A, Murray to David Thorburn, MPP, 17 Sept. 1842
67 Ibid., Incoming General Correspondence, Charles Friend to Murray, 13 Dec. 1842. See ibid., William Erskine, Smithtown, to Murray, 13 Jan. 1843: 'Had I it in my power to get any other situation I assure you I would not be a teacher of a Common School.'
68 OA, Education Office, Letterbook A, Murray to Rev. D. McKenzie, Woodstock, 18 May 1843
69 Ibid., Murray to Edward Lane, secretary, Teachers Society of Johnstown District, 14 March 1843
70 Ibid., Incoming General Correspondence, John Tilt, Township of Toronto, to Murray, 19 April 1843
71 Letter to editor from Murray, *Christian Guardian,* 22 Feb. 1843. Originally published in *Kingston Chronicle & Gazette*
72 OA, Education Office, Letterbook A, Murray to John Giles, aspiring teacher, Ancaster, 10 Jan. 1843
73 Ibid., Murray to chairman and Committee of Teachers in Townships of Charlottenburgh and Lancaster, 16 Sept. 1842. In their letter to Murray the committee had demanded an income for teachers 'at least double that of a Mechanic's – without a competent salary he can command the Esteem and respect of neither Parents nor Children.' Incoming General Correspondence, 10 Sept. 1842
74 Ibid., subscribers and teachers in Esquesing to Murray, 3 Sept. 1842. P.C. Campbell in his 1839 'Memorandum on Common Schools' suggested in rural school districts the provision of a house and perhaps five acres of good land for the schoolmaster (Wilson edition, 68)
75 DHE, III, 273, Murray to McCaul Commission, 23 Dec. 1839

76 OA, Education Office, Letterbook A, Murray to Robert Mowbray, teacher, Aldborough, 22 Dec. 1842

77 *Christian Guardian*, 22 Feb. 1843

78 OA, Education Office, Letterbook A, Murray to William Hutton, Kingston, 14 July 1842; to School Commissioners of Tarbolton, 12 Dec. 1842. See also Murray to James Strang, Galt, 17 Sept. 1842. P.C. Campbell in his 'Memorandum' made the point that disagreements often took place as to the site of a proposed school. The solution normally was to erect two schools 'where one would be amply sufficient' (Wilson edition, 66)

79 OA, Education Office, Letterbook A, Murray to William Erskine, Peterboro, 19 Jan. 1843

80 Charges of incompetency against commissioners were common enough, but one report to Murray even mentioned cases of nepotism, whereby wives, sons, daughters, and brothers of the commisisoners were appointed to the best schools, 'no matter how unfit or unexperienced.' Ibid., Henry Livesley, Simcoe, 27 May 1843

81 Ibid., teachers of the District of Brock to Murray, 17 June 1843

82 Ibid., school teachers and commissioners of Gore District to Murray, 1 April 1843

83 Ibid., teachers of the Brock District to Murray, 17 June 1843. The warden of Victoria District, however, opposed the idea of excluding alien (American) teachers on the grounds that 'some of our best teachers [are] females from the States.' Ibid., William Hutton to Murray, 2 July 1842

84 Ibid., teachers of the Brock District to Murray, 17 June 1843. For other letters to Murray expressing concern over the hiring of female teachers, see Rev. William Reid, Grafton, 15 June 1843; president, Police Board, Belleville, 26 June 1843; clerk of police, Cobourg, 31 July 1843; Henry Livesley, Simcoe, 27 May 1843

85 Ibid., George S. Tiffany to Murray, 20 Feb. 1843

86 Ibid., Ahira Blake to Murray, 16 Oct. 1843

87 Ibid., Robert Roy Mackie, Richmond, Bayham, to Murray, 1 Nov. 1842. Also James Strang, Galt, chairman, common school commissioners, 14 Sept. 1842

88 2356 men and 663 women. DHE, VII, 154

89 For example, OA, Education Office, Letterbook A, Strang, 14 Sept. 1842; school teachers and commissioners, Gore, 1 April 1843; Samuel Armour, chairman, Cavan teachers, 17 Dec. 1843; teachers of Brock district, 17 June 1843

90 Ibid., John Burns, Esquesing, to Murray, 19 Jan. 1843. Same charge of illiteracy made in Henry Livesley to Murray, 27 May 1843; Johnston Neilson to Murray, 16 Aug. 1843

91 Ibid., Murray to Thornton, Hamilton, 27 March 1843

92 Ibid., Incoming General Correspondence, teachers, Sidney Township, 26 June 1842; John Treffrey, chairman, school board, Norwich Township, 4 July 1842; Thomas Alexander, teacher, Cobourg, 29 July 1842; Richard Fowler Butt, clerk of Wellington District, 25 Feb. 1843; A. Mitchell, teacher, Bothwell, 7 July 1843; John McKay, township clerk, Thorah, 10 Feb. 1844

93 See ibid., 'A.B.' (teacher), Markham, to Murray, 4 Feb. 1843

94 Ibid., Teachers of Brock District to Murray, 17 June 1843. Also '... let nothing of a pecuniary nature as to education of children be left voluntary.' Johnston Neilson, teacher, Smith's Falls, 3 Aug. 1842

95 Draft bill of 1846, DHE, VI, 76. At the time Ryerson described this clause as 'the *poor man's* clause, & at the very foundation of a system of public education.' The main objection to the clause, he predicted, would come from the rich and quoted a Methodist magistrate as saying he did not wish 'to be compelled to educate *all the brats* in the neighbourhood.' Ryerson's reply was to emphasize that 'to educate "all the brats" in every neighbourhood is the very object of this clause of the bill; & in order to do so, it is proposed to compel selfish rich men to do what they ought to do, but what they will not do voluntarily.' Ryerson to W.H. Draper, 20 April 1846, as quoted in C.B. Sissons, *Egerton Ryerson: His*

Life and Letters (2 vols., Toronto 1947), II, 101. 'In every good government and in every good system,' Ryerson urged, 'the interests of the whole society are obligatory upon each member of it.' Draft bill of 1846, DHE, VI, 76

96 PAO, Education Office, Incoming General Correspondence, subscribers and teachers of Esquesing to Murray, 3 Sept. 1842
97 Circular to the Common School Teacher, 14 Aug. 1850, DHE, IX, 215
98 Ibid.

The English Public School Tradition in Nineteenth-Century Ontario

J.D. Purdy

'... brave, helpful, truth-telling Englishmen' are what we want, said Squire Brown. So he sent his son, Tom, to public school to acquire these qualities. And so did many of Squire Brown's contemporaries in Victorian England. The renowned English public school, often regarded as a unique creation of the English nation, enjoyed an immense popularity in the nineteenth century. The volume of literature devoted to analyzing its ethos and special characteristics is voluminous[1] and has been perpetuated to the present day. Many of these schools possess a history which is deeply intertwined with the emergence of the English nation. Stretching back to the mediæval era and the days of the Tudors and Stuarts, they were founded by members of the aristocracy, the higher clergy, and the gentry and were often identified as schools for poor boys. Over the centuries the nobility and upper classes gradually secured control of these institutions and transformed them into instruments for preserving and enhancing their own power and status.[2]

Even in the midst of the political, religious, and social turmoil of Victorian England, the public school retained its traditional role of producing England's leadership elite, especially for the political and military spheres, the professions, and, later in the century, the proconsuls of the new empire. Generally speaking the boys were not encouraged to enter the business world or the newly emerging scientific and technological careers, a trend which is claimed to have had an adverse effect upon Britain's position of world industrial leadership.[3] By 1900 the public school had acquired a distinctive image in the national mythology and a mystique which is perceptibly captured in the words of the most recent government commission which investigated these schools.

The Edwardian public school with its fanatical zeal for team games and athleticism, its philistinism, its hierarchical system of prefects and boy-made customs reflecting seniority, gloried in cultivating what was called the public school spirit. This spirit defies definition because it has always meant different things to different people. To some it meant the Christian virtues, the patriotism and sense of duty, which was preached often from the pulpits by generations of headmasters and housemasters. To others, such as Kipling in *Stalky & Co.* it meant the resourcefulness, the freedom from cant, the rigid control of emotions and the refusal to betray comrades which boys learnt in their eternal conflict with the official rules of the school enforced by masters.[4]

A similar appraisal argues that the public school boy possessed a particular accent, certain mannerisms, and habits of thinking which constituted '... an elite shorthand.'[5] In short, the boarding school graduate had been subtley transformed from the Christian and scholarly gentleman of Thomas Arnold, headmaster of Rugby School (1828–42), to a person who displayed manliness, good manners, and sportsmanship.[6] Squire Brown would have been satisfied with the results.

Schools of this type flourish in a socio-economic environment decidedly different from the harsh pioneer atmosphere of early Upper Canada. Institutions espousing the ideals of the English public schools could only emerge in a society which possessed a more mature economy, a stable political structure, and a more clearly delineated class system. These ingredients were lacking in a frontier community. Private schools for both day students and boarders of both sexes abounded in Upper Canada in the decades before the 1840s when a publicly financed and regulated system of education was established, but it is doubtful if any of them were deliberately modelled on the English public schools. Not even John Strachan's Cornwall Academy, probably the most famous boarding school in the colony where many of the members of the Family Compact, the colony's ruling elite, were educated, was influenced by the Etonian approach.[7]

The first institution established along English lines was Upper Canada College opened in 1829 through the initiative of the lieutenant-governor, Sir John Colborne. Shortly after his arrival in the colony, the governor decided that Upper Canada needed such a school.[8] His motives were not unmixed. He earnestly wanted a school which would impart a superior academic education and would serve as a model for the flagging district grammar schools established by the colonial government as early as 1807. But he was also attempting to defuse the heated controversy generated by John Strachan's charter for the University of King's College, York, granted in 1827, which, owing to its Anglican character, had antagonized a large portion of the local community. This is a story which has been told many times. Colborne correctly argued that there was an insufficient supply of scholars for a university and therefore a boarding school in the capital would assist in correcting this situation.[9]

While his efforts were greeted enthusiastically by the reform element, the somewhat peculiar origins of the school ultimately created a hostile reaction from many sources which was to bedevil the college's existence for the remainder of the century. Strachan and his Tory followers were extremely critical of the college's curriculum and ethos. All opponents deplored granting it an endowment of 66,000 acres from the school lands. For a few years in the decade of the 1830s the school became a political football in a series of contentious conflicts between Tories and Reformers, and, while it survived the onslaught of its critics, it did not achieve a peaceful existence until near the end of the century when it shed its official ties with the provincial government.

During this time there were several investigations into the college conducted by government commissions and select committees of the legislature. Various proposals concerning its future were mooted, including elevating it into the provincial university. Egerton Ryerson once suggested making it the provincial model grammar school where grammar school teachers could be trained. The vexatious land endowment was finally confiscated by the government in 1887. Certainly these attacks had an adverse effect upon the school's morale but, nonetheless, in spite of these difficulties Upper Canada College survived and in doing so became a pattern for other boarding schools to follow.

The schools referred to in this essay are boys' schools modelled on the English pattern: Upper Canada College, Toronto; Ridley College, St Catharines; Trinity College School, Port Hope; and Hellmuth College, London. The one exception is the Quaker school, Pickering College, Pickering (later Newmarket), which attempted to be a truly Canadian institution and provides a good comparison and contrast with the other schools.[10] The founders of these schools, apart from Pickering College, were drawn from the ranks of Anglican clerics and businessmen, and as in nineteenth-century England,[11] they were stimulated by a variety of motives, not all of which were concerned with the academic needs of the province's youth. Religious idealism, sentimental attachment to an old English institution, patriotic emotions, the yearning to keep Canada within the British empire, the desire to create a leadership class embued with the ideals of Christian service, the search for an alternative form of education to the state system – all were factors which contributed to the creation of Ontario boarding schools.

Trinity College School was the product of mixed motives, primarily educational need and the desire to have a boys' school linked to a party within the Anglican church. Actually, Trinity grew out of a small private school operated by the Rev. W.A. Johnson, Anglican rector of St Phillip's, Weston, who, dissatisfied with the public system, decided to educate his sons and some local boys in his home.[12] Johnson, a convinced Tractarian and ritualist, enlisted the support of some faculty members of the high church University of Trinity College, Toronto, and in November 1864 the corporation officially designated his school as Trinity College School.[13] This affiliation with a university of high church persuasion was further strengthened when, at the incorporation of the school in 1872, the list of the board members included many officials of Trinity College and other leading high churchmen.[14] Yet, for Trinity College School, party affiliation does not seem to have been as blatant nor conspirative as for Hellmuth College and Bishop Ridley College.

Hellmuth College, London, was part of grandiose scheme devised by Issac Hellmuth, an ardent Anglican Evangelical, who, as dean and later bishop of Huron (1872–83), hoped to make his see city a major educational centre. His aspirations included a university, a theological seminary (actually Huron College founded in 1862), and boarding schools for boys and girls.[15] The boys' school, originally known as the London Collegiate Institute, later renamed Hellmuth College, and later still Dufferin College,[16] was opened in September 1865 'for the sons of gentlemen' who were to receive an 'education commensurate with the requirements of the time.'[17] Furthermore, as its brochure indicated,

THE DISCIPLINE OF THE COLLEGE [sic] is based, as nearly as possible, upon the model of the great public schools of England and Germany in which the military system has been adopted.

The utmost care and attention are bestowed on the Moral and Religious Training of the Pupils, who are treated in every respect as gentlemen, and encouraged to prove themselves deserving of confidence.[18]

While this innocuous statement of intentions did not openly confirm the school's evangelical tendencies, Hellmuth adopted certain measures to ensure the evangelical purity of the school's ethos. Members of the corporation were leading low churchmen, most masters possessed a similar background, and Hellmuth and his institution maintained a lively intercourse with the evangelically oriented diocese of Ohio of the American Episcopal church. Curiously, Hellmuth College attracted a disproportionately large number of American boys.[19] One possible explanation is the desire of American Episcopal parents of evangelical leanings to send their sons to an institution that could guarantee them this atmosphere, for Tractarianism was increasing in the Episcopal church in the latter decades of the nineteenth century.[20]

The founding of Bishop Ridley College[21] in the fall of 1889 perhaps best of the three schools exemplifies a mixture of motives. In a somewhat defensive tone the opening paragraph of the school's first prospectus paid a glowing and fulsome tribute to the provincial schools, but quickly asserted that despite the system's successes '... it is necessarily limited in certain respects, and cannot provide for all the exigencies of modern civilization.'[22] The increasing pace of life made it difficult, if not impossible, the authors argued, to impart the proper kind of religious education and moral discipline to youth. These cherished values could only be inculcated by sending boys '... away to school where they will receive the best education possible, religious, intellectual and physical.'[23] The founders' aim was to produce

Christian gentlemen for 'The Christian character is the highest type of character; the true Christian is the true gentleman.'[24] This is certainly reminiscent of Arnoldian Rugby, but the prospectus goes on to betray a more limited purpose than any Arnold ever envisaged. The kind of religious training to be imparted was to be '... based upon sound Protestant Church of England principles.'[25] The list of individuals who were connected with the founding of Ridley constitutes a roll call of leaders of the Evangelical party, many of them possessing old and respected Canadian names. Among them were T.R. Merritt, N.W. Hoyles, A.H. Campbell, the Hon. S.H. Blake, Herbert Mason, Sir Daniel Wilson (president of the University of Toronto), Sir Casimir Gzowski, Homer Dixon, the Rev. J.P. Sheraton (principal of Wycliffe College), and the Rev. W.J. Armitage (later Archdeacon of Halifax).

Ridley College, in part, grew out of a campaign of the low church Evangelicals in southern Ontario, especially Toronto, to establish a number of institutions which could offset and hopefully undermine the Tractarian sympathies of the hierarchy and many of the clergy in that area. The Evangelicals were strong and possessed influence and wealth, but had been contained by the Tractarians. They established a number of educational institutions where the youth of both sexes could be indoctrinated, including, in Toronto, Wycliffe College to train divinity students; Havergal School for girls; and the Deaconess' College. Many of the same men were associated with the founding of all or some of these schools. They formed a kind of interlocking directorate motivated by typical Victorian evangelical earnestness.[26] The appointment of the Rev. J.O. Miller, a recent graduate of Wycliffe College and associate editor of the *Evangelical Churchman*, as headmaster of Ridley College, and the decision to call it after Bishop Ridley, one of the Marian martyrs and the darling of the Evangelicals, added a delicious barb to their campaign and underscored their real intention.[27] Thus, while the Evangelicals could rightly assert that they were establishing a new church college along the lines of an English boarding school and were extending educational facilities for Ontario boys, it is also manifestly evident that they ardently anticipated that the school would be of great assistance in checking the spread of Anglo-Catholicism in the Canadian church and that while the graduates of Ridley College would be Christian gentlemen, they would be proper Evangelical Anglicans who would, hopefully, provide a leadership cadre for this party.[28]

The Society of Friends (Quakers) has always exhibited a warm interest in education and in England operated a number of boarding schools (mostly co-educational), beginning with Ackworth College, Yorkshire, in 1777.[29] It was only natural that Canadian Friends would attempt to carry on this tradition. Spurred on by the exhortations and financial contribution of Joseph John Gurney, a leading English Quaker and the brother of the well-known English Quakeress reformer, Elizabeth

Fry, the Society opened a school in the fall of 1842 on a farm near the village of Bloomfield, Prince Edward County. Originally called the West Lake Friends' Seminary, it remained at this location until it was closed in 1865 owing to a decline in student numbers, the difficulty of obtaining teachers, and the lack of sufficient funds. Thirteen years later it was reopened in the town of Pickering and took its name, Pickering College, from this town.

The seminary attempted from the beginning to be a distinctive Canadian-style school and yet at the same time displayed many of the distinctive features of an English Quaker institution. The techniques of discipline, the broader curriculum, the co-educational aspect, and the practice of having the students do manual labour on the school farm were characteristics of a Friends' institution. Actually, the seminary was modelled on the Nine Partners School, Duchess County, New York, which, in turn, had formed itself on the lines of Ackworth College.[30]

In establishing their school, the Quakers were motivated by some of the same impulses as were the founders of other boarding institutions, in addition to special reasons of their own. Stung by the imputation of disloyalty at the time of the Rebellion of 1837 because they often sent their children to American Quaker schools, they deemed it prudent to have their own in Upper Canada. They also anticipated that it would help fill a gap in the colony's shaky educational structure. Moreover, as Canadian Quaker historian A.G. Dorland has pointed out, the Friends had suffered a major schism in 1828 (the Hicksite Separation) which indicated to many the need for a school that would provide for '... the lack of trained leadership within the Society.'[31]

Quaker spokesmen generally eschew any elitist element in their educational philosophy, but, as with their Anglican counterparts, the founders of Pickering College fully expected their school to train youths for a specific kind of leadership.[32] No doubt this concern was one of the causes of the spirited controversy which beset the Quaker community during the 1850s over this issue of restricting enrolment solely to Friends' children.[33] It was finally decided to accept any child regardless of religious affiliation, financial considerations playing a prominent role in this decision.[34] This liberal policy was retained when the school was moved to Pickering.

So, in summary, the Quakers, like their Anglican brothers, were impelled to undertake the task of building a boarding school for reasons that transcended purely educational needs and aspirations. Political feelings, the hope of acquiring proper religious instruction, the need for leaders were motives that, combined with a desire to provide a sound academic education for their children, sparked all of them to establish these institutions.

While educational need and religious training were obvious motives for opening these schools, another factor which helps to explain the increasing popularity of boarding schools in England and the United States in the latter part of the Victorian period was the declining role of the family as an educative institution coupled with a changing conception of the nature of childhood and adolescence.[35] Many explanations have been offered for this phenomenon. The English historian, F. Musgrove, suggests that it was a result of the Industrial Revolution. As one means of offsetting the pressures imposed upon the family by this societal change, many English middle class families began to send their sons away to schools to receive the appropriate type of education and child care which they felt they could no longer provide at home. With the widespread railway network which stretched across England it was easier to send youths away for their education.[36] James McLachlan in his study of American boarding schools noted a similar trend on the part of middle class parents, especially in the New England region.[37] Although to date no concrete work has been done in this area for Canadian society, it is reasonable to assume that a similar process was manifesting itself here, especially as southern Ontario became more industrialized with the passing of the nineteenth century. Moreover, an extensive system of railroads was built during this era which linked the cities and towns of this area more closely together. As a result people became more accustomed to travelling and were, therefore, less inhibited about sending their sons away from home.

The authors of the first prospectus of Ridley College were certainly aware of this trend when they wrote:

... The great majority of those immersed in the professions, in business, and in social life, find it impossible to give that time to systematic religious training of their children which they feel is necessary. Apart from that difficulty, children who have not the constant supervision of their parents, acquire too much facility of individual movement, and chafe under restraint because of the lack of a wise discipline. If parents could themselves supply this deficiency by the definite and continuous instruction of their children there would be no difficulty; but in these days of immense and ceaseless activity, many parents find it impossible and the question of the education of their children is thus a serious problem. The only solution lies in placing their children where they will receive all the advantages of the best home training. Of boys this is especially true, and hence the desire of parents to send them away to school where they will receive the best education possible, religious, intellectual and physical.[38]

Here was the justification for boarding schools. To parents they were attractive because their sons could receive a specific type of education. Not only could they receive sound academic instruction and perhaps an introduction to commercial training[39] but, hopefully, the boys were also exposed to proper religious and moral values and these, it was assumed, were ingredients which the public schools of the province could not impart. Furthermore, these institutions were all located in railway towns which, as noted, made them easily accessible but kept the lads out of the reach of the evil influences of urban areas and permitted the schools to foster a family-like atmosphere in a relatively pleasant town or rural area.[40]

It would seem appropriate at this point to discuss in some detail the kind of education an adolescent received at these schools. What were its purposes? For what vocations and professions was he prepared? What attemps were made to include the so-called newer subjects, sciences and business in particular? To what extent did chapel, extra-curricular activities, and athletics reinforce the attitudes and values imparted in the classroom? Perhaps the most important question is what did the parents, especially businessmen, expect the boarding schools to accomplish for their sons?

Allusion has been made to the fact that English public schools did not prepare boys for the commercial or scientific world even though many graduates entered these realms. The New England schools, as McLachlan has decisively demonstrated, deliberately trained their students to enter business careers.[41] The Ontario approach fell between these two positions. Ontario headmasters and their allies lauded the benefits to be derived from an exposure to Horace, Caesar, and Cicero. The Rev. Dr J.H. Harris, first principal of Upper Canada College (1829–38) and an ardent advocate of classical education, admitted on one occasion that while it might appear to be very impracticable '... the mind is, nevertheless acquiring materials and strength for future efforts and success ...'[42] Yet, striking enough, even while pleading the cause of the classics, he realized that 'I am not insensible to those particular circumstances of the province which render it desirable, that the course of instruction to be adopted at such a Seminary, should ... be so arranged as to afford pupils, not finally destined for the University, or for learned professions, the means of acquiring, by preceding through a certain portion of the system, such an education as would be suitable for every member of respectable society ...'[43]

Unfortunately, Harris did not elaborate on that tantalizing phrase 'the particular circumstances of the province.' Apparently he perceived that the social and economic conditions of the colony were different from those of England and that while these factors created the need for a different kind of education they did not preclude the objective of producing gentlemen.[44] Early in his regime at the college Harris introduced a more extensive curriculum which included mathematics, science, and, perhaps more importantly for the local scene, a special form, known as the partial form, which taught bookkeeping along with other subjects but omitted the classics. The partial class also took English composition, history, geography, writing, arithmetic, French, and geometrical drawing. To enter this form a boy had to have attended the college for two years or to have passed through the third form. At the time this was considered a sufficient background for entry into a business career.

Even with this concession to local conditions the classical forms were the haven of most of the students.[45] Almost forty years later Principal Cockburn in his address of welcome to Lord Dufferin, when he visited the college in October 1872, commented on the commercial form that '... we believe we may safely appeal to the leading merchants of the Dominion as to the energy, ability and Christian character displayed by those who preferred a Mercantile career.'[46] Cockburn went on to note that since many Canadian boys left school early they needed a course more suitable for the particular needs of the country.[47] He claimed that UCC had adopted the recommendations of the English Public Schools (Clarendon) Commission of 1864 which had advocated a more flexible and practical curriculum. Interestingly enough Dufferin, an old Etonian, made no reference to business ethics in his reply but paid a glowing tribute to the ideals and values of English public schools. Perhaps Cockburn was attempting to allay current criticisms about the impractical nature of the college's type of education. He may also have been trying to rehabilitate the commercial course in the eyes of the students, who, according to one prominent old boy, John Ross Robertson, were wont to refer to it in typical schoolboy derisive fashion as '... the refuge of the destitute.'[48] Nonetheless, UCC initiated a significant step which was a signal departure from the English model.

Most of the other schools found it necessary to follow this lead. At Ridley College the prospectus indicated that 'Those who intend going into business will receive a thorough commercial training.'[49] Hellmuth College advertised that 'This institution provides a Classical, Scientific, and Commercial education of the first class ...'[50] Students could not enroll in the commercial subjects at Hellmuth College until they had advanced to the fifth and sixth forms of the collegiate department.[51] The lack of school records makes it impossible to derive any conclusions about the number of boys who took the commercial courses or to what extent the authorities actually emphasized them. Some definite recognition was accorded this section in the annual prize list as awards were granted for penmanship and bookkeeping.[52]

When Pickering College was opened in 1878 a curriculum similar to that given in the provincial collegiates was adopted. The college administration recognized that '... Many boys and young men are anxious to obtain a thorough business education without being forced to study those subjects required only for entrance into the learned professions.'[53] As a result, a very comprehensive business course was offered and the college prided itself on this aspect of its programme even boasting, unashamedly, that '... In the past the Commercial Form has been one of the most satisfactory departments of the College. Students in it have made very creditable progress ...'[54] No doubt this pride was justified as the public schools did not offer courses of equal quality. A further indication of the emphasis placed on the commercial form was the annual examination conducted by external examiners '... to give to meritorious students an opportunity of securing a fitting testimonial of their attainments in the studies pursued by them in the College ...'[55] These brochures also reported that courses in phonography (short hand) and telegraphy were given. With respect to the latter the Montreal Telegraph Company opened an office in the college and instruction was given by a 'first-class operator.' Certainly no stigma was attached to these classes, for the school's records indicate that a large number took them and that these subjects were granted almost the same number of hours in the time-table as the academic subjects.[56]

During the 1890s the school's board of management came under the sway of the Rogers family, leading Quakers in Toronto.[57] They were important rising entrepreneurs who would over the years exert a powerful and beneficial influence on the school's development. It is interesting to speculate what degree of influence they had over the provision of this extensive business course. At any rate, Pickering College certainly made a creditable attempt to provide its students with the kind of education suitable to the social and economic conditions of Ontario.

As is well known, however, the English public schools always claimed that they were interested in providing more than an academic education. Character building, the development of the all-round man, the preparation of future leaders, the perfecting of the Christian gentleman was their primary consideration.[58] This meant the inculcation of certain values, principally placing service to one's fellow man and the nation before self-interest. This is the area where chapel, athletic field, cadet drill, and extra-curricular activities made their contributions to a boy's education. While it is relatively easy to describe a classical or commercial curriculum and perhaps speculate on its potential benefits, it is much more difficult to analyze the overall effects of the teaching of moral and spiritual values. It is quite conceivable that a boy could have imbibed similar attitudes if he had remained at home, attended church and Sunday school, and enrolled in the local public schools.

There does not seem to be any adequate test or criterion by which to measure this aspect of a boarding-school education. The absence of any significant number of autobiographies or other forms of reminiscences by Ontario old boys eliminates one potential source of information. Another possible test of the impact of this value structure, especially of the service ideal, lies in tracing the careers of graduates. One of the major claims of English public school protagonists was that their former students could be found in positions of leadership in the government and military and even more clearly in the civil service. Of course, it is a commonplace that the ranks of the British parliament and cabinet were populated with public school boys. They possessed an almost automatic entrée into the inner circles of power. The fact that they attended one of these institutions was only one factor in this phenomenon. Wealth and family position were probably more significant factors.[59]

In Ontario, as in the rest of the dominion, this tradition did not take root. Only a handful of Ontario boarding school boys served in the federal parliament between Confederation and the end of the century. A perusal of *The Canadian Parliamentary Directory* shows that twenty-one members of parliament and two senators graduated from boarding schools in this province and of these only one became a cabinet minister.[60] In stark contrast to the British experience, no English-speaking prime minister in the nineteenth or twentieth centuries ever attended boarding school in Ontario.[61] While a few boys entered the imperial service, none ever succeeded in becoming a major colonial administrator, although a few became successful military leaders.[62]

This situation poses two questions. Why didn't these young men enter public service? In what areas did the majority of boys seek their vocations? At the outset it would seem easier to answer the second question, although the two are inter-related. Although more extensive research is needed in this area, a perusal of biographical dictionaries and similar material strongly indicates that for many boys business and law were the major choices of occupation. As A.H. Young, a former student of UCC, wrote, 'Many of the "Old Boys" have taken to Law or to business; and in both they have attained great prominence.'[63]

This is not entirely surprising. Historians refer to this era as the age of the great barbecue, the period of exploitation of the country's natural resources. Fortunes were being made in railways, mining, manufacturing. A business career, no doubt, was a more attractive outlet for a youth's energies and ambitions. A man could practice noblesse oblige more easily after he had accumulated a fortune than he could from a parliamentary seat in Ottawa or Toronto. The barons of Bay and St James Streets were as heroic to Canadian boys as the imperial demi-gods of Rudyard Kipling or G.A. Henty. To be a leading industrialist or businessman in a small Ontario community was a more honourable (and more profitable) career than to be a political figure. Undoubtedly, it was safer, and besides, if rich, one could become a king-maker behind the scenes in party politics.[64] Professional men also shared in society's esteem in those days and were certainly accorded more respect than politicans.[65] Unfortunately, however, there is, as yet, no adequate study of the social and educational backgrounds of the professions in this country to enable one to draw firm conclusions about their status, but again the biographical dictionaries substantiate this argument.

A factor in the choice of careers was the essential pragmatism and materialism of Canadian society. As Peter Waite has recently noted, '... This commercial ambience went right through Canadian society.'[66] Sir George Parkin, principal of Upper Canada College (1895–1902) and an ardent advocate of the English public school, suggested in his study *The Great Dominion* that one of '... the greatest obstacles to the attainment of the highest educational results in Canada, as in other young countries, is the haste to rush into professional and business life without allowing time for thorough mental training.'[67] Furthermore, as he stated later in this book, '... But there is absolutely no sympathy with the establishment of an hereditary nobility or aristocracy on Canadian soil. I think I am right in saying that objection to it is marked.'[68] The implication is that the more open (but not classless) society of Canada resisted the creation of class and educational barriers or privileges which would prevent the ordinary boy from making his mark. Business then became one obvious route for advancement for a youth be he a graduate of a fee-paying boarding school or of the state-supported system. Parkin claimed that the free school attended by all classes was '... a method of social co-operation for obtaining the best educational results with the least waste of force.'[69]

There was no guarantee that a boarding school graduate would become a captain of industry. On the other hand, the movement of youths into the business world created a Canadian tradition whereby the successful entrepreneur sent his sons to these schools to acquire the right social ideals and contacts. The first generation of capitalists did not emerge from these institutions but the second and third generations often attended these schools.[70]

The failure of 'old boys' to enter political life can only partly be ascribed to this desire to seek rewards in economic life. From the earliest days of the province young men of all classes entered politics at all levels and ascended to the higher echelons of leadership in parliament and party. Again social class and education (or the lack of it) did not inhibit aspirants for public office. Parkin reminded his readers that '... It is almost universally found that the men selected [for county government in Ontario] represent the most solid and reliable portion of the farming and trading community: they need no guidance of an upper and specially educated class as in the English county council ...'[71] Politics in this new country was a somewhat sordid scramble for patronage, a rough and tumble affair not always regarded, in certain social circles, as a proper sphere of activity for a gentleman. Chapel and prize-day speakers might extol the virtues of public service but the reality of Canadian politics told a different tale.[72]

Basically the Christian gentleman concept was not compatible with the individualistic competitiveness of nineteenth-century Ontario industrial society or the rude political struggles of the era. Such a figure might be out of place amid the harsh bargaining of the board room or the crude atmosphere of backroom politics. If the aim of Ontario boarding school founders in the nineteenth century was to produce leaders for the province and the nation and to infuse Canadian life with certain particular values and attitudes, then the attempt must be deemed a failure.

The socio-economic milieu of the new environment rejected this transplant and ultimately in characteristic North American fashion transformed the school into a somewhat different institution. The private school in the twentieth century may have played a different and more dynamic role. Further research is needed to prove or disprove this contention. Yet, the boarding school offered a viable alternative to the public schools for those parents who sought an institution that offered more than an academic education. No doubt many boys drank deeply of their school's ideals and cherished memories of their years in those ivied halls. Ontario boarding schools in the Victorian era did contribute a small element of leadership to the province's life, but so far the evidence does not point to a significantly large representation. These schools, by and large, were isolated, both geographically and socially, from the main trends of development in nineteenth-century Ontario.

NOTES

1 For an excellent discusssion of novels dealing with these schools see John R. Reed, *Old School Ties: The Public Schools in British Literature* (Syracuse 1964).
2 The best general histories of the public schools are T.W. Bamford, *The Rise of the Public Schools* (London 1967), and E.C. Mack, *Public Schools and British Opinion, 1780–1860* (London 1938) and *Public Schools and British Opinion Since 1860* (New York 1941).
3 Bamford, *Rise of the Public Schools*, Chapter 5 and David Ward, 'The Public Schools and Industry in Britain after 1870,' in Walter Laquer and George L. Mosse, eds., *Education and Social Structure in the Twentieth Century* (New York 1967), 37–53
4 *Public Schools Commission,* First Report (London 1968), i, 18
5 T.J.H. Bishop, *Winchester and the Public School Elite* (London 1967), 17
6 For a brilliant discussion of the transformation of the concept of the public school boy see David Newsome, *Godliness and Good Learning* (London 1961), Chapters 1 and 4.
7 G. Spragge, 'The Cornwall Grammar School under John Strachan,' Ontario Historical Society, *Papers and Records,* xxxiv, 1942, 63–84, and J.D. Purdy, 'John Strachan and Education in Canada, 1800–1851' (unpublished PHD thesis, University of Toronto, 1962)
8 Colborne himself was an old boy of Christ's Hospital and Winchester College and as governor of the Guernsey Islands had been responsible for reviving an Elizabethan foundation, Elizabeth College.
9 Public Archives of Canada [PAC], Q series, 351-1-2, 94, Colborne to Hay, private, 2 April 1829
10 It is true that Roman Catholic and Protestant groups founded boarding schools but it is not clear whether these institutions were consciously modelled on their English counterparts. For studies of this kind of school see *Woodstock College Memorial Book* (Woodstock 1951) and Alex McGregor, 'Egerton Ryerson, Albert Carmen, and the founding of Albert College, Belleville,' *Ontario History,* LXIII, 4, Dec. 1971, 205–16.
11 Bamford, *Rise of the Public Schools,* Chapter 2
12 Ontario Archives [OA], F. Keith Dalton, 'A Biography of the Rev. William Arthur Johnson,' revised July 1964, typescript, and A.H. Humble, *The School on the Hill* (Port Hope 1965)
13 Humble, *School on the Hill,* 1
14 The school was moved to Port Hope in 1868. Johnson soon crossed swords with the evangelical rector of the town, the Rev. F.A. O'Meara, for his mild ritualistic practices.

15 A.H. Crowfoot, *The Dreamer: Life of Isaac Hellmuth* (Toronto 1963), especially Chapter 5

16 There is a local legend that Egerton Ryerson took the title collegiate institute from this school and applied it to the high schools throughout the province.

17 University of Western Ontario [uwo], Lawson Library, Regional History Room, Hellmuth College Collection, *Collegiate Institute*, London, Canada West, prospectus

18 The reference to Germany is curious. While there were boarding schools in that country, they did not resemble the English pattern. One possible explanation is Hellmuth's European background. He was born near Warsaw and educated at the University of Breslau.

19 Hellmuth College Prospectus, 1871–2, shows that 43 per cent of the enrolment were American boys. Other years indicate a similar trend.

20 This development is discussed in any standard history of the Episcopal church. See, E. Chorley, *Men and Movements in the American Episcopal Church* (New York 1946) and W. Manross, *A History of the American Episcopal Church* (New York 1959)

21 This was the original name of the school until 1900 when it was changed to Ridley College. See Kim Beattie, *Ridley: The Story of a School* (2 vols., St Catharines, nd), II, 108

22 Prospectus, Ridley College, 1888, reprinted in ibid., I, 13

23 Ibid.

24 Ibid.

25 Ibid.

26 For an English parallel see Ford K. Brown, *Fathers of the Victorians* (Cambridge 1961), especially Chapter 9

27 For an explanation of the reason for using Ridley's name see Ven. Archdeacon W.J. Armitage, 'Related Institutions,' in *Jubilee Volume of Wycliffe College* (Toronto 1927). Armitage claimed that he was personally responsible for choosing this title.

28 The Rt Rev. Charles Hamilton, bishop of Niagara (1885–96), wrote to T.R. Merritt deploring the use of the phrase 'sound Protestant principles of the Reformation' which, he argued, was at variance with the Prayer Book. He went on to state that he would object to a school which invoked the phrase '... the Catholic principles of the Reformation.' Clearly the bishop, a decided high churchman, objected to identifying the school with a specific church party. See letter, bishop of Niagara, Hamilton, 7 May 1889 to T.R. Merritt quoted in Beattie, *Ridley*, II, 1028

29 For a discussion of Quaker educational ideas see W.A.C. Stewart, *Quakers and Education* (London 1953).

30 A.G. Dorland, 'A Hundred Years of Quaker Education in Canada: The Centenary of Pickering College,' Royal Society of Canada, *Transactions*, Section II, 1942, 51–91

31 This split, which occurred in the American branch of Quakerism, was concerned with different emphasis being placed upon orthodox evangelical doctrine by one group and upon the Quietistic tendencies in Quakerism by another group. Ultimately the conflict led to a serious division which eventuated in the Hicksite separation in 1828, and which manifested itself also among Canadian Friends. See A.G. Dorland, *A History of the Society of Friends (Quakers) in Canada* (Toronto 1927), Chapters 8 and 9

32 This desire is shown even more clearly in later years. In December 1905 the school building was destroyed by fire. After discussion the Friends decided to rebuild for a number of reasons, among them being the need for a leadership cadre for the Society so that it could maintain Quaker influence in Canada. uwo, Pickering College Collection, typed mimeograph essay, nd, no author indicated

33 Pickering College Collection, Minutes of Board of Management, 1841–65, several meetings

34 Ibid.
35 Philippe Ariés, *Centuries of Childhood: A Social History of Family Life* (New York 1962)
36 F. Musgrove, *The Family, Education and Society* (London 1966), Chap. 1; see also Musgrove's articles, 'The Decline of the Educative Family,' *Universities Quarterly*, XIV, 1960, 377–404; also 'Population Changes and the Status of the Young in England since the Eighteenth Century,' *Sociological Review*, II, 1963, 69–93; 'Middle Class Education and Employment in the Nineteenth Century,' *Economic History Review*, series 2, no 12, 1959, 99–111
37 J. McLachlan, *American Boarding Schools* (New York 1970), Chapter 6
38 Beattie, *Ridley*, I, 13
39 See below for a discussion of commercial curriculum.
40 The official histories of Ridley College and Trinity College School note that they were located in areas removed from urban influences. See Beattie, *Ridley*, I, 6–7 and Humble, *School on the Hill*, p. 33
41 McLachlan, *American Boarding Schools*, pp. 169, 184–5
42 Rev. Dr J.H. Harris, DD, *Upper Canada College* (Toronto 1836), p. 21
43 Ibid., p. 13
44 For a delightful view of the training of gentlemen at Upper Canada College see Stephen Leacock, 'The Struggle to make us Gentlemen,' *My Remarkable Uncle* (Toronto 1965). As with so many of Leacock's essays, social criticism of a high merit is mingled with his humour. Leacock was an old boy and a former English master at UCC, so had first-hand experience of the situation.
45 The Rev. Dr John McCaul, second principal (1839–43), claimed that Harris disliked adding this form and the newer subjects and only did it under public pressure. See Rev. Dr McCaul's 'Reminiscences of Upper Canada College,' in J.G. Hodgins, *Documentary History of Education in Ontario* 28 vols., (Toronto 1907), XX, 286–7
46 Ibid., XXIV, 78
47 Ibid., 78–80
48 Quoted in Geo. Dickson and G. Mercer Adam, *A History of Upper Canada College* (Toronto 1892), 230
49 Beattie, *Ridley*, I, 14
50 UWO, Hellmuth College Collection, Prospectus, nd
51 Hellmuth College had three departments, primary, academic, and collegiate. If a boy passed through the first four forms, that is, the primary and academic departments, he was, in the collegiate section, exposed to a considerable training in Latin, Greek, mathematics, and other subjects. A very diversified programme was offered a boy who stayed for the entire six forms.
52 See, for example, *London Free Press*, 24 June 1880
53 UWO, Pickering College Collection, brochure, 1879–80, 5
54 Ibid., 1881–2, 9
55 Ibid., 10. This brochure, and its successors, listed the names of the examiners who were often prominent educational figures. In 1881, for example, such men as John E. Bryant, principal of Galt Collegiate Institute, and Inspector James L. Hughes of Toronto were the examiners.
56 *Ibid.* Lists of students and their courses are given in each year's brochure along with time-tables. In some years approximately one-quarter of the students were taking commercial courses.
57 The Rogers family was involved in a number of enterprises including coal, oil, railroads, and finances.
58 For an interesting discussion of the gentleman concept see Edmund King, '"The

Gentleman": The Evolution of an English Ideal,' *Year Book of Education* (London and New York 1961)

59 See Rupert Wilkinson, *The Prefects* (London 1964)

60 J.K. Johnson, ed., *The Canadian Parliamentary Directory* (Ottawa 1968)

61 Two English-speaking prime ministers from Nova Scotia, Sir Charles Tupper and Sir Robert Borden, attended boarding schools in their native province. The former went to Horton Academy and the latter to Acacia Villa.

62 All of these schools, except Pickering College, boast of a military tradition. A good example of this is A.H. Humble, *School on the Hill*, 48, where he lists several Trinity boys who became military leaders, but, interestingly, most of these men served in the imperial forces, not in the Canadian army. One would suspect that Ontario boys became leaders of the local militia companies but did not generally serve in the army as regular professional officers.

63 A.H. Young, *The Roll of Pupils of Upper Canada College* (Kingston 1917), 33. Other biographical dictionaries consulted were H.J. Morgan, *Canadian Men and Women of the Time* (Toronto 1898 and 1912); Johnson, J.K. ed., *Canadian Parliamentary Directory* (Ottawa 1968); Sir C.G.D. Roberts, ed., *A Standard Dictionary of Canadian Biography* (Toronto 1938), Vol. 2; W. Stewart Wallace, ed., *The Macmillan Dictionary of Canadian Biography* (3rd edition, Toronto 1963)

64 Most boarding school boys probably returned home and became solid respectable citizens in the local community.

65 A.R.M. Lower, *Canadians in the Making* (Toronto 1958), 308–9

66 P.B. Waite, *Arduous Destiny: Canada 1874–1896* (Toronto 1971), 280. As Waite also noted, a good study of local Ontario society at this time is Sara Jeanette Duncan's novel, *The Imperialist* (Toronto 1971).

67 G. Parkin, *The Great Dominion* (London 1895), 222–3. Parkin's career at UCC is a case study in the failure of the English public school ethos to be adopted in Canada. See C. Berger, *The Sense of Power: Studies in the Ideas of Canadian Imperialism 1867–1914* (Toronto 1970), 35–6, 210–13, for an excellent discussion of Parkin's expectations for boarding schools in this country.

68 Parkin, *The Great Dominion*, 240

69 Ibid., 216–17

70 R. Cook in his essay 'Stephen Leacock and the Age of Plutocracy, 1903–1921,' in J.S. Moir, ed., *Character and Circumstance* (Toronto 1970), lists eight leading industrialists at the turn of the century, of whom none had attended a private school.

71 Parkin, *The Great Dominion*, 238

72 Interview, Mr Robert Mainwarring, Brockville, with the author, 29 Dec. 1970. Mr Mainwarring, the son of the last headmaster of St Alban's School, Brockville (1901–47), stated that politics was never held up as a profession to the students.

Myths in some Nineteenth-Century Ontario Newspapers

James Reaney

One thing about which fish know exactly nothing is water, since they have no anti-environment which would enable them to perceive the element they live in.
Marshall McLuhan, *War and Peace in the Global Village*

The importance of this form of literary fiction ... is that it studies society from the point of view of its popular or cliché mythology, its accepted ideas.
Northrop Frye, *The Modern Century*

During the last four or five years I have been reading the nineteenth-century files of such newspapers as *The St Marys Journal-Argus*, the *Stratford Beacon-Herald*, and the *London Free Press*. With the last-named I have read some decades continuously day after day, week after week so that I might possibly share, if not the minds of all those long-dead readers, at least the minds of the editors, journalists, and advertisers who hoped to shape the mind of their community. In honour of Dr Talman, in whose library I did a great deal of the reading, I would like to describe what I think those minds were like.

Swift has a scene in *Gulliver's Travels* where the Lilliputians opine that, since he consults it so often, Gulliver's God must be his pocket watch; Gulliver had never thought of this before, nor would nineteenth-century London, Ontario, if an outside observer were to point out similar hidden deities, traces of whose worship appear all over their newspaper. As I invite the reader to step back and regard the environmental bubble the *Free Press*,[1] in particular, must once have formed, I am hoping to show that the newspaper kept expressing certain popular myths, certain clichés or accepted ideas which editors and readers alike may never have examined objectively, from the outside. And from the outside some of them seem merely curious, some sinister, some inviting more skill in speculation than I possess.

First of all, the newspaper itself is always seen as a sort of god. Heretics and atheists who now call TV the Idiot's Lantern no doubt asked in 1857, 'You don't believe everything you read in the newspapers, do you?' Their feeble protests occasionally surface in the correspondence column or even in such forms of reader-rejection as the type-riot that knocks a hole in the files of Mackenzie's *Colonial Advocate* or the arson with political motive that destroys the *Free Press* office in 1849. Protests are insignificant in the face of what seems a silent mass acceptance of the newspaper as a producer of knowledge and power: to be civilized is to read the newspaper. The Irish Catholic settlers of Biddulph are said[2] to be so notoriously backward that they do not read the newspapers; their primitive tribal state (1857) had just revealed itself in the xenophobic murder of a cattle drover (the Brimmacombe murder) who made the mistake of sleighing through their settlement. The implication here is that those who forget about feuds, tribal loyalties, ballads, superstitions, and so on, straighten out, become normal, and like everyone else. Ironically, of course, it was these Biddulph settlers not reading newspapers who produced in the Donnelly Tragedy (1880) the most sensational 'story' the *Free Press* ever printed. Those who read the newspapers are not as newsworthy as those who don't? Yes, this seems to be true when it comes to the stories of Negroes, Indians, the eccentric, and the extremely poor. The newspaper is a god. Read it, or miss out on the rules.

Therefore, ornamental cuts which portray a printing press floating deified in clouds of glory are to be expected. So is this banner motto which appears on the front page of the *Free Press* from the 1850s: 'Let it be impressed upon your minds, let it be instilled into your children, that the Liberty of the Press is the Palladium of all our Civil, Political and Religious Rights.' The Palladium cannot solve all problems though, for in the one month of February 1856, for example, a boiler explosion kills 'a man dressed in the garb of a farmer,' a Malahide farmer digs a deep well and hangs himself down it, and a toll gate keeper is beaten up by Hughes Wilson with a maple stick. Not only that, female typesetters had just been advertised for (12 February 1856); they were needed to break a strike by printers who had been worried about their civil right to a living wage!

Libel suits against the Palladium sometimes try to bring it down from its clouds of glory. In 1852 Colonel Prince, a renowned Tory (one of the sort who had six rebels executed without trial in 1838, yet moved for annexation to the States in 1849) sued the *Free Press* for saying this at a time when the colonel was hoping to get a judgeship. John Wilson, the last speaker for the defence, had this to say:

Gentlemen ... In all free countries, the press has become the representative of the public voice, and the action of the Government is made to bear upon the public in accordance with it. In the History of England rebellions were frequent but never amounted to much for want of concerted action. A rising now would be quite a different matter. Looking closely into history we find that the grossest abuses prevailed. It was perhaps one or two months after an event before any considerable portion of the people heard of it. – Now by means of the press everything is made public at once.

An appointment is no sooner made or a candidate appears, than his qualifications
are at once canvassed through the press ... The Defendant has a duty imposed upon
him to keep you informed on all public matters ... We boast of our freedom. What
makes us free? As long as the press is left at liberty to canvass the public acts of public
men, and no longer; for the press is the means by which you exercise that freedom.
(*Free Press*, 15 May 1851)

In the same issue, the editor further expands on the identity of people and paper:
'The improved sense of the community of interest existing between the public and
the press, as manifested by the intelligent and self-reliant jury which gave this ver-
dict will have its due weight in restraining future prosecutions.'

Whether the press always deserved its freedom and its claims for great influence
or not, one has to admit in looking at some individual copies of the earlier newspapers – say the *London Gazette* in the 1830s – that their appearance is most
elegant. The paper is still white, the type is well set, and the letters it printed are
still jet black; how a dreary, provincial backwoods filled with stumps, frogs, and
mud has been transformed by Caslon, lower and upper case! We see the same
triumph of order here that would have been visible at that time in the new straight
railroads with their parallel rails and the roads that meet at right angles which the
surveyors' instruments had produced. Perhaps now we are a bit dehydrated by all
the mechanical precision around us, but at the time it must have been exhilarating.
Again, there are faint outcries from the long-distance carters[3] who lose their profession after the Great Western is completed; in London, Ontario, the town crier
disappears although I suspect that he becomes a bill poster. Another oral art seems
to be affected; the very early newspapers in the thirties hardly bother with local
news, which presumably can get itself spread by word of mouth, but in the forties
when a fight between prominent businessmen takes place on Ridout Street, extra
copies of the paper describing the event were called for. Do even those who must
have seen the fight want to read about it? Is it becoming true that nothing really
happens unless it is printed? One can catch a glimpse of the modern situation in
which the newspapers decide for us what will be and has been and is happening.
In possession of this much potential power and prestige, what else can we do but
agree with the newspaper that it is a god and that the printing press should appear
angelic.

At this point, since we are talking of angels and similar divine messengers, it is
natural to ask, 'What about advertising?' Since it wished to survive, the *Free Press*
never faltered in its belief that advertising was good for you. During the depression
of 1857 special attempts to persuade merchants to advertise have to be made and
an American paper is quoted (30 December 1858) on the subject of an entrepreneur named Bonner who as the depression got worse took more and more

advertising space: '... was crazy enough to advertise still more extensively than ever, filling column after column with the announcements of the contents of his paper' with the result that 'he is a rich man, with a country house, 2 or 3 fast horses and we soon expect to see him sailing his own yacht ... Who are the crazy men? – Bonner who advertises a great deal, or the old fogies who advertise not at all?' A local dry goods merchant had earlier understood the message and taken a whole page (remember that this is in a four-page newspaper) to advertise his fall imports. Other newspapers take note and their doing so is reprinted in the *Free Press* (5 October 1857): 'The monster advertisement which appeared in the FREE PRESS, of Saturday last, to see *one whole page* devoted to *one whole advertisement*, viz., that of Mr. Alexander Hamilton's Dry Goods Merchant there. This immense advertisement is what we call, in the words of that paper, "the most effective that can be called to mind," and "a forerunner of success" ... Any man who studies human nature will be convinced that the *sure way to success in business* is to make it well known, *and that there is no better way of doing so than by advertising in the newspapers*.' Others are not so sure about advertising. It may bring Mr Bonner a new yacht and Mr Hamilton increased custom, but it also may tempt those without cash to make themselves miserable. The merchants of London were accustomed to put their goods out on the sidewalks so that the customers could see what they had to offer. In a case involving theft, a Mr Justice Burns took occasion to 'reprehend in severe terms this practice' and he was supported by an anonymous correspondent ('Andrew') who (6 November 1858, 'The Sidewalk Nuisance') even went so far as to say that 'the merchant is more to blame than the thief, and ought to be treated accordingly.' Several days later (10 November) indignant correspondents call this latter idealist a 'would-be local Paley' who is advocating that the 'merchant ought to be fined, and the poor victim, that is, the thief, we suppose, should be rewarded for being the means of bringing him to justice.' Equally scathing and more revealing of a dominant myth, we have also: ' "Andrew" is evidently far behind the age. Go-a-headism, is a peculiarity of the New World, and has almost become incorporated in our institutions; and what "Andrew" condemns, is practised throughout the length and breadth of this great continent, but his knowledge, like his ideas, appears to be very limited. What he censures as a sad want of proper business habits, just proves that business men know their business, and can therefore afford to laugh at the absurdities of a Merry Andrew.' Except to terminate the correspondence exchange because he fears it will descend to personalities, the editor makes no comment either way. I suppose he might be thinking that if the merchants would put their goods into some more monster advertisements instead of on the sidewalk the problem might be solved. One feels that the problem would not be solved, however, but simply transferred to a more elusive realm. It is fairly easy for society to regulate a 'sidewalk nuisance'; it becomes much more difficult when it disappears into a printed rhetoric that was just beginning to wrap itself around Canadian life with the ideals of a technological 'go-aheadism' that is eventually destructive of not only man, but of the newspaper itself. Actually, the technique of the 1850s advertisement (and for long after) is mainly a matter of size – the use of Fat Face type and similar devices. Verbal distortion on a grand scale only enters into the copy for the patent medicines (written in New York or Buffalo, I suspect) and beyond that and the Globe Foundry calling its stove 'The King of Stoves' there is really nothing that might be regarded as the ancestor of today's cigarette ads. Still, at this stage the newspaper has its own special format and design, both tied to the wheels of progress or 'go-aheadism.' For example, it is not a book (say by a thoughtful, 'would-be Paley'), in which case the reader would meet the medium on more or less even ground; if it were a book the newspaper would have to give up its display type, its various sizes of type. This comes out in a report (1 December 1858) on 'Setting Types by Machinery': '... He used to declare that he would do away with the wearisome work of composition; and from day to day for years he employed his moments of leisure, if such men can be said to have leisure, in devising how the work could be performed by machinery.' The invention succeeds, but it is best applied to books for, 'where a great variety of letter is employed, it could not be adopted to so much advantage.' The phrase 'great variety' is worth noticing; it is part of a manipulation which some social critics have pointed out is like magic. If the community of subscribers is not hypnotized by the reportage and the editorials (which have a great many more hidden myths than we have so far pointed out) it will certainly not survive the 'go-ahead' stimulation of the ads, no matter how many justices and 'Would-be Paleys' enquire if there is not something wrong somewhere; if, as a matter of fact, anyone knows for sure just where we might be 'going ahead' to.

At any rate, we are not going backward; backward, far-away, and foreign countries are sometimes called 'sealed' lands,[4] and are either horrible or curious or laughable, sometimes all three at once. What is it like to be 'unsealed'? Well, for one thing, it is to read the newspapers, and the best key word here seems to be 'enlightenment.' The *Free Press* (30 September 1852) reprints a late eighteenth-century account of the Portuguese royal family under the heading 'Stupidity of the Old Royal Families of Portugal and Spain.' The corpulent queen is falconing in 'leather integuments', and is a 'regular attendant at mass'; the article talks of the '... miserable monotony and superstition of the family!' 'These Portugese princes with their primitive, patriarchal ideas, should have lived somewhere before the Flood. They are fit for no other period, apparently.' A comforting glow still rises from the page these observations are printed on; the middle class 'go-ahead' reader can look down on royalty. For he is not a regular attendant at mass; no falconer he, when more massive techniques can knock down passenger pigeons and trap a whole river of fish (26 October 1858) at the Wardsville dam. The queen of Portugal has cousins not so far away, however; ' "Removal of the London Post-Office, Great Public Meeting"/The usual quiet routine of Juvenile Cockney life when political excitement has not called the hordes from the "uncivilized concessions" has been varied by an intense excitement regarding the removal of the Post-Office' (5 August 1852). Here, the bourgeois reader knows already about contemporary countrymen who come into town to get drunk, disgrace themselves at brothels, and hold dangerous parades on the twelfth of July. After reading (*Free Press Weekly*, 12 February 1880) about the stealing of relics (skulls and teeth of the victims) by country people during the Biddulph Tragedy, one hastens to agree with the *Free Press*. But then, how it smarts when a British journal finds all of Canada – concession and town, rural and urban – barbaric. This produces editorial hints that perhaps the American Revolution did bring civilization to this continent and should be joined, though late. But, in the end, as an 'unsealed' land, it is Britain that is chosen as a source of values and images rather than the States. British affairs, before the American Civil War at least, dominate the *Free Press*; London Major's streets are assumed to be as familiar to *Free Press* readers as those of their own London Minor; and all the better since not all Americans are like Mr Emerson (28 December 1858), who is 'entirely devoid of that abominable Yankee slang and self-consequence so peculiar to the Americans.' But the reader of the *Free Press* is invited to take part in more complex 'who has the more enlightenment' games than this (3 November 1857): '... supposing he did, there are few young men of Beaton's age and station who would not ... especially so when it seems that Mrs. Russell had a fierce passion for him which would induce her, as she said, "to go to the middle of hell for him." ' The servant class ('station') should find their masters (in this case, mistress) irresistible. Under the heading 'Black Virtue in Distress' (15 October 1857) we find this: 'The complainant promptly mounted the witness box, and was attired in a yellow dress surmounted by a jacket of green print; the whole set off with a superfluity of skirt distended by hoops, after the most approved fashion. The gloves were blue – the sun bonnet, one of very long proportions, white, – and the head was enveloped in a turban which might have become Nena Sahib.' Negroes shouldn't dress so colourfully and besides their dancing[5] is fascinating, but somehow wrong: 'On a Saturday night all the Town's on the heel/Here to see niggers dance and to hear Lucy Neal' (11 April 1845, *London Times*). The Oneida squaw (19 April 1869) who tramps in to the market square from Muncey, a good fifteen miles down the river from London, has somehow no business to be so ridiculously loaded down with twenty baskets, four hickory door mats, and her children. Occasionally a correspondent ('Hibernicus' on 26 April

1856) will remonstrate about the image of the Irish in recently declared criminal statistics: 'I do not believe that the Council would allow an employee to cherish such "Know-Nothing" principles. At all events, I hope that some of my fellow countrymen in the City Council who desire to uphold the reputation of Irishmen will bring the matter up ...' The editorial reply is not clear cut; nor was it at an earlier date (14 August 1846, *London Times*) when 'An Irishman & a Subscriber' pointed out that murders committed in Ireland were written up as Irish murders, indicative of national ferocity; murders committed in England, however, are reported simply as 'murders': 'Had it been an Irish woman who had destroyed her children by throwing them into the Liffy [sic], there would have been no one to excuse her crime on the plea of poverty.' But 'go-aheadism' and its 'enlightenment' have seldom been able to understand poverty; all the less when it is connected with cultural differences.

In pursuing the key word 'enlightenment' in a somewhat different area we find (29 April 1856):

INVOKING SPIRITS. – We thought that London did not contain a believer in spiritualism, but since the mysterious disappearance of Mr. Bacon and his supposed murder pine tables and other appliances used for invoking the manes of the departed have been called into requisition by several persons in this city ... After such instances of superstition who will boast of the enlightenment of the nineteenth century?

A day later a would-be clairvoyant is said to have been assured about Farmer Bacon's whereabouts by 'a spirit of the seventh circle.' However, it seems to depend on what social power the departure from 'enlightenment' can muster (15 July 1852):

Brethren Ladies and Gentlemen, – in addition to the important duties that I have been this day called upon to perform, viz., to lay the corner stone of the County of Elgin Municipal buildings in ancient Masonic form, that of addressing a few words to you in reference to the ceremony you have just witnessed, has also devolved *upon me*, it is one that however agreeable to my inclination; I should yet have much preferred to see intrusted to some one more able to do justice to a most noble theme.
Having, however, undertaken this duty, I will endeavour in a brief space, to afford you, in addition to a short glance at the origin of ancient masonry *some* slight explanation of the ceremony we have just performed, and of the reasons for which, our Fraternity, are so often called upon to officiate upon similar occasions, and while confident that the subject, however feebly handled in the present occasion, will possess great interest for the minds of the Brethren present, I will endeavour to ... etc.
... the first authentic accounts we possess of their proceedings are during the erection

and completion of the most sumptuous and costly building that probably ever was formed by man – this building is no other than the Temple commenced by Solomon, King of Israel, in the 4th year of his reign etc.

The speaker goes on (the *Free Press* diminishing the type size in order to squeeze it all in) to equate the temple site with Mount Moriah and Golgotha, to add that 'the great importance of a knowledge of the ancient Arts & Cabala of the Craft induced Kings and Princes to seek admission' to Masonry, and that according to the dictates of 'Speculative Masonry' the Corner Stone is generally 'that in the northeast corner if practicable.'

One would think that if the occultism of a spirit in the 'seventh circle' must go, so should that of laying the Corner Stone 'in the northeast corner if practicable.' But there is still a thin line[6] between a completely mechanical rationalist view of time and space, and the older microcosm-macrocosm world-pictures. You can see the thin line in the following (16 October 1857):

IGNORANCE OF PHYSICAL TRUTH. – How few men really believe that they sojourn on a whirling globe, and ... how very few believe that the solid pavement of the globe upon which they nightly slumber, is an elastic crust, imprisoning fires and forces ... Were these great physical truths objects of faith as well as deductions of reason, we should lead a better life than we do, and make a quicker preparation for its close.

I guess that the editor of the *Free Press* who thoughtfully reprinted this from a British journal could hardly foresee Hitler's 'planet baccilli'; that a century later the 'physical' truth would indeed be an object of faith and also, when most of the implications of 'enlightenment' had been ravelled out, of the most numbing despair; but in 1857 the eventual nihilism of science is not yet glimpsed. Instead, man's increasing power over nature through science is greeted with the same gasp of pleasure as the news that the 'Iron Horse [is] at Shakespeare. Already we can almost hear his shriek' (*Stratford Beacon*, 1 August 1856), that copper has been discovered on the North Shore of Lake Superior, or that a mammoth walnut tree (12 October 1860) in Metcalfe Township has been cut down and sold to American entrepreneurs who will turn it into thousands of rifles. On 21 December 1859, after its being advertised for some months, a book by a Canadian geology professor[7] ('a working naturalist') at McGill University called *Archaia* is reviewed; the review agrees with the author's own summing up of his work when he says that 'the reader has, I trust, found, in the preceding pages, sufficient evidence that the Bible has nothing to dread from the revelation of geology, but much to hope in the way of elucidation of its meaning and confirmation of its truth.' Actually on reading the book this reader did not find 'sufficient evidence'; what can be found is a writer unconscious of how damaging the science he pursues really is to fundamentalism;

geology is just about to part company with the Bible forever. The power geology gives to find oil in Lambton County and iron at Marmora will soon seem much more important than the imaginative power the first chapter of Genesis can produce in a society which used to see the week, particularly the first week of time, as having a pattern that shaped life, shaped it in a human-divine relationship quite unlike the ratrace time of the busy printer inventing machines which will put him out of work or of a factory operative whose goods must be consumed by a society madly producing too many such goods already. Not far away waits a world in which the idea that the County Court House is modelled on Solomon's Temple will seem very strange; the *Free Press* cannot see that its very prose, its very type perhaps, builds up the destruction of the world picture it supposedly favours. So, for the time being, the old world of symbols and meaning is not quite gone; the new world of nothingness and Vanity Fair has not quite conquered.

Speaking of Vanity Fair, one of the favourite books of this newspaper's society is *Pilgrim's Progress,* if the good press (3 November 1857) the visiting Bunyan Panorama receives is any indication; what the paper itself never comes to grips with it that almost the whole society says it is on its way to Jordan; a great deal of that society, including its newspapers, is quite happy to stay at Vanity Fair. The ambivalence of 'enlightenment' – just as one wants to ask, 'Go ahead where?' so one also wishes to ask, 'Enlightened as to what?' – comes out in the description of Robert Stephenson's burial in Westminster Abbey. God is called the 'Great Engineer of the Universe'; 'Commerce has girdled the earth with its iron roads' and Robert Stephenson, like William Shakespeare, is survived by no lineal descendants! This latter seems to imply that the folio and the rocket are masterpieces with similar effects. Certainly it could be part of a genuine enlightenment, no doubt, to have a railway or two around; but as a substitute for the Bible, Shakespeare, and religion it sounds rather fetischistic. The newspapers report many incidents of trees falling on both people and railway tracks; ' "A Timely Warning"/A summons was granted by the magistrates on Saturday ... against a person named Popple, for causing an obstruction to the due working of the trains. It appears that this person and others are in the habit of using the railway tracks as a highway, so that human life is constantly endangered by the practice.' But sometimes underneath this and many other excerpts I could present, one detects a rather waspish tone of: 'How dare they get in the way of the Iron Horse, our holy beast!' From the old lady who sits down on the London and Port Stanley Railway and falls asleep to the fiend in human form who in Biddulph Township (24 January 1870) broke one of the rails the Grand Trunk Sarnia Express was to have passed over – 'Of course there is no blame to be attached to anyone!' – there are some human beings too stupid or too atheistical to worship at the shrine. No doubt, they are not newspaper readers! One may ask though what alternative was there in that society to 'go-aheadism' and 'enlightenment'? Since Arnold, Ruskin, and Flaubert are rather far away we will have to make do with the local Roman Catholic bishop (his Anglican equivalent seems to be obsessed with real estate) : 'His Lordship Bishop Walsh' said (1 July 1869) at the Sacred Heart Convent at a graduation exercise: 'The child when brought to school is not only an ignorant being, but it is also a being inclined to evil ... This house does not pretend to turn out what are known as strongminded women ...' As his lordship continues by saying that he hopes to raise 'the temple of knowledge on the eternal foundations of religion' one can't help feeling that he is describing just one more set of railway tracks; in despair one would almost prefer a spirit from the seventh circle.

'Her levity of character ... forbade members ... receiving her as a visitor' (4 December 1858). 'Polite society' is the phrase used further on that defines the excluders of levity. Indecent bathers (21 July 1857) are denounced. The accepted idea seems at first to be that polite society is against indecency and illicit passion. 'He had lived with Lydia on the Platonic system' (10 June 1843, *London Times*) implies, however, that he was a bit of a mollycoddle and 'Boxer will stand for more' (10 April 1843, *London Herald*) shows how open and straightforward the animal world could be; the human world could not so that although 'polite society' seems to be ranged against 'levity' and 'indecency' it is actually more than interested in them. Take the association around a recurring phrase such as 'stripped' ('mutilated' could also be used) and what emerges is the image of some shadowy erotic demon, cruel and delightful, obscene and beautiful, who rules another part of the soul completely from that tyrannized over by the mechanical geometry of 'go-aheadism' and 'enlightenment.'

William Wright (6 April 1868), a drunkard, is 'stripped' and tortured by some Caledon Township maenads. A sick prostitute in Toronto (20 December 1858) describes herself being stripped, then her attacker stripping himself. Sadism in Shakespeare, Ontario (14 February 1870) involves 'stripping' two drunkards and tying them to horses. One London arsonist (31 August 1860) is tarred and feathered down by the river and the *Free Press* approves Judge Lynch's actions. This is the era of Father Chiniquy, the renegade priest, whose *Maria Monk* thrilled Protestant readers with its revelations of the confessional; his presence (8 December 1858) is always heralded favourably and a priest (2 January 1857) who attempts to violate a married parishioner is given the ultimate rhetorical treatment of dotted lines just as he is about to lift up his frock. One feels a powerful sense of gloating; particularly with reference to 'mutilation' in the long and detailed description of the Taeping Massacre (7 August 1857) where the effect is to transform the reader into both victim and torturer: with reference to 'stripped' there is a long account of one Mark (16 October 1860) who returning to the Chatham area from Kansas with a bowie knife was about to go back there with four local girls. A mob prevents him '... arriving here, Mark was, *sans* ceremony, rooted out – he was not in bed – and ordered to strip to the buff ... a number of other parties ... were looking on ...' After throwing off the original attackers, one of whom he knifes in the groin, the victim is beaten, tarred, and feathered by those who were originally more passive onlookers. By reporting these Sadeian scenes the newspapers involved seem to fulfill some sort of need in their readers.

In a lighter way, news items about the Glasgow poisoner, Madeline Smith, or the courtesan, Lola Montez, fulfill the same need for having your cake (how disgusting – evil lust, promiscuous dancer, Caledon maenads with red hot pokers etc.) and eating it too: 'I, bourgeois newspaper reader strip the arsonist, tar and feather him, though I have just forbidden the village boys to strip naked for swimming.' Obviously one longs for more direct statements about Eros at this time; well, there were advertised in the papers of the 1850s books that sounded as if they might help citizens with the 'shadowy demon.' Such a book ('A Book for the Million') is advertised in the 1854 *Stratford Beacon* and it is called Dr W.C. Lispenard's *Practical Private Medical Guide*/'Know Thyself.' If the formerly mentioned *Archaia* tried to mend a split in the macrocosm between Genesis and geology, Dr Lispenard's book tries to do the same thing for a microcosm torn between 'polite society' and 'stripped': 'enlightenment' versus 'mutilated.' Here are some of Dr Lispenard's phrases: 'this most imperious of all their appetites' (32); 'The anticipations of wedlock are crowded with misgivings, and often-times, the dark hour hangs upon him, and forbids him making the advance on which hinges his earthly happiness.' Yes, indeed; so how do we young men caught in the intolerable neither-nors of our progressive society, with gleet hanging over our heads if we approach prostitutes ('three prostitutes followed by 50 boys' [21 September 1859]), court cases for adultery ('hired men had connection with her [13 October 1859]) and no less than early death promised by Dr Lispenard for masturbation and nocturnal emissions? Sphinx-like, Dr Lispenard can only add, 'Nature demands the nude frame dressed and armed with all the vigor, desire, and freshness of manhood – with physical power and nervous correspondence – conviction of conquest – a certainty of triumph.' From all the preceding 'stripped' quotations one can see how Nature does demand 'the nude frame' (Blake's 'lineaments of gratified desire') but one can't quite see, given all the 'polite society' taboos, how Nature is ever going to receive this glorious sight.

In closing, I would like to move to yet another kind of myth, and it is of a far pleasanter kind, showing a release from the tension we have been dealing with. Occasionally the newspaper will let itself go, and simply respond to something powerful or beautiful. The effect is of suddenly entering a Fairyland (Blake would call it the state of Beulah) and this effect is brought on usually by wind or thunderstorms, or by the approach of winter, or by the Christmas market: 'The gusts of wind (28 November 1859) followed one another in rapid succession ... woke the whole fraternity of sleepers ... drove in the large door of the Market House.' At last the class divisions, the separation of non-reader and reader collapse before the phrase 'fraternity of sleepers.'

Hibernation./Written for the 'Free Press'; At this season the bears are asleep, living quietly on themselves ... How strange it would be if we, in this northern latitude, were subject to the same ordination! ... At the beginning of December, in ordinary circumstances, the somnolence would begin, and as the thermometer descended, the sleep would deepen. About this period of the season our busy city would be silent as Pompeii – and only wolves and foxes going about the streets; each house having its complement of slumberers, who never kick and never snore ... In the window of a newspaper office, you would see this announcement, – Yesterday, the Editor succumbed in his easy chair, but the Sub-Editor hopes by the use of onions and sal-volatile to issue another number ... Messrs. Simpkin and Co., would call attention to their new elixir, which has the effect of securing sleep at once, when nature is a little dilatory in completing her design. They would hint the advantage of a family getting somnolent together, and dwell pathetically on the disagreeableness of baby keeping awake after mamma had become helpless ... (20 February 1856)

In reading the 1860 file of the *London Free Press* I suddenly noticed a new phrase – 'the Storm King' a phrase used for blizzards and rainstorms alike. Incognito he visits picnics (27 July 1869) and causes greendawns (26 July 1869) and he appears at the very end of this quotation:

Lost in the Snow/Being the Dismal Experience of a Young Man on Sunday Night./ ... any one who was abroad on Sunday night, say between the hours of eleven and twelve o'clock, fully deserved all the commiseration he could get from every well regulated, snug and comfortable family fireside. It was an awful night and no mistake ... The snow pelted down, and eddied about with cutting force in the strong 'baffling' wind from the North-west. One had to grope his way more by instinct than any knowledge he might have had of localities and the names of streets and houses ... And as for any intelligent reckoning of distances, by the grocery signs, or observation of the fixed planets, let me tell you, my lords and ladies, it was out of the question; for neither could be seen, it being so powerfully dark, behold you, that you couldn't tell a locomotive headlight from a copper candle stick more than three feet and quarter before you ... Then a savage blast of wind came down, howling like a pack of wolves, and which he could only resist by bracing himself well up against a neighboring garden gate ... At last, in the classic language of the Strathroy *Dispatch* 'the weary traveller discerned a dim light far in the distance,' namely, about five feet ... and chuckled defiance to the Storm King and his wintry hosts. (4 January 1869)

At the very opposite pole to this happy exuberance there is a chilling story (2 September 1858) that belongs with the less happy myths we discussed previously: 'Determined Suicide/The Unfortunate man whose name is Nathan Young, was a clock cleaner, and might have been seen walking through the streets dressed in black clothes, with a small box in his hand, in which he carried his tools ... "I ever intended doing this as soon as I could not take care of myself ... I have no friends, therefore bury me, and sell my things to pay the expenses ... I write this as calmly as anything I ever wrote/Nathan Young (London, August 30, 1958)" ... the deceased was a native of New Haven, Connecticut.'

Two days after this report of an ultimate rebellion against machinery, progress, and enlightenment, the *Free Press* carried a description of the celebrations in Montreal for the completion of the Atlantic Telegraph. There is a parade; note the position of those to do with newspapers:

Butchers on Horseback.
Sailors from Steamers and Ships in Port.
BAND
Workers in Iron, Brass, Copper, Tin, and other metals.
Managers, Clerks, and Men from Grand Trunk Works.
Musical Instrument Makers, Carpenters, Grocers.
Cabinet Makers, Coach Makers, and
all Workers in Wood.
BAND
Mason, Stonecutters, Bricklayers, Plasterers,
Slaters, etc. etc.
Leather and India-rubber Manufacturers, Shoemakers and all
Workers in Leather.
Sugar Workers, Millers, Brewers, Tobacconists,
Pipe-Makers.
BAND
Bakers and Confectioners,
Tailors and Clothiers,
Furriers, Hatters, and Brush Makers,
Printers, Bookbinders, and Type-Founders.
The Press.
BAND
Citizens
Mayor and Corporation of Montreal.

The Strathroy paper (1 September 1858) is quoted as saying that the completion of the Atlantic Telegraph was a 'triumph of mind over matter, of light over darkness, of knowledge over ignorance, of truth over error, of science over space. It has ushered a new era into the history of our world.'

Perhaps we, slightly sick of new eras ushered in by this or that technological breakthrough, would not have joined the torch-light procession that was held at Strathroy nor joined the Montreal parade either. When it's far too late, of course, we can point out where the parade really led, where the advertising got ahead to, how two-sided the enlightenment was, how good it is to find people getting such pleasure out of something free and unmanufactured like a snowstorm and so on. In short, we are in a position to read these nineteenth-century newspapers in a way they could not, to see myths and shapes they were only dimly conscious of if at all. But there is so much more to be done; the papers involved are an endless world which can be returned to again and again, each visit bringing up some more insight not only into the structure of their mental world (what McLuhan would call the water they lived in) but of our own.

NOTES

1 There are so many references to the *London Free Press* that a bracketed date in the text simply means that particular issue of the *Free Press*. With some exceptions I have kept well back into the early files of this newspaper since the shapes I am looking for seem clearer then – that is, in the 1850s. After the reports of John Brown's execution and the start of the American Civil War, the tone of the *Free Press* changes in some still undefined way.
2 University of Western Ontario Library, clerk of the peace, Huron County, Ontario, correspondence, Cooper to Macdonald, 25 March 1859
3 *Free Press*, 8 Sept. 1857
4 *Free Press*, 16 July 1857, in a reference to Persia
5 See the item in 'Police Intelligence' on the Negro musician and vagabond, Dick Chrystler, *Free Press*, 18 Aug. 1869
6 'The Orange Demonstration at Strathroy' (*Free Press Weekly*, 27 Jan. 1860.) contains an even richer set of symbols and correspondences. 'It seems that signs were well known to God's ancient heritage, the Jews ...' and to present day Orangemen as well. William of Orange as a latter-day equivalent to Moses is a bit hard to take, though.
7 Sir John William Dawson

The Illustrated Historical Atlases
of Ontario with Special Reference
to H. Belden & Co

Lillian Rea Benson

The year 1975 will mark the one hundredth anniversary of the publication of the first of the illustrated historical atlases for the counties and districts of Ontario. There were thirty-four of these volumes published, all but two of which appeared in a seven-year period beginning in 1875 and ending in 1881. The later ones, second atlases for Wentworth and Wellington counties, appeared in 1903 and 1906.

These atlases were a specialized type of publication which had originated in the United States a decade earlier and were designed to replace the county wall map. Their production was made feasible by the introduction of new techniques in lithography and the steam-driven press. In the United States some map publishers became atlas publishers, and dozens of new companies were formed to promote, publish, and sell the county atlas.[1] Soon a few of these publisher-promoters began moving across the border into Ontario. However, with the exception of J.H. Meacham & Co's atlas of the counties of Frontenac, Lennox, and Addington, which was printed and engraved in Philadelphia, the printing, lithographing, and engraving of Ontario atlases was done in Toronto.

There were two types of atlas. All those published prior to 1880 and the two published in the early 1900s contained only county material, except for a few general maps; those published in 1880 and 1881 were atlases of the Dominion of Canada with a supplement containing material relevant to a specific county. To differentiate between them, they will be referred to as 'county atlases' and 'supplements.'

All except the *Guide Book & Atlas of Muskoka and Parry Sound Districts*[2] were large volumes, approximately 45 × 36 centimetres, awkward to handle and difficult to store. In both types the county material fell into the same general pattern: an historical sketch of the county, followed by records of the founding and development of each municipality within its borders, portraits of pioneers and prominent citizens, hundreds of short biographical notices, dozens of illustrations of farm and village homes and business establishments, and maps – township maps and plans of towns and villages, all of which were very detailed. Locations of schools, churches, grist and saw mills, post offices, and even orchards were indicated. Farm boundaries were delineated on all township maps. The owner's name was printed on his lot on maps in county atlases; only the names of subscribers were shown on lots marked in the supplements.

Research has proven that the material contained in the atlases is remarkably accurate considering the speed with which the data collectors and mappers must have worked to cover the large areas as thoroughly as they did. As one geography professor remarked to the writer: 'Despite the unquestioned commercialism which inspired their publication, the result was a surprisingly accurate compilation of useful data in convenient form.'

Certain features were designed to be revenue producing. Space was sold for portraits and illustrations. The inclusion of biographies was limited 'in accordance with the usual practice ... to those who have supported the work by ordering views or portraits or otherwise aiding in our enterprise.'[3] (An exception to this practice was made by the publishers of the Wellington County atlas of 1906 who stressed the completeness of their biographical coverage.) The canvassers have been criticized for high-pressure salesmanship, but from the vantage point of a century later perhaps we should be grateful for their skilful and effective use of flattery and persuasion. Otherwise, many features of historical interest today would have been reduced in scope, or publication might even have been abandoned.

The canvassers have also been charged with making fraudulent statements in their eagerness to obtain subscriptions and, indeed, such was the case. S.R.G. Penson, the artist of the Muskoka atlas, described the technique used by salesmen: 'The canvassers used to lead the farmers to believe that the book would cost them but $8.00, whereas it always cost them $12.00. The plan was to sell on a contract that read $12.00 if no more than 2000 were sold – $10.00, if 3000 were sold – and $8.00 if 4000 were sold. The canvassers always stated that the highest number had already been sold, and this is where the fraud came in, for the lowest number was never reached in any county in Ontario.'[4] No doubt there was much grumbling but in the end the subscribers paid the price and were proud to possess a copy of their atlas.

Some of the success of the atlas publishing venture may be attributed to its timing. In most sections of Ontario, settlement was emerging from the pioneer stage, and foundations had been laid for a prosperous agricultural and industrial society. Perhaps for the first time there was an inclination and desire to pause and assess what had been achieved. Although few may have given conscious thought to the recording of the struggles and accomplishments of the past, the atlas makers presented an opportunity to do so, and their arrival was welcomed.

For the generations which observed or participated in its preparation, the atlas was a treasured possession. But years went by and in the period of social and economic change between the two world wars many ideas and possessions of the past were cast aside. Among the casualties were not a few of these old publications, thoughtlessly discarded as out of date and worthless impedimenta.

In the early forties students of Ontario history, knowing well the value of the atlases and their potential uses in connection with new and growing studies of the history and development of this province, feared that a most useful resource might disappear. The number originally published was small, fewer than 2000 according to Penson, and probably closer to 1200 in most counties. There was an urgent need to locate existing copies and to encourage their preservation in libraries and reference collections. In 1944 a preliminary survey of holdings in the larger libraries of Ontario revealed that none of the co-operating libraries had anything approaching a complete collection.[5]

The survey had the effect of drawing attention to these publications, and efforts were made to complete holdings in reference libraries. In the process further information was uncovered regarding the atlases and their publishers. This, in turn, stimulated even greater interest.[6] At the same time the growing emphasis on Ontario studies, especially in such areas as land use, urban history and development, and social history, produced a dramatic increase in the use of these volumes in research. Resulting demand pushed the average price of a volume from a modest $10 in the thirties and early forties to $80 by the end of the fifties. Add to this a growing general interest in Canadiana, and by 1970 prices ranged from about $175 to $250 – when copies could be found.

Today the situation has changed. Another generation of entrepreneurs are using new, inexpensive techniques to reproduce these atlases. Basically the new publications are reprints of the county material included in the original atlases. Some, however, have introductions added; some have minor changes in the positioning of illustrations. Many are slightly reduced in size, and to more than one a relevant map has been added. The first reprint, the York County atlas, appeared in 1969. Others followed rapidly and it seems certain that long before the anniversary year of 1975 all thirty-four volumes will have been reprinted.

The reappearance of these volumes has been greeted with satisfaction by librarians, teachers, and students in many fields. The popularity of the reprints beyond this circle has been encouraging and raises a hope that citizens of Ontario may become more interested and better informed regarding the rich heritage which is theirs.

As previously stated many of the atlas publishers who worked in Ontario were citizens of the United States. Penson specifically mentions Page, Miles, and the Belden brothers as being in this category.[7] Of these the Beldens alone seem to have acquired a Canadian identity based in part upon the volume of their atlas publishing but more especially upon their later activities as publishers of *Picturesque Canada,* described in contemporary journals as being a great Canadian publishing achievement,[8] and by their continuing presence on the Toronto business scene as agents for the Home Knowledge Association of New York and Chicago.

The H. Belden & Co imprint appeared on seventeen of the thirty-four Ontario county atlases or supplements. The brothers, Howard Raymond and Reuben Booth Belden, who formed the partnership came to Canada in 1876 from Chicago where they had already gained considerable experience in this specialized field of publishing.[9] Indeed, in that same year their Chicago firm, Howard Belden & Co., published three illustrated historical atlases – Milwaukee County, Wisconsin; Wayne County, Michigan; and the combined counties of Ottawa and Kent, Michigan.

An act of the Ontario Legislature (1869) required the registration of co-partnerships and business firms. Unfortunately, not all atlas publishers seem to have complied with the law. However, the Beldens together, singly, or with other partners filed no less than eight declarations in Ontario between 1877 and 1910. Only three are pertinent to the atlas story. The first of these, filed in the County of Ontario Registry Office, was registered under the firm name of J.H. Beers & Co.[10]

For almost a century it has been thought that the *Illustrated Historical Atlas of the County of Ontario, Ont.* is an example of the work of J.H. Beers & Co, one of the dozen or so Beers companies which dominated the atlas publishing field in the United States. When the preliminary check-list of Ontario atlases was being prepared, only a Beers atlas was reported for Ontario County. Since then, however, copies with a Belden imprint have been discovered. Both have a publication date of 1877, and a comparison of the two volumes shows the contents to be identical, the only difference being the publisher's name on the title page. Thus, it now seems that the atlas bearing the Beers name is really a Belden publication, their first Canadian production.

Although a number of possible reasons may suggest themselves, any attempt at this time to explain why the Beldens began their Canadian operation under a business name not their own would be pure conjecture and is not relevant to their later work. They used the Beers name for only a few months. Presumably before all copies of the Ontario atlas had been bound a new title page was substituted with the name H. Belden & Co replacing J.H. Beers & Co. A probable date for this change, October 1877, is suggested by the new declaration of partnership under the Belden name.[11]

During 1878 the Beldens published two county atlases, one for Northumberland and Durham, the other for Hastings and Prince Edward counties. These were followed in 1879 by four more county atlases, one each for Carleton, Huron,

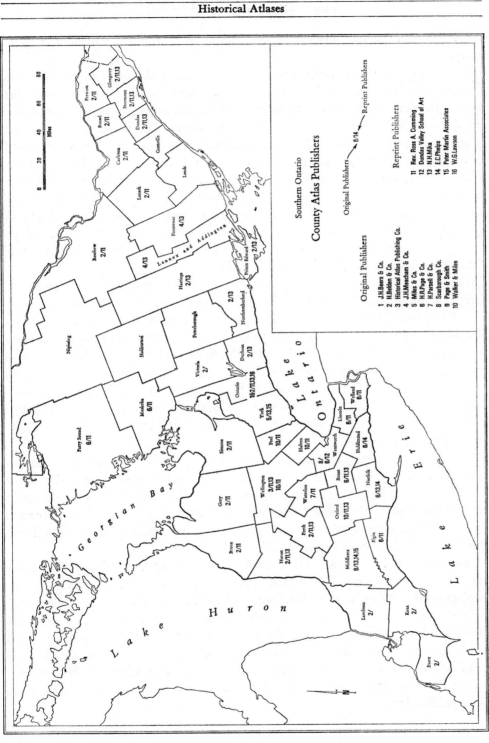

Southern Ontario
County Atlas Publishers

Original Publishers → 6/14 ← Reprint Publishers

Original Publishers

1 J.H.Beers & Co.
2 H.Belden & Co.
3 Historical Atlas Publishing Co.
4 J.H.Meacham & Co.
5 Miles & Co.
6 H.R.Page & Co.
7 H.Parsell & Co.
8 Scarborough Co.
9 Page & Smith
10 Walker & Miles

Reprint Publishers

11 Rev. Ross A. Cumming
12 Dundas Valley School of Art
13 N.H.Mika
14 E.C.Phelps
15 Peter Martin Associates
16 W.G.Lawson

and Perth counties and another for the counties of Stormont, Dundas, and Glengarry.

By the end of the seventies the only other atlas publisher still operating in Ontario was H.R. Page & Co whose final atlas appeared in 1879. This left the field to the Beldens. In 1880 they introduced general atlases incorporating county supplements, a possible cost-saving change in content. The major difference with respect to county material lay in the treatment of township maps. Those contained in the supplements were neither as large nor as detailed as those in the county atlases. The scale was reduced so that one map could be accommodated on a single page rather than being spread over a double page. Only the names of subscribers to the atlas appeared on the township maps. Although the addition of general material may have been welcomed by subscribers at the time, today's user cannot view the change as an improvement. These new atlases bore the title *Illustrated Atlas of the Dominion of Canada.*

Four of these atlases were produced in 1880 containing supplements for Bruce, Grey, Lambton, and Lanark counties; others for Essex, Kent, Prescott and Russell, Renfrew, Simcoe, and Victoria appeared in 1881. One point of interest should be noted about the six 1881 publications. For the first time the Beldens had engaged a civil engineer, D. Macdonald, to supervise the preparation of local maps. Hitherto they, themselves, had prepared or supervised both maps and written material relating to the counties. Soon after the final Belden atlas of 1881 was published the firm of H. Belden & Co, map and atlas publishers, ceased to exist. However, Belden involvement with atlas publishing in Ontario was not to end for another twenty-five years.

Late in 1881 a new publisher, H. Parsell & Co, printed a Dominion of Canada atlas including a supplement for Waterloo County. Its appearance and content suggest that it belonged to the Belden group of 1881, and D. Macdonald again had supervision of the local maps. The explanation of the similarity becomes evident from a reading of the Parsell partnership registration. Henry Parsell and Reuben Booth Belden were partners.[12]

The reason for the Parsell partnership and the engagement of a civil engineer may have been related to the Beldens' plan for another important and ambitious project – the publication and distribution of *Picturesque Canada,* for which they formed a new partnership in 1882 under the name Belden Bros.[13] It is probable that one of the partners – presumably it was Howard – had to drop some of the work connected with the atlas programme to organize the work ahead. It is possible also that they may have needed to withdraw capital from H. Belden & Co to get the new project under way and that Parsell was invited to finance the final publication.

The second atlas of Wellington County is a twentieth-century publication and, as such, is outside the period to be covered in this essay. Nevertheless, in the interest of completeness it seems desirable to include a brief mention of this very good county atlas. It was published by the Historical Atlas Publishing Co, of Toronto, for which no partnership registration seems to exist. Neither could a listing for the business be found in Toronto city directories. The principals of the company, therefore, remain unidentified. However, some information about the publication of the volume is available. It is known that the atlas was being distributed to subscribers in the first week of August 1906.[14] It has been reported that the work of preparation and production extended over a two-year period; that a civil engineer worked for fifteen months on the township maps; that the engraving required ten months. The same report stated that the biographical sketches were 'absolutely free,' a departure from the already noted practice of limiting such entries to subscribers or those who purchased space for other features.[15] Another source reported that R.B. Belden was in Palmerston in January 1905 gathering information for the forthcoming atlas.[16] There is evidence that Reuben B. Belden established residence in Guelph, the county seat, while the work was in progress.[17]

We know that Reuben Belden, at least, had some part in the publication of the Wellington County atlas of 1906. Was he merely an employee, a 'data collector,' as the Palmerston correspondent to the *Stratford Herald* described him, or was he a partner in the enterprise, a 'publisher' as stated in the assessment records? It may or may not be significant that the brothers reappeared on the Toronto scene a short time after the completion of the atlas – after an absence of over ten years. A similarity between the imprint 'The Art Publishing Company,' used on the title page of the Beldens' *Picturesque Canada*, and 'The Historical Atlas Publishing Company' is suggestive, as is also the fact that the wording of the introduction to the Wellington atlas is strangely reminiscent of that used in the introductory portion of Belden's atlas of Perth County (1879). But, regardless of what may have been the Beldens' connection with the Wellington atlas, there can be no question that in the course of their Canadian publishing careers the two young men from Chicago made valuable contributions to the historical records of the Province of Ontario.

Neither the Beldens nor their contemporaries, Messrs Page, Miles, Walker *et al*, are likely to have envisaged the new uses for their publications and none would have dreamed of the resurgence of interest culminating in the reprinting of the series. Although not specifically designed for that purpose, the present reprinting programme serves well to draw attention to the centenary of historical atlas publishing in Ontario and to the debt which is owed to those enterprising nineteenth-century publishers.

APPENDIX A: ORIGINAL PUBLICATIONS

Counties	Publishers	Date
Brant	Page & Smith	1875
Bruce	H. Belden & co	1880
Carleton	H. Belden & co	1879
Elgin	H.R. Page & co	1877
Essex	*H. Belden & co	1881
Frontenac, Lennox, and Addington	J.H. Meacham & co	1878
Grey	H. Belden & co	1880
Haldimand	H.R. Page & co	1879
Halton	Walker & Miles	1877
Hastings and Prince Edward	H. Belden & co	1878
Huron	H. Belden & co	1879
Kent	*H. Belden & co	1881
Lambton	*H. Belden & co	1880
Lanark	H. Belden & co	1880
Lincoln and Welland	H.R. Page & co	1876
Middlesex	H.R. Page & co	1878
Muskoka and Parry Sound districts	H.R. Page & co	1879
Norfolk	H.R. Page & co	1877
Northumberland and Durham	H. Belden & co	1878
Ontario	J.H. Beers & co	1877
Ontario	*H. Belden & co	1877
Oxford	Walker & Miles	1876
Peel	Walker & Miles	1877
Perth	H. Belden & co	1879
Prescott and Russell	H. Belden & co	1881
Renfrew	H. Belden & co	1881
Simcoe	H. Belden & co	1881
Stormont, Dundas, and Glengarry	H. Belden & co	1879
Victoria	*H. Belden & co	1881
Waterloo	H. Parsell & co	1881
Wellington	Walker & Miles	1877
Wellington	Historical Atlas Publishing co	1906
Wentworth	Page & Smith	1875
Wentworth	*Scarborough co	1903
York	Miles & co	1878

* Not reprinted as of 30 April 1973

APPENDIX B: REPRINT PUBLICATIONS

Counties	Publishers	Date
Brant	Mika	1972
Brant (with Oxford)	Cumming	1972
Bruce	[Cumming]	1970
Carleton	Cumming	1971
Elgin	Cumming	1972
Frontenac, Lennox, and Addington	Mika	1971
Grey	Cumming	1971
Haldimand (with Norfolk)	[Phelps]	[1972]
Halton	Cumming	1971
Hastings and Prince Edward	Mika	1972
Huron	Cumming	1972
Huron	Mika	1972
Lanark (with Renfrew)	Cumming	1972
Lincoln and Welland	Cumming	1971
Middlesex	Peter Martin Associates	1970
Middlesex	Mika	1972
Middlesex	Phelps	1972
Muskoka and Parry Sound districts	Cumming	1971
Norfolk (with Haldimand)	[Phelps]	[1972]
Northumberland and Durham	Mika	1972
Ontario (J.H. Beers)	W.G. Lawson	[1971]
Ontario (J.H. Beers)	Cumming	1972
Ontario (J.H. Beers)	Mika	1972
Oxford	Mika	1972
Oxford (with Brant)	Cumming	1972
Peel	Cumming	1971
Perth	Cumming	1972
Perth	Mika	1972
Prescott and Russell (with Stormont, Dundas, and Glengarry)	Cumming	1972
Renfrew (with Lanark)	Cumming	1972
Simcoe	Cumming	1970
Stormont, Dundas, and Glengarry	Mika	1972
Stormont, Dundas, and Glengarry (with Prescott and Russell)	Cumming	1972
Waterloo (with Wellington, 1877)	Cumming	1972

APPENDIX B: REPRINT PUBLICATIONS (CONTD)

Counties	Publishers	Date
Wellington, 1906	Cumming (for the Corporation of the County of Wellington)	1972
Wellington, 1906	Mika	1972
Wellington, 1877 (with Waterloo)	Cumming	1972
Wentworth, 1875	Dundas Valley School of Art	1971
York	Peter Martin Associates	1969
York	Mika	1972

NOTES

1 [Bates Harrington,] *How 'Tis Done: A Thorough Ventilation of the Numerous Schemes Conducted by Wandering Canvassers Together with the Various Advertising Dodges for the Swindling of the Public* (Syracuse 1890), 13–80

2 The Muskoka atlas was unique in several respects. The smaller size (30.5 × 23.5 cm) was probably dictated in part by its potential use as a guide book and also by the lesser amount of historical material available in an area newly opened to agricultural settlement. Although it was published by H.R. Page & Co, all the work of preparation was done by three local people, John Rogers, S.R.G. Penson, and W.E. Hamilton. Advertisements within the volume itself indicate that sales were not limited to subscribers.

3 H.R. Page & Co, *Illustrated Historical Atlas of the County of Norfolk, Ont.* (Toronto 1877), 3

4 S.R.G. Penson, 'Records of the Penson Family' (1910). Penson (1857–1945) recorded his reminiscences for his family, and the unpublished manuscript was loaned to the writer by his daughter, Miss Elizabeth Penson. Penson also made the drawings for Page's Haldimand atlas.

5 Lillian Rea Benson, 'Historical Atlases of Ontario: A Preliminary Check-List,' *Ontario Library Review*, xxviii, Feb. 1944, 45–53

6 One of the most useful studies to result from the awakened interest in these atlases is *County Atlases of Canada: A Descriptive Catalogue*, compiled by Betty May and published in 1970 by the National Map Collection, Public Archives of Canada. Another interesting study, although it has no reference to Ontario atlases, is George Sitwell's 'County Maps of the Nineteenth Century as Historical Documents: A New Use,' published by the Association of Canadian Map Libraries in the *Proceedings of the Second Annual Conference 17–9 June 1968*. It is a careful examination of the accuracy of the maps and related information in J.H. Meacham & Co's *Illustrated Historical Atlas of Pictou County Nova Scotia.*

7 Penson, 'Records of the Penson Family'

8 *The Week* (Toronto), i, 6, 10 Jan. 1884, 91 and 'Review of Literature, Science and Art,' *Dominion Annual Register*, 1880–1, 308

9 Information from Chicago city directories, supplied through the courtesy of L.A. Viskochil, Chicago Historical Society, shows that in 1871 Howard Belden was an agent for Warner, Higgins & Beers, atlas publishers. By 1874 he was a partner in Higgins, Belden & Co, for which firm his brother Reuben was a salesman. A final entry in 1875 lists the brothers as proprietors of Howard Belden & Co, county atlas publishers.

10 Registry Office, County of Ontario. Co-Partnership Register, Document 224, 12 April 1877. The Beldens are described as civil engineers of Toronto. It was stated that they were

carrying on business as county atlas publishers, that the partnership had subsisted since 15 October 1876 and was to exist for two years from that date.

11 Registry Office, City of Toronto. Co-Partnership Register, Document 1613, 7 March 1878. Howard Belden was described as a map and atlas publisher; Reuben was again described as a civil engineer. The partnership, it was stated, had been in existence since 1 October 1877.

12 Ibid., Document 2551, 26 Jan. 1882

13 Ibid., Document 2629, 1 May 1882

14 Drayton *Advocate*, 2 Aug. 1906

15 *Guelph Mercury*, 30 May 1906

16 *Stratford Herald*, 11 Jan. 1905

17 City of Guelph, Assessment Records, 1906, 1907. Reuben B. Belden is listed as a tenant and his occupation is given as publisher.

The Frontier Politician

M. Elizabeth Arthur

In the bitter contests between closely matched political parties in the tenth parliament of Ontario (1902–5) Robert R. Gamey, the recently elected member from Manitoulin, made his charges of corruption against members of the government.[1] Suddenly provincial attention was focused for the first time on politics and politicians in Northern Ontario, which for thirty-five years before Gamey was elected, had been represented at Queen's Park. The choosing of representatives, attempts to influence government in such vital matters as land grants, timber and mining policy, the determination of party allegiances, and the laborious tasks of party organization when a small electorate was spread over such an enormous area had all been going on since Confederation. These processes, however, had seldom attracted much attention from the rest of the provinces.

In 1867 the newly created constituency of Algoma stretched from the Quebec boundary on the east to the edges of Hudson's Bay territory on the north and west. With the purchase of company land two years later began a prolonged battle over the new limits of the province of Ontario but, wherever they might eventually be fixed, they were recognized in the 1870s as the boundaries of the gargantuan provincial riding. From 1876 on,[2] the difficulties of one man attempting to represent such an area were being described to the legislature, as petitions for the subdivision of the riding were presented. Repeatedly the government acknowledged the force of the argument, particularly in view of the growth of population that marked the 1870s,[3] but deferred action. As Premier Mowat smoothly put it on one occasion as he stressed the general interest in northern development: 'The representatives of the whole Province were in one sense the representatives of Algoma.'[4] In 1885 Algoma East and Algoma West were established as provincial ridings,[5] and in 1902 a further sub-division occurred, giving northern Ontario a total of five seats, one of them Manitoulin,[6] whose first representative was the controversial Mr Gamey.

For the purposes of this study, discussion will be confined to that part of the original riding known for seventeen years as Algoma West, and to four men who represented it: Frederic William Cumberland, Simon J. Dawson, Robert A. Lyon, and James Conmee. The votes for these four from 1867 to 1902, as well as the party affiliation of the winner in each election, as set out in Table 1, give some preliminary concept of the unique problems of the north and of anyone attempting to analyze northern elections a century ago.[7] At this stage, a few tentative conclusions emerge.

TABLE 1

	ELECTION	WINNER	PARTY AFFILIATION	MARGIN OF VICTORY	TOTAL VOTES CAST
Algoma	1867	F. W. Cumberland	Conservative	224	517
	1871	F. W. Cumberland	Conservative	acclamation	
	1875	S. J. Dawson	Independent	227	783
	1878	R. A. Lyon*	Liberal		
	By-election			acclamation	
	1879	R. A. Lyon	Liberal	155	2017
	1883	R. A. Lyon	Liberal	114	3136
Algoma	1885	James Conmee	Liberal	83	737
West	By-election				
	1886	James Conmee	Liberal	acclamation	
	1890	James Conmee	Liberal	59	1513
	1894	J. M. Savage†	Conservative	6	2268
	1895	James Conmee	Liberal	269	2527
	By-election				
	1898	James Conmee	Liberal	291	3155
Port Arthur-Rainy River	1902	James Conmee	Liberal	559	1689

*Resigned 1884 after protests re election.
†Unseated by recount and new election called.

At no time could Algoma be regarded as a safe seat, and the post-Conmee years show that any impression of growing Liberal strength was illusory. Up to 1900 there were never as many as 3200 votes cast in northwestern Ontario. Even in the later elections, individual scattered polls recorded such minute numbers of voters that any mysteries created by the introduction of vote by ballot were transparent indeed. In almost every election, whether because of chicanery or the vagaries of weather, or both, returning officers failed to arrive at some of these polls with the ballot boxes,[8] and some voters were accordingly denied the franchise. Charges of corrupt practices were legion, yet the unseating of two members in a period of thirty-five years (one of them reinstated in the ensuing election in the riding of Algoma East) hardly marks frontier election practices as conspicuously more dubious than those of the more thickly populated areas of the province.

Similar to other areas also was the virulent partisanship of the local press. The Thunder Bay *Sentinel* began publication in 1875, proclaiming its commitment to the interests of the Conservative party and the special interests of the village of

Prince Arthur's Landing (later Port Arthur). Efforts to establish an equally partisan Liberal newspaper began also in the 1870s[9] but it was another decade before the *Weekly Herald and Algoma Miner* poured forth its praises for the Mowat government and the interests of the Ontario community to which Algoma West was seen to belong. The *Herald* had begun publication in 1882 as an avowed supporter of the Conservative party, focusing its interest on mining and local affairs,[10] but within a few months it was calling itself independent, then defending the conduct of the Liberal member, R.A. Lyon, against the federal Conservatives. The appointment as editor of James Dickinson, former reporter for the Toronto *Globe* and secretary of the Ontario Press Gallery,[11] had, by 1887, brought to the paper considerable talent, extended political reportage, and a predictable point of view. The only other newspaper before 1890, of which more than isolated issues survive, was the Fort William *Journal* which began its career in 1887 with an attempt at more objective reporting of the federal election of that year,[12] but its objectivity was usually noticeable only in comparison with its older-established rivals, and then only in its treatment of federal politics. To base estimates of the effectiveness or honesty of the Queen's Park representatives from western Algoma upon the descriptions given of them in the local press would be foolhardly indeed – yet, on some issues, these frenetic accounts contain the only contemporary evidence.

For the first eight years after Confederation, Algoma's member in the Ontario legislature was Toronto resident F.W. Cumberland – engineer, architect, railway promoter, friend of the Ottawa and Toronto Conservative establishment, surely an unusual 'representative' for the frontier. His links with his constituency were minimal. He never lived in it, and seldom visited it. His election was apparently secured through the interest of his associates in the federal Conservative party.[13] He was entirely dependent for information about local issues on individuals and groups that tried to maintain correspondence with him in Toronto, in spite of the difficulties in communication. It must be remembered that, throughout his years in the Ontario legislature, there was no telegraph or railway within two hundred miles of the Lakehead area,[14] and any contact with Toronto from November to April was 'tedious and uncertain.'[15] Letters sent during those months, when the legislature was traditionally in session, were routed by way of Duluth and took about two months to reach their destination.

Although no outright attack on Cumberland's effectiveness as a representative has been found, there are at least indications that individuals and pressure groups within Algoma were not relying solely upon his support in the early 1870s. W.B. Frue, the manager of the Silver Islet mine, represented an American syndicate working for advantageous provincial legislation and the protection of its interests. Frue's letters make it plain that, although he might give Cumberland formal and brief notification of events, he was expending his energy where he thought it would do the most good – on detailed presentations to members of the Ontario cabinet.[16] Similarly, Peter McKellar, member of a Fort William family deeply involved in the mining developments of the time, made use of his business trips to Toronto to get in touch with members of the cabinet, as well as to hold brief conversations with Cumberland.[17]

By 1875, the Algoma electorate seems to have come to two conclusions, one of them virtually unanimous, the second widely enough held to determine the outcome of the election. The voters desired a representative who had closer ties with the district, who lived in it for at least part of each year. Such a man was unlikely to have the provincial reputation of a Cumberland; success in elections in the district might well depend on the very qualities least likely to produce a provincial reputation. Those nominated to contest the seat in 1875 were Edward Biggings, a Sault Ste Marie newspaper editor, and Simon J. Dawson, a surveyor long associated with the western part of the district. Both men emphasized in their campaigns their connections with the district itself and the issues of purely local interest upon which they were prepared to do battle in Toronto.[18]

The second conclusion seems to have been that the Mowat government would continue in office, and that it would be desirable for Algoma to elect a supporter of the government. The acceptance of this point of view would depend not only on the strength of individual devotion to the Conservative party, but also upon certain local issues. The Conservative candidate came from Sault Ste Marie and would poll some votes in eastern Algoma by virtue of his place of residence alone. In the Thunder Bay area, fierce rivalries had grown up in which it was popularly believed the Liberal Mackenzie government at Ottawa had deliberately chosen a railway policy favourable to Fort William.[19] This circumstance made it unlikely that many residents of Prince Arthur's Landing would vote for an avowed Liberal. A crisis of conscience was avoided by having Dawson run as an Independent, on the understanding that he would support the Mowat government in the House. This ploy won him the election.

Dawson's political career in Ontario was a brief one, but both the causes he espoused and the circumstances of his move to the federal arena in 1878 are significant in considering the role of the frontier politician. In the legislature, the change from the Cumberland approach became evident almost immediately. Within a few days of the opening of the 1875 session Dawson challenged the statement that stipendiary magistrates were overpaid and underworked, and cited the particular difficulties attending the administration of justice in Algoma.[20] Henceforth, he seldom missed an opportunity to draw to the attention of the House the special application of the legislation under discussion to northern conditions – the malfunctioning of the contract system when used for small expenditures on Thunder Bay colonization roads,[21] the desirability of permitting timber licences to be issued in free grant townships,[22] the application of the Licence Law in regard to sales of liquor to Indians,[23] the need for extending the franchise to the Indians of Algoma, whether they lived on reserves or not.[24] But it soon became clear that these interventions struck few sympathetic chords in the minds of his audience. Again and again the next speaker would continue the debate, as if after a digression. There were no comments upon his remarks, no questions addressed to him; there was not even the publicity of ridicule, unless some of the cheers punctuating his longer speeches could be so interpreted.

For the first of his full-scale orations Dawson chose a subject which was to become familiar to his listeners for years to come – the miracles of Algoma development, the potential value of its natural resources, the beauty of its scenery, the magnificent future that awaited his constituency.[25] The same speech, with variations, appeared at least once a year and, in 1883, the *Herald* claimed he was still using it in the dominion Parliament.[26] There is at least a suggestion that the enthusiastic recitation of the glories of Algoma was beginning to pall in Toronto when, after a very long speech by Dawson, Premier Mowat commented: 'Every member of the House had listened with deep attention to the remarks of the hon. gentleman who had just taken his seat, as indeed they always did to his speeches regarding the resources and the progress of the district he represented. (Hear, Hear)'[27]

As an Independent, Dawson was not committed to support the Mowat government on every occasion and there were examples of some restiveness from the beginning.[28] In time, his divergence from party orthodoxy undermined any possibility that he might become an effective spokesman for Algoma at Queen's Park, for his stand on the Manitoba boundary question alienated most of his colleagues. His statement that reports concerning the Hudson's Bay Company territory were all one-sided and framed in a spirit of antagonism to the company[29] did get reported, but does not seem to have been well received. Further comment on the tenuous historical links binding Algoma to southern Ontario was not officially reported, and only chance references to it survive in contemporary accounts.[30] One can assume that he was less explicit on the subject of separatism in Algoma than in his 1880 speech before the House of Commons[31] which brought down upon his head the wrath of the Toronto *Globe*. Then he was denounced as one of the members of Parliament who were 'traitors to themselves and their constituents.'[32]

It is impossible to gauge precisely to what extent Dawson's concern with the boundary issue and dissatisfaction with his ambivalent position at Queen's Park influenced his decision to resign his seat and contest the 1878 election in the federal riding of Algoma. He was successful, and continued to represent the district, first as an Independent, and then as a Conservative, until 1891. The question of provincial boundaries, the conflict between federal and provincial powers, the development of east-west transport were all matters in which he and his constituents had vital interests, but when he spoke on these matters he was not solely or uniquely a frontier politician. Still less did he represent the only frontier area in the dominion of the 1880s. It is thus within the context of Ontario provincial politics that Algoma's representation can most effectively be studied.

When Dawson resigned, an avowed Liberal was chosen by acclamation to succeed him. Robert A. Lyon was a lumberman and merchant from Michael's Bay, Manitoulin Island, to which he had moved from Milton some years before. His knowledge of the western half of his constituency was slight, even though communication with many parts of his riding was improving as railway and telegraph lines were being constructed. In 1879 his brother W.D. Lyon (MPP for Halton, 1875–9) became the stipendiary magistrate for Thunder Bay at a time when conflicts of jurisdiction between provincial and federal authorities were occurring in the Rat Portage (Kenora) area,[33] but the new member for Algoma did not need accounts of his brother's difficulties to convince him of the justice of the Ontario cause. Not for him were heretical thoughts of secession. Not for him either were the Dawson flights of oratory. Introduced in the legislature 9 January 1879, R.A. Lyon spoke rarely and briefly. Once, he mentioned the need for more roads in Algoma and the desirability of buying all supplies (except pork and flour) in Toronto, where they were 26–30 per cent cheaper than in the north.[34] Rather perfunctorily, he moved the annual resolution for a select committee to inquire into the possibility of subdividing the Algoma Riding,[35] then sat silent as the discussion swirled away out of his control. Mowat wished to wait for the next census returns, but before Lyon could withdraw his motion, John C. Miller of Muskoka-Parry Sound suggested the creation of a new province instead, and quoted Simon Dawson's views on the matter. Lyon's own position was expressed a week later when Miller was claiming that disaffection with Ontario rule was strong in the north, and that a resolution asking for separation had been sent to Ottawa. Lyon said that this was 'a buncombe resolution and did not express the feelings of his constituency generally.'[36] He added that he was pleased that so much new territory was to be added to Ontario as a result of the award of the boundary commissioners.

In each of the sessions from 1879 to 1884, the striking point about Lyon seems to have been his conformity to party and his silence in debate. Brief comments such as those brushing aside any suggestion of corruption in the awarding of colonization road contracts[37] formed most of his contributions. Certain phrases like 'colonization roads' seem to have awakened him to make a conditioned response. Sometimes he did not even hear the first pealing of the bell and his mouth watered only when another member made specific reference to events in Algoma. In the debate on the Sault Ste Marie railway line, he was at last moved to indicate the advantage this enterprise would confer on eastern Algoma.[38] Only once or twice in these years did he make any comment on matters of particular concern to the western part of his riding. The hostile Thunder Bay *Sentinel* may have been extreme in describing him as 'neither ornamental nor useful,'[39] but the records of the assembly up to the spring of 1884 do make him appear the model backbencher.

Then, however, the Wilkinson bribery case erupted in the legislature and it soon became clear that Lyon had been subject to much more complicated pressures than his record would have led anyone to suspect. Two members of the legislature presented to the Speaker the money they claimed had been received from John Wilkinson and F.S. Kirkland as the price for voting against the government, bringing down the Mowat ministry, and taking part in a coalition with the Conservatives.[40] It was alleged that a number of Liberal members, including Lyon, had been offered a variety of inducements to join in such a scheme, in fact that a round robin bearing the signatures of these members was in existence, although the interesting document was never produced. In these early revelations, primary interest was naturally centred upon the two representatives of southern Ontario constituencies who had made the affair public. The *Globe*, predictably, applauded their public spirit for leading the 'conspirators' on until sufficient evidence had accumulated.[41] The *Mail*, whose editor was one of those charged with conspiracy, was equally predictable in questioning the motives of these members.[42] As the revelations continued, the role of the frontier and of the member from Algoma became clearer, and important sidelights upon northern attitudes toward government policy can be discerned along with the personal dilemma that confronted Lyon in 1883–4.

Among those accused of conspiracy in this case, F.S. Kirkland was unique in two ways. He was an American citizen and he had business connections in the Thunder Bay area. He had formed a lumber company, in which Thomas Marks of Port Arthur was one of the directors, to operate on the Canadian side of Pigeon River, only to find that, under Ontario law, he must bid at public auction for the timber he thought had been acquired with the purchase of the land on which it stood.[43] When he was arrested, he was carrying letters from Marks, as well as from Thomas A. Keefer of Port Arthur and R.J. Peters of Manistee, Michigan, two men who were closely connected in mining enterprises in Thunder Bay. The *Globe* gleefully published all these letters, but Peters' was the only one that was at all explicit about the nature of the business dealings between the men. It referred to money available for securing favourable timber legislation in Canada, and also to his desire to buy pine lands in Canada.[44] It was claimed that Peters had already bought 10,000 acres on the Canadian side of the boundary, and that he was hostile to the Mowat government because he could not get a patent for the timber upon it. There seems little doubt that, irrespective of party allegiance, interested northerners, including Lyon, wanted the lands sold at a fixed price and giving the purchaser the right to standing timber,[45] which was what Peters wanted as well. Those caught up in the mining enthusiasm of the Thunder Bay area in the early 1880s had an additional reason for urging the change, as they negotiated for American capital to finance their projects.

Pressure groups within his constituency and his own interests inclined Lyon to the Peters view. Was such pressure enough to cause him to oppose government policy? On 28 September 1883 he had been re-elected by a narrow majority over his Conservative opponent, William Plummer of Sault Ste Marie. Almost at once reports of irregularities in election procedures throughout the riding began to come in. By early February, W.R. Meredith, the leader of the opposition, was scathing in his comments on fortuitous equinoctial gales that prevented the delivery of ballot boxes at certain points in Algoma.[46] In view of the later charge that Lyon was plotting with the Conservatives to dethrone Mowat, it is interesting to observe the harassment to which he was subjected by those with whom, it was claimed, he was about to throw in his lot. It was alleged that Edward Meek, a Toronto lawyer acting for Algoma Conservatives, promised Lyon that protests over the 1883 election would be dropped if he joined the Liberals defecting from Mowat. It was also alleged that Lyon was one of the signers of the round robin. It would appear that Lyon's desire to have the protests stopped and his agreement with the timber policy advocated by the 'conspirators' represented substantiated facts, but any relationship between these facts remains obscure.

In July 1884 Lyon testified before the commissioners investigating conduct of the members of the legislature, and he made it quite clear that he had been prepared to cast a vote against the government on the timber question.[47] He admitted attending a meeting in which Edward Meek had made some observation about dropping protests over the 1883 election, but doubted that Meek had any authority to make an offer in such a matter and denied that he had ever taken the remark seriously or allowed it to influence his decision in the matter of timber policy. Lyon subsequently announced his resignation, just as an election court convened to consider one of the more than eighty petitions to controvert the 1883 election.[48] With the subdivision of the Algoma riding, a by-election was required in any case. In 1885 R.A. Lyon was returned for the new riding of Algoma East, which he continued to serve until 1890.

The charges against the 'conspirators' were referred to the spring Assizes of 1884. There Chief Justice Hagarty noted the absence of precedents in British law to guide the court in such a case, and granted a defence motion to move the case to the Court of Queen's Bench. Various delays meant that the final disposition of the case did not come up until May of 1885, when all were acquitted.[49] The case then faded from the public view. Hector Charlesworth judged it significant in delaying a development of Conservative power in Ontario, believing that the public reacted against the 'conspirators' even if they were guilty of no offence known to the law.[50] The parallels with the much better known Gamey case of twenty years later are intriguing ones. But for frontier politicians certain points of special significance emerged. Party affiliation might mean little before the compulsive local force of a particular issue. Party leaders in Toronto might well be dubious of the loyalty of northern representatives after their experience with the ebullient Dawson and the apparently tractable Lyon.

In James Conmee, Algoma West found its first representative at Queen's Park and a man whose background seemed to fit more closely the stereotype of the frontier politician. He had been born in Grey County, where his father engaged in the lumber trade. As a boy in his teens, he had served in the 8th New York cavalry under General Custer, and had seen service in the American Civil War. By the early 1870s he had appeared in the Thunder Bay region to install machinery in the Oliver-Davidson lumber mill. In the next decade he became involved in numerous business enterprises in the community, cutting timber along the CPR right of way, establishing a planing mill, setting up the first telephone communication in Port Arthur, and promptly moving to make this enterprise a monopoly, purchasing a hotel.[51] In December 1884 he was elected mayor, to the disgust of the *Sentinel* which claimed that he had promised every hotel keeper in town a liquor licence if he were elected.[52] (Contemporary sources suggest that even if this were true and the promise had been kept, there would have been little perceptible change in the Port Arthur landscape.) Only a few months later Conmee made his bid for election to the provincial assembly, and the *Sentinel* delighted in reporting that he was facing charges of smuggling and of perjury.[53] But the Grand Jury returned no bill on either indictment.

The most celebrated legal case in which Conmee was ever involved did not, surprisingly enough, become grist for the political mill. Along with John D. McLennan, he held a contract for the building of part of the Lake Superior section of the CPR and when, late in 1885, the company held up payment on the grounds that its specifications had not been met, Conmee and McLennan sued for the sums they alleged were owing to them – at that time nearly $300,000. The company launched a counter suit alleging fraud or, at the very least, inaccuracy in the progress certified by the contractors' manager. The case was first heard in Toronto in early November 1886, and Judge Cameron agreed with the CPR contention that the matter should go to arbitration. The report of the arbitrators satisfied neither party to the dispute and the case did eventually go to trial; in August 1889 the CPR was ordered to pay $251,732.53 plus costs, and their counter suit was dismissed. The case then went to the Ontario Court of Appeals which upheld the judgment of the lower court.[54] The amounts of money involved (said to be the largest in any suit in Ontario up to that time)[55] and the battery of legal talent enlisted (B.B. Osler and Dalton McCarthy were among the counsellors for Conmee and McLennan, Samuel Blake and Christopher Robinson for the CPR) were sufficient to draw much attention to the case, at least at the beginning. As it dragged on, however, it became evident that this incident in the business career of James Conmee could not be used politically against him. He emerged the victor in too many rounds of the battle; public sympathy in his district could too easily be aroused in favour of a knight battling the CPR dragon;[56] and the case cut across political party lines. Conmee was a Liberal MPP while his partner's father was the Conservative MP for Glengarry.[57]

The succession of hearings in the case of Conmee and McLennan *v* the CPR kept Conmee's name before the public and, to some extent, merely to have been accused of being party to such a monumental fraud may have been of political advantage to him. On the other hand, if he were to become involved even on the periphery of some government scandal like the unhappy Lyon, his name would be blazoned before the public, probably as an arch-conspirator. It would never be possible for him to assume the near-anonymity of his predecessor, yet he arrived at Queen's Park with virtually no political experience and with few highly selective political contacts, for he had been removed from the southern Ontario ecumene since his teens. He was in the unenviable position of the political neophyte of whom much is expected, or suspected. In his first session in the legislature he was asked to second the address in reply to the Speech from the Throne, and *Globe* used this occasion to praise the new member. 'It is no disparagement to Mr Conmee to say that his best friends were delighted at the fluency with which it was delivered and the full and accurate knowledge of public matters possessed by the speaker. It is not often that a maiden speech is better received.'[58] It would appear that Conmee's conduct in the House in this first session became a matter of close scrutiny for political friends and enemies alike.

His record in the many years he represented Algoma West at Queen's Park justified neither the hopes nor the suspicions of 1886. By the 1890s he had survived two general elections and his business interests were burgeoning and spreading over most of northern Ontario. His interventions in debate were brief, often delivered with a bluff good humour, sometimes taking the form of quips at the expense of his opponents.[59] His vote was cast consistently in support of his party. Perhaps the most arresting feature of Conmee's record during his first five years in Toronto was his silence on issues that were being fiercely debated in his constituency, but upon which public opinion was so sharply divided that a strong stand by the representative of Algoma West could only lose him votes in some quarter. While Port Arthur battled the CPR over taxation of property – an issue that might effect the transfer of the divisional point to Fort William, and while the two towns squabbled over the right of a Street Ralway Company from one of them to run within the jurisdiction of the other, Conmee found it judicious to say so little that the *Sentinel* proclaimed its suspicions that the former mayor of

Port Arthur was a secret supporter of Fort William aspirations and that one protagonist in the celebrated Conmee and McLennan suit was now being supported by the CPR.[60] But the *Sentinel* had a long record of not being able to prove its case against Conmee, and neither could any other group of voters in Algoma West at this stage in his career.

But in the early 1890s, with the end of the silver boom and the closing down of the Thunder Bay mines whose future had seemed bright only a decade before, Algoma West was a constituency facing an economic crisis so acute that its representative could no longer afford to be silent. In the legislature, from the spring of 1891 on, seldom a day passed without his voice being heard. On 21 March, for example, 'There was a heavy gust of private bills. Mr Conmee fathered four.'[61] A few days later Conmee rose to the defence of the Ontario government's practice in the letting of contracts for colonization roads and, out of his own practical experience in construction work, he spoke 'with stinging vigor of the enormities of the tender system as exemplified by Ottawa.'[62] The climactic break came when the Hon. A.S. Hardy, commissioner of crown lands, was presenting the government's amendment to the Mining Act and Conmee's criticism of the existing practice was almost as severe as that of the leader of the opposition.[63] Attack on what was being superseded might, in the simple northern mind, be equated with support for the idea of amendments, but nevertheless the spectre that had haunted Lyon walked again.

The *Globe's* editorial position throughout the continuing debate was not personally critical of Conmee, nor was his loyalty to the party called into question, but there was real reluctance to accept his arguments or his descriptions of the plight of prospectors and miners. Approval was expressed, on the other hand, for the position Hardy adopted in the debate – that, in spite of the pleas of special interest groups, a fair share of the wealth derived from the mines must be secured to the people of the province generally.[64] Conmee continued his attack on the royalty clause, and urged the setting up of a mining commission to collect information and report to the House.[65] He criticized the attorney general and the commissioner of crown lands and referred to a 'Cabinet of lawyers' but, when members of the opposition seemed inclined to applaud this remark, he quickly added that it was all the worse when the leader of the opposition, another lawyer, assented to what was being done. Nonetheless, it was constantly Meredith and Conmee who were leading the attack on proposed government legislation, with A.F. Campbell (Liberal, Algoma East) mildly critical, but hedging his bets much more than the representative of the hard-hit mining region around Thunder Bay. Two of Conmee's motions went down to defeat, as did one of Meredith's.[66]

In the following year, with the Thunder Bay economic crisis continuing to deepen, Conmee was equally voluble in the assembly. He returned to the fray on the subject of the mining laws,[67] and also commented upon such diverse matters as provincial fisheries (30 March), the Liquor Licence Act (7 April), the qualifications of locomotive engineers (7–8 April), the duties and payment of High Court judges, the flag and the coat of arms (6 April). Some of these topics had long been of interest to him; his daughter stated, for example, that he had composed words for a national anthem which placed second in a competition to Alexander Muir's 'The Maple Leaf Forever,'[68] but the spate of utterances in these two sessions of the legislature cannot be explained on grounds of breadth of interest alone. Somehow, and quickly, he had to overcome a reputation for silence in Queen's Park proceedings – a silence which, no matter how judicious it had been earlier, now threatened his political future. He had constantly to keep reminding the House of Algoma West's 'dissatisfaction with the so-called mining policy of the government. It was too meagre and it was unworthy of the province.'[69] At the same time the *Herald*, of which he was now a co-owner,[70] described his efforts in detail for the benefit of his constituents. Perhaps the best use of Conmee's talents for publicizing an issue came when the government agreed to suspend the collection of royalties in certain circumstances for five or even seven years. The Conmee chorus of 'Make it ten' resounded through the House whenever any number was mentioned by any speaker on this issue – and there were many opportunities for such an intervention during the session. Eventually, Hardy had to take official note of the falling off of mining activity in the early 1890s, but he chose to blame the situation on the world decline in silver prices, not on Ontario mining policy.[71]

That Conmee emerged from these debates an unquestioned supporter of government policy in other areas without embittering his relations with his own party seems to have been due both to the understanding of men like Hardy and to Conmee's own manner of handling the problem. Pressure from his constituency demanded a certain stand, and Conmee carried the matter off with a certain burly grace. No one cried 'Conspiracy' when he introduced a motion, later carried, strongly advocating raising the pay of the leader of the opposition who had so frequently joined him in his attacks on the Mining Act amendments.[72] Conmee was asked to second the address in reply to the Speech from the Throne in 1894,[73] and, although his general theme was the prudence and moderation of the government, he was able to insert a brief sketch of what the Speech from the Throne would have included on the subject of mining legislation had he had the drafting of it. It was a deft and sometimes witty reconciliation of the demands of his party and his private view. Later, his opponents were to interpret Conmee's performance of 1891–4 as an attempt to secure cabinet office, and a threat of desertion from the ranks unless such an appointment were forthcoming.[74] This interpretation Conmee denied and his denial carried a good deal of conviction. In the last days of the 1894 session, with an election in the offing, the member from Algoma West was prominent in his defence of the government on every issue except mining policy. It would appear that it was intense local pressure and not disappointment in a search for promotion that guided his conduct.

In the 1894 election in Algoma West, the Conservatives were triumphant, but the margin of victory was only six votes. The victor was then unseated, a by-election was called for 9 February 1895, and James Conmee re-elected before the Eighth Parliament of Ontario met. But never again did he enjoy the kind of prominence in Queen's Park he had achieved in the early 1890s. During 1895 and 1896 he seemed to be confining his attention to business enterprises, often with specific northern companies or conditions in mind. He led a large delegation on behalf of a bonus for the Rainy River Railway Company.[75] He spoke briefly on the general regulations for street railway companies,[76] and on a resolution concerning municipal fire insurance.[77] Then, in 1897, the muted performance of the preceding two years was at least partially explained, and the unhappy defensive mood of his last years in the Ontario legislature was foreshadowed. It became clear that Conmee's interests were now shifting to federal politics. He had contested the Nipissing riding in the 1896 federal election, and had placed his resignation from the Ontario House in the hands of his solicitor with instructions to forward it to the Speaker. What other instructions Conmee had given were never made clear. What did emerge was that the letter was not forwarded, Conmee lost his bid for a federal seat, and remained a member of the provincial assembly. Months later he did offer to resign, but at that time the attorney-general, who professed ignorance of all the preceding events at the time at which they had occurred, advised him that resignation was neither necessary nor advisable. The Conservative party in Ontario now had a new leader, J.P. Whitney, who was reorganizing the opposition forces and scenting afar off the possibility of electoral victory. In the post-Mowat era that was just dawning, Whitney even found a quotation from Mowat that was appropriate for the occasion, one reflecting on the illegality of running for a federal seat without resigning from a provincial one. Conmee's conduct was embarrassing to the Liberals and the Hon. George Ross could only say that he 'could see no good in going to the expense of an election in the vast constituency of West Algoma. The mistake had occurred, and holding an election would not rectify it.'[78]

This incident had revealed Conmee as a vulnerable target for opposition attack. Long before their concentration upon special issues in 'new Ontario' helped Whitney and his party to achieve power, they looked closely at the career of the member from Algoma West, his personal financial dealings, and his alleged attempts to influence government illegally. From 1897 on, although Conmee might be flippant on one occasion and wear a mantle of injured innocence on another, his speeches were far too often defences of his personal conduct against opposition attack. He denied that he had used his position on the Railway Committee to further his own interests.[79] Against the charges of corrupt practices in the winning of his election campaigns, he flung back reminiscences concerning Conservative tactics at Rat Portage.[80] As early as 1901 his connection with the Algoma Central and Hudson's Bay Railway had come to the interested attention of J.P. Whitney.[81] Three years later, when a government subsidy to that railway was proposed, there was a dramatic effort to prevent Conmee and one other member of the House from voting on a matter in which, the opposition claimed, they were personally interested. Since each of the members mentioned was allowed to vote on the question of excluding the other, the Liberal party managed to assure each of them the right to vote on the railway subsidy and then the subsidy itself was granted, by a majority of three.[82]

The same session of the legislature was marked by an attempt to show how financially rewarding had been Conmee's transactions in Port Arthur real estate. W.R. Smyth (Conservative, Sault Ste Marie) demanded minute details about a government land deal in 1903 involving an exchange of property granted to St Joseph's Hospital and a piece of land already sold to Conmee for $500.[83] But the the repeated questions reveal more about the anxiety for evidence than the answers provide in the way of useful information. In the intense atmosphere of the 1904 session, with the Gamey charges against the Liberals stimulating heated discussions, most of the incidents involving Conmee seem anticlimactic.

During much of the session, he was deeply concerned over the passing of a private bill respecting waterpower development on the Kaministikwia River. This bill limped through committee in March and was eventually passed, with Premier Ross declaring it the worst tangled piece of waterpower legislation ever to come before the House. Snappishly, on the last day of a difficult session, he expressed his regret that 'Mr Conmee did not say what he had to say in less time.'[84] It was Conmee's last day in the legislature of Ontario; it was also the last occasion on which a Liberal premier of Ontario faced the legislature for twenty-nine years. But Conmee was not involved in the disasters of the Ontario Liberals. He resigned his seat and then contested successfully the federal riding of Thunder Bay-Rainy River in the 1904 election. He continued to represent the district at Ottawa until 1911 when ill health forced him to retire from politics and from winters on the frontier. He died in Arizona in 1913.

Conmee's survival in politics bears testimony to his shrewdness. In the legislature the issues upon which he chose to speak were those least divisive within his constituency; almost without exception they were issues of interest to his constituency. The desirability of maintaining official party support if he were to win elections had been impressed upon him from the beginning; the careers of Dawson and Lyon carried their particular lessons for any representative from northwestern Ontario. The Liberal party label Conmee wore could assure him some crucially important votes from others who had carried their party allegiances north with them. At the same time, he dared not allow that label and the obvious advantages of party support to push him into unquestioning acceptance of any government policy that was almost unanimously condemned in the north. The whole record of his battle over mining policy and his temporary removal from the political scene in 1894 bear testimony to that fact.

But what of the political philosophy that animated him, the most successful frontier politician of his time? Perhaps something of the erosive influence of the frontier on abstract theory emerges from the statement of J.A. Mathieu, who later represented the Rainy River district at Queen's Park for sixteen years. Mathieu was an American who first arrived in northwestern Ontario in 1900, without any party allegiance, and recalled his experiences in an interview many years later:

Q 'How did you become a Conservative?'
A 'Conmee, the Liberal, he asked me for support, and I wouldn't give it to him. I was cutting on Indian land at the time, and he had my contract cancelled. I didn't like that kind of liberalism, so I became a conservative – just got my citizenship papers and I was drafted for the next election.'[85]

In spite of the party differences between the two men, it can be questioned whether their concept of political power and its uses differed markedly. Conmee, like Mathieu after him, was a business man in politics. His business interests antedated and informed his political career. His political career made possible a vast expansion of his business interests. Power seemed to consist of a licence to operate financial enterprises remote from scrutiny, but Conmee was to find that Sault Ste Marie and even Port Arthur were not so remote from the Toronto of the twentieth century as they had been in the nineteenth. West of Port Arthur, Mathieu discovered that obscurity lasted another few years, until the timber scandals of 1919 erupted and menaced the career of his friend, G. Howard Ferguson.[86]

From all his public pronouncements and private business dealings, it is clear that Conmee was an ardent supporter of laissez-faire and of the free flow of goods and capital across the Canadian-American border. One of the rare occasions on which he referred to any other articles of his political creed was the debate over the Separate Schools Act, in which he discussed the rights of minorities embodied in Gladstone's Home Rule Bills and identified the liberality of the treatment of Canadian Catholics with the Liberal party of Canada.[87] But there is no indication that this concern for minorities extended any farther – to the French Canadians who constituted about 25 per cent of the labour force in the lumbering industry in northwestern Ontario around 1900,[88] for example. Still less did his earlier personal battle over the practices of the CPR move him to consider the labour practices of that company within his riding.[89] In the increasing social unrest of the Thunder

Bay area after 1900 he apparently perceived no cause for alarm; secure in his economic and political success, he saw no reason for change.

At first glance, the differences between Cumberland, Dawson, Lyon, and Conmee seem to preclude any possibility of generalization concerning the genus *frontier politician*. Two of these men were Roman Catholic, two were Protestant. Two were Liberal party supporters, one Independent, one Conservative. Two were Scottish by birth, one English, and one Irish-Canadian. The social classes from which they had come, their education and cultural interests, their personalities and their manners were so different that any stereotype of the frontier politician becomes absurd. Yet, a pattern does emerge, – that of the entrepreneur in politics. All these men were speculators in northern real estate; all were gambling upon the development of natural resources they saw as unlimited; all turned to politics as a means of securing more rapid development of the area as a whole or some particular segment of it. Their real story, in so far as it can be pieced together, is to be found not in the debates of the assemblies to which they were elected, but in scattered and fragmentary records of business dealings involving the north.[90] The size of the provincial riding they represented and the diversity of their interests tended to obscure the fundamental similarities between them. It was only when the north came to be represented by five men after 1902, when the diamond became fragmented, that the various facets became clearer and more easily scrutinized. Douglas Cameron, elected member for Fort William-Lake of the Woods in 1902, was a spokesman for an easily identifiable pressure group; his business association was clear – with the Rat Portage Lumber Company and the western lumbermen's organization.[91] Dr T.S.T. Smellie, who defeated Cameron in 1905, was soon seen to be a representative deeply concerned about social issues on the frontier, a somewhat crotchety humanitarian. But when men like Cameron and Smellie were elected, one stage of frontier development had already passed – an age in which the very range of economic possibilities had created its own enthusiasm, in which the extractive and exploitative nature of the area they represented was reflected in the attitudes of the politicians it served.

NOTES

1 Charles W. Humphries, 'The Gamey Affair,' *Ontario History*, LIX, 1967, 101–9; Hector Charlesworth, *More Candid Chronicles* (Toronto 1928), 137–8
2 Ontario Archives [OA], Ontario, Legislative Assembly, *Debates* [newspaper Hansard], 26 Jan. 1876, 30 Jan. 1878 (microfilm)
3 Ibid., 2 March 1878
4 Ibid., 26 Jan. 1876
5 Ontario, Statutes, 1885, 48 Vic, c 2, s 8

6 Ibid., 2 Ed. vii, c 4, s 2

7 Most of this material is derived from Roderick Lewis, comp., *A Statistical History of all the Electoral Districts of the Province of Ontario since 1867* (Toronto 1967) with some details from the *Parliamentary Guide* and newspaper accounts. Lewis, for example, lists Dawson as a Liberal but the biographical note provided for the *Guide* as well as the accounts in the Thunder Bay *Sentinel* and the Algoma *Pioneer* (Sault Ste Marie) leave no doubt of his party affiliation.

8 Newspaper Hansard, 7 Feb. 1884

9 G.B. Macgillivray, *A History of Fort William and Port Arthur Newspapers from 1875* (Toronto 1968), 6–7

10 *Weekly Herald and Algoma Miner*, 15 April 1882

11 Toronto *Globe*, 30 Jan. 1886

12 Fort William *Journal*, 31 March 1887, 12 Nov. 1887

13 Newspaper Hansard, 14 Jan. 1868 includes letter, dated 29 June 1867, from Hon. Alexander Campbell *in re* first elections in Algoma.

14 Thunder Bay *Sentinel*, 29 July 1875 (first issue)

15 OA, Education Department, Incoming General Correspondence, 1873, Amos Bowerman (of Prince Arthur's Landing) to the Chief Superintendent of Schools, 5 Sept. 1873

16 Public Archives of Canada [PAC], MG 28, iii–19, Algoma Silver Mining Company Papers, W.B. Frue to Cumberland, 4 April 1872; Frue to Hon. Adam Crooks, 4 April 1872

17 Diary of Peter McKellar, 1874, entries of 6, 8, 9, 15, 24, and 28 Oct. (MSS in possession of Mrs Gordon McLaren of Thunder Bay)

18 PAC, MG 29 E–I, Algoma *Pioneer* Extra, 16 July 1875, Edward Biggings to the electors of Algoma; 26 Nov. 1875, interview with S.J. Dawson

19 *Prince Arthur's Landing and the Terminus of the* c.p.r. (Toronto 1878), 8; John King, 'c.p.r. Construction in Fort William,' Thunder Bay Historical Society, *Papers*, 1909–10, 46–7; M.E. Arthur, 'The Landing and the Plot,' *Lakehead University Review*, 1968, I, 2–9

20 Newspaper Hansard, 13 Dec. 1875

21 Ibid., 17 Dec. 1875

22 Ibid., 27 Jan. 1876

23 Ibid., 2 Feb. 1876

24 Ibid., 15 Feb. 1877

25 Ibid., 15 Dec. 1875

26 *Weekly Herald*, 16 May 1883

27 Newspaper Hansard, 30 Jan. 1878

28 OA, Col. Charles Clarke Papers, Dawson to Clarke, 7 May 1878; newspaper Hansard, 27 Feb. 1878

29 Newspaper Hansard, 4 Feb. 1876

30 James C. Hamilton, *The Prairie Provinces, sketches of travel from Lake Ontario to Lake Winnipeg* (Toronto 1876), 192 contains additional detail on the 4 Feb. 1876 speech.

31 Canada, House of Commons, *Debates*, 1880, I, 61–2, 18 Feb. 1880

32 Toronto *Globe*, 23 Feb. 1880

33 Ontario, *Sessional Papers*, 1887, no 19, letters of W.D. Lyon to Oliver Mowat, 23 Feb. and 1 April 1881; OA, Irving Papers, Hugh Sutherland to Hon. T.B. Pardee, 26 Sept. 1883

34 Newspaper Hansard, 24 Feb. 1879

35 Ibid., 26 Feb. 1879

36 Ibid., 5 March 1879

37 Ibid., 15 Feb. 1881

38 Ibid., 1 March 1881

39 Thunder Bay *Sentinel*, 2 March 1885
40 Toronto *Globe*, 19 March 1884
41 Ibid., 20 March 1884
42 Toronto *Mail*, 19 March 1884
43 *Weekly Herald*, 27 March 1884
44 Toronto *Globe*, 19 March 1884
45 Ibid., 24 March 1884; *Weekly Herald*, 17 April 1884
46 Newspaper Hansard, 7 Feb. 1884, 22 Feb. 1884, 7 March 1884
47 Toronto *Globe*, 18 July 1884
48 Thunder Bay *Sentinel*, 1 Aug. 1884
49 G.M. Rose, ed., *A Cyclopedia of Canadian Biography* (Toronto 1888), 726, Edward Meek entry
50 Charlesworth, *Chronicles*, 132–3
51 Lakehead University Library, Whalen Papers, 'Incidents in the Life of James Conmee 1848–1913,' a speech delivered to the Thunder Bay Historical Society, 25 Feb. 1936, by Laurel Conmee Whalen.
52 Thunder Bay *Sentinel*, 19 Dec. 1884, 8 Jan. 1885
53 Ibid., 12 June 1885
54 Ibid., 3 April 1891. This is the best summary of the various stages through which the case had progressed up to that time, betraying none of the newspaper's usual anti-Conmee bias, but merely reporting an important story. Publicity around the beginning of a celebrated case is illustrated by the Toronto *Mail*, 6 Nov. 1886.
55 Toronto *Mail*, 9 Dec. 1886
56 *Weekly Herald*, 8 Aug. 1886
57 Ibid., 18 Dec. 1886
58 Toronto *Globe*, 30 Jan. 1886
59 eg, Newspaper Hansard, 3 March 1886, 9 March 1886, 6 April 1887, 27 Feb. 1889
60 Thunder Bay *Sentinel*, 1 and 23 April 1892
61 Toronto *Globe*, 22 March 1891
62 Newspaper Hansard, 22 April 1891
63 Ibid., 29 April 1891
64 Toronto *Globe*, 23 April 1891
65 Newspaper Hansard, 28 April 1891
66 Ibid., 1 May 1891
67 Ibid., 23 March 1892, 6 April 1892, 9 April 1892
68 Whalen Papers, Laurel Conmee Whalen copied the words of this anthem from a manuscript in her possession.
69 Newspaper Hansard, 25 May 1893
70 Macgillivray, *Newspapers*, 73–5
71 Newspaper Hansard, 10 April 1894
72 Ibid., 2 May 1891
73 Ibid., 15 Feb. 1894
74 Ibid., 12 Aug. 1898
75 Ibid., 4 April 1894
76 Ibid., 8 April 1895
77 Ibid., 18 March 1896
78 Ibid., 19 March 1897
79 Toronto *Globe*, 30 March 1901
80 Newspaper Hansard, 6 Feb. 1902
81 Toronto *Globe*, 30 March 1901
82 Ibid., 21 April 1904

83 Ontario, Legislative Assembly, *Journals*, 1904, 195–6, 23 March 1904; 218, 28 March 1904
84 Newspaper Hansard, 24 April 1904
85 OA, interview with Mathieu by L. Waisberg and V. Nelles, 29 July 1965, research notes for the history of the Department of Lands and Forests, *Reviewing Nature's Wealth*, by Richard S. Lambert and Paul Pross.
86 Peter Oliver, 'Howard Ferguson, the Timber Scandal and the Leadership of the Conservative Party,' *Ontario History*, XLII, 1970, 166
87 Newspaper Hansard, 23 April 1894
88 OA, J.P. Bertrand, 'The Timber Wolves,' 12 (unpublished manuscript)
89 See Jean Morrison, 'Community in Conflict: a study of the working class in the Canadian Lakehead, 1903–1913' (unpublished MA thesis, Lakehead University, forthcoming.
90 A number of references to Dawson's and Lyon's business interests are to be found in PAC, RG 10 C–3, Indian Affairs Department Letterbooks. In the Ontario Archives, the fragmentary Dawson Papers, as well as the Alexander Campbell Papers and the Col. Charles Clarke Papers, and the Crown Land Papers for the townships of Neebing and McIntyre throw some light on the extent of Dawson's private interests. For Conmee, the sources are even more diverse and the evidence they present extremely difficult to interpret. PAC, RG 16 A 5–7, Port Arthur Customs Records, and RG 12 A–1, Port Arthur Shipping Register, 1886–1913, contain some references as do OA, Lands and Forests Papers, Applications for Timber Licences, Ground Rent Journals. The Minutes of the Port Arthur Town Council from 1884 on touch upon some of his local enterprises, as do the James Whalen Papers. Conmee's habit of forming companies with his son-in-law, James Whalen, and others, and later withdrawing from the partnership, makes a study of his direct financial interest in particular pieces of legislation before the Ontario House difficult to ascertain.
91 OA, Lumbermen's Association Minutes. Lists of members, copies of briefs submitted by western lumbermen, 1898 and 1905

Edward Barnes Borron, 1820-1915
Northern Pioneer and
Public Servant Extraordinary

Morris Zaslow

Few Ontario residents recognize the name of E.B. Borron or can guess his claim, if not to fame, then at least to be remembered with appreciation. Yet few men of his time played a more important part in shaping the present-day province. Borron makes an interesting subject for study for his contributions to the provincial programmes of northern expansion and resource management. His life also sheds light on another area of concern in this age of 'big government' – the impact of the individual on government policy formulation and the shaping of public opinion. A study of E.B. Borron's career is timely, too, because of current interest in the contributions of lesser figures in government, industry, and the arts; and in the general problem of the role of the individual in shaping the course of history.[1]

Edward Barnes Borron's background was that of the early nineteenth-century English country gentry. His father, John Arthur Borron of Wooldon Hall near Warrington, Lancashire, was a man of the Industrial Revolution who engaged in agricultural, manufacturing, and mining enterprises, with which he associated his many sons. His mining interests included salt-making, coal-mining, and the management of lead mines in Scotland, notably one at Leadhills in Lanarkshire. Edward, the sixth son, was intended for a mining career, and with that in mind was enrolled in Dr Bruce's Academy in Newcastle-on-Tyne, which had an enviable reputation for scientific training. From there Borron proceeded to the University of Edinburgh, but withdrew because of illness after a single term. He entered his father's businesses as a youth of fifteen in 1836, working in several mines, particularly at Leadhills (from 1838). When his older brother left the business, the twenty-one-year old Edward began eight years as manager of the Leadhills mine (1842–50) and returned for a second period (1858–61), until the family disposed of their interest in it.

North America with its wonderful opportunities beckoned to members of the large Borron family. At least two brothers and one sister moved to the United States, while Edward and another sister settled in Canada. Edward came out in 1850 and found employment in the mining industry, mainly as manager from 1852 to late 1857 of the copper mine at Bruce Mines, north of Lake Huron. This was the largest undertaking of the Montreal Mining Company, which had secured title to many promising mining locations along the shores of Lakes Superior and Huron. Attracted by the rich surface showings, the company had invested a large sum on buildings, mine workings, and the ore-dressing plant, most of which was wasted because of bad planning and a failure to select a suitable concentrating process. Borron's main innovation was to change the method of miner payment from the 'tut-work' system, based on the quantity of rock brought to surface, to the 'tribute' system, where payment depended on the amount of dressed ore mined. This led the miners to concentrate on the richest veins, and, coupled with higher copper prices, made the operation profitable at intervals from 1852 to 1865 when, as Borron had long advised, the mine was finally sold. Borron had resigned over this and other policy matters at the end of 1857 and had returned to Scotland to manage the Leadhills mine.

He was back again in the upper Great Lakes country in 1862, however, engaging in local mining activities. In 1869 the Province of Ontario, under the General Mining Act of that year, appointed him its land agent and mining inspector for the Lake Superior Mining Division based at Sault Ste Marie. He was empowered to grant or renew miners' licences, register mining claims, and, as an *ex officio* justice of the peace, to settle disputes relating to licences, claims, locations, and boundaries. There was very little mining activity; in four years he issued fifty to sixty licences and granted a few claims. He resigned in 1873, disgusted by the ineffectiveness of the office, and no successor was appointed. This experience, however, familiarized him with each mining property and gave him an unmatched knowledge of the geological, mining, and economic conditions of the district.

The position also contributed to his election in 1874 as member of parliament for Algoma, which he carried easily (Borron 436, W.J. Scott 258, P.J. Brown 18) as a supporter of the Liberal government of Alexander Mackenzie, his majority coming mainly from Bruce and Wellington mines and Manitoulin Island. He had a narrower lead at Sault Ste Marie, while Scott headed the poll at Fort William.[2] He did not take his seat in the House of Commons until 7 April 1874, almost midway through the session. Three other MPs from remote constituencies were also introduced to the House at the same time, and all four received the full sessional indemnity 'as if they had been present and taken their seats in this House on the 26th March last, under the special circumstances connected with the Election and Return in these cases.'[3] Though some fifty elections went before the courts over various allegations of irregularities, Algoma was not one of them. The contest had not lacked its worrisome aspects, however; Borron wrote much later of 'having been completely ruined by the expenses of my election in 1873–74.'[4]

He was a useful if unspectacular member of parliament, attending to his constituents' needs before ministers and departments, serving on two Commons committees, and voting on most recorded divisions. Even some of his abstentions may have been deliberate, such as on a prohibition amendment or opposition resolutions against the government's Pacific Railway policy. The work on the Committee on Expiring Laws was not very onerous, but that of Immigration and Colonization was another matter. He asked a few questions of the immigration officials and experts on the Prairies or British Columbia who appeared before the committee. He also took a hand at advertising his own district by placing reports on local conditions at several settlements on record in the committee's printed annual report for 1877.

In the House of Commons he spoke once or twice per session, usually on questions of concern to his district. The Pacific Railway project, which would have to pass through the constituency, was the most important of these. In 1875, while discussing the location of the route, he argued in favour of a Lake Superior terminus at Thunder Bay rather than at Nipigon Bay, and for a route that stayed close to the Lake Huron shore and came within thirty miles of Sault Ste Marie. Later, in 1878, when the government's policy became one of building the railway in sections as a public work, Borron urged the importance of pushing ahead with the part of the railway north of Lake Huron: 'Surely the people of Montreal and Quebec could not be so blind to their own interest or to the interest of the people of Manitoba, and the North West, as not to perceive the immense importance of the extension westward of the Canada Central Railway and Georgian Bay Branch, two most important links in this great chain of railway communication.'[5] Such a location, he contended, would provide an easy, direct rail route east to the Atlantic via Montreal, plus a useful lake port to attract the traffic of both the American and the Canadian Northwests. Because of the time required to complete the all-Canadian railway, this would be a useful practical solution for the foreseeable future:

He hardly thought there was an hon. member in this House so sanguine as to believe that the section of our Canadian Pacific Railway lying north of Lake Superior would be completed in less than twenty-five years. It will tax the whole energies of this Dominion to construct the railway from the head-quarters of Lake Superior to the Pacific Ocean, and it was impossible to predict when the intermediate section between the head of Lake Superior and Lake Nipissing could be finished. In the meantime, we would be dependant on other lines of communication passing to a greater or less extent through United States territory, and that for nearly six months of each year.[6]

Such pessimism was widespread, and no doubt was genuinely felt by Borron. He was using it, however, for the benefit of his constituency, for the effect it might have on trade patterns and building up its ports.

Another subject he raised more than once involved the Indians' annuities under the Robinson Treaty of 1850.[7] That treaty had promised that these were to be increased to $4.00 per head if government revenue from the territory ceded reached the point where such payment was justified. Borron argued that as the area was now yielding about one million dollars a year in land sales, leases, rents, royalties, and dues (to Ontario), the time was overdue for raising the Indians' annuities: 'They were peaceable and law abiding; perhaps if they had not been so peaceable their interests would not have been so long neglected.'[8] The government referred to legal complications as reason for delay, but after the session ended Edward Blake, then minister of justice, advised Borron he would try to have the increase paid at once: 'I hope to put the matter in train for judicial investigation as to the respective liabilities of Ontario and Canada but meantime it seemed to me the Indians ought not to suffer.'[9] The Indians secured the added sums, and eventually the courts ruled that Ontario would have to reimburse the dominion government for increases in the annuities to Indians under the Robinson Treaty. Borron's airing of the question reflected his lifelong sympathy for the Indian.

Borron spoke infrequently in the House on other matters, most notably in 1877 in the debate on the tariff, which was becoming the central issue of federal politics. His address followed the traditional Liberal arguments – that tariffs were highly exploitative because they were transferred in greatly increased amounts to the final consumers, unlike direct taxes which were the only equitable form of taxation. Tariffs also constituted favouritism, and led to monopolies and the exploitation of the public for private benefit: '... re-adjustment of the tariff with a view to benefiting and fostering manufacturing industries although called "protection" was really legalized spoliation, and class legislation in its most specious form.'[10]

Borron's political career ended in a mystery. In the spring of 1877 he sought to resign his seat, perhaps because of reluctance to face the hazard and expense of another general election. He applied to the government leaders for a suitable position in the public service in return for opening up his seat. Places discussed included those of immigration agent at Duluth, inspector of weights and measures in British Columbia, and dominion stipendiary magistrate for the District of Keewatin. Borron's request was considered, then declined, perhaps out of party considerations. As David Mills, minister of the interior, advised him: 'I have your private letter of the 8th inst. Mr Mackenzie had before mentioned the matter to me, and we had discussed it. There is nothing at present that we could do, and perhaps it would not be well to open your constituency up at the present moment, even if there was an opportunity. But since the receipt of your letter your case has been discussed by Mr Mackenzie, Mr Blake, and myself, and it will at a fitting opportunity receive the most favourable consideration.'[11]

The prime minister's reply was more direct and more specific: 'Mr Mills &

myself have been considering since the Session closed if we could find some position for you in connection with the North-West or the business of that Department [ie, Interior]. In the event of a vacancy I would like very much to know who is likely to be elected in Algoma as it would be very awkward at present to have an election lost in that constituency where we are doing so much work. I would be glad to hear from you on this point.'[12] Perhaps Borron could not give Mackenzie the desired assurance. At all events, he did not resign and create a vacancy, nor did he receive a federal appointment. He did not contest the next general election of 1878 either, and Algoma was easily carried, 885 to 480 votes, for the Conservative government of Sir John Macdonald by Simon J. Dawson, the explorer for whom the Dawson Route between the lakehead and Manitoba was named.[13]

Borron's quest failed with the federal government, but not long afterwards, in May 1879, he was offered a very important position for which he proved ideally suited. Through the good offices of his dominion colleagues and their Ontario government connections he secured the appointment in the provincial public service of stipendiary magistrate for Northern Nipissing, in which position he was to enter on the most significant phase of his career and the source of his future importance.

Borron's appointment reflected a stage in the progression of Ontario's claim to the Disputed Territory – the region north of the height of land beyond the Great Lakes and Ottawa River and west to Lake of the Woods – a dispute in which the province was engaged with the dominion from 1871.[14] In 1878 a commission of three, jointly appointed by the two governments, accepted Ontario's claims and awarded the province a northern boundary along the line of the English and Albany rivers, James Bay, thence due south to Lake Timiskaming. Though the dominion government, once again in the hands of the Conservatives under Sir John Macdonald, refused to accept the award, Ontario proceeded to organize its new territory into provisional districts and appointed two stipendiary magistrates to administer the added lands, with the 87th meridian as the dividing line between their jurisdictions. W.D. Lyon, the magistrate for the District of Thunder Bay, took charge of Ontario interests in the country west of Lake Superior, and E.B. Borron, appointed for the northern part of the District of Nipissing, was given charge of the area north of Lakes Superior and Huron and west of Lake Timiskaming. The purpose of these appointments was to provide for the administration of justice, and also, in the language of Borron's commission, '... to procure and forward information, and to advise and assist in settling all matters relating to our new territory.'[15]

In practice, Borron's work as stipendiary magistrate consisted of a series of annual inspection tours to study and report on conditions and prospects in parts of his vast district, and to make the best arrangements for carrying out the Ontario government's responsibilities in the territory, notably the administration of justice.[16] He made annual visits each summer from 1879 to 1886 inclusive, in the course of which, as he reported in 1887, he travelled 17,000 miles, nearly 8000 of them in birchbark canoes along the northern rivers and lakes. These were mainly traverses from southern Ontario to Moose Factory, the principal settlement of the region, by way of the rivers of the Great Lakes and Ottawa drainage basin, and the various tributaries of the Moose and Albany rivers. He also explored the coasts of James Bay and the adjoining James Bay Lowland region. In 1881 he took the census of population at many points, for the purpose making a special return journey along the entire length of the Albany River.

His title of stipendiary magistrate seemed to imply that the position would be a judicial one and should therefore have been given to a man with legal experience, not to a practical mining man whose legal training was limited to his service as a local justice of the peace. This resulted in an attack against his appointment that came to a head in the legislature on 1 April 1887,[17] when the government was accused of having appointed Borron from political motives. The opposition implied he had evaded his responsibility by not taking up residence with his family in the region, and that he did almost nothing to earn his $1200 annual salary. The government defended the appointment as justified by Borron's special skills and the value of his services, contended that he had not been able to take up residence because the status of the territory continued in dispute between the province and the dominion, and argued that his appointment as stipendiary magistrate gave the province a higher status in the territory than if he were simply an explorer in government pay. The opposition called for a report on Borron's judicial work, which the government broadened to include his entire work. The result was Borron's report for 1887,[18] in which he tried to refute the criticisms by demonstrating that his work could hardly have been performed by an ordinary lawyer, and that it '... will compare favourably with the time occupied and labour performed by any other Stipendiary Magistrate (Dominion or Provincial) in the North-West.'[19] The activities for each year since 1879 were presented under two headings, 'Return Shewing the Number of Cases brought before E.B. Borron ...' under which a variation of the short statement 'No cases brought before me this year' was repeated, and 'Other Duties Performed,' under which his travels and other work for the year were summarized.

The critics implied that Borron's failure to deal with any cases at all represented some shortcoming on his part. In fact, there was very little crime in the region, the Indians being naturally very law abiding and quite effectively supervised by the Hudson's Bay Company officers and the Church of England and Roman Catholic missionaries, the principal white men with whom they were in contact. The company left the native population to settle their own disputes and did not intervene except when its own men or property were involved. The few whites were also under the control of these superiors; a dispute in 1881 between the factor at Moose Factory and an employee was settled simply by shipping the servant back to Scotland. The company officers at Moose and Albany were unwilling to give up their authority to an outsider, partly for selfish reasons, but also out of fear that giving a foothold in the country to an Ontario government agent would hasten the pace of settlement and development, and in the long run would undermine the company's position. The continuing claim of the dominion government to the territory was a further complication. Borron realized that unaided he could not uphold Ontario's authority on the remote James Bay coast, separated from the settled parts of the province by a broad band of wilderness; and he considered it would be most unwise for Ontario to assert its authority prematurely without having sufficient force to make it effective in that area. He felt, moreover, that the existing situation was satisfactory, since the company in following its own interest had instituted practices that were suited to the local situation, as for example on the liquor question.[20] The province should consider seriously whether it was desirable to introduce the full apparatus of justice in a regular form to such a primitive land; if it did, it should begin by building a jail at Moose Factory and appointing at least one constable there. As for himself, in 1879, 'Finding it impossible to administer justice under the circumstances, and that there was an indisposition on the part of the Hudson's Bay Company's officers and servants to afford information, or to furnish me with the means of obtaining it otherwise, under the impression that such might be injurious to the interests of the Company, I concluded to return and report, before the navigation closed.'[21]

On Borron's advice, the government decided the best answer would be to associate the company with the provincial judicial system, and it arranged to appoint the two officers, J.L. Cotter at Moose Factory and W.K. Broughton at Fort Albany, as provincial justices of the peace. Borron was instructed to attend to the commissioning of the two gentlemen during his 1883 tour. Since the most convenient judicial centre for these posts was Sault Ste Marie in a different judicial district from his own, Borron needed a special commission 'per dedimus potestatem in and for the Provisional Judicial District of Algoma' to swear in the two new justices.[22] This was done, and the James Bay settlements were thus brought within the framework of the Ontario judicial system. That trip of 1883 was Borron's last to the James Bay coast; in the following seasons he devoted himself to examining the country farther south and west, along the route of the Canadian Pacific Railway.

In the main, as Borron was at pains to point out, his function was to describe conditions and assess the present and future situations from the provincial standpoint. He reported directly to Premier Oliver Mowat, and these reports, published as sessional papers by the legislature, were an invaluable source of information on the new territories. Borron furnished realistic descriptions of the settlements and their inhabitants on such subjects as the missions, education, Indian-white relations, economic conditions, and present and future threats to the stability of the region. Besides, in almost every report he suggested ways of aiding the inhabitants. In his ninth report, for 1890, he urged the province to press the dominion government to relieve the inhabitants of the heavy customs duties burden, to provide at least a monthly mail service, to bring the Indians in districts adjoining the railway under treaty, and to build a hospital in Moose Factory. The province should appoint a medical man to visit the Indians in the inland settlements, establish public schools where needed, introduce legislation to protect native hunting and fishing rights, regulate the fur trade, and work out appropriate land-use programmes for the country, especially as between lumbering and fur trapping. He even made an impassioned plea in 1886 against the cruel suffering inflicted on animals by steel traps, and pleaded for a return to the use of deadfalls and traditional methods of trapping as more humane.[23]

But the public was interested mainly in the settlement and development of the region by, and for, the modern industrial state that represented the idea of progress of that day. Borron's knowledge of the region made him cautious about proposing hasty, unwise development. Instead, he insisted on accuracy, and often called for further investigation and research into possible uses of the various resources. His evaluations of the natural resources of the territory were a most important side of his work, particularly in the later reports after 1885 that summarized his studies and travels and presented his conclusions.

Agricultural and timber possibilities were an important subject of his investigations. He differentiated among the several subregions – the unprepossessing James Bay coast; the first steppe inland from the coastal strip, which held better prospects for forestry and agriculture based on hardy field crops and stock raising; and in the valleys of the Abitibi and Albany rivers, pockets of good soil, capable of producing farm crops and lumber. Later Borron concentrated his attention on a wide band of highly favourable agricultural and forest land, forty miles or so north of the Canadian Pacific Railway – the earliest reports on what was to be known as the Great Clay Belt some fifteen years later. From his travels north by various routes he perceived the existence of a vast area of arable land extending more or less continuously from west of Lake Nipigon east to Lake Abitibi. In his reports of 1885 and 1886 which described this new fertile belt he advised the province to open experimental farms to ascertain the true qualities of the various areas, suggested simple drainage works to increase the amount of arable soil, and called for experimenting with uses for common woods like poplar. Above all, he appealed for transportation facilities to open up the country north of the railway, which he felt had been built a little too far south to lead to the fullest development of the country. The zones of good soils and forests should be tapped by a series of roads and railway branches, by using the navigable portions of the northward-flowing rivers that had served him so well, and by the development by the dominion government of the navigation of Hudson and James bays to open trade routes with the outside world.

Borron's later reports, based on the experience of his field investigations, offered proposals which were influential on future government policies. The time was propitious. The first wave of conservationist thought had emerged, and there was considerable public interest in natural resource questions. The provincial government, responding to this sentiment, after 1888 appointed commissions on natural resources matters – on fish and game, mineral resources, and Algonquin Park – and took noteworthy steps to establish other provincial parks as well.

It is somewhat surprising that the mining man Borron did not devote one of his final reports to the subject of mineral resources, even though his various reports referred to indications of iron ore, lignite coal, china clay, gypsum, peat, petroleum, and natural gas. Perhaps he did not do so because of the appointment in 1888 of a Royal Commission on the Mineral Resources of Ontario. His testimony before that commission was the full equivalent of one of his annual reports, and it coincided with a gap for 1889 in his series of reports.[24] His presentation drew on his fifty years' experience with mining. He was optimistic about the mining future of a large part of the region in view of the many known occurrences of copper, silver, gold, iron, and other metals. These, he felt, would be developed in their proper time – when the geology became better understood, processes and equipment were improved, transportation facilities opened the country, skilled labour became available, and good, close markets were developed. He suggested an educational programme to produce much-needed middle management and technical staff; also the importance of accurate records and statistics as guides to wise investments.

The federal tariff, he felt, hampered the advance of the industry by adding to mining costs. To encourage development, there should be no tariffs on mining machinery and other industry needs. Government policy should help to reduce costs; in general, 'It is only by aiding in the construction of railways, by liberal land laws and by furnishing thoroughly reliable information that the provincial government can assist the capitalists.'[25] To protect the public, railways should be built only after known resources warranted their construction; in return for governmental aid, the railways should be obliged to haul primary produce of the region at special low freight rates. In a later report (1895) to the Ontario Bureau of Mines that reiterated many of the foregoing points, he wrote more strongly of the need for absolutely accurate information, and avoiding extravagant mining booms in favour of steady, sound growth.[26]

Borron's final report to the legislature in 1891 was devoted entirely to a discussion of a subject that had been largely overlooked in his previous reports. The epochal *Report on the Lakes and Rivers, Water and Water-Powers of the Province of Ontario* reviewed the various uses of water resources, especially as a source of electric power. He pointed to the incalculably rich resource arising from the large, relatively even water flow of the interior plateau, and the vast amounts of electric power generated by the 1000 foot fall to the Great Lakes or James Bay, for which power new uses were constantly being developed. Such a vast property should be used in the public interest to secure adequate revenue, offset shortages of coal and other fuels, provide a cheap, reliable source of energy to attract manufacturers from high power cost countries (such as Britain), and give Canada some of the impetus that made Britain so great a manufacturing centre. Borron proceeded to enunciate a principle for the management of the resource that was one of the earliest such expressions in Canada:

CONSERVATION OF PUBLIC RIGHTS.

This report shows, or is intended to show, the importance of the water-powers of the province to the farmer, the manufacturer and the miner; in fact not only to the employer but the employees engaged in every industry, trade or pursuit. It is thus, a franchise in which the people at large, now and hundreds of years hence, are and will be deeply, nay, vitally interested. It is one, consequently, in which the rights of the Crown, or in other words, of the people, are to be most jealously and carefully guarded. The writer would, therefore, respectfully but strongly urge that in all future sales of land the water, whether of lakes or rivers (with the exception of that which may be required for domestic or sanitary purposes), should be reserved to the Crown as trustee for the benefit of the people of the province generally. And that water-powers should not be sold, but leased for a term of years, the rent charged varying according to circumstances; the position of the fall or rapid, the difficulties to be overcome before it can be applied or utilized, and even the purposes to which it is to be put, being all taken into consideration.[27]

The publication of this report was perhaps deliberate on the part of the government in order to build public support for what was to become official policy. Once instituted, the leasing – as opposed to selling – of water-power resources made it possible to proceed, fifteen years later, to the almost revolutionary experiment in public ownership of hydro-electric power resources that has been one of the most vital steps in the growth of twentieth-century Ontario.

Borron, who was now past the age of seventy, was less in the public eye after 1891, though he was by no means idle. Indeed, he made at least two further reconnaissance trips in 1895 and 1896 into northern Ontario. The first of these was on behalf of the newly-founded Bureau of Mines, whose director, Archibald Blue, sent him to report on the mineral resources of a district adjacent to a 100-mile section of the Canadian Pacific Railway between White River and Missinaibi stations. In the midst of the series of examinations along the interconnected rivers and lakes Borron took sick and had to return home by railway while his long-time assistant, John Driver, completed the work. The other journey was on behalf of the federal Department of Indian Affairs, to help with the Indian census in the Fort Frances district, perhaps because of his well-known *rapport* with the native peoples.

Though his work as stipendiary magistrate lost whatever *raison d'être* it might have had with the final abandonment of the dominion's claims to the Disputed Territory in 1889, Borron continued to be listed in the public accounts of Ontario under that designation till 1897, his salary being increased to $1300 in 1893. In 1899, however, the salary was reduced to $750, and in 1903 it apparently disappeared from the provincial accounts. He may have remained a little longer on the provincial payroll, for in 1904, in applying for a position in the dominion civil service in connection with the new railways across northern Ontario, Borron wrote of being '... greatly in need of a position the emoluments of which are good – if only for one year ... I am in the enjoyment of wonderfully good health, and next year if I live will be in a position, I hope, to retire from the public service and spend the remainder of my life (if any) in a milder climate.'[28] This letter to Sir Wilfrid Laurier was written in a firm hand and showed clarity of thought and expression, but Borron's age (83) made his request a hopeless one, even if the prime minister's reply was a courteous, '... I will, with pleasure place your application before them.'[29]

Borron seems to have retired around 1904, and to have lived in moderately comfortable circumstances in Toronto thereafter. City directories show him after 1905 residing in a series of houses, all in the Avenue Road district, notably 57 Lonsdale Road, where he lived after 1913 and which after his death continued to be occupied until 1936 by his widow and then by one of their daughters. He enjoyed reasonably good health, despite his advanced years, until the first winter of the Great War, when he broke his hip from a fall and died in his bed, probably of pneumonia, on Friday, 23 April 1915. Burial was on Monday, 26 April, in Mount Pleasant Cemetery.

It is surprising that the passing of a ninety-four-year old retired gentleman, so long out of the public eye, should have received the notice it did. In the spring of 1915 newspapers were filled with diplomatic and military operations, and with the first heavy Canadian casualty lists, for Borron's death coincided with the Battle of Ypres in which Canadian troops first encountered poison gas. In Toronto both the *Globe* and the *Evening Telegram* carried short obituary pieces on 24 April that emphasized his explorations: 'The first man to explore the great wilderness of the James Bay slope for the Ontario Government'; his reports, which '... are treasured not only for their valuable information but for the fine style in which they were written'; and his influence: '... he was a potent factor in the development of that new country.' The *Sault Daily Star* based its obituary mainly on the Toronto articles while adding a few details from local sources – such as the information that a street, Borron Avenue, was named for him; and that he had lived about ten years at Sault Ste Marie (presumably in the sixties and seventies), and was still fondly remembered in the city. Sheriff Richard Carney, who had been the returning officer in 1874, recalled that 'Mr. Borron was an honorable man ... He was a tall, fine looking man ...' and told how they had gone together to Manitoulin Island before the 1874 election, where Borron almost lost his life when his cutter went through the ice.[30]

What manner of man was Edward Barnes Borron?[31] His grandson and granddaughter recall a handsome, erect, tolerant, kindly, understanding gentleman, which agrees with the respectful obituaries that also stressed his gentlemanly qualities. Obviously he was endowed with remarkable physical health, being able to undertake arduous bush travels in his mid-seventies and continuing active until well in his eighties. His public career showed he was conscientious in performing his duties and possessed a sense of obligation to serve the public that was typical of his English background. Undoubtedly he used his political connections to secure an appointment where he would be able to fulfil his capacities while serving the public, but he only sought a position the duties of which he could fill acceptably, and which could satisfy his sense of purpose.

A strong faith in reason characterized Borron's attitudes towards the problems of his day and marked him as a true nineteenth-century liberal. He had an abiding belief in the power of the truth to direct men to proper courses of action. On specific questions his views were moderate, pragmatic, and realistic, and featured a sense of equity and fair play. He possessed the liberal's optimistic belief in orderly progress through the unobstructed operation of normal natural forces. Thus northern Ontario was bound to achieve a dazzling future when conditions became right – as they inevitably would: '... if our Canadian copper mines be such that if situated in Europe they would have realised very large profits and been considered very valuable, it necessarily follows that so soon as those favorable conditions arise in Ontario, then ... will copper-mining in this province become profitable, and the vast deposits of that metal in the copper-bearing belt north and west of the great lakes become in the fullest sense of the term valuable.'[32]

Borron's liberalism was not inconsistent with a humane sympathy and concern for the welfare of the northern peoples. He was tolerant of, and sympathetic towards, the native peoples of the region, who were entitled to be treated fairly by governments and helped to better their condition. They needed to be given every assistance from the provincial and federal governments to prepare the way for a smooth upward progression towards the civilized standards of the outside world.

But he was no uncritical disciple of the cult of progress; changes should be guided and tempered by the need to protect the interests of these people.

In his concern for the region and its people, he departed somewhat from more extreme laissez-faire positions. He conceived of an active role for the state in frontier development, to provide necessary public works and set up systems that facilitated and encouraged participation by entrepreneurs and private capital. The province should make special efforts to provide social amenities, facilities, and regulations appropriate to the welfare of the existing inhabitants.

His concept of public responsibility also led him to espouse certain restraints on the free operation of natural economic principles. This could be seen in the proposals to prevent the unnecessary tying-up of unworked mineral resources, the advocacy of special freight rates to help northern products to reach markets, and, especially, the proposition that water-power resources were too vital to the community to be allowed to pass irrevocably into private hands. Thus, like other advanced liberal thinkers of the period, Borron was beginning to perceive a need for the state to give a higher priority to the public welfare than to private interests.

E.B. Borron's career is thus very significant in terms of the history of Ontario. He informed and advised the provincial government on appropriate policies for northern development at a time when the region had little or no political power and needed to have its interests represented on the highest level of policy determination. His background, experience, and especially his direct access to Premier Mowat made him an important force in keeping the government of Ontario aware of the opportunities and problems of the new northern hinterland. Borron described the relationship with Mowat in the following terms: 'Sir Oliver allowed me much greater latitude in regard to the treatment of the subjects on which it seemed to me – in the interest of the province – that information and advice was necessary – than is usually allowed the most trusted public servants: and from the time of my appointment in 1879 until ... 1896 all my reports, whether public or confidential, were carefully read and considered by him. And in no instance that I remember did he express doubt or disapprobation of any assertion or statement contained therein.'[33]

Borron's influence on the public through his published reports was especially strong in the 1880s and 1890s, when southern Ontario was entering the modern industrial age and its interest in the north's potentialities was regressing somewhat from the previous generation's enthusiasm for conquering the frontiers of the Huron and Ottawa tract or those of the great Northwest. Along with a few other Ontarians, Borron helped keep this interest alive until the next period of popular awareness and concern that arose in the days of the Laurier boom. When new railways and technological innovations (pulp and paper, hard-rock mining, and hydro-electric power generation) were bringing the north into the economic nexus of the province, northern enthusiasm came easily to Ontario's people and governments. That renewed interest could then build, in some degree, on the information and ideas collected and published earlier by Borron.

Borron's advice undoubtedly helped shape the realistic policies of northern development of the Mowat government that were so progressive and effective for their time, and that managed the public domain so well – at least in comparison with the other jurisdictions of the day. He educated the people to a knowledge of the province's resources and made it aware of the importance of conserving the public domain in the interests of the people. The appointment of Borron, the miner and northern pioneer, as stipendiary magistrate in the Ontario civil service – a striking example of the great flexibility of the provincial administrative system of the time – reflected the highest credit on the government of the day. It yielded rich dividends for the province while giving a public-spirited citizen a unique opportunity to devote his special gifts to the service of the state, not as a run-of-the-mill civil servant, but as a public servant extraordinary.

NOTES

1 This sketch of Borron's early life is based on his own accounts in Ontario, *Sessional Papers,* 1891 no 3, 13–15, and Ontario, Royal Commission on the Mineral Resources of Ontario, *Report* (Toronto 1890), 92–100, 316–17, 402–4; also copy of a family genealogy, in possession of Dr R.J.M. Borron, Toronto.
2 Canada, *Sessional Papers,* 1874 no 59, 4
3 Canada, House of Commons, *Journals,* 1874, 322 (23 May)
4 Public Archives of Canada [PAC], MG 26, G 1(a), Laurier Papers, vol. 333, 89114, Borron to Sir Wilfrid Laurier, 18 Aug. 1904
5 Canada, House of Commons, *Debates,* 1878, 2510 (7 May)
6 Ibid.
7 Ibid., 1875, 1026–7 (1 April)
8 Ibid., 1026
9 Ontario Archives, Blake Papers, Letterbook no 1, 255, Blake to Borron, 30 Aug. 1875
10 Canada, House of Commons, *Debates,* 1877, 971 (23 March)
11 University of Western Ontario, David Mills Papers, Letterbook, 767, Mills to Borron, 13 June 1877
12 PAC, RG 5, B 9, Alexander Mackenzie Papers, Letterbook no 7, 578–9, Mackenzie to Borron, 18 June 1877
13 Canada, *Sessional Papers,* 1879 no 88, 5–6
14 See, M. Zaslow, 'The Ontario Boundary Question,' in Edith G. Firth, ed., *Profiles of a Province* (Toronto 1967), 107–17
15 Ontario, *Sessional Papers,* 1880 no 22, [5]
16 The travels, and the findings that resulted from them, gave rise to ten annual reports, printed as Ontario, *Sessional Papers,* 1880 no 22, 1881 no 44, 1882 no 53, 1882–3 no 39, 1885 no 1, 1886 no 1, 1887 no 64, 1888 no 1, 1890 no 87, 1891 no 3
17 *The Globe,* 4 April 1887; *The Mail,* 2 April 1887
18 Ontario, *Sessional Papers,* 1887 no 64

19 Ibid., 4
20 Ontario, *Sessional Papers*, 1880 no 22, 36
21 Ibid., 1887 no 64, 5
22 Ontario, Provincial Secretary's Department, General Correspondence, 1882, files 1068 and 1069, 19 May 1882
23 Ontario, *Sessional Papers*, 1886 no 1, 32–5
24 Ontario, Royal Commission on the Mineral Resources of Ontario, *Report*, 69–70, 92–100, 114–15, 147, 194–5, 238–9, 242, 316–17, 402–4, 428–9. A transcript of Borron's complete testimony is found in PAC, MG 29, C 23, Robert Bell Papers, vol. 41, Subject Files – Ontario Mining Commission. The published report appears to include nearly the whole of Borron's submission.
25 Ontario, Royal Commission on the Mineral Resources of Ontario, *Report*, 242
26 Ontario, Bureau of Mines, *Fifth Report* (1895), 257–8
27 Ontario, *Sessional Papers*, 1891 no 3, 35
28 Laurier Papers, 89118, Borron to Laurier 18 Aug. 1904
29 Ibid., 89119, Laurier to Borron, 1 Sept. 1904
30 *Sault Daily Star*, 4 May 1915, 3
31 Records dealing with Borron's private life – such as personal diaries and family letters – are disappointingly few in number. In the 1850s, probably while he was living at Bruce Mines, he married Marie Delorimier, a native of St Joseph Island, who survived him by a few years. Their four daughters were living at the time of their father's death in North Bay (Mrs Mary Leask), Toronto (Mrs Ainslie Hime who kept house for her parents), Kansas City (Mrs Katherine Douglas, who afterwards returned to Toronto to live with her sister), and Hawaii (Mrs Claire Brandt). There was one son, Edward, who was born in 1859 and died in 1902. He, too, was a northerner, settling at French River, where he was the local harbourmaster, lighthousekeeper, and justice of the peace. I am indebted for this information to two of the younger Edward's children, Dr R.J.M. Borron, Toronto (interview and documents), and Mrs May B. View, Lomita, California (letter).
32 Ontario, Royal Commission on the Mineral Resources of Ontario, *Report*, 100
33 Laurier Papers, 89116, Borron to Laurier, 18 Aug. 1904

Ontario Denied:
The Methodist Church
on the Prairies 1896-1914

George N. Emery

In 1896 a wheat boom on the Canadian prairies sparked a massive immigration and a great expansion of settlement. From a mere quarter of a million people, most of whom were located in southeastern Manitoba, the prairie population increased more than five-fold over the next two decades, occupying a vast triangle bounded by Winnipeg, Lethbridge, and Edmonton. Impressive too were the prospects for the prairie west; with its vast amount of fertile land – much more than existed in Ontario – western Canada seemed destined for an enormous population.

The immigration, which originated from Britain, the United States, and continental Europe as well as from eastern Canada, brought to the prairies a veritable mosaic of traditions, cultural values, and institutions. Political parties, labour unions, fraternal societies, and churches were examples of institutions which came into the west. A major institutional thrust largely from Ontario came from the Methodist Church of Canada.

Like the surrounding population, the Methodist population on the prairies grew substantially during the late 1890s and early twentieth century. In the dominion census of 1901 nearly 206,000 prairie residents professed to be Methodist – nearly a six-fold increase from 1891. In the meantime, the number of actual church members increased to 57,000 in 1914 – more than three times the church membership of 1896.[1] A result of this growth was the division of the Manitoba and Northwest Conference into three in 1904: the Manitoba, Assiniboia (renamed Saskatchewan in 1905), and Alberta conferences. By 1914 both the Manitoba and Saskatchewan conferences were larger in church membership than the original conference had been in 1896, and the Alberta Conference was nearly as large.[2]

Most of the human and financial resources for Methodist expansion on the prairies came from the Methodist conferences in Ontario. In addition, the Ontario conferences exercised important administrative controls over prairie church expansion, and they were a major source of prairie Methodist religious culture. However, by 1914 prairie Methodism was less completely the outreach of its Ontario parent than church leaders in the Ontario and prairie conferences desired. Canadian Methodist traditions and perspectives on the prairies had been diluted to some extent by the importation of scores of clergy from Britain, a development made necessary by the inability of the Ontario conferences to meet fully prairie ministerial needs.[3] The greatest disappointment to church leaders, however, was that, in terms of proportionate strength and of influence over its own people, the church failed to achieve on the prairies the stature that it had won in Ontario. In the period 1896 to 1914 the Canadian Methodist church showed how the institutions and culture of Ontario could reach into an adjacent pioneer environment. The church also showed how Ontario's reach could exceed its grasp.

In 1896 the Canadian Methodist church was a young institution, the product of a union of four separate and distinct Methodist churches just twelve years before. It was also the largest Protestant denomination in Canada, chiefly because of the unequalled support which it enjoyed in Ontario – a province in which, in 1901, nearly one in three professed to be Methodist.[4] No other major religious institution was so orientated to Ontario. In 1891 Ontario congregations accounted for 77 per cent of Canada's Methodists but only 60 per cent for each of Canada's Anglicans and Presbyterians. By 1911, despite two decades of rapid church and population growth in western Canada, 62 per cent of Canada's Methodists could still be found in Ontario as opposed to only 47 per cent for each of the Anglicans and Presbyterians in Canada.[5]

The large membership of the Ontario conferences resulted in a majority of Ontario men at the General Conference, a national body which met every four years and which determined policy for the entire Canadian Methodist church. At the General Conference of 1902, 64 per cent of the delegates were Ontario men, and in 1910 Ontario men accounted for 57 per cent of the delegates.[6] Predictably, Ontario Methodists dominated the internal structure of the General Conference as well; for example, at the General Conference of 1906, nineteen of the thirty chairmen of committees were Ontario men.[7] In contrast, Ontario delegates were never a majority at the General Synod, the national body of the Anglican church, and, by 1910, Ontario men had ceased to be a majority at the General Assembly, the national body of the Presbyterian Church. Similarly the internal structures of the Anglican and Presbyterian national bodies were considerably less dominated by Ontario men than was the case with the General Conference.[8]

Together with the church's highly centralized polity, such power at the General Conference gave Ontario men great influence in mission work. The headquarters of the Missionary Society was in Toronto, and Ontario men were usually a majority at the annual meeting of the General Board of Missions, the governing body of the society. More importantly, the executive committee which exercised the General Board's authority throughout the year was completely dominated by Ontario men during the period under study. In 1906, for example, the Rev. James Woodsworth of Winnipeg was the only member of the twenty-four man executive who was not from Ontario, and even he was originally from that province; fully half the executive were from Toronto.[9] The result was extensive Ontario control over western church expansion. Although the authority to create missions rested with prairie conference missionary committees, as well as with prairie mission superintendents who were responsible to the General Board, officials in Toronto decided which missions would receive grants – without which survival was difficult or impossible. Oversight of all financial expenditures was the price of this support; only by becoming financially self-supporting could a congregation become independent of eastern officials.[10]

The Women's Missionary Society, a separate and distinct organization which was not controlled by the General Board of Missions, was also heavily centred in Ontario. The WMS headquarters was in Toronto, and in 1910 the society drew 76 per cent of its members and 66 per cent of its revenues from the five Ontario conferences.[11] However, the WMS gave most of its attention to the Asian mission fields, and it was far less important to prairie church expansion than was the Missionary Society.

The general superintendent of the Methodist church, elected by the General Conference for an eight-year term, was another arm of Ontario Methodist influence. He was the visible symbol of unity within the church, and he acted as the church's official spokesman; in addition, he was responsible for co-ordinating church activities and for arbitrating disputes. As exercised by the Rev. Albert Carman of Ontario, general superintendent from 1884–1915, the position acquired many of the characteristics of a bishop's office. When a second general superintendency was created in 1910, the Rev. S.D. Chown, another Ontario man, was appointed.[12]

Church journals provided a final manifestation of Ontario Methodist strength. With the exception of the *Wesleyan*, a weekly for the Maritime conferences, the official Methodist journals were published in Toronto. The most important was the *Christian Guardian*, the official weekly for the Ontario and western conferences, where it reached an average of one in nine church members. Through articles, editorials, and letters to the editor, the paper, which Egerton Ryerson of Upper Canada had founded in 1829, now helped to impart Ontario Methodist goals to the pioneer areas of the prairies; together with conference news columns, the same sources informed Ontario readers as to the problems of the western regions which the church was trying to develop.[13]

Within the Ontario-centred organizational framework of their church, Methodist leaders in Ontario and the west hoped to perpetuate on the prairies the religious culture which had evolved in the older conferences. This religious culture included a weakening of commitment to personal salvation for the world to come, a deepening of commitment to the Christianization of life on earth, and strong ascetic traditions such as total abstinence from alcohol and a strict sabbath observance.[14] These values were popular too in many British and American Protestant churches, as well as in other Canadian denominations such as the Presbyterian church. Nevertheless, the ingredient of Canadian nationalism distinguished the Methodist cultural mix from Anglo-Saxon protestantism in general, and other ingredients, such as Methodist institutional loyalty, distinguished the church to some extent from other Canadian denominations. In general, Methodist goals for the west represented the outreach of a Canadian protestantism, part of which was distinctively Methodist; especially in the Methodist church, that outreach came largely from Ontario – the province with the geographical proximity and the resources to develop prairie Methodism, and the source of so many of the church's institutional controls.[15]

Central to the Methodist perspective on the west was the Old Testament belief that God was the God of nations as well as of individuals; to this was added the assumption that Protestant Christian values, such as those expressed by Canadian Methodism, were vital to the nation-building process.[16] Church leaders feared the destruction of Protestant values throughout the dominion if the west, with its enormous material potential, were not won for Christ. On the other hand, if the west were given Christian foundations, Canada could be a powerful base for exporting the gospel on a world-wide scale.[17] At this point Methodist ambitions for the west merged with a broad Anglo-Saxon crusade to bring about the millennium, but the church's Canadian perspective nonetheless remained conspicuous. Despite an eagerness to interpret the physical strength of the United States and Britain as a sign that God was working through these nations to bring about His kingdom on earth, Methodist leaders anticipated a still greater role for their own country. In their view, Britain and the United States were old countries which had reached their prime and which had failed to solve serious internal problems; neither had prevented urban slums, and the United States had done too little to Christianize its west and to assimilate its European immigrants.[18] Canada, in contrast, was a young country which could learn from and avoid the mistakes of others; moreover, the vast fertile lands of the prairies suggested that Canada had enormous potential for growth and that it would one day be second to none as a world power. In 1905 the Rev. J.H. Riddell, an Ontario native and the principal of Alberta College, Edmonton, predicted that fifty million people would live in the North Saskatchewan valley alone.[19] However, it was essential that this material growth be accompanied by Protestant Christian foundations, and Methodist leaders were deeply conscious of the prairies as being a Canadian responsibility. They were convinced by their nationalism that Canadian clergy were better suited to the population and physical environment of the prairies than were foreigners; they were also reluctant to use British or American resources which might otherwise go to mission fields in non-Christian lands.[20]

A part of the religious culture which the church imparted to the prairies was distinctively Methodist. The class meeting and the itinerant system for locating clergy were examples of traditions which were unique to the church, and the prairie conferences were also given a distinctive selection of priorities. For example, neither of the Anglican or Presbyterian churches equalled the Methodist church in zeal for prohibition, nor did they match the advanced position on the social gospel which the General Conference expressed after 1906.[21] Ancestor worship provided another distinctive ingredient; many Ontario clergy who moved west thought of themselves as repeating on the prairies what Methodist 'saddle bag' preachers had done for Upper Canada some two generations before.[22] Finally, Methodist attitudes to the west were shaped by pride in the church's size and influence. Fully conscious that their church was the largest denomination in Ontario and the largest Protestant denomination in Canada, Methodist leaders expected their church to enjoy the same premier position on the prairies.[23]

The corollary to Methodist hopes for the west was the church's opposition to rival languages, cultures, and religious traditions. Most Methodists fought the extension of French-Canadian culture west of Quebec, and the church's modest programme of French-Canadian evangelization suggested an underlying hope that even Quebec might one day be Protestant and English-speaking.[24] The problem of French Canada was aggravated by a second challenge: the heavy immigration of continental Europeans to the prairies. From the Methodist viewpoint, the Europeans were an immoral, docile, ignorant people who were imprisoned in decadence by avaricious, mediæval, authoritarian churches. Unless something was done the newcomers would drag Canadians down to their level. The immigrant's acceptance of low wages and living standards produced slums; his vote threatened to pollute Canadian politics; his morality was a bad example for Canadian youth; and the heterogenous society which would result from failure to assimilate him was a threat to Canadian nationhood.[25] Thus, with the Ontario conferences in the forefront, the church sought legislation which would compel the attendance of the European children at English-language public schools.[26] To further Anglicize the Europeans, Methodist missions were established among them. Prior to 1914 missions in Winnipeg and Alberta received about $200,000 in grants for this field of work.[27]

To a large extent the prairie conferences became vehicles for the Methodist and Protestant culture of Ontario, though not always in the manner anticipated by mission officials in Toronto. As far as can be determined most of the prairie laymen came from Ontario, including the great majority of prominent laymen. The latter were especially important for their continuity of leadership; unlike the clergy who were subject to the itinerant system, the laymen were not forced to move every three years.[28] The dependence upon Ontario men in the prairie conferences, while admirable from the viewpoint of perpetuating Ontario Methodist traditions, represented a disappointment to another Methodist hope: to benefit from all sources of immigration, a key requirement if the prairie conferences were to match the Ontario conferences in proportionate strength.

The prairie clergy were less decisively the outreach of Ontario than were the laymen. Of 641 ministers who can be identified, fully a third were from Britain.[29] Nevertheless, a majority were Ontario men, including a decisive majority of the senior clergy who served as chairmen of Methodist districts and as ministerial delegates to the General Conference.[30] The faculties of the prairie theological colleges were also dominated by natives of the Ontario conferences. Like the key prairie laymen, the clergy on the college staffs were exempt from the itinerancy and were able to provide important organizational leadership.[31] Presumably they also helped to assimilate the many British-born candidates for the ministry in Canadian Methodist traditions.

Ontario's outreach was evident in the financial as well as the human resources behind prairie church expansion. Grants to prairie mission fields were controlled by officials in Toronto, and the Ontario conferences were vital sources of money. Collectively the prairie conferences had a debtor relationship with the Missionary Society prior to 1914: prairie missions consumed more in grants than was contributed back to the Missionary Society by self-supporting congregations. Conversely, the Ontario conferences alone gave substantially more to the Missionary Society than they received back in grants.[32] Newly rich urban laymen provided the bulk of Methodist contributions to missions. In Toronto, a city with more than thirty Methodist churches, 40 per cent of the money raised came from the three wealthiest congregations.[33] The role of the wealthy was further enhanced by special funds which they raised over and above the regular fund of the Missionary Society.[34]

Through their contribution of resources and their institutional controls, the Ontario conferences were a major source of prairie Methodist religious culture. As far as can be determined from conference minutes, Methodist publications, and correspondence from church officials in the west, the values, goals, and distinctive features of the prairie conferences were generally the same as those in the Ontario conferences. Even Protestant influences from outside the country were likely to reach the prairie conferences through the Ontario channels of the church. This was illustrated by the visit of the American evangelists, Torrey and Alexander, to Toronto in 1906; although they had been hitherto largely ignored by Canadian Methodists, despite the world-wide fame which they had earned from their triumphant tour of the globe in 1901, their visit to Toronto's Massey Hall sufficed to ignite Torrey-Alexander revival services in Calgary and in Grenfell, Saskatchewan, and to stimulate Winnipeg Methodists into helping to promote a Torrey-Alexander mission to their city in the following year.[35]

Insofar as they were an outreach of Ontario, the prairie conferences of the Methodist church also tell a story of Ontario hopes denied. Prior to 1914 the church's accomplishments in the west fell short of the expectations of church leaders, both in Ontario and on the prairies.[36] The church was weaker and less influential in prairie society than in the society of Ontario. In the dominion census of 1901, 30.5 per cent of Ontario's population professed to be Methodist; in 1911 only 15.5 per cent of the prairie population expressed the same preference. Whereas the Methodist church was the largest denomination in Ontario, Presbyterians, Roman Catholics, and Anglicans outnumbered Methodists on the Prairies. In consequence, the Presbyterian church had displaced the Methodist church as the largest Protestant denomination in Canada.[37]

A more serious Methodist failing in the west, relative to Ontario, was the weakness of the church's hold on its own supporters. A comparison of church and census statistics suggests that Methodists whose church life had lapsed were proportionately more numerous on the prairies than in Ontario. In Ontario the church membership, as reported to the General Conference, was equal to 34 per cent of the Methodist census population. On the prairies the proportion who were church members dropped to 26 per cent in Manitoba, 21 per cent in Saskatchewan, and 19 per cent in Alberta.[38] Allowing for non-members who were children or regular adherents, the remainder, the lapsed Methodists, seem to have increased proportionately from east to west. The only consolation was that the numbers of lapsed Presbyterians on the prairies were even greater; in terms of church membership the Methodist church was actually larger than its Presbyterian counterpart in Saskatchewan and Alberta and was nearly as large in the prairie region as a whole.[39]

By comparison with the heroic saga of Methodism in Upper Canada a century earlier, the period 1896 to 1914 was a disappointing chapter in Canadian Methodist history. A major factor was the pattern of immigration. About half of the prairie population came from Britain, the United States, and continental Europe, lands in which Methodist supporters were proportionately fewer than in Ontario. Whereas the church claimed more than 30 per cent of Ontario's population, fewer than 10 per cent of the British and American immigrants were likely to be Methodist, and none of the European immigrants were likely to join the church.[40] The Anglican and Presbyterian churches were the major beneficiaries of the British immigration, and the Roman Catholic church was the major beneficiary of the American and European immigration.

An additional disadvantage for prairie Methodism was the Canadian church's lack of appeal for many British and American Methodist immigrants. For example, Wesleyan Methodist immigrants from Britain were alienated by the different name of the Canadian church, by the absence of some of their favourite hymns in the Canadian Methodist hymn book, and by the cool reception which Canadians often gave them on account of their accent, dress, and other old country characteristics.[41] In the new society of the prairies, these factors were reinforced by the weakness of social constraints which encouraged church attendance in older communities. Methodist immigration chaplains documented the result for the period 1906–10; of more than 19,000 British Methodist immigrants who were given letters of introduction, only 441 were reported to have joined the Canadian church while another 813 became adherents.[42]

A decline in the spiritual life of the church also worked against Methodist success on the prairies. Symptoms of this malaise were the erosion of commitment to personal salvation, the decline of the class and prayer meetings, the loss of church members, and the shortage of candidates for the ministry.[43] Although the decline of spiritual life had no simple explanation, certain factors stood out. Not the least was the materialism which underlay the western boom and from which the church had hoped to profit. To one Saskatchewan clergyman the wheat-hungry settler's motto seemed to be 'Goodbye God, we are going West.'[44] In urban congregations church life was further weakened by competition with secular entertainments. More importantly, proximity to magazines, newspapers, and other sources of information gave urban congregations exposure to new intellectual currents which were wracking the very foundations of evangelical Protestantism.[45] The spirit of scientific enquiry, the examination of the Scriptures in the light of historical and archeological findings, and the discoveries of Darwin suggested that much of the Bible was not literally true, and they undermined acceptance of the supernatural, upon which the Methodist's traditional conversion experience rested.

Spiritual decline in the church was accelerated by the urban bias of the requirements for the ministry. By the 1890s ordination required college training, and the Methodist theological colleges were orientated to what were essentially urban problems – for example, the retention of faith in the face of the new intellectual currents. Unfortunately for the prairie conferences, graduates of this training were sent not only to urban middle-class congregations but also to the congregations of rural, frequently psychologically insecure people to whom the 'old time religion' was still attractive.[46] The irony was that most of the clergy were from rural congregations in the first place.

Somewhat related to the spiritual decline was the middle-class character which had come to the church. In the west as in the east, the need for money and organizational talents gave a dominant role to wealthy urban laymen. Yet the urban working class were not reached by Methodism, perhaps because they felt uncomfortable amidst the fine dress of the church members and the prosperous air of the large city churches. In rural areas, tenants, hired men, and others who were marginal to local society were also neglected; surveys of two rural districts in Manitoba found that the clergy gave most of their time to established, better-off farmers.[47] Class barriers were not surmounted by proselytizing in the style of the 'saddle bag' preachers of the Upper Canadian frontier; save for immigration, the major source of new church members was the Sunday School rather than the ranks of the unchurched.[48]

Another source of weakness for prairie Methodism was the chronic shortage of resources, both human and material. The need for resources was exceptional. In its scope and rapidity, the expansion of settlement on the prairies was without precedent in Canadian history, and the low population densities of the rural west added to the problems of church support. Despite assistance from the Ontario conferences, Methodist resources were seldom equal to the task at hand. Prior to 1914 the Missionary Society was unable to provide its missionaries with the minimum salary required by church law, even though the minimum was calculated to cover no more than the barest essentials of life.[49] Also for want of money, scores of churches and parsonages went unbuilt, enormous circuits were imposed upon inexperienced clergy with virtually no supervision, and few married clergy could be accepted for prairie service.[50] That a shortage of ministers resulted was not surprising. Only the most dedicated and adventurous clergy in eastern Canada were willing to transfer into such harsh conditions, and, lured away to more lucrative secular careers or to the higher salaries of American churches, an astonishing number of prairie clergy left the church entirely. In the period 1905–14, 167 prairie clergy left the church – fifty-two more than in the five Ontario conferences which had twice as many ministers.[51] The deadly crossfire of expansion and resignations forced the Missionary Society to seek more than one hundred new clergy annually after 1907. When the eastern conferences failed to provide clergy in the necessary numbers, the General Board executive reluctantly recruited more than two hundred lay preachers from Britain in the period 1905–14, on the understanding that the recruits would prepare for ordination.[52] Still the shortages persisted. In December 1907, with recruiting from all sources exhausted, the general secretary for the Department of Home Missions reported that about thirty organized fields were left unsupplied while another twenty men could have been employed to open up new and promising work.[53]

The decline of the church's evangelical firepower does not alone explain the shortage of resources on the prairies. The continuing glamour of the Asian mission fields siphoned off thousands of dollars and some of the most promising young men in the ministry. The Woman's Missionary Society best illustrates the orientation to the overseas work. In a typical year, 1914, this organization gave $144,000 to Asian missions and yet largely ignored pressing needs in home missions, despite a financial reserve of nearly $150,000.[54] Mission work among the European immigrants also slowed Methodist growth in the west. Although this field of work absorbed more than $200,000 which might have been profitably invested in ordinary domestic missions, no more than a handful of European immigrants became Methodist.[55] Finally, the shortage of resources stemmed from the parochialism of Methodist congregations. In 1910, for example, the average contribution to missions per church member was only $2.19, and a Manitoba Methodist estimated that three-quarters of the church membership gave nothing to missions.[56] Despite the vision and generosity of wealthy laymen in Toronto, the parochialism was most striking in Ontario. In four of the five Ontario conferences, the average contribution to missions was less than the national average in 1910; on the other hand, three of the four conferences in which the average contribution exceeded the national average were in the west.[57]

In 1914 the era of Methodist expansion on the prairies came to a close, as suddenly as it had begun some two decades before. Partly for want of sufficient resources, church officials adopted a programme of consolidation rather than the taking up of more new territory.[58] The outbreak of war in Europe then confirmed the change of direction. Over the next four years clergy and laymen left the prairies for the front, and the cost of the war effort brought about a sharp decline in the revenues of the Missionary Society. The war also ended temporarily a major Methodist problem – the immigration of Europeans to the prairies.[59] As mentioned, the church's achievement on the prairies was less than church leaders had hoped for. The church was weaker and less influential on the prairies than in Ontario, and the Methodist identity was modified by the prairie environment as well. The traditional loyalty of Methodists to their church as an institution was undermined by movements for co-operation and church union with the Presbyterians, both of which grew partly out of the church's problems of growth in western Canada.[60] At the same time the prairie conferences had attained a degree of maturity which was likely to secure an increase of autonomy for western Methodists in the years to come. Thus in its prospects for the future as well as in its record of the past, the Methodist church on the prairies represented Ontario denied. In this respect, studies of other institutions on the prairies may show prairie Methodism to have been a microcosm of prairie societal development in general.

NOTES

1 Computed from *Canada Year Book*, 1912, 28ff; Journal of Proceedings, General Conference, 1914
2 Computed from Journal of Proceedings, General Conference, 1898 and 1914

3 See United Church Archives [UCA], Home Mission Reports, Rev. F.H. Langford, Regina, to Rev. T.A. Moore, Toronto, 2 June 1914; UCA, Allen Papers, Rev. James Allen, Toronto, to Rev. C.H. Cross, Saskatoon, 10 Feb. 1914

4 Computed from *Canada Year Book*, 1912, 3, 28

5 Ibid.

6 Computed from Journal of Proceedings, General Conference, 1902 and 1910

7 Ibid., 1906

8 Computed from Journal of Proceedings, General Synod, Anglican Church of Canada, 1896–1915; Acts and Proceedings, General Assembly, Presbyterian Church in Canada, 1906 and 1910. Ontario influence was considerably reduced at the Anglican General Synod by the division of all standing committees into eastern and western sections; Ontario men were eligible only for the former, and in 1911 six of the ten eastern section chairmen were Ontario residents. At the Presbyterian General Assembly three of the most important committees were divided into eastern and western sections, with Ontario men eligible only for the latter; in 1911 all three western section convenors were Ontario men; for the remaining committees seventeen of the thirty-two convenors were Ontario men.

9 Computed from Annual Report, Missionary Society of the Methodist Church, 1905–06, iii. In 1906, 23 of the 44 members of the General Board were Ontario residents; however, the Ontario majority at the annual meeting of the General Board was made certain by the failure of the western members to attend regularly. See Allen Papers, Rev. James Allen, Toronto, to J.H. Ashdown, Winnipeg, 14 Sept. 1909; *Christian Guardian*, 21 July 1909, article by the Rev. F.B. Stacey.

10 In time the prairie conferences won some autonomy in the administration of missions. In 1906 the General Conference authorized the formation of local city mission boards in urban areas, and the first local board was duly formed in Winnipeg; however, although the local boards were empowered to raise and expend monies locally, the approval of expenditures by officials in Toronto was still necessary in the event that the local boards required financial assistance from the Missionary Society, and prior to 1914 the Winnipeg local board failed to become financially independent of the society

A second change was authorized by the General Conference of 1910. Henceforth the General Board of Missions allotted fixed sums to conference missionary committees which were empowered to make grants as they saw fit. However, contributions to missions from prairie congregations were directed to the General Board as before, and the General Board determined how large the allotments to the conferences would be. The inadequacies of these allotments, which were partly attributable to the priorities and decisions of mission leaders in Ontario, in turn crippled western initiative in opening up work in new areas, especially in the expensive mission work among the Europeans. See Journal of Proceedings, General Conference, 1906, 119–20; ibid., 1910, 104 and 394–5; *Christian Guardian*, 2 Feb. 1910, supplement; ibid., 6 Nov. 1912, Saskatchewan Conference news

11 Computed from Annual Report, Woman's Missionary Society, 1909–10, xxx

12 Journal of Proceedings, General Conference, 1910, 71, 74, 380–1. The second general superintendent was appointed for four years and resided west of the Great Lakes.

13 Other journals included the *Missionary Outlook*, the monthly publication of the WMS; the *Missionary Bulletin*, quarterly which contained letters from missionaries in the field; and the *Epworth Era* and the *Banner*, the publications for the youth organizations and the Sunday schools respectively.

14 For ascetic values see The Doctrine and Discipline of the Methodist Church, 1906, sections 31 and 35, and Journals of Proceedings, General Conference, reports of committees on temperance, prohibition, and moral reform and committees on sabbath observance. For declining of commitment to personal salvation see Minutes, Toronto Conference, 1896, pastoral address; Minutes, Saskatchewan Conference, 1910, 64–6; Journal of Proceedings,

General Conference, 1910, 335; *Christian Guardian*, 25 Jan. 1905, Rev. W.H. Hincks, Toronto Conference, to editor; ibid., 1 March 1905, Rev. W. McMullen, Florence, Ontario, to editor; ibid., 29 March 1905, 'A Pioneer Layman' to editor. For examples of the growing commitment to the Christianization of life on earth see Rev. Alexander Sutherland, 'The Twentieth Century and Missions,' *The Methodist Magazine and Review*, January 1901, 19; *Christian Guardian*, 17 Dec. 1913, article by Rev. S.D. Chown; *Canada's Missionary Congress*, Addresses Delivered at the Canadian National Missionary Congress, Toronto (Toronto 1909).

15 Like the western conferences, the Maritime conferences were short of clergy throughout the period under study. See *Christian Guardian*, 21 Jan. and 13 May 1903; ibid., 11 May 1904; ibid., 15 Feb. 1913, Rev. James A. Spenceley, Rosetown, Saskatchewan, to editor

16 See Minutes, Toronto Conference, 1896, pastoral address; Home Mission Reports, Rev. Oliver Darwin, Saskatchewan Conference mission superintendent, to Rev. James Woodsworth, Winnipeg, 30 June 1906; Canada, House of Commons, *Debates*, 1906, 5603, statement by T. S. Sproule, Ontario Methodist MP; *Christian Guardian*, 7 Dec. 1898; ibid., 31 March 1911, article by Rev. R.O. Armstrong, Winnipeg

17 See Annual Report, Missionary Society, 1907–8, 55–6; *Canada's Missionary Congress*; *Christian Guardian*, 28 March 1902, Rev. James Woodsworth, Winnipeg, to editor.

18 See Home Mission Reports, Rev. Arthur Barner, Alix, Alberta, to Rev. James Allen, Toronto, 27 Jan. 1907; ibid., Rev. T.J. Johnston, Clover Bar, Alberta, to Rev. James Allen, 15 Sept. 1908; *Missionary Outlook*, June 1906, article by H.H. Fudger, Toronto; ibid., Oct. 1912, article by 'T.A.P.'; J.S. Woodsworth, *My Neighbor* (Toronto 1911), 69

19 *Christian Guardian*, 26 July 1905

20 See Home Mission Reports, Rev. T.C. Buchanan, Alberta Conference mission superintendent, to Rev. James Allen, Toronto, 18 Dec. 1909; ibid., Rev. James Woodsworth, Manitoba Conference mission superintendent, to Rev. James Allen, 22 July 1909; Allen Papers, Rev. James Allen to Rev. T.C. Buchanan, 20 March 1911; ibid., Rev. James Allen to Rev. John Corbett, Bowmanville, 27 March 1908; UCA, Carman Papers, Rev. James Allen to Rev. Albert Carman, 15 Dec. 1903

21 The Anglican church was openly for temperance rather than total abstinence, and its most ascetic position merely called for close regulation of the liquor traffic. Like the General Conference, the Presbyterian General Assembly officially supported total abstinence, but the church, by reputation, included many who drank in moderation; unlike the General Conference, the General Assembly never formed a separate committee on the liquor problem, and it had difficulty attracting laymen to the committee which was charged with the liquor question. See Journal of Proceedings, General Synod, Anglican Church of Canada, 1896–1915; Acts and Proceedings, General Assembly, Presbyterian Church in Canada, 1896–1914; *Christian Guardian*, 1 Feb. 1899, address of Principal William I. Shaw of Wesleyan Theological College, Montreal; ibid., 17 Sept. 1902, fraternal address to the General Conference by Dr Bryce, moderator of the Presbyterian church. Unlike the General Synod, the General Assembly advanced considerably in the direction of the social gospel; however, unlike the General Conference, the Presbyterian national body stopped short of condemning the existing social order. Admittedly the Methodist social gospel in the west developed partly in response to local conditions in the west; however, the prairie social gospel also evolved from general trends that were well established in the Ontario and Maritime conferences – the declining of commitment to personal salvation and the growing emphasis on the Christianization of life on earth.

22 See *Christian Guardian*, 16 Nov. 1898, Manitoba and Northwest Conference news; ibid., 1 Feb. 1899; ibid., 6 Nov. 1911, article by Rev. John Maclean. Attempts to resurrect the camp meeting were another throwback to the church's Upper Canadian past; see ibid., 7 and 28 Aug. 1901

23 See *Christian Guardian*, 26 Nov. 1902, address by the Hon. Clifford Sifton at Metropolitan Methodist Church, Toronto; ibid., 8 Feb. 1911, Rev. Wellington Bridgman, Manitoba Conference, to editor; Home Mission Reports, Rev. John Maclean, Morden, Manitoba, to Rev. C.E. Manning, Toronto

24 See *Christian Guardian*, 16 June 1897, article by Rev. W.H. Withrow; ibid., 7 July 1897, editorial; Annual Report, Missionary Society, 1898–9, xii; ibid., 1900–1, xii; ibid., 1906–7, cxi; *Missionary Outlook*, March 1900 and August 1903. See also Minutes of the Methodist annual conferences for uncompromising stands on the Manitoba and Northwest schools questions. For reference to the church programme of French evangelization see Edmond H. Oliver, *His Dominion of Canada* (Toronto 1932); Paul Villard, *Up to the Light* (Toronto 1928).

25 See Home Mission Reports, Proceedings of the Commission on Foreign Missions in Western Canada, Winnipeg, 28 Aug. 1909; ibid., address by Irving Grok at Wiarton, Ontario; Annual Report, Missionary Society, 1912–13, viii–x; *Christian Guardian*, 21 May 1902, Manitoba and Northwest Conference news; ibid., 2 Feb. 1910, supplement; ibid., 23 Feb. 1910, article by Rev. S.D. Chown; *Missionary Outlook*, June 1912, article by Rev. J.S. Woodsworth

26 See Minutes of the annual conferences, 1896 and 1905; Carman Papers, Rev. Hamilton Wigle, president of the Assiniboia Conference, to Rev. Albert Carman, 15 Feb. 1905; ibid., Rev. T.C. Buchanan, Alberta Conference, to Rev. Albert Carman, 15 Feb. 1905; ibid., Rev. Albert Carman to Rev. C.H. Huestis, president of the Nova Scotia Conference, 7 March 1905; ibid., Rev. James Woodsworth, Winnipeg, to Rev. Albert Carman, 25 Feb. 1905; *Christian Guardian*, 8, 15 Feb. and 21 June 1905

27 Computed from Annual Reports, Missionary Society, 1899–1914; Annual Reports, Woman's Missionary Society, 1900–14

28 Of 296 laymen who can be identified through biographical dictionaries, 222 were Ontario natives. Special fund drives of the church (eg, the Twentieth Century Fund of 1898 and the Mission Plant and Extension Fund of 1910) illustrated the organizational leadership provided by these Ontario men, as did educational campaigns such as the Laymen's Missionary Movement, which was founded in 1909. Ontario natives who became prominent in the prairie conferences included J.A.M. Aikins of Winnipeg, a millionaire corporation lawyer; H.W. Hutchinson of Winnipeg, a farm implements manufacturer; J.H. Ashdown of Winnipeg, the millionaire president of a hardware store chain; the Hon. G.W. Brown of Regina, a lawyer, businessman, and the lieutenant-governor of Saskatchewan; W.G. Hunt of Calgary, a Massey-Harris Company executive; and the Cushing brothers of Calgary (W.H. and A.B.), manufacturers of windows, sashes, and doors. For patterns of organization see Home Mission Reports and Allen Papers; *Canada's Missionary Congress*

29 More than 1200 clergy served in the prairie conferences in the period 1896–1914; 641 were identified through biographical dictionaries, conference obituaries, and pension records in the UCA, Toronto. Of these, only one was from the United States – a result of the shortage of ministers and higher wages which prevailed in the American Methodist churches.

30 Computed from Journals of Proceedings, General Conferences, 1898–1914; Minutes, Manitoba, Saskatchewan, and Alberta conferences, 1905–14. Of the twenty-eight prairie clergy who attended the General Conference of 1910, 16 were originally from Ontario, two were from other provinces, eight were from Britain, and two cannot be identified. In the Saskatchewan Conference, which had more British clergy than the other two prairie conferences, seven of the eleven district chairmen for 1912 were originally from Ontario, one was from another province, two were British in origin, and one cannot be identified.

31 Of nine clergy on the faculties of prairie theological colleges who can be identified, seven were raised in Ontario and six took degrees at Victoria College, Toronto. College staff who provided important organizational leadership included Principal J.W. Sparling of Wesley

College, Winnipeg, and Principal J.H. Riddell of Alberta College, Edmonton. Another notable organizational leader was the Rev. G.W. Kerby of Calgary, principal of Mount Royal College, a Methodist secondary school. See Home Mission Reports and Allen Papers, for the organizational contributions of these men.

32 Computed from Annual Reports, Missionary Society, 1898–1914

33 Computed from Minutes, Toronto Conference, 1902, 1908, and 1912. As new churches were built in the city, the percentage of contributions coming from the Sherbourne St, Metropolitan, and Central Methodist churches gradually declined, from 41 per cent in 1902 to 37 per cent in 1912.

34 See Home Mission Reports, Mission Plant and Extension Fund receipts to January 1914

35 *Christian Guardian*, 19 April 1905; ibid., 7 March and 11 April 1906; ibid., 7 Oct. 1907. The Laymen's Missionary Movement, which was both international and interdenominational, was another influence which reached the west by way of Ontario. See Journal of Proceedings, General Conference, 1910, 284–8; *Canada's Missionary Congress*, 243ff

36 Home Mission Reports, D.H. Kennedy, High Bluff, Manitoba, to Rev. C.E. Manning, Toronto, 16 Feb. 1911; ibid., Rev. John Maclean, Morden, Manitoba, to Rev. C.E. Manning, 8 Feb. 1911; ibid., Rev. Wellington Bridgman, president of the Manitoba Conference, to Rev. James Allen, 11 Sept. 1908; *Christian Guardian*, 2 April 1913, editorial and Clark Keane to editor; ibid., 9 April 1913, George C. Wood to editor; ibid., 23 April 1913, C.W. Swallow to editor and T.R. Clarke to editor.

37 See *Census of Canada*, 1911, 2–3

38 Computed from ibid.; Journal of Proceedings, General Conference, 1914, 333

39 Journal of Proceedings, General Conference, 1914, 333; *Acts and Proceedings*, General Assembly, Presbyterian Church in Canada, 1912, 472

40 Since no denominational census was taken in Britain during the period under study, denominational strengths have been estimated on the basis of the 1851 religious census for England and Wales and from secondary sources. See K.S. Inglis, 'Patterns of Religious Worship in England and Wales,' *Journal of Ecclesiastical History*, 1960, II, 74–6; K.S. Inglis, *Churches and the Working Classes* (Toronto 1963); Desmond Bowan, *The Idea of the Victorian Church* (Toronto 1968). For denominational strengths in the United States in the primary states of emigration to the Canadian prairies, see Karel Dennis Bicha, 'The Plains Farmer and the Prairie Province Frontier, 1897–1914,' *Proceedings of the American Philosophical Society*, 1965, CIX, 6, 422; US Department of Commerce, *Bureau of the Census, Religious Bodies, 1916*, Part I (Washington 1919), 109–11

41 See Journal of Proceedings, General Conference, 1914, 226; *Christian Guardian*, 15 Feb. 1911, Walter Giddings, Gleichen, Alberta, to editor; Lloyd G. Reynolds, *The British Immigrant: His Social and Economic Adjustment in Canada* (Toronto 1935). The absence of American immigrants from among the prominent laymen of the prairies suggests the church's low appeal among American Methodist immigrants.

42 Home Mission Reports, Quadrennial Report of the Committee on Immigration, July 1910

43 The dwindling numbers of class leaders attested to the decline of the class meeting. In 1898 the church had 7309 class leaders, or 1 leader for every 38 church members; by 1910 there were only 5464 class leaders, or 1 for every 62 church members. Computed from Journal of Proceedings, General Conference, 1898 and 1910

44 *Missionary Bulletin*, 1910, VI, 3, 488, letter from Rev. R.R. Morrison, Outlook, Saskatchewan

45 See *Christian Guardian*, 25 Jan. 1905, Rev. W.H. Hincks, Toronto Conference, to editor; ibid., 14 Oct. 1912, article by Rev. S.D. Chown; ibid., 16 Oct. 1907, Rev. L. Lashley Hall, Fernie, BC, to editor; Minutes, Toronto Conference, 1896, pastoral address; Nathanael Burwash, *A History of Victoria College* (Toronto 1927), Chapters VIII, XI, and XII

46 See Burwash, *History of Victoria College*; W.E. Mann, *Sect, Church and Cult in Alberta*

(Toronto 1955); J.H. Riddell, *Methodism in the Middle West* (Toronto 1946), 169–70, 262; *Journal of Proceedings*, General Conference, 1902, 96; ibid., 1906, 129

47 See *Missionary Outlook*, March 1910, article by the Rev. J.H. Gundy, and S.D. Clark, *Church and Sect in Canada* (Toronto 1948), Chapter VIII, for Methodist difficulties in urban working-class areas; for the Manitoba studies see Departments of Social Service and Evangelism of the Methodist and Presbyterian churches, *Rural Survey, Swan River Valley, Manitoba* (1914), 58–9; ibid., *Turtle Mountain District, Manitoba* (1914), 61

48 See *Christian Guardian*, 25 Jan. 1905, article by Rev. W.H. Hincks; ibid., 11 Jan. 1911, article by Rev. C.H. Cross, Saskatchewan Conference; ibid., 11 Oct. 1912, editorial; ibid., 8 Jan. 1913, editorial. Despite the immigration factor, Methodist Sunday Schools accounted for 60 per cent of new church members in 1914 as compared with only 40.5 per cent in 1898. Computed from Journal of Proceedings, General Conferences, 1898–1914

49 Allen Papers, Rev. James Allen to Rev. R.L. Dawson, PEI, 20 April 1914. See also *Christian Guardian*, 22 May 1912, Alberta Conference news

50 For problems of supervision see *Christian Guardian*, 29 Sept. 1905, Assiniboia Conference news; ibid., 19 Feb. 1913, Rev. James A. Spenceley, Rosetown, Saskatchewan, to editor; Home Mission Reports, Rev. Arthur Barner, Alix, Alberta, to Rev. James Allen, 29 Jan. 1907; ibid., report of Rev. Oliver Darwin, Saskatchewan Conference mission super-intendent, for the year ending June 1910; ibid., Rev. C.H. Cross, Saskatchewan, to Rev. James Allen, 28 July 1913; Allen Papers, Rev. T.P. Perry, Alberta Conference president, to Rev. James Allen, 23 Aug. 1912. For difficulty in accepting married clergy from the east see Home Mission Reports, Rev. James Woodsworth to Rev. James Allen, 22 July 1909; Allen Papers, Rev. James Allen to Rev. C.H. Cross, Saskatoon, 14 Feb. 1910.

51 Computed from Minutes, annual conferences, 1905–14

52 Computed from Annual Report, Missionary Society, 1909–10, 41; ibid., 1913–14, xiv; *Christian Guardian*, 11 Sept. 1912; ibid., 26 Oct. 1910

53 Allen Papers, Rev. James Allen to Rev. J.I. Dawson, Sackville, NB, 31 Dec. 1907

54 Annual Report, Woman's Missionary Society, 1914

55 Computed from Annual Reports, Missionary Society, 1898–1914; Annual Reports, Woman's Missionary Society, 1900–14

56 *Christian Guardian*, 8 Nov. 1911

57 Average contributions to missions were computed from Journal of Proceedings, General Conferences, 1898–1914, and contributions to the WMS are included in the calculations

58 A key factor in consolidation was the necessity of raising missionary salaries to the church's minimum level. See Allen Papers, Rev. James Allen to Rev. W.W. Andrews, president of Regina College, 26 May, 1911; ibid., Rev. James Allen to Rev. J.A. Doyle, Saskatchewan Conference president, 11 April 1913

59 See ibid., Rev. James Allen to Rev. W. Hollingsworth, Calgary, 26 Aug. 1914; ibid., Rev. James Allen to Rev. T.C. Buchanan, 17 Oct. 1914; ibid., Rev. James Allen to Rev. Walter A. Cooke, Winnipeg, 24 Dec. 1914; Annual Report, Missionary Society, 1913–14, v, xxiv

60 See *Christian Guardian*, 15 July 1903, article by Rev. G.W. Kerby; ibid., 20 April 1904, Rev. James Woodsworth to editor; ibid., 14 Feb. 1906, report of congregational meeting at Grace Church, Winnipeg. In 1912 86 per cent of church members over 18 years of age endorsed church union, including more than 93 per cent of the church members on the prairies; see ibid., 17 July 1912

Bookmen and Scholars

Carl F. Klinck

When Sir Robert Falconer reviewed 'the intellectual life of Canada as reflected in its Royal Society' in 1932, he had a good deal to say about research in 'the scientific sections,' but very little about scholarship in the humanities.[1] Fourteen of the chapters in the society's fiftieth anniversary volume (1882–1932) dealt with progress in the natural sciences; three with the literature, history, and 'economic sociale' of French Canada; four (written in English) on history, archaeology, statistics, and political and economic science; and one on 'English Canadian Literature.'

Sir Robert appears to have recognized the aims and achievements of the scholars of French Canada who were Fellows of Section I, but he was somewhat confused about the disciplines represented in Section II. 'From the beginning,' he wrote, 'its aims were vague.' Literature, particularly, was loosely defined. Some of the literary fellows elected to the society in the early years – men like William Kirby – were 'zealous amateurs' in historical research. Evidently poets like Archibald Lampman and Charles G.D. Roberts were expected to produce poems worthy of Canada's 'academy.' 'Except for a few contribution[s] by two or three of our national poets, Section II has indeed not produced much pure literature,' Sir Robert said, and then, in the same sentence, turned to archeology and history.[2] Fortunately, the creative writers had Lorne Pierce to praise them in the chapter on English-Canadian literature.

This fiftieth anniversary volume yields almost no details about the state of scholarship in Canadian literature in 1932 for comparison with the very evident progress in research in Canadian history accomplished before that same year. The theory I wish to advance in this essay is that literary history – the systematic discovery and explanation of facts *about* the lives, times, and works of authors – had made a start, albeit a slow one, under conditions similar to, and influenced by, contemporaneous research in general Canadian history.

Toward the end of his presidential review, Sir Robert noted that Section II was being 'broadened' in the 1920s 'by more frequent papers from Canadian scholars on criticism both of classical and modern literatures, and on philosophical subjects.'[3] Canadian literary scholarship, of course, had to wait for the systematic study of English literature to take hold. The term 'Canadian' was not coupled with 'modern' by Sir Robert, but he did refer to Duncan Campbell Scott's presidential address in 1922, in which Scott had found 'evidence for the progress of Canadian literature in the growing independence of our literary judgment as to our own poets, which has been generally accepted by the outside world.'[4] This stage in progress was understandable: creativity comes first, criticism next, scholarship third, and criticism supported by scholarship as maturity arrives.

At the time of the anniversary in 1932 Lorne Pierce could hint at the third of these developments:[5] 'Poets and artists have emerged to supplant European Traditions with a native achievement nourished by the Canadian soil. This native art is neither a miracle nor a mystery; we know its beginnings, and we can trace its evolution.' 'The Evolution of Canadian Literature' was the title which Pierce had given to the introductory chapter of his own handbook, *An Outline of Canadian Literature (French and English)*, published in 1927.

The work of tracing the 'evolution' had not gone far beyond identification of authors and the grouping of them by periods and topics. The pre-Confederation era was not arousing much interest, although a great deal of precise information about early writers had been provided in *Bibliotheca Canadensis: or A Manual of Canadian Literature* (published 1867) by Henry J. Morgan, a professional researcher and biographer, at the very beginning of such Canadian studies. He was followed by some semi-professionals and occasionally by teachers and professors trained in English literature. The first survey in the twentieth century, Archibald MacMurchy's *Handbook of Canadian Literature (English)* (1906) was published by a Scot teaching school in Toronto, a year after *Roberts and the Influences of His Time* (1905), a critical study by James Cappon, MA, Glasgow, professor of English at Queen's (1888–1919). Evidently a slight demand for information was then rising in the schools and universities.

Thomas G. Marquis, a Toronto schoolteacher and journalist, contributed a survey of a broad range of Canadian literature to *Canada and its Provinces* (1914),[6] the series sponsored by historians Adam Shortt and Arthur Doughty. A cautious report on his country's literature was given in a chapter of the *Cambridge History of English Literature* (1916) by Professor Pelham Edgar of Toronto, who was born and educated in that city, and who also held a doctorate in philosophy from Johns Hopkins. 'Our literary past,' he wrote about Canada, 'is the literary past of England; we have not yet had time to strike root for ourselves.'[7] Later he became celebrated as one of those who helped to 'discover' Marjorie Pickthall, E.J. Pratt, and Northrop Frye.

Ray Palmer Baker, a graduate of the University of Western Ontario in 1906 (later a professor of English in the United States), published his excellent Harvard

PHD thesis, *A History of English-Canadian Literature to the Confederation*, in 1920. Another survey, *Headwaters of Canadian Literature*, appeared in 1924, the work of Archibald MacMechan, a native of Berlin (Kitchener), Ontario, but a Maritimer and professor of English at Dalhousie since 1889. The year 1924 also welcomed a very large, handsome, and popular book by John D. Logan (a journalist and literary editor with a PHD from Harvard) and Donald G. French, a schoolteacher and journalist. This 'synoptic introduction to the literary history of Canada (English) from 1760 to 1924' bore the title of *Highways of Canadian Literature*; it displayed categorization and critical terminology with an air of authority which awoke pride and appreciation in several generations of readers. Pierce's more concise *Outline* came out in 1927, and *A Handbook of Canadian Literature* by Professor V.B. Rhodenizer of Acadia in 1930. Meanwhile, special studies had begun to appear, notably Alexander Clark Casselman's invaluable notes in his edition of [Major John] *Richardson's War of 1812* (1902); V.L.O. Chittick's Columbia University thesis, *Thomas Chandler Haliburton* (1924); Lorne Pierce's *William Kirby* in 1929; and James Cappon's *Bliss Carman and the Literary Currents and Influences of his Time* (1930).

This first shelf of scholarship in Canadian literary history should not be overrated, but its existence in 1932 indicated that a dent had been made upon the exclusiveness of English studies concerned with the United Kingdom. Many people could remember when there had been professorial chairs in the universities labelled jointly for 'English literature and history,' a practical demonstration of the nineteenth-century view that history was a category of literature or literature a category of history, especially with reference to England. If 'Canadian' was ever to become a university subject, one might have expected, by analogy, the introduction of chairs of 'Canadian literature and history.' One need only look at T.G. Marquis's chapter in *Canada and Its Provinces* (1914) to guess at this possibility from the literary side; his sub-sections of 'English-Canadian Literature' were, in this order, history, biography, travels and exploration, general literature, fiction, poetry.[8] Pierce's *Outline* (1927) dealt, not only with the novelists, poets, dramatists, and essayists, but also with religious and devotional literature, nature writers, humourists, journalism, biography, travel and exploration, and history. 'History in its broadest sense,' Pierce explained, 'includes the total record of man's experience and thought. Thus understood every book mentioned in this *Outline* is a work of history.'[9] And every book, paradoxically, was also literature in the broadest sense. In Dr R.E. Watters' *A Check List of Canadian Literature and Background Materials, 1628–1950* (published in 1959), and in the massive *Literary History of Canada* (1965), very nearly the same sub-divisions were still being used.

What happened to the dual chairs at Toronto in 1894, at Queen's in 1910, and at Western (Ontario) University in 1920 was separation of disciplines by the appointment of professors of modern history. Some of these scholars made their separateness an opportunity for the introduction of Canadian into the 'modern' category. While students of literature were still keeping the family of books together, and practising literary history or emphasizing criticism of *belles lettres,* the historians were beginning to put their scholarly houses in order. Pelham Edgar clearly saw this happen, as he said in his *Cambridge History* article: 'History is more successfully organized in Canada at the present time [1916] than any other branch of literature. Our archives are being systematically explored, and societies exist for the purpose of editing old, and publishing new, material of a historical nature.'[10]

Busy with their documents, the historians were eager to release fact from fables, but they were collecting everything of native origin. They soon dominated the libraries of universities and large urban centres, serving as chief librarians and also in the role of historian-cum-collector-cum-professor, typified by men soon to be named in this article. Among the Canadiana rescued in this way were compositions of an imaginative as well as an informative kind, which would some day appear in the strict canon of Canadian literature. Conversely, works acknowledged to be creative took on enriched meaning under explanations by historians. So the romance of facts and the facts underlying romance were being recovered for Canadian readers.

Orderly arrangements had been made for history and the social sciences. George M. Wrong had been professor of modern history at Toronto only a few years before he issued, in 1897, the first of the annual instalments of the *Review of Historical Publications Relating to Canada.* This became in 1920, under the late W.S. Wallace, the *Canadian Historical Review.* The Canadian Historical Association was organized in 1922, and the *Canadian Journal of Economics and Political Science* began to serve its special group of researchers in 1935. The impression which these examples made upon the literary scholars may be seen, not in immediate attempts at organization of societies, but rather in a new journal devoted to their common needs. The *Queen's Quarterly* in the 1920s and the *Dalhousie Review* (established 1921) still welcomed their articles. In October 1931, however, another university journal, the *University of Toronto Quarterly,* gave promise of more opportunities for specialized publication. Its purpose was to support the humanities, and it could make, as Professors Watson Kirkconnell and A.S.P. Woodhouse stated in 1947, 'the history of Canadian literature its special, and the history of literature and of ideas, its general preoccupation.'[11] Of prime importance was the introduction into this quarterly of an annual review of 'Letters in Canada,' beginning in the issue of April 1936 with notes on the production of the year 1935. The scope of this survey was generous: the editors said that it 'does not stop short with imaginative literature, but extends to the literature of criticism and comment, and also to scholarship in the humanities ... including some important work in history and sociology, with reference for further information in the Canadian field to the appropriate sources.'[12]

Thus, soon after the Royal Society's anniversary review in 1932, the *University of Toronto Quarterly* announced the beginning of the modern period of Canadian literary criticism and scholarship. Some of the most influential works which followed may be named. In 1936 Professor W.E. Collin of the University of Western Ontario published *The White Savannahs*. In 1943 Professor E.K. Brown, who had reviewed 'Poetry' in the first issue of 'Life and Letters,' brought out *On Canadian Poetry*. In the same year Professor A.J.M. Smith's overhauling of opinions about literary history appeared in *The Book of Canadian Poetry*. Professor Desmond Pacey's *Creative Writing in Canada* (1952) was a modern survey, soundly based on research and critical judgment. The comprehensive *Literary History of Canada*, which appeared as late as 1965, was the work of a team of scholars. Norah Story's *The Oxford Companion to Canadian History and Literature* (1967) is a useful guide to information which has been gathered by investigators in both of these disciplines. Critical articles are now a feature of *Canadian Literature*, the University of British Columbia quarterly edited by Dr George Woodcock which began publication in the summer of 1959. Biographical, historical, and critical monographs are now appearing by the dozens, and the preparation of theses in this field has become a major operation in the graduate schools.

There is not yet a society specifically organized for the advancement of scholarship in Canadian literature. Those engaged in such writing associate with other professors in the meetings of the Humanities Association of Canada and the Association of Canadian University Teachers of English. They share with others the assistance of the Humanities Research Council of Canada (founded in 1943 under the sponsorship of the Royal Society and the closely-related Canadian Social Science Research Council), and, since the Massey Report of 1951, the patronage of the Canada Council (founded in 1957).

Dedicated librarians assisted in this development at every stage, not only by collecting, purchasing, and preserving, but also by setting examples of professional scholarship: many of them were historians, writers, and teachers. In this distinguished line, which includes Fred Landon and James Talman, the classic types appear to be Adam Shortt (1859–1931), George M. Wrong (1860–1948) and William Stewart Wallace (1884–1970). It so happens that both Shortt and Wrong were born in southwestern Ontario, not far from London. They were contemporaries of the whole group of Confederation poets and novelists born between 1858 and 1862; regional pride prompts one to name those who got their start in this area: Archibald Lampman at Morpeth, Wilfred Campbell at Berlin (Kitchener), Sara Jeannette Duncan and E. Pauline Johnson at or near Brantford. Sadly one must record that Shortt had to be lost to Queen's, Wrong to Toronto,

Lampman and Campbell to Ottawa, S.J. Duncan (Cotes) to India and England, and E. Pauline Johnson to Vancouver. They all contributed to a national movement, as Dr Landon also did in the following generation, and Dr Talman in the next.

Adam Shortt was a noted historian, archivist, teacher, and political economist. His birthplace at Kilworth (in 1859) can almost be seen from London. He left for Walkerton as young boy, and then became successively a student and tutor in philosophy at Queen's (when lectures in political economy were given by instructors in philosophy); a professor of political science in 1891; an authority on Canadian banking, preferential trade, and industrial disputes; and chairman of the Board of Historical Publications at the Public Archives of Canada. He is best known for a major series of historical volumes. In editorial partnership with Arthur G. Doughty [later Sir Arthur] and with Robert Glasgow as publisher, he produced *Canada and Its Provinces, A History of the Canadian People and their Institutions by One Hundred Associates*. Space was given to Canadian literature, and T.G. Marquis made the most of his opportunity to act as literary historian, confirming the remark of a biographer that Shortt put his faith in men and libraries.[13]

George MacKinnon Wrong was born on a farm at Grovesend, near Port Bruce. He became a very distinguished professor of history at the University of Toronto. Under his inspiration, professional scholarship in Canadian history flourished there after 1894. Not only was he a founder of the *Review of Historical Publications Relating to Canada* (1895) but he also helped to organize the Champlain Society in 1905. His own historical works were of a very high standard, and, as a biographer pointed out, 'for their essays students found themselves – often for the first time – reading long, standard books, and learning to evaluate evidence. They learned, too, something of the art of writing.'[14]

Dr Landon was born in London in 1880, two years before the founding of the Royal Society, and he lived through the whole development which has been sketched. He was eighteen years of age when the Ontario Historical Society was founded in 1898, and forty-two when the Canadian Historical Association was organized in 1922. In all of these societies he and James Talman, who had studied under Landon at Western and Stewart Wallace at Toronto, took an active part. Together, and one after the other, they served Western through a total of forty-seven years, from 1923 until 1970. Assisted for many years by Miss Lillian Benson, they built up a collection of rare and current Canadiana which now amply sustains specialized postgraduate and faculty research in both history and literature. Meanwhile, they never ceased activities in teaching, writing, and the pursuit of meticulous scholarship. Among their accomplishments were the enlargement of the specialist's field for investigation in Canadian-American relations and into the materials of regional history (newspapers and periodicals as well as archives), including much that was potentially as useful to the literary man as to the historian.

Fred Landon wrote articles far beyond the date of his retirement, and Dr Talman will probably do the same. Old historians never die; they only write away. It is characteristic of the achievement of this kind of scholar that he has not time to use all his hoard of discoveries. I have been a beneficiary of notes and clippings collected by Dr Landon, and I have been a co-worker with the knowledgeable Dr Talman. Footnotes have been my special inheritance from the historian-librarians, for they may be depended upon to place, at the bottom of each page, hints of information which they could not enlarge upon just then; these have been profitable for the purposes of literature. Since there is room for only one example, it will be from that master of information, the late W. Stewart Wallace of Toronto.

A footnote of his attached to an historical article on the North-West Company led me to forgotten files of Samuel Hull Wilcocke's *The Scribbler* and opened up for me the biography of one of Canada's earliest critics together with a fascinating view of Montreal journalism in the 1820s. The temper of such a scholar as Wallace is revealed in *The Pedlars from Quebec and Other Papers on the Nor'Westers* (1954), a whole volume of supplements or 'postscripts' to the Champlain Society volume which he had published twenty years earlier. Subsequent research had given him new information which his conscience would not allow him to ignore. His introduction[15] ought to be obligatory reading for all young historians of Canadian literature.

NOTES

1 Royal Society of Canada, *Fifty Years Retrospect: Anniversary Volume 1882–1932* (1932), 9–25
2 Ibid., 22
3 Ibid., 23
4 Ibid., 24
5 Ibid., 55
6 Adam Shortt and Arthur G. Doughty, eds., *Canada and its Provinces* (Toronto 1914). For Marquis's article see Vol. XII, 493–589
7 *Cambridge History of English Literature* (Cambridge 1916), XIV, 343–60; reference to 344
8 Shortt and Doughty, eds., *Canada and its Provinces*, XII, 493–589
9 Lorne Pierce, *Outline* (Toronto 1927), 217
10 *Cambridge History*, XII, 358
11 Watson Kirkconnell and A.S.P. Woodhouse, *The Humanities in Canada* (Ottawa 1947), 190
12 *University of Toronto Quarterly*, V, 3, April 1936, 360
13 W.A. Macintosh, 'Adam Shortt, 1859–1931,' in *Canadian Journal of Economics and Political Science*, IV, May 1936, 164–76; reference to 169
14 W.S. Wallace, 'The Life and Work of George M. Wrong,' *Canadian Historical Review*, XXIX, 3, Sept. 1948, 229–39; reference to 233
15 Toronto 1954, v–viii

Bibliography of
the Academic and Journalistic Writings
of James J. Talman

Hilary Bates

1927

1 The position of the Church of England in Upper Canada, 1791–1840.
Unpublished MA thesis, University of Western Ontario, 1927
2 The Reverend Richard Flood, Indian missionary and rector of Delaware,
1834–1865. London and Middlesex Historical Society, *Transactions*,
Part 12, 1927, 21–5

1929

3 Church of England missionary effort in Upper Canada, 1815–1840. Ontario
Historical Society, *Papers and Records*, XXV, 1929, 3–14
4 Early immigration to Adelaide township in Middlesex County. London and
Middlesex Historical Society, *Transactions*, Part 13, 1929, 48–54
5 Social conditions in Upper Canada, 1815–1840. Unpublished PHD thesis,
University of Toronto, 1929
6 Travel literature as source material for the history of Upper Canada,
1791–1840. Canadian Historical Association, *Annual Report*, 1929, 111–20

1931

7 Agricultural Societies of Upper Canada. Ontario Historical Society, *Papers
and Records*, XXVII, 1931, 545–52
8 Narrow escape for rector in river tragedy. *London Free Press*, 2 May 1931
9 edited with M.A. Garland: Pioneer drinking habits and the rise of the
temperance agitation in Upper Canada prior to 1840. Ontario Historical
Society, *Papers and Records*, XXVII, 1931, 341–64
10 When Ontario fought drink demon. Toronto *Mail & Empire*, 12 November
1931
11 Review: Catharine Parr Traill, *The Backwoods of Canada. Canadian
Historical Review*, XII, 1931, 76–7
12 Review: The Diary of Reverend William Fraser (1834–1835), with an
introductory essay on Early Presbyterianism in Western Ontario by Harry E.

Parker from London and Middlesex Historical Society, *Transactions*, Part 14, 1931, 1–156. *Canadian Historical Review*, XII, 1931, 318–19

1932

13 Accused horse thief becomes legislator. *London Free Press*, 13 February 1932

14 The Diary of Captain John Thomson ... *Orillia Packet and Times*, 26 May 1932

15 Indian killed, wrestling at barn raising ... *Orillia Packet and Times*, 2 June 1932

16 Cut piece off tail of cow to cure hollow horn. *Orillia Packet and Times*, 23 June 1932

17 First agricultural society organized in Orillia in 1836. *Orillia Packet and Times*, 14 July 1932

18 *Extracts from the diary of Captain John Thomson, who settled in Orillia, Ontario in 1832.* Orillia, Packet and Times, 1932

19 Ebenezer Allan had shady reputation in his Delaware deals. *London Free Press*, 8 October 1932

1933

20 The first Church of England Sunday school paper in Canada. *Church messenger*, September 1933. Continued in *Church messenger*, October 1933

21 Strachan found London people lamenting fact of having no clergyman. *London Free Press*, 25 March 1933

22 Held by storm, Strachan spent night in woods. *London Free Press*, 1 April 1933

23 Strachan found youth ignorant of the Church. *London Free Press*, 8 April 1933

24 Negro settlement in Waterloo County. *London Free Press*, 2 December 1933

25 A secret military document, 1825. *American Historical Review*, XXXVIII, 1933, 295–300

26 Suggestions for instructors: *A plan for teaching the material contained in M.W. Bro. Herrington's book on "The History of the Grand Lodge of Canada in the Province of Ontario."* Committee on Masonic Education of the Grand Lodge of Canada, A.F. and A.M. in the Province of Ontario, 1933

27 Travel in Ontario before the coming of the Railway. Ontario Historical Society, *Papers and Records*, XXIX, 1933, 3–20. Part reprinted in Early Stage Travel in Western Ontario *London Free Press*, 6 December 1933

28 Western Ontario in 1836 described by Robert Davis. *London Free Press*, 30 December 1933

29 When the Penetanguishene Road was laid out. *Orillia Packet and Times*, 16 March 1933

30 Review: Walter S. Herrington, *The History of the Grand Lodge of Canada in the Province of Ontario, 1855–1930. Canadian Historical Review*, XXIV, 1933, 469

31 Review: [Paquin, Rev. J.] *The tragedy of old Huronia (wendake ehen). Canadian Historical Review*, XIV, 1933, 244

1934

32 Anglican missionary's visit to Orillia 100 years ago. *Orillia Packet and Times,* 5 April 1934

33 Bishop Strachan's visit to Orillia in 1842. *Orillia Packet and Times,* 18 January 1934

34 Burning of St. Paul's took place in 1844. *London Free Press,* 21 February 1934

35 The Church of England in Fingal ninety years ago. *St. Thomas Times-Journal,* 22 September 1934

36 Early years of Church of England in Port Burwell and Vienna. *St. Thomas Times-Journal,* 25 August 1934

37 Historic Ontario. *Kiwanis magazine,* May 1934, 195–6

38 Movies may prove handmaid of history. *London Free Press,* 26 September 1934

39 The Position of the Church of England in Upper Canada, 1791–1840. *Canadian Historical Review,* xv, 1934, 361–75

40 St. Paul's corner stone laid ninety years ago. *London Free Press,* 22 June 1934

1935

41 Archibald Hope Young [obit]. *Canadian Historical Review,* XVI, 1935, 219–20

42 Grant of land to St. John's made in 1834. Peterborough *Examiner,* 20 March 1935

43 Local church histories. *Canadian Historical Review,* XVI, 1935, 340–1

44 The Ontario Archives. *Ontario Library Review,* XIX, 1935, 64–6

45 A peek behind the scenes. *Orillia Packet and Times,* 1935

46 Review: Le Comte de Colbert Maulevrier, *Voyage dans l'intérieur des Etats-Unis et au Canada. Canadian Historical Review,* XVI, 1935, 426–7

47 Review: Mrs John Graves Simcoe, *The diary of Mrs. John Graves Simcoe. Canadian Historical Review,* XVI, 1935, 231

1936

48 Alexander Fraser [obit]. *Canadian Historical Review,* XVII, 1936, 90

49 Le Révérend John Ogilvie. *Bulletin des Recherches Historiques,* XLII, 1936, 682–3

50 Valuable records in obscure places. *Ontario Library Review,* XX, 1936, 147–8

51 The value of crown lands papers in historical research, with an illustration of their use. Royal Society of Canada, *Transactions*, 3rd series, xxx, 1936 Section 2, 131–6

52 Review: Elizabeth H. Davidson, *The Establishment of the English Church in Continental American Colonies*, and W. Stanford Reid, *The Church of Scotland in Lower Canada: Its Struggle for Establishment. Canadian Historical Review*, xvii, 1936, 445–6

1937

53 Clerical Accidents in Upper Canada. *Canadian Churchman*, 15 April 1937

54 From Moscow to Whitby: The Romantic Career of the First Rector of Markham and Vaughan. *Canadian Churchman*, 4 March 1937

55 The Mysterious John Bryan, an unsolved problem in Canadian Church History. *Canadian Churchman*, 18 March 1937

56 The printing presses of William Lyon Mackenzie, prior to 1837. *Canadian Historical Review*, xviii, 1937, 414–18; Collingwood *Enterprise Bulletin*, 20 January 1938

57 Review: Sara L. Campbell, *Brooke township history, 1833–1933. Canadian Historical Review*, xviii, 1937, 237

58 Review: Oswald C.J. Withrow, *The romance of the Canadian National Exhibition. Canadian Historical Review*, xviii, 1937, 234

1938

59 Founder had hopes Louisville would be leading metropolis. *London Free Press*, 3 December 1938

60 ...letters of James Elliott ... 1844 ... *London Free Press*, 29 January 1938

61 The newspapers of Upper Canada a century ago. *Canadian Historical Review*, xix, 1938, 9–23

62 Some notes on the clergy of the Church of England in Upper Canada prior to 1840. Royal Society of Canada, *Transactions*, 3rd series, xxxii, 1938, Section 2, 57–66

63 The treasure room iii, Province of Ontario archives. *Canadian Bookman*, xx, 1938, No. 3, 11–13

64 Review: Adolph B. Benson, ed., *The America of 1750: Peter Kalm's Travels in North America. Canadian Historical Review*, xix, 1938, 418–9

65 Review: P. Campbell, *Travels in the interior inhabited parts of North America in the years 1791 and 1792*, edited H.H. Langton. *Canadian Historical Review*, xix, 1938, 207

66 Review: *Fort Klock papers, 1762–1845. Canadian Historical Review*, xix, 1938, 337

67 Review: Milton W. Hamilton, *The Country Printer, New York State,* *1785–1830. Canadian Historical Review,* xix, 1938, 333

68 Review: John Wolfe Lydekker, *The faithful Mohawks. Canadian Historical Review,* xix, 1938, 417–18

69 Review: Welland County Historical Society, *Papers and Records,* Volume 5, and W.V. (Ben) Uttley, *A History of Kitchener. Canadian Historical Review,* xix, 1938, 427–8

1939

70 A Canadian view of parties and issues on the eve of the Civil War. *Journal of Southern History,* v, 1939, 245–53. [Letters from George Sheppard]

71 Chief Brant's gift repeating rifle... *London Free Press,* 4 November 1939

72 Church society great help to Huron Diocese. *London Free Press,* 29 July 1939

73 The first bishop of the Diocese of Toronto. *Canadian Churchman,* lxvi, 1939, 292, 303

74 First dailies in Ontario in the 1850's largely owed success to the telegraph. *London Free Press,* 21 June 1939

75 First election of Bishop of Huron Diocese... *London Free Press,* 23 September 1939

76 George Brown was promoter for Bothwell. *London Free Press,* 21 October 1939

77 George Sheppard able newsman made headway. *London Free Press,* 12 August 1939

78 The newspaper press of Canada West, 1850–1860. Royal Society of Canada, *Transactions,* series 3, xxxiii, 1939, Section 2, 149–74

79 No day of rest on sabbath for clergy of 1879. *London Free Press,* 15 July 1939

80 Noble Catfish Creek Henry Dalley's choice for port development. *London Free Press,* 18 November 1939

81 Ontario's first newspaper 'ad' was about a brewery. *London Free Press,* 29 April 1939

82 Printing presses of William Lyon Mackenzie. *London Free Press,* 1 November 1939

83 Railway 'daily' issued weekly unique as paper. *London Free Press,* 9 September 1939

84 Sioux Indian Chief who lived and died here 100 years ago. *Orillia Packet and Times,* 9 March 1939

85 Two clergymen encountered in journey of 1820. *London Free Press,* 23 December 1939

86 with M.A. Garland: William Pope, bird lover ... *London Free Press,* 26 August 1939

87 Year of confederation saw Presbyterians of Middlesex flourishing. *London*

Free Press, 4 February 1939

88 Review: Mable Burkholder, *The story of Hamilton. Canadian Historical Review*, xx, 1939, 350

89 Review: Edward Godfrey Cox, *A reference guide to the literature of travel. Canadian Historical Review*, xx, 1939, 338

90 Review: Historical Records Survey, Division of Women's and Professional Projects, Works Progress Administration, *A description of the manuscript collections in the Massachusetts Diocesan Library. Canadian Historical Review*, xx, 1939, 460

91 Review: Roland Wild, *Macnab the last laird. Canadian Historical Review*, xx, 1939, 452

1940

92 Bruce, as frontier, small population at Confederation. *London Free Press*, 24 August 1940

93 Chaplains in Upper Canada. *Canadian Churchman*, 20 March 1940

94 Charged rival clergy too fond of pleasures of their parishioners. *London Free Press*, 30 March 1940

95 Facts of value and inaccuracies found in directories of 1860's ... *London Free Press*, 22 June 1940

96 Galt site pleased Bishop Strachan as first parish of Huron District ... *London Free Press*, 2 September 1940

97 Hurons were gamblers ... *London Free Press*, 10 February 1940

98 John West's visit to Ontario. *Canadian Churchman*, LXVII, 1940, 452

99 Johnson and his companion Gamelin in 1761 visited Port Dover, Long Point, Port Stanley ... *London Free Press*, 3 February 1940

100 Lone white man occupied large region in Bruce. *London Free Press*, 13 January 1940

101 Loyalists had reward but suffered severely in standing by Empire. *London Free Press*, 19 October 1940

102 Mud roads, discomfort overcome by Strachan on journey century ago. *London Free Press*, 16 November 1940

103 Nathan Bangs most famous circuit rider. *London Free Press*, 17 February 1940

104 Our debt to the Mother Country. *Canadian Churchman*, 19 September 1940; *Greater Britain Messenger*, November/December 1940

105 Owen Sound looks over 100 years ... *London Free Press*, 5 October 1940

106 Pressing worries of Bruce, new settlers, taxes, roads, revealed in old directory. *London Free Press*, 2 March 1940

107 Protest from Chatham over rumors, neglect preceded boom of '52. *London*

Free Press, 16 March 1940

108 contributing editor: George Brown, ed., *Readings in Canadian history.* Toronto, Dent, 1940

109 Residents of London celebrated great occasion of formal entry of first official railway train. *London Free Press*, 20 July 1940

110 Rum and fur business thought by missionary to be linked together. *London Free Press*, 25 May 1940

111 Shovels and champagne played part in hectic railroad-building days. *London Free Press*, 27 April 1940

112 Son of indian warrior bitter toward whites ... *London Free Press*, 11 May 1940

113 Strachan's first visit to Huron ... *London Free Press*, 7 September 1940

114 Sydenham found boat service vile ... *London Free Press*, 10 August 1940

115 Tradition of early day old age shattered by scattered records of church registers and newspapers. *London Free Press*, 8 June 1940

116 Troy, Kent Hamlet, had prosperous days. *London Free Press*, 13 April 1940

117 Review: *Acton's early days. Canadian Historical Review*, XXI, 1940, 334

118 Review: Jean Delanglez, *Frontenac and the Jesuits. Church History*, IX, 1940, 392

1941

119 Angry words with bitter charges featured Upper Canada's election preceding rebellious clash of '37. *London Free Press*, 12 July 1941

120 Bishop Strachan. *Canadian Churchman*, LXVIII, 1941, 516

121 Early missions on Monck road. *Orillia Packet and Times*, 13 February 1941

122 Opened 90 years ago, old school goes to war. *London Free Press*, 19 July 1941

123 Review: Florence B. Murray and Elsie McLeod Murray, *Preliminary Guide to the Manuscript Collection in the Toronto Public Libraries. Canadian Historical Review*, XXII, 1941, 327

124 Review: Milo Milton Quaife, ed., *War on Detroit. Canadian Historical Review*, XXII, 1941, 203–4

1942

125 Energetic yeomen and quality liquor won praise for St. Thomas. *London Free Press*, 14 March 1942

126 Found 'spiritual destitution' in 1842 ... *London Free Press*, 24 February 1942

127 ... opening Great Western, Hamilton to London. *London Free Press*, 6 July 1942

128 Hunger, illness attended voyages of pioneers. *London Free Press*, 14 November 1942

129 Joseph Brant's interest in masonry in the early days. Brantford *Expositor*, 25 August 1942

130 London newspaper venture ... *London Free Press*, 28 February 1942

131 The origins of freemasonry in the Niagara District. *Historical sketch to commemorate the sesqui-centenary of freemasonry in the Niagara District 1792–1942*. Toronto, Grand Lodge A.F. and A.M. of Canada, 1942, pp. 3–13

132 A pioneer war production in Upper Canada. *Western Ontario Historical Notes*, I, 1, 1942, 2–5

133 Railway wrecks ... *London Free Press*, 21 March 1942

134 Recognition was slow in coming to importance of local history. *London Free Press*, 4 July 1942

135 edited: *Report of a missionary journal made by the Honourable and Reverend Charles James Stewart through Upper Canada in 1820*. London, University of Western Ontario, 1942

136 St. Thomas 'Hill' tough problem ... *London Free Press*, 17 January 1942

137 St. Thomas man touring in '46 believed own district best. *London Free Press*, 26 December 1942

138 Westminster free and happy with taxes for year only $464.00. *London Free Press*, 24 January 1942

139 Review: *Libraries in Canada, 1938–1940. Canadian Historical Review*, XXIII, 1942, 91

140 Review: Antoine Roy, *Rapport de l'Archiviste de la Province de Québec pour 1940–1941*, and *Guide to Depositories of Manuscript Collections in New York State (exclusive of New York City)*, Volume I. *Canadian Historical Review*, XXIII, 1942, 329–30

1943

141 Building of London's first Anglican Church ... *London Free Press*, 21 August 1943

142 ... London's big fire. *London Free Press*, 20 November 1943

143 Cholera, high prices and shortage of food included in worries of over century ago. *London Free Press*, 13 November 1943

144 Early London taverns boasted all comforts. *London Free Press*, 10 July 1943

145 Exploiting by white residents hampered Moravian settlement. *London Free Press*, 5 June 1943

146 105 years in Canadian canal work through three generations record of the family of A.L. Killaly. Peterborough *Examiner*, 28 January 1943

147 Hunters helped out food supply of Fairfield settlers. *London Free Press*, 25 September 1943

148 Introducing an editor [S.B. Herbert]. *Ontario Library Review*, xxvII, 1943, 459

149 Laying of cornerstone was memorable event for London. *London Free Press*, 6 November 1943

150 Leaders of Fairfield community held promoters under suspicion. *London Free Press*, 3 July 1943

151 Library for 'clerks and students' shown scant respect. *London Free Press*, 11 December 1943

152 Local history value stressed. *London Free Press*, 28 October 1943

153 London given definite form as municipality with Burwell survey. *London Free Press*, 3 January 1943

154 Major Nelles was mystery figure along Grand River. *London Free Press*, 27 March 1943

155 Missed guess when Laurier chosen chief of Liberals. *London Free Press*, 16 October 1943

156 Ontario's first paper started 150 years ago. *London Free Press*, 17 April 1943

157 Preserving local war records. *Ontario Library Review*, xxvII, 1943, 15–17

158 St. Paul's nearing century mark ... *London Free Press*, 11 September 1943

159 Site for Fairfield settlement ... *London Free Press*, 19 June 1943

160 Society formed in 1830 to civilize Indians ... *London Free Press*, 30 October 1943

161 Some books about Latin America. *Ontario Library Review*, xxvII, 1943, 472–4

162 ... diary of Zeisberger. *London Free Press*, 29 March 1943

163 They talked of old times at gathering back in '60's. *London Free Press*, 24 July 1943

164 Trek of youth to u.s. west and gold fields gave Canada manpower worries century ago. *London Free Press*, 14 August 1943

165 War backfire gave Thames area uneasy time in 1794. *London Free Press*, 3 July 1943

166 White Village now 'missing' ... *London Free Press*, 28 August 1943

167 Introduction and edited with E.M. Murray: Mrs Anna Jameson, *Winter studies and summer rambles in Canada*. Toronto, Nelson, 1943

168 Yuletide brought little break in routine of settlement days. *London Free Press*, 24 December 1943

169 Review: A.J.H. Richardson and Helen I. Cowan, eds., *Rochester Historical Society Publications*, xx. *Canadian Historical Review*, xxiv, 1943, 68–9

1944

170 Brant Museum has excellent record of local history. Brantford *Expositor*,

1 April 1944

171 Bogus money arrests gave London thrill and some fun. *London Free Press*, 29 January 1944

172 Charlevoix was great press agent ... *London Free Press*, 18 November 1944

173 Christmas stocks from Quebec hauled by sleigh to Sandwich. *London Free Press*, 16 December 1944

174 Circus of century ago toured country roads ... *London Free Press*, 24 June 1944

175 Doan's old school in Norfolk played part in Ontario's major advances in education. *London Free Press*, 18 March 1944

176 Famous Clinton Hotel marked junction of roads. *London Free Press*, 1 April 1944

177 Found London growing town of 75 houses 113 years ago. *London Free Press*, 10 June 1944

178 Gay parties marked passing of old year ... *London Free Press*, 1 January 1944

179 History of Woodstock Baptist Church told in notable volume. *London Free Press*, 22 April 1944

180 Home comfort late in reaching upper section of Bruce County. *London Free Press*, 14 October 1944

181 Light in London tavern window during storm was welcome beacon when city in making. *London Free Press*, 13 March 1944

182 New society will collect district lore, [unidentified] 1 April 1944

183 Perth pioneers were proud of holdings after 10 years of work. *London Free Press*, 23 December 1944

184 Railway journey 90 years ago ... *London Free Press*, 19 February 1944

185 Rush of 'draft dodgers' from u.s. Civil War into Canada described by Press as stampede. *London Free Press*, 5 February 1944

186 Strange story of Mary Jemison ... *London Free Press*, 11 March 1944

187 Tale of vast pigeon flights of early days amazed writer. *London Free Press*, 8 July 1944

188 Two-preacher circuit grew into powerful church. *London Free Press*, 16 September 1944

189 Value of local history. *London Free Press*, 21 July 1944

190 Review: Mattie M.I. Clark, *The positive side of John Graves Simcoe. Canadian Historical Review*, xxv, 1944, 455

191 Review: F.H. Dobbin, *Our old home town. Canadian Historical Review*, xxv, 1944, 329–30

192 Review: Antoine Roy, *Rapport de l'Archiviste de la Province de Québec, pour 1941–1942. Canadian Historical Review*, xxv, 1944, 209–10

193 Review: James Everett Seaver, *A narrative of the life of Mary Jemison, the*

white woman of the Genesee, revised by Charles Delamater Vail. *Canadian Historical Review*, xxv, 1944, 438–9

194 Review: Louis B. Wright and Marion Tinling, eds., *Quebec to Carolina in 1785–1786. Canadian Historical Review*, xxv, 1944, 207–8

1945

195 Backwardness of carriage styles annoyed traveler of century ago. *London Free Press*, 18 August 1945

196 Fingal dates right to fame long previous to war flying. *London Free Press*, 17 March 1945

197 Lacking brewery or distillery, Mitchell rated lone dry town. *London Free Press*, 27 January 1945

198 Lake transport made Port Stanley thriving spot in pre-railway days. *London Free Press*, 8 September 1945

199 Lieutenant-Governor Simcoe dined well on porcupine on site of London. *London Free Press*, 2 September 1945

200 Plank road gave luxury to travel ... *London Free Press*, 25 July 1945

201 Rumor of gold find along Thames gave thrill to Londoners of 1853. *London Free Press*, 1 September 1945

202 Troops rehabilitation old problem for Canada. *London Free Press*, 24 March 1945

203 Review: T.A. Reed, *The blue and white. Canadian Historical Review*, xxvi, 1945, 456–7

204 Review: Bertus Harry Wabeke. *Dutch emigration to North America 1624–1860. Canadian Historical Review*, xxvi, 1945, 457

1946

205 An episode in Latin American and Canadian relations. Ontario Historical Society, *Papers and Records*, xxxviii, 1946, 51–5

206 Introductory notes. *Western Ontario Historical Notes*, iv, 1946, No 2, 27–30

207 edited with introduction and notes: *Loyalist narratives from Upper Canada*. Toronto, The Champlain Society, 1946. Reprinted: New York, Greenwood Press, 1969

208 Review: Lucien Brault, *Ottawa old and new*, and W.P. Percival, *The lure of Montreal. Canadian Historical Review*, xxvii, 1946, 325–6

209 Review: Central United Church, Stratford, Ontario, *Centennial history, 1845–1945. Canadian Historical Review*, xxvii, 1946, 337

210 Review: *Rapport de l'archiviste de la Province de Québec pour 1942–1943. Canadian Historical Review*, xxvii, 1946, 67

1947

211 Immigrant travel becomes less arduous. *London Free Press*, 29 October 1947

212 Old Red School records hold key to much district history. *London Free Press*, 8 February 1947

213 The pioneer press in Western Ontario. *Western Ontario Historical Notes*, v, 1947, No 2, 43–8

214 The Rise of the University of Western Ontario. *Western Ontario Historical Notes*, v, 1947, No 2, 26–31

215 Three Scottish-Canadian newspaper editor poets. *Canadian Historical Review*, xxviii, 1947, 166–77

216 Review: Province of Saskatchewan, *First Report of the Saskatchewan Archives for the Period April 1, 1945 to May 31, 1946. Canadian Historical Review*, xxviii, 1947, 446–7

1948

217 Eyewitness account of British Columbia Floods. *London Free Press*, 5 July 1948

218 The Great Western railway. *Western Ontario Historical Notes*, vi, 1948, No 1, 2–7

219 Some precursors of the Ontario Historical Society. *Ontario History*, xl, 1948, 13–21

220 Review: *Les cahiers des dix, no 12. Canadian Historical Review*, xxix, 1948, 427–8

221 Review: R. MacGregor Dawson, *The Government of Canada. London Free Press*, 15 April 1948

222 Review: Isabel Skelton, *A man austere: William Bell, Parson and Pioneer. Canadian Historical Review*, xxix, 1948, 86–7

1949

223 The first Prince Edward Island literary journal. Royal Society of Canada, *Transactions*, series 3, xliii, 1949, Section 2, 153–6

224 Introduction to: Richard Cockrel, *Thoughts on the education of youth (1795)*. Toronto, Bibliographical Society of Canada, 1949

225 Review: M.E. Nichols, *(cp) The story of the Canadian Press. Canadian Historical Review*, xxx, 1949, 166–7

1950

226 Ontario Archives. *Canadian Historical Review*, xxxi, 1950, 341

227 The visitation of Bishop Strachan to the western parts of the diocese of

Toronto in 1840. *Western Ontario Historical Nuggets*, XIV, 1950

228 Early Ontario land records as a source of local history. *Western Ontario Historical Notes*, VIII, 1950, No 4, 130–4

229 George Sheppard, Journalist, 1819–1912. Royal Society of Canada, *Transactions*, 3rd series, XLIV, 1950, Section 2, 119–34

230 compiler: History of South Western Ontario: A selected list. *Ontario Library Review*, XXXIV, 1950, 119–22, 291–6

1951

231 The Jeffery stamp collection. Address at the 152nd convocation, University of Western Ontario, 19 September 1951. Typescript

232 Migration from Ontario to Manitoba in 1871. *Ontario History*, XLIII, 1951, 35–41

233 Travel time in early Western Ontario is uncovered. *London Free Press*, 19 May 1951

234 Review: Alexander De Conde, *Herbert Hoover's Latin American Policy*. *Canadian Historical Review*, XXXII, 1951, 171

235 Regional Ontario history as an imaginative experiment. Review of F.C. Hamil, *The valley of the Lower Thames, 1640–1850*. *Western Ontario Historical Notes*, IX, 1951, 156; Toronto *Globe and Mail*, 4 August 1951

1952

236 The Canada Company paid 300,000 pounds for the Huron Tract. ... *Goderich Signal-Star*, 31 July 1952

237 1952 meeting place [of the OLA]. *Ontario Library Review*, XXXVI, 1952, 3–4

1953

238 Introduction: Thomas Magrath, *Authentic letters from Upper Canada*. Toronto, Macmillan, 1953

239 The development of the railway network of Southwestern Ontario to 1876. Canadian Historical Association, *Annual Report*, 1953, 53–9

240 Oxford colonization experiment part of world history. *London Free Press*, 15 August 1953

241 with Ruth Davis Talman: *"Western" – 1878–1953*. London, Ontario, The University of Western Ontario, 1953

1954

242 *Early Freemasonry in Ontario*. Halifax. Canadian Masonic Research Association, 1954

243 Review: Claude T. Bissell, ed., *University College: A Portrait, 1853–1953.* *Canadian Historical Review*, xxxv, 1954, 68–9

1955

244 The impact of the railway on a pioneer community. Canadian Historical Association, *Annual Report*, 1955, 1–12

245 Review: Hugh G.J. Aitken, *The Welland Canal Company: a study in Canadian enterprise. Canadian Historical Review*, xxxvi, 1955, 155

246 Review: Hamilton Ellis, *British Railway History. Business History Review*, xxix, 1955, 282–3

247 Review: D.C. Harvey, ed., *Journeys to the Island of St. John, or Prince Edward Island, 1775–1832. Canadiana*, vi, 1955, Nos 4, 9

248 Review: H. Holcroft, *The Armstrongs of the Great Western*, and C. Hamilton Ellis, *The Midland Railway. Business History Review*, xxix, 1955, 203–4

1956

249 Western honours London librarian [Richard E. Crouch]. *Ontario Library Review*, xL, 1956, 4

250 Review: Edgar Andrew Collard, *Canadian Yesterdays. Canadian Historical Review*, xxxvii, 1956, 190–1

251 Review: Fred Coyne Hamil, *Lake Erie Baron: the story of Colonel Thomas Talbot. Canadian Historical Review*, xxxvii, 1956, 272

252 Review: Neil F. Morrison, *Garden gateway to Canada, one hundred years of Windsor and Essex County, 1854–1954. Canadian Historical Review*, xxxvii, 1956, 182–3

1957

253 Africa's expanding universities. *London Free Press*, 9 July 1957

254 Bruce 'cruel' to missionary in 1887. *London Free Press*, 21 December 1957

255 John Dearness, 1852–1954 [obit]. Royal Society of Canada, *Proceedings*, 3rd series, LI, 1957, 79–83

256 Letter from Nigeria: congregation swings and sways. *London Free Press*, 21 June 1957

257 Review: Charles Truk Currelly, *I brought the ages home. Canadian Historical Review*, xxxviii, 1957, 75–6

258 Review: William Kilbourn, *The firebrand: William Lyon Mackenzie and the rebellion in Upper Canada. Canadian Historical Review*, xxxviii, 1957, 149–50

1958

259 How to enter your books for G-G judging [Governor-General's Award]. *Canadian Author and Bookman*, XXXIV, spring 1958, 28, 30, 32

260 entries on London and Middlesex County in *Encyclopedia Canadiana*, 10 volumes. Toronto, Grolier, 1958

261 Review: A.W. Currie, *The Grand Trunk Railway of Canada. American Historical Review*, LXIII, 1958, 1046–7

262 Review: H.M. Jackson, *Justus Sherwood: soldier, loyalist and negotiator. Vermont History*, XXVI, 1958, 311–12

1959

263 edited: *Basic documents in Canadian history*. Princeton, New Jersey, Van Nostrand, 1959

264 *Captain Thompson Wilson and early freemasonry in London, Ontario.* Halifax, Canadian Masonic Research Association, 1959

265 Review: Richard A. Preston, ed., *Kingston before the War of 1812. Canadian Historical Review*, XL, 1959, 347–8

1960

266 Champlain as an explorer in inland North America. *Vermont History*, XXVIII, 1960, 22–3

267 *Convocation address, University of Waterloo, 18 June 1960*, University of Waterloo Convocation, 1960, 9–14

268 Loyalty, nationalism and the American Revolution: Nova Scotia and Quebec, 35 pp. A paper read and distributed to the Seminar on the American Revolution, Colonial Williamsburg, Williamsburg, Va., 10 September 1960

269 Ontario. Chapter XI in Part 3 of Milton Rubincam, ed., *Genealogical research methods and sources*. Washington, American Society of Genealogists, 1960

1961

270 Review: J.M.S. Careless, *Brown of the Globe.* I: *The Voice of Upper Canada, 1818–1859. American Historical Review*, LXVI, 1961, 1099

1962

271 Railway promoter Zimmerman entertained in lavish style ... *London Free Press*, 10 February 1962

1963

272 *Huron College, 1863–1963.* London, Ontario, Huron College, 1963

1964

273 Review: Florence B. Murray, ed., *Muskoka and Haliburton, 1615–1875.*
Canadian Historical Review, XLV, 1964, 72–3
274 Review: J.M.S. Careless, *Brown of the Globe.* II: *Statesman of Confederation,*
1860–1880. American Historical Review, LXX, 1964, 278
275 Review: Ramsay Cook, *The Politics of John W. Dafoe and the Free Press.*
American Historical Review, LXIX, 1964, 560–1

1965

276 Review: Charles M. Johnston, ed., *The Valley of the Six Nations. American
Historical Review,* LXXI, 1965, 294
277 Review: *Nil Alienum: the memoirs of C.B. Sissons. Canadian Historical
Review,* XLVI, 1965, 256–7

1966

278 Review: *Dictionary of Canadian Biography.* I: *1000–1700. Journal of the
Canadian Church Historical Society,* VIII, 1966, 21–3
279 Review: Robert L. McDougall, ed., *Canada's Past and Present: A Dialogue.
American Historical Review,* LXXI, 1966, 1473–4
280 Review: Hazel C. Mathews, *The Mark of Honour. American Historical
Review,* LXXII, 1966, 342–3

1967

281 The United Empire Loyalists in *Profiles of a province: Studies in the history
of Ontario.* Toronto, Ontario Historical Society, 1967, 3–8
282 Review: Edith G. Firth, ed., *The Town of York, 1815–1834: A further
collection of documents of early Toronto. American Historical Review,*
LXXIII, 1967, 628–9

1968

283 Ontario: a product of the American Revolution. *Historical Magazine of the
Protestant Episcopal Church,* XXXVII, 1968, 129–34; reprinted in *Loyalist
Gazette,* autumn 1968, 20–1
284 Twenty-two years of the Microfilm Newspaper Project. *Canadian Library,*
XXV, 1968, 140–8

285 Review: Merrill Denison, *Canada's First Bank: A History of the Bank of Montreal. American Historical Review*, LXXIV, 1968, 334–5

286 Review: Lillian F. Gates, *Land Policies of Upper Canada. The Journal of American History*, LV, 1968, 693–4

287 Review: John Howison, *Sketches of Upper Canada. Canadian Literature*, No 36, spring 1968, 98–100

1969

288 Fred Landon [obit]. *Canadian Historical Review*, L, 1969, 488

289 Review: (unsigned) G.P. de T. Glazebrook, *Life in Ontario: a social history. Choice*, VI, 1969, 430

290 Review: (unsigned) Loraine Spencer and Susan Holland, *Northern Ontario, a bibliography. Choice*, VI, 1969, 194

1970

291 *The journal of Major John Norton, 1816* (bibliographical introduction by C.F. Klinck and historical introduction by J.J. Talman). Toronto, Champlain Society, 1970

1971

292 Introduction: George Heriot, *Travels through the Canadas (1807)*. Edmonton, Hurtig, 1971

293 Review: (unsigned) Harold Adams Innis, *A History of the Canadian Pacific Railway*, 2nd ed. *Choice*, VIII, 1971, 903

1972

294 Benjamin Cronyn, in Marc La Terreur, ed., *Dictionary of Canadian Biography*. X: *1871–1880*. Toronto, University of Toronto Press, 1972, 205–10

295 Hannibal Mulkins, ibid., 536

296 with Daniel J. Brock, John Talbot, ibid., 671

297 Introduction to: Edward Ermatinger, *Life of Colonel Talbot and the Talbot Settlement* [1859]. Belleville, Mika Silk Screening Limited, 1972

298 Review: Pierre Berton, *The Last Spike. American Historical Review*, LXXVII, 1972, 600

Contributors

FREDERICK H. ARMSTRONG was educated at Toronto and now teaches at Western. His main field of interest is urbanization. He has written articles for *Ontario History* and the *Dictionary of Canadian Biography*, edited Henry Scadding's *Toronto of Old*, and prepared the *Handbook of Upper Canadian Chronology and Territorial Legislation*.

M. ELIZABETH ARTHUR is a native of Orangeville who studied at Toronto and McGill and is now head of the History Department at Lakehead University, Thunder Bay. She has written for *Ontario History* and the *Revue d'histoire de l'Amérique française*, and has edited *Thunder Bay 1821–1892*, recently published for the Ontario Series of the Champlain Society.

HILARY BATES is Humanities Librarian at Memorial University, St John's, Newfoundland. A native of Toronto, she was educated at Sarnia and Western and has written for *Ontario History*. She has just completed an index to the publications of the Ontario Historical Society.

LILLIAN REA BENSON was born in Guelph and educated at Western where she joined the staff of the library and was assistant librarian in charge of administration from 1950 until her retirement in 1970. She was president of the Ontario Historical Society in 1956–8, and is presently helping with the 'spade work' for the centennial history of Western.

A native of Simcoe, Ontario, DANIEL J. BROCK studied at the University of Western Ontario and Hamilton Teachers' College. He is presently working on his doctorate at the University of Guelph. He has written for *Ontario History* and *The Dictionary of Canadian Biography* and is a frequent contributor to the historical column of *The London Free Press*.

MAURICE CARELESS is a Torontonian who studied at the University of Toronto and Harvard University before returning to Toronto, where he was head of the History

Department for some years. A former president of both the Ontario Historical Society and the Canadian Historical Association, he has received two Governor General's awards and the Tyrrell Medal of the Royal Society. The best known of his many works is probably his two-volume biography of George Brown. He is currently working on a history of urbanization in Canada.

GEORGE N. EMERY was born at Alliston, Ontario, and educated at Ingersoll, Queen's University, and the University of British Columbia before coming to teach at Western. His main interest is social history. He has written on Methodist missions for *The Alberta Historical Review* and is presently studying the relationship between Canadian Protestantism and European immigration with the support of the Canada Council.

DAVID GAGAN is from Owen Sound and studied at Western and Duke University before joining the History Department at McMaster. He has written several journal articles and has done considerable editorial work, including launching the new *Canada: An Illustrated Quarterly of our Past* and acting as general editor for the Canadian History Through the Press series. As well, he has written *The Denison Family of Toronto, 1792–1925,* published by the University of Toronto Press.

The Rev. M.A. GARLAND comes from Cargill, Ontario, and was educated at Walkerton and the University of Western Ontario, where he studied theology at Huron College. He has written widely on the history of Western Ontario. He is now retired from the Protestant Episcopal Church of the United States and lives in Fredonia, New York.

One of the deans of Canadian history, GEORGE P. DE T. GLAZEBROOK is a native of London who was educated at Upper Canada College, the University of Toronto, and Oxford University before entering a career divided between the University of Toronto and the Canadian Department of External Affairs. He has received many honours including the Tyrrell Medal. His histories of Canadian external relations and transportation in Canada have long been standard references, and since his retirement he has written several books including *Life in Ontario: A Social History* and *The Story of Toronto*. He is now working on a history of local government in Ontario.

A native of Haynes, Alberta, LEO A. JOHNSON studied at the Universities of Waterloo and Toronto before returning to the History Department of the University of Waterloo to teach. His interests include both Manitoba and Ontario history, and he was co-editor of *Ontario History* from 1966 to 1970. He is currently working on pioneer settlement and has published several articles on this subject and the development of economic class in Canada. For one such article he received the Cruikshank Medal of the Ontario Historical Society in 1971.

CARL F. KLINCK has just retired from the English Department of the University of Western Ontario, where he was head for many years. Born in Elmira, Ontario, he was educated at Western and at Columbia University. A Fellow of the Royal Society of Canada, he has written widely on Canadian literary history; the *Literary History of Canada*, which he edited, is the standard work in the field. Recently he and James J. Talman edited *The Journal of Major John Norton 1816* for the Champlain Society.

FRED LANDON (1880–1969) spent most of his long life at London, Ontario. He was a graduate of Western, who enjoyed varied and successful careers as a sailor, journalist, librarian, historian, and author. After a decade at *The London Free Press*, he was chief librarian of the London Public Library and then librarian and vice-president of Western. He was president of the Ontario Historical Society and the Canadian Historical Association as well as a recipient of the Cruikshank and Tyrrell medals. The best known of his books is probably *Western Ontario and the American Frontier*.

The late MAX L. MAGILL grew up at Woodstock, Ontario. On graduating from Queen's, he attended the London Teachers' College and then went into law. After his retirement he turned to writing history, sometimes under the pseudonym of John Ireland. Although he always described himself as an amateur historian, the three Cruikshank medals he won for his articles in *Ontario History* testify to the quality of his work. When he died at Toronto in March 1973, he was well along with a history of the Bank of Upper Canada.

JUDSON D. PURDY is from St John, NB, and is a graduate of the Universities of New Brunswick and Toronto. He is now a member of the History of Education Department at Althouse College, University of Western Ontario. His main interests lie in educational history, particularly the role of Bishop John Strachan, about whom he has written in *Ontario History*.

JAMES REANEY comes from South Easthope, Ontario, was educated at the University of Toronto, and now teaches in the English Department at Western. Well known as a literary figure and playwright, he has received three Governor General's awards. His works include *The Red Heart, A Suit of Nettles, Twelve Letters to a Small Town, The Killdeer,* and *Colours in the Dark.* He has written the biography of the Black Donnellys for the *Dictionary of Canadian Biography* and in 1973 New Press published his collected poetry under the title *Poems.* He is currently working on a collection of documents concerning the Biddulph Tragedy, which has grown out of writing his play *Donnelly.*

Born in Ottawa, ALLAN SMITH was educated at the Universities of Manitoba and Toronto and now teaches in the History Department at the University of British Columbia. Articles by him have appeared in the *Canadian Historical Review,* the Canadian Historical Association *Annual Report,* and the *Dictionary of Canadian Biography.*

HUGH A. STEVENSON, a native of Peterborough, teaches in the History of Education Department of Althouse College, University of Western Ontario. In addition to articles on Canadian historical and educational topics appearing in professional and popular journals, he is the author of *Writing an Historical Essay: A Guide for High School Students* and has contributed two chapters to *Canadian Education: A History,* edited by J.D. Wilson, R.M. Stamp, and L.-P. Audet. As a collaborator with other colleagues, he has edited and compiled *Approaches to Teaching Local History, Canadian Education and the Future: A Select Annotated Bibliography, 1967–1971,* and *The Best of Times/The Worst of Times: Contemporary Issues in Canadian Education.*

CHARLES F.J. WHEBELL was born in Nassau in the Bahamas and educated at Western and the London School of Economics. He is an historical geographer who teaches with the Geography Department at Western. He has written for several journals and is currently chairman of the Ontario Geographic Names Board.

W. ROBERT WIGHTMAN comes from Sudbury, Ontario, and was educated at Welland, Western, and Durham University in England. He is now a member of the Geography Department at Western. His interests and writings include both English and Ontario historical geography, and he is currently accumulating statistical material on the colonial and later development of Ontario, 1826–91.

J. DONALD WILSON was born in Hamilton and educated at Western and the University of Toronto. He is presently a member of the Department of History at Lakehead University. Among his interests are the history of education and ethnic history, on which he has written a wide variety of articles, as well as contributing to the *Dictionary of Canadian Biography.* He has also co-edited two books: *Canadian Education: A History* and *The Best of Times/The Worst of Times: Contemporary Issues in Canadian Education.*

MORRIS ZASLOW comes from Rosthern, Saskatchewan, and was educated at the Universities of Alberta and Toronto. He is now a member of the History Department at Western. The recipient of fellowships from the Canada Council, Nuffield Foundation, and Killam Foundation, he is a former editor of *Ontario History* and past president of the Ontario Historical Society. He has edited *The Defended Border: Upper Canada and the War of 1812*, written *The Opening of the Canadian North, 1870–1914*, and acted as general editor for the Champlain Society.

This book

was designed by

ROBERT MACDONALD

under the direction of

ALLAN FLEMING

and was printed by

University of

Toronto

Press